Alen Hwch

9. XII

THE RECORD SOCIETY OF LANCASHIRE AND CHESHIRE

FOUNDED TO TRANSCRIBE AND PUBLISH
ORIGINAL DOCUMENTS RELATING TO THE TWO COUNTIES

VOLUME CXXXVI

The Society wishes to acknowledge with gratitude the support
given towards publication by
Lancashire County Council

ISBN 0 902593 43 9

Produced by Sutton Publishing Limited, Stroud, Gloucestershire.
Printed in Great Britain
by
Henry Ling Ltd at the Dorset Press, Dorchester, Dorset.

Liverpool Town Books
1649–1671

Edited by
Michael Power

PRINTED FOR THE SOCIETY
1999

CONTENTS

ABBREVIATIONS

LRO   Liverpool Record Office

OED   Oxford English Dictionary

THLC   Transactions of the Historic Society of Lancashire and Cheshire

MAPS AND ILLUSTRATIONS

MAPS

ILLUSTRATIONS

INTRODUCTION

Publication of the Town Books

The Liverpool town books are a major source for the history of the town from 1550, when they begin, to 1835, when the municipal corporations act changed the way towns were run. During this period some sixteen large manuscript volumes were compiled from which a basic history of the town can be written.[1] The earliest two books are already in print. J.A. Twemlow edited the first manuscript volume, and part of the second, in a lavish and scholarly edition for the corporation early this century.[2] The series was continued by the careful transcription of the rest of volume two, to 1625, by Eveline Saxton, and the first part of volume 3, to 1649, by E.K. Wilson, misleadingly published under the titles *Liverpool under James I*, and *Liverpool under Charles I* by George Chandler, the city librarian, in the 1960s.[3] The present volume presents the second part of volume three covering the years 1649 to 1671. With it some 121 years of the 285 years of town books up to 1835, and three of the sixteen volumes, are now available in print.

It is a debatable point whether the transcription and publication of source material is worthwhile at a time when other methods of photographic reproduction are available and electronic storage and retrieval are in prospect. Microfilm is, however, not as easy on the eye as the printed page, nor as easy to reproduce and make available, and computer scanning of this kind of local record has hardly begun. If local records are to be made widely available the traditional method of printed publication is still the best way. Extending the run of printed town books makes available the detailed record of the activities of the townsmen and women which take on an additional interest during a period when Liverpool began its major commercial growth. The time transcription takes is great, however, and it is unlikely that Twemlow's original vision of seeing the whole corporation record up to 1863 printed will ever be realised.[4]

Edited highlights of the town books are available in print. Sir James Picton's four volumes of extracts were published in the 1870s and 1880s. James Touzeau provided a more useful collection in 1910 which has provided the principal access

---

1   These are kept in Liverpool Record Office in the Central Libraries: 352 MIN/COU 1–16. They are usually not issued to readers but eight microfilms which cover the series are available.
2   J.A. Twemlow, *Liverpool Town Books 1550–1862: 1 1550–71*, Liverpool, 1918; *II 1572–1603*, Liverpool 1935.
3   G. Chandler, *Liverpool under James I*, Liverpool 1960; ibid. *Liverpool under Charles I*, Liverpool 1965.
4   The council began printing its minutes in that year, and Twemlow's intention was to begin publishing transcriptions of the municipal record to that date, as the title of his volumes, *Liverpool Town Books 1550–1862*, indicates. See his introduction to volume one, xxxix–xl.

Liverpool in the late seventeenth century (sketch, William Fergusson Irvine).

to the town record for most historians.[5] Neither is wholly satisfactory. Picton attempts a history of the town, using brief extracts from the source to illustrate his points. Touzeau is better in reproducing entire sections of the record, but even he rearranges extracts to fit the themes he concentrates on. Both are partial in what they include, focussing on such dramatic episodes as charter disputes and significant council policy decisons, and ignoring the 'dull' round of lists of freemen, or portmoot court presentments. The result is a record which misses out the majority of items in the original record. The 198 pages of original manuscript covering the decade 1651–1660, for example, is accorded only twenty-five pages in Touzeau.

Picton and Touzeau both relied on the labours of T.N. Morton, the record clerk to the corporation from 1880 to 1898, who transcribed fuller extracts from the town books into thirteen volumes.[6] On first sight these beautifully handwritten volumes seem to offer an alternative to battling with the original town books, especially since they are indexed. Alas, Morton too was selective. For the year 1649, for example, he omits the entire election court and a list of burgesses and, though mentioning portmoot courts, includes less than one fifth of the items dealt with in them. The labours of an earlier clerk of the corporation in the early-nineteenth century, Charles Okill, also exist in a series of manuscript indexes to the town books, but these too, turn out to be partial; his indexes of townspeople's names are limited to their appearance as officers or leaseholders of the corporation, and not in any other context.[7]

It is clear that the published extracts from the town books, and even the manuscript transcriptions available in Liverpool Record Office, give a most inadequate insight into the main municipal record.[8] There is no substitute for consulting the original record if a serious history of the town, or any of its denizens is to be written, which is the justification for this continuation of the publication of the town books.

Town Books and the Government of Liverpool

The town books consist of minutes of the meetings held to govern, to make town policy and to enforce local laws. From their inception in the mid-Tudor period till the period of this volume the business recorded followed a traditional pattern.

5   Sir James Picton, *Memorials of Liverpool*, 2 vols., Liverpool 1873; ibid. *The city of Liverpool; selections from the municipal archives and records*, 2 vols., Liverpool 1883–6. James Touzeau, *The rise and progress of Liverpool from 1551 to 1835*, Liverpool 1910. For comments on their work see Twemlow, *op.cit.*, clv–clvi, clxvii.

6   LRO, 352/CLE/TRA 2/1–13. See Twemlow, *op.cit.*, pp. cliv–clv; and T.N. Morton 'A concise account of the charters, muniments and other records of the Corporation of Liverpool in 1897', *THLC*, 49, 1897, 71–86.

7   LRO, 352/CLE/TRA 1/5; for comment on Okill see R. Stewart Brown, 'The Pool of Liverpool', *THLC*, 82, 1930, 134–5.

8   The best survey of manuscript and printed transcriptions from the town books is contained in Twemlow, *op.cit.*, cxlix–clxix.

There was always an election court held on the feast of St Luke, 18 October, at which the new mayor, bailiffs and other senior officials were elected. Four portmoot courts, sometimes described as quarter sessions of the peace, were usually held in October, January, April and July. There a jury presented transgressors against the peace, against borough regulations on freedom, marketing and manufacturing, those neglecting the upkeep of buildings and water courses, those misusing the common and failing to control animals, and those failing to clear rubbish. More often than not in the period 1649 to 1671 fewer than the four portmoot courts appear: in ten years only three portmoots appear, in six years only two, and in one year, just one.

The other main business recorded was the minutes of assembly or council meetings, at which the mayor, bailiffs, aldermen and councillors were present, in theory a total of forty-one people.[9] On average the council met about eight times a year in the 1650s and 1660s, though its activity varied from only two meetings in 1651 to eighteen in 1657. It had a wide remit. An important function was to defend the rights of the town, as in pursuing Irish lands promised to the town in compensation for damage during the Civil War, seeking a new charter, defending the town against the claims of the incumbent of the parish church of Walton on the Hill, contesting control of the the lordship of the town with Lord Molyneux and advancing the claim of the town to be a port independent of Chester. Much of its time was spent making decisions on more mundane matters, the tenancy of town property, allowing enclosures on the common, nominating new councillors to replace those who had died, issuing orders about plague infection, levying taxes, keeping watch on incomers to the town and so on.

The other items appearing in the town books were more sporadic: freemen admissions were most common, appearing in twenty years (lists of freemen appear in three years); there were thirteen audits of previous years' accounts, five elections of M.P.s, occasional rentals of corporation property or inventories of books and plate.

All this activity was engaged in by a town which derived its authority during the mid-seventeenth century from the charter of Charles I granted in 1626, but it is clear that traditions, or the 'ancient laws and laudable customs' often referred to by portmoot juries, were as or more important in determining how the town governed itself and what was recorded in the town books of this activity. The charter made the mayor, bailiffs and burgesses (i.e. all freemen) the supreme authority in the town; in fact, most major policy decisions seem to have been made in this period by the council or assembly, the body of forty-one, which is not mentioned by the charter. The mayor and senior aldermen are named justices of the peace in the charter, with all the usual powers. Yet the the major judicial record in the town

9   R. Muir and E.M. Platt, *A history of municipal government in Liverpool*, Liverpool, 1906, 87, 105. This study of the charters and other fundamental documents contains the text of the charters and the clearest guide to the history of the constitution of the borough.

books, the portmoot court, is less of a quarter sessions than a court leet and is not mentioned in the charter.[10]

It is not, of course, unusual for a historic town government to diverge from the formal provisions of charters. Liverpool resembles many other town governments in the seventeenth century in its officers, the tight control of a council, and a court structure which mixed different judicial functions. Its mayor and bailiffs (one for the king or commonwealth, one for the town) are the commonly found chief officers of towns. It lacked a chamberlain or treasurer but such duties were carried out by bailiffs and appraisers. Its mixture of agricultural, market, taxing and cleansing officers (barleymen, aletasters, leavelookers, leathersearchers, scavengers and so on) was much the same as in many other towns, and more specific officers, like water bailiffs and customers, were appropriate additions for a port. The exercise of power by a council (often a body of twenty-four or forty-eight) was common; the exercise of democratic control by the whole body of burgesses the exception. And it was not unusual for there to be one borough or portmoot court which developed jurisdiction over an indiscriminate range of petty criminal and civil matters, over elections and the enforcement of borough regulations.[11]

There is one respect in which the way the town was governed was notably affected during the period 1649 to 1671. A town corporation which had supported the parliamentary side in the Civil War and been quick to adopt loyalty to the Commonwealth and Protectorate governments developed political and religious attitudes which sat uneasily with the restored monarchy. In 1662 Charles II's commissioners used the Corporation Act to root out six aldermen, seven councillors and the town clerk who were puritan enough to refuse renouncing the Solemn League and Covenant. With the admission of new freemen in the same year, supporters of church and king, a powerful impetus was given to the development of a 'court' controlled town, a change confirmed by a new charter of 1677 which increased the council from forty to sixty members, fifteen of whom were intended to be countrymen and loyal. Within the continuing traditional control exercised by the council in the mid-seventeenth century there was, then, an imposed political change from parliamentary to royal allegiance, from puritan to anglican.[12] Such labels are rather crude. But there is no doubting the change in the social and political complexion of the council. It is reflected in the appearance of no fewer than four aristocratic mayors in the 1660s, a most unusual concentration.

The Town Clerks

The recording of minutes and their care was the responsibility of a central official of the corporation, the town clerk. Elected each year with the mayor and bailiffs,

---

10   R. Muir and E. Platt, *op.cit.*, 91–4; 165–89. S. & B. Webb, *English Local Government from the revolution to the municipal corporations act: the manor and the borough*, I, 1908, 351.

11   S. & B. Webb, *op.cit.*, 303–27 (officers); 360–83 (councils); 337–58 (courts).

12   R. Muir & E. Platt, *op.cit.*, 101–6.

his principal duties were to keep the town records safe, and 'record or cause to be recorded all matters and things fit and necessary to be recorded in every mayor's time agreed upon and set down in writing at every assembly by the council of the said town'.[13] The town clerk acted as both secretary and archivist to the corporation, and was obviously a central figure in its smooth working. Although elected, the officeholder usually paid a fee or annual payment to the corporation from the various emoluments enjoyed. Fees for drawing up documents of actions commenced in the mayor's court or recording admissions to the freedom or of apprentice indentures guaranteed the town clerk a steady income.[14] Some thirteen individuals held the office between 1550 and 1750. Some served for long periods, guaranteeing continuity. Adam Pendleton and John Hewett held the office for twenty-six and thirty-five years successively from 1550 to 16ll; John Winstanley, who was town clerk at the beginning of this volume, held office for twenty-two years from 1641 to 1663; Ralph Peters held the office for thirty-five years from 1707 to 1742. Relations between clerk and council were not, however, always harmonious.[15]

During the period of this volume there were three town clerks: John Winstanley was elected on 15 October 1641, William Blundell appointed on 10 November 1662, and Samuel Fazakerley elected on 28 January 1663/64, continuing in post until 1677.[16] Winstanley was elected in 1641 to replace Richard Welles who had asked to be discharged of the office. In a contested election he was chosen over Arthur Burrow and Andrew Taylor. The terms of his appointment included a fee of £10 per annum to be paid to the bailiffs from his emoluments, a condition he had waived on 15 January 1647 'in regard of his suffering condition with the rest of the townsmen who have deeply suffered from cruel enemies in these sad times'.[17] His tenure was a long and apparently successful one. It counted for nought when on 10 November 1662 he was summarily removed from office and the council by commissioners enforcing the Corporations Act, along with six aldermen and seven common councillors. The puritan establishment in the town was purged, and, in the words of the commissioners, 'public safety and encouragement of loyalty' advanced.[18]

William Blundell of Liverpool, gentleman, was appointed by the commissioners in his place on the same day, 10 November 1662, and hurriedly admitted a freeman and councillor three days later. Politically sound though this appointment might have seemed it was an impractical choice. After little more than a year in office

13   Oath recorded in 1625: G. Chandler, *Liverpool under Charles I*, 108.
14   J.A. Twemlow, *op.cit.*, lxxx–lxxxiv; G. Chandler, *Liverpool under James I*, 45–6; Chandler, *Liverpool under Charles I*, 48–9.
15   Robert Brooke, 1613–23, and Robert Dobson, 1627–37, seem to have been particularly troublesome: see G. Chandler, *Liverpool under James I*, 46; G. Chandler, *Liverpool under Charles I*, 48–9.
16   G. Chandler, *Liverpool under Charles I*, 284; and see text below, 148, 164.
17   G. Chandler, *Liverpool under Charles I*, 282–4, 354–5.
18   See below, 148.

Blundell resigned in January 1664 because, living in Prescot, he 'could not answer the full service of the office because of his remoteness'. Samuel Fazakerley, a gentleman of Liverpool, was chosen 'on mature deliberation' by the mayor, aldermen and council on 28 January 1664, and continued in post until 1677. He paid £5 per annum for the office.[19]

These upheavals in the office are reflected in the palaeography of the town books. There seem to be two hands at work in the period of Winstanley's office up to 1662. The most frequently occurring, presumably Winstanley's, is large with emphatic flourishes. A smaller hand alternates, clearly demonstrating the existence of an assistant clerk, although such an office did not formally exist. Who this might have been there is no means of discovering. Both scribes record the range of business, portmoot court presentments, assembly minutes and so on, though it is noticeable that the large hand consistently records the election court minutes each 18 October, the occasion when the tenure of the office of town clerk was renewed.[20]

The hands become more varied when Blundell was appointed. Five different hands are discernible during his period of office, a reflection perhaps of his difficulty in getting in to Liverpool to take minutes.[21] Order is restored when another large hand, with a rather thinner stroke than Winstanley's, commences in September 1663 before Blundell had formally resigned. This becomes the most common hand to the end of the volume in 1671, and presumably belongs to Fazakerley. But once again there is a deputy, for a smaller neater hand appears with some regularity, though not for minuting election courts.[22]

The variety of scribes, known and unknown, who recorded business in the town book has a bearing on the care with which the town book was compiled. During 1662–63, with Blundell nominally in control, much seems to be missing. Only one portmoot court was recorded, for example. This might have been the effect of the disorder resulting from the upheaval on the council as the Corporations Act cut a swath through the aldermen and councillors. As likely an explanation is that Blundell was frequently absent from meetings and the formal recording of proceedings was neglected.

Even in settled periods the standard of recording varied. Winstanley had evolved a method of always recording the portmoot courts immediately after the election court each mayoral year. Assembly minutes and other business then followed. This regular arrangement gives the impression of an organised minuting system at work which encourages confidence in the integrity of the record. The

19 See below, 164.
20 See original town book volume three. Winstanley's hand is clear on page 470, and frequently thereafter; the deputy's hand appears on page 476.
21 *Ibid.* A mannered hand appears on page 743; a different hand on page 747; a large hand on page 749; a small hand on page 752; a large hand which resembles Fazakerley's hand on page 753.
22 *Ibid.* See the presumed hand of Fazakerley on page 783 and frequently thereafter; the much smaller and neater hand on page 811 and thereafter.

overall orderliness of the manuscript and general absence of blank pages (an average of less than two gaps each year) add to the impression of recording carefully done. After the year of Blundell's confusion Fazakerley imposed a different system somewhat less convincing than Winstanley's. He adopted a chronological approach in which portmoot court minutes appear interspersed with assemblies and other business. The record seems thinner (an average of only six or seven assembly minutes each year compared to about nine under Winstanley) and blank pages intrude much more obviously (an average of over four gaps each year).

Overall, then, the standard of recording by the three town clerks of this period varied. It is difficult to assess how seriously this vitiates the record. It is probably true to say that it creates problems in 1662–63, and that activity later in the 1660s was a little less efficiently recorded than in the 1650s.[23]

Editorial Conventions

The transcription of the town book in this volume departs from the practice employed by Twemlow (1550–1603), Saxton (1603–1625) and Wilson (1625–1649) in not being verbatim. The principle has been to include all factual material in the original record, in its exact order and remaining as close to the original phraseology as possible, but omitting much common form in order to expedite transcription and reduce the bulk of the record. It is hoped that nothing has been lost for the reader except philological exactitude, and that for most historical purposes this text will be as complete as is necessary. Plate 2 (see p. xviii) shows the character of the standard page in the town book. Most of the original text is in English, and the occasional Latin entries, indicated in footnotes, have been translated.[24]

The format of the original document has been broadly retained. Each new mayoral year is prefaced by a heading with the new mayor's name and the year he began his office, as is usually the case in the original. Dating by the Old Style, with the year commencing at the Annunciation (25 March) is retained. Where the document does not include this it has been added, and the mayoral year, not included in the original, has also been inserted in square brackets. Each separate meeting within a year (each portmoot court, assembly, audit and so on) is preceded by a blank space (as is usually the case in the original) and headed in capitals. Indenting in this edition does not copy the original and has been employed to make

---

23 Even in the 1650s recording could be very thin. The sparsest year of activity in this volume is, for example, the mayoral year 1651–52.

24 I am very grateful to Elizabeth Danbury, lecturer in the School of Library, Archive and Information Studies at University College London, for her assistance with passages I found difficult, particularly those on manuscript pages 760 and 929.

each item distinct. Manuscript page references are included on the left hand side of the printed page.[25]

The principle in editing the text has been to remain close to the original but to make it as easy as possible to read. To this end spelling has been modernised, except for surnames which have been transcribed exactly as they appear. Christian names have been standardised and presented in full except in cases where they form part of a signature when the original form has been retained. Placenames which survive today have been rendered in their modern form; those which do not, retain the original spelling. Abbreviations have usually been extended and modern punctuation imposed. Words missing in the document are usually indicated by a dash; text missing because of marginal damage to the manuscript in the final mayoral year, 1670–71, is also denoted by a dash.

Additional commentary on the text has been deliberately kept sparse. Unlike Twemlow's edition footnotes are not used to elucidate the text or supply additional commentary on people and events but wherever some characteristic of the language, format or condition of the original document seemed significant it is noted.

25   Volume three of the town books is a large paper volume of almost 500 leaves, about half of them containing the material for the years contained in this edition, 1649–1671. The manuscript volume is for the most part paginated. During Thomas Ayndoe's mayoralty (1655–56) this changes briefly to foliation. Page 615 is followed by folios 616–20, each with a dorse, the equivalent of ten pages. Page 621 succeeds folio 620, and the normal page sequence resumes. From page 927 to the end damp has attacked the margins of the pages, and some gaps occur in the mayoral year 1670–71.

Liverpool Town Book, *p. 699 (below pp. 122–4). The Portmoot of 24 October 1659.*

THOMAS HODGSON, GENTLEMAN, MAYOR, 1649 [1649–50]

p. 470
LIVERPOOL. COURT OF ELECTION HELD ON THE FEAST OF ST LUKE, 18 OCTOBER 1649, BEFORE WILLIAM WILLIAMSON, GENTLEMAN, MAYOR, AND EDWARD LYON AND THOMAS STORIE, BAILIFFS.[1]

Thomas Hodgson, gentleman, is elected mayor, sworn
Gilbert Formby, mariner, head bailiff for the mayor and republic of England, sworn
Evan Marshe, shoemaker, the other bailiff for the town, sworn.[2]

    Officers chosen by the mayor and council:
John Fogg, minister
John Winstanley, town clerk
John Kirk, serjeant at mace
Richard Dwarrihouse, water bailiff
George Glover, schoolmaster
Richard Rose, church clerk
John Williamson, hall keeper[3]
Town customer suspended
Richard Poultney, subcustomer
Richard Crompton, Robert Fleetwood, stewards of the hall, sworn
Gilbert Tarleton, Thomas Rainford, supervisors of the highways
Thomas Copprill, heyward, provided he keep one to look to the sea bank from seed time to harvest
Thomas Lurting, George Potter, churchwardens

p. 471
    Officers chosen by the jurors:
Roger Jones, Thomas Storie, Peter Lurting, Richard Parcivall, merchant appraisers, sworn
Thomas Burton, Thomas Nicholson, registers of leather, sworn
William Mosle, Thomas Leaver, aletasters, sworn
Thomas Carr, Richard Holland, Richard Kenion, cooper, Richard Coppull, barleymen, sworn
Edward Horrobine, murenger[4]
Edward Ashton, William Chorley, Robert Hall, William Bushell, scavengers, sworn
Roger Rose, John Boulton, leavelookers, sworn

1   Preceding text in Latin; henceforth such instances noted simply as Latin.
2   Latin.
3   Latin.
4   Variously spelled at election courts; most often murenger, but sometimes mallinger.

John Barton, Edward Rycroft, porters
John Formby, Edward Rycroft, boardsetters
John Ryce, Richard Widdowes, boothsetters

p. 472

Names of the free burgesses[5] of the town[6]

Thomas Hodgson mayor, Thomas Stanley bart., John Moore esq. ald., John Holcroft esq., William Langton esq. recorder, Thomas Hockenhull, John Walker ald., John Williamson, Thomas Bicksteth, James Williamson, Thomas Blackmoore, Thomas Tarleton, William Williamson

Sir Francis Willoughby, Sir Walshingham Cooke

Richard Shutleworth esq., Henry Brook esq., John Braddill esq., John Bradshawe esq., Ralph Ashton esq., William Bankes esq., John Leightborne esq., Thomas Longworth esq., William Morgell esq., Bartholomew Hesketh esq., William Lingford, James Chantrell, Geoffrey Holcroft esq., Nehemiah Brettargh

Richard Holland esq., Sir John Booth, Sir Gilbert Ireland, George Ireland gent., Richard Crosse esq., Peter Egerton esq., Thomas Felle esq., George Dodding esq., Edward Butterworth esq., Matthew Allyreade esq.

George Key lt col., Michael Richardson, Thomas Worsley, George Smithson, Thomas Tolbortt, Ralph Ashton esq., William Ashurst esq., John Jackson lt col., Roger Pheinwick, John Hewetson, James Pitson, John Blagreave

Ministers: James Hyatt clerk, Nevill Kay, Thomas Sixsmith, Peter Shawe, Henry Shawe, Joseph Tompson, Edward Lapage, Thomas Walleworth, John Coe(clerk), Richard Lyon, William Bell, John Fogg, David Ellison, William Ward, Henry Nayler, William Dunne, Thomas Boulton, Richard Pickering

Bailiffs, reeves and council: Gilbert Formby, Evan Marshe bailiffs, Robert Moore gent., John Winstanley town clerk, John Kirk serjeant, John Chantrell, Robert Lurting, John Higinson, Edward Chambers, Roger Jones, Edward Alcock, Ralph Massam, John Williamson, John Woods, Edward Formby, Thomas Williamson, John Tarleton, Edward Williamson, Robert Cornell, John Sandiford, Richard Williamson, John Sturzaker, Edward Lyon, Thomas Storie, Richard Dwarrihouse, Richard Rose, Richard Blevine, Robert Peares, Thomas Ayndoe, John Walle, William Lurting smith, Thomas Shepard, Robert Greene, Richard Parcifall, Peter Lurting

p. 473

Thomas Clayton, Richard Duckenfield, Thomas Warburton, Henry Blundell, Richard Fleetwood, Edward Starkley, Thomas Blackburne, John Brookes, Richard

---

5   This list is divided into sections, indicated by the indentation. It has been much annotated in a different hand to the original compiler, some names underlined, others crossed out, some with 'mort', 'dead', 'd' or 'ex' added, some with crosses added. These annotations have been omitted since they are not part of the original list, and were perhaps generated at later dates when the list was used for checking on attendance or local taxation. Where the annotation adds an occupation this is noted in round brackets.
6   Latin.

Hockenhoolle, George Halley, Allen Walley, Arthur Burran, Edward Moore, William Rigby, Thomas Mossock (chirurgeon), Edward Dicconsand, William Patten, William West, Richard Sankey, John Sharples senior, Hamnett Holcrofte, Peter Stanley, George Topping, Hugo Cooper, Nicholas Sherburne, Joseph Ward, Edmund Smoult, Peares Gerrard, Ralph Shorrock, John Beswicke capt., Robert Clark capt., Thomas Morgan capt., Robert Philpott capt., Leonard Rollinson capt., William Swanley capt., John Sorrocold capt., William Carrington lt col., John Birch capt., John Atherton esq., Henry Stanley gent., Robert Wingreene capt., William Lea capt., George Cannage capt., Andrew Ashton capt., Geoffrey Birchall capt., John Eaton, Peter Fleetcrofe, Robert Pynington, John Newton, John Daniell (esq), Edward Starkey capt., Edward Ogle capt., Robert Roe, Richard Radcliffe esq., William Massey, John Church, Alexander Bonner, William Fyfe (physician), Henry Ashton, Gregory Holcroft, John Greene (mariner), Robert Ireland, Edward Garrett, James Massey, Robert Gardner, William Edwards, Philip Watson, Alexander Greene, Thomas Baxter, Edward Manne, William Toxteth, John Ashhurst lt col., John Fox capt., Thomas Horton (merchant), Henry Porter, James Johnson, John Chandler, John Formby, Richard Washington senior, John Goore, John Bankes senior, Hugh Houghton

p. 474

Richard Brookes, Henry Rolline, John Sympson, William Sympson, Thomas Coppull, Henry Johnson alias Nickson, Ralph Winstanley, Edward Winstanley, Edward Finney, Thomas Scale, Giles Mercer, Thomas Chapman, Edward Fisher, Thomas Plombe, John Lurting (mariner), Robert Rose senior, Thomas Leivsley, Richard Higinson cutler, Richard Higinson husbandman, Robert David alias Macatere, Richard Turner (mariner), John Barrow, Humphrey Webster, Edmund Ogden, John Waide, Gilbert Fairclough, Richard Holland, Brian Mercer, Richard Lunte, Richard Poultney, Robert Johnson, Henry Webster, John Birchall, Richard Martine, Thomas Balive, John Henshawe, Henry Goore, Samuel Halle, Edward Winstanley, Robert Clark, Thomas Radcliffe, Thomas Farren, John Tompson, Robert Bicksteth junior, Henry Birchall, Robert Fleetwood, Richard Higinson butcher, George Prescott, Francis Wallworth, William Lurting senior, William Hawkshead, Robert Seacome, William Eccleston senior, John Knape, Roger Rose junior, Thomas Haskaine, John Harrison, John Mathew, Robert Egads, Thomas Duke, Robert Taylor, Richard Kenion sailor, Robert Fidler, Thomas Greenes, Richard Walker (smith), James Burton, Roger Harrison, Thomas Worrall, Thomas Barker, Edward Dodd, Richard Bankes, Richard Browne, Henry Radcliffe (shoemaker), Thomas Taylor (skinner), Thomas Preeson, James Watson, William Daintith, John Bankes junior, Edmund Lyon, Richard Parr, William Widnes, Peter Parr, Henry Fearnhead, Thomas Bankes, William Topping, Richard Barker, John Johnson alias Fleeming, William Rymmer (sailor), Thomas Gardner, Michael Barker, Robert Farrington, William Webster, John Lurting, smith, Richard Fazakerley, William Horrockes, Edward Horrobine, Joseph Dixon skinner, Richard Morecrofte, John Bate, Edward Taylor, Henry Ambrose, William Sympson, Richard Farrer, James Patrick, Henry Cooper (shoemaker), John Hussie, William

Smithells, John Barton, Thomas Burton, Lucas Harrison, Richard Leivsley, Thomas Cheaney, Thomas Carr, John Lunte, John Eccleston, John Evererd, William Sutton, Thomas Rainford, Henry Rydeing

p. 475

Edmund Lyon (maltster), John Johnson (of Everton), Richard Parsifall, Richard Williams, Peter Lurting, Thomas Lurting, Peter Boulton, Robert Lyon, William Chantrell, Thomas Hancock, Edward Rycrofte, William Chorley, John Carr, Adam Leathes, William Gardner, Richard Widowes, Thomas Nicholson, John Ryce, Abel Lyon, John Sharples junior, Henry Wilcock, John Owen, Augustine Yong, James Woodward, William Jumper, John Cook, Rowland Ashton, Thomas Morecroft, Thomas Taylor, Richard Kenion cooper, Peter Kennard, Henry Kilshawe, William Middleton, William Litherland, James Aynsdalle, Henry Craine, John Royle, Edward Plumer, Anthony Hunte, Thomas Croper, John Halles, Thomas Greene, John Crosse capt., Thomas Croste, Tracie Cater, Thomas Mollineux capt., John Burges, Robert Goulborne, William Mosse, Edward Bell, Edmund Tyrer, Thomas Shepard, William Bankes, John Haskins, William Wray, Oliver Fairhurst, William Eccleston junior, Darby Caton, Thomas Lancellott, Thomas Derbisheire, Robert Fairehurst, Alexander Moore gent., Peter Farrer, Edward Tarleton (mariner), George Potter, Thomas Gallaway, Gilbert Tarleton, William Darwen, John Dickfield, John Mannwaring, Christopher Brookbank, William Bushell, Richard Tyrer, Richard Coppull, Edmund Leivsley, Anthony Beck, Richard Washington junior, Richard Crompton, Thomas Croper, Peter Seddon, William Seddon, John Brookbank, Richard Williamson mason, Edward Ashton, Alexander Greene junior, William Duckenfeild, Thomas Birch, Edward Tarleton, Anthony Carr, John Bird (gent.), Thomas Heyes (gent.), John Lyon tanner, Christopher Bennett merchant, Thomas Leaver, Robert Halle, Thomas Fazakerley, Cuthbert Holland, Abraham West, Richard Barrowclough, William Ryding (cooper), Thomas Roe (shoemaker), Robert Ball (sailor), George Formbie, William Higinson (smith), George Glover, John Smith (shoemaker), Gilbert Coote, John Tennant, Edward Lea, William Newis, George Tarleton, Jeremy Berstowe, William Olive, Richard Rymer, Humphrey Mercer, Henry Ogle, Michael Tarleton, Robert Barrowe, John Sutton, Edward Sutton, Henry Corles, John Eccles, William Reynold, Richard Gallaway, Thomas Chapman, James Barton, John Cocker, James Hey (miller), Thomas Parcivall, Robert Swifte, William Fleetwood.

p. 476
LIVERPOOL. GREAT PORTMOOT COURT OR SESSION OF THE PEACE, 22 OCTOBER 1649, before the mayor and Gilbert Formby and Evan Marsh, bailiffs.

Inquest held before the mayor and bailiffs on the oath of Edward Lyon, Edward Alcock, John Tarleton, Robert Gornell, John Johnson, John Tompson, John Birchall, John Hunshall, John Bankes, Edmund Leivesley, Thomas Rainford, Richard Lunte, Thomas Croppe, Gilbert Tarleton, Edward Rycroft, William Midleton and William Mosse.

We present:

Robert Barker for abusing Mr William Williamson during his mayoralty, saying he was a traitor, £5

William Strangwais for abusing Mr William Williamson saying he was an unworthy fellow, £5

The same for saying the aldermen were unworthy men and dealt very unjustly with him, 20s

The same for reserving a distress from Edward Lyon and Thomas Storie, late bailiffs, which they took for a fine in pursuance of their office, 13s 4d

John Slack of Ditton, shoemaker, for abusing Thomas Nicholson, one of the registers of leather, taking with violence a pair of shoes in open market which were seized, not being of good leather, 6s 8d

James Bradshawe, shoemaker, for working unlawful leather, 2s 6d

James Boulton, John Bullocke, Peter Leather, John Slake, Thomas Fazakerley, Edward Lyon, Evan Marsh, John Birchall, Thomas Nicholson, Thomas Burton, Henry Radclive and Henry Cooper for the like offence, 2s 6d apiece

Jane, wife of John Higinson, butcher, for being drunk and calling Thomas Storie a knave, 15s

John Higinson for suffering muck to lie before his house in Dale Street wherein Alice Halloway lived, 12d

Margaret Potherne, widow, Margery Barker, widow, and John Eccleston for the like offence, 12d apiece

Richard Widdowes for not cleaning the standing place for stalls in the market according to his office and for abusing the chapmen that stand there, 12d

William Leece for using the faculty of a freeman, not being free, 6s 8d

Archibald Findley, Elizabeth Barker, Thomas Parker and Richard Taylor for the like offence, 3s 4d apiece

Thomas Bicksteth, alderman, Dorothy Sandiford, widow, and John Eccleston for the like offence, 6d apiece

Gilbert Coote, William Leece, Edward Leece for the like offence, 3s 4d apiece

Thomas Duke for entertaining inmates in his house in Water Street, 3s 4d

George Tarleton, mariner, Ellen Blevine, widow, Edward Chambers, William Strangwais, Dorothy Bicksteth, widow, Margaret Banester, widow, Ellen Eccleston, widow, Richard Higinson, butcher, John Owen, John Chandler,

p. 477

Jane Hoskeine, widow, Henry Craine, Thomas Tarleton, Anthony Hunt, Richard Kenion, John Lurting, mariner, Henry Kilshawe, John Sturzaker and William Sutton for the like offence, 3s 4d apiece

Richard Johnson of Everton for shearing grass and leasowing cattle in the town field, 5s

Roger Hey, William Seacome and Margery Barker, widow, for the like offence, 5s apiece

Richard Washington junior for a tussle on one Browne, 3s 4d

Browne for tussle on said Washington junior, 3s 4d

Edward Halsall for tussle on Edward Lyon, 3s 4d

Thomas Duke for suffering his wall to fall to annoyance of John Sturzaker, 12d

William Dicconson of Wavertree for engrossing corn in the market, 6s 8d

All who owe suit and appearance to this court and have not appeared nor excused themselves, as named in the bailiff's estreat, 3s 4d apiece

We order:

The water course and ditch between the bridge at Town's End and the end of Ellen Blevine's croft be scoured by 11 November next on pain of 10s to bailiff

Edward Chambers to scour ditch by Hogs Hey Common that water can flow to the sea by the last of November on pain of 5s

John Eccleston to remove timber and ashlars in Dale Street, by his garden, by 1 November, and bailiffs to see that great marble stones nearby are moved, 5s

John Syre and Thomas Warton to scour their ditches in Akers Lane before 11 November for they are a great annoyance to the highway on pain of 5s apiece

John Higinson to give security that his tenant, Robert Stringer, nor his wife nor children, in case their parents die, shall be burdensome to the town on pain of 20s

Mr Strangwais to pay yearly rent to town, as ordered, for the house he has set on town's land at the heath side or it is to be pulled down before 29 October of this month on pain of 10s

The encroachment on the town's land near the park gate be removed and bailiffs to see the wall set in its ancient place before 2 February on pain of 10s

We conceive upon view that Mr Walker may put lights in the gable end of house where William Middleton dwells, towards the back side of Margery Barker's house on pain of —

We agree to all ancient orders and laudable customs.

p. 478

PORTMOOT COURT OR SESSION OF THE PEACE, 5 FEBRUARY 1649, before the mayor and Gilbert Formby and Evan Marsh, bailiffs.[7]

Inquest taken on the oath of Thomas Storie, Robert Lurting, Edward Chambers, Ralph Massam, Richard Washington junior, William Lurting, smith, Thomas Burton, Richard Higinson, husbandman, George Potter, Thomas Leaver, Richard Holland, Richard Higinson, cutler, Richard Kenion, cooper, Edward Horrobine, Thomas Carr, Robert Halle, Richard Widdowes.

We present:

John Poultney for a tussle on William Bennett, nil

William Bennett for a tussle on John Poultney, nil

Henry Wilcock for a tussle on John Higinson, 3s 6d

7   Latin.

William Newis, Thomas Parker, Robert Gowborne, William Leece, Richard Taylor, John Poultney, Richard Blevine and Robert Stringer for using the faculty of freemen, not being free, 3s 4d apiece

Edward Formby, Gilbert Formby, John Bird, Jane Haskaine, James Williamson, John Higinson, William Newys, Anthony Hunte, Oliver Fairehurst, Elinor Sharples, Elizabeth Heapey, widow, William Gardner and Henry Ryding, for having swine unrung, 6d apiece

John Chandler for letting muck lie in the street, 2s

Thomas Boulton, Mr John Walker, Henry Moore, Mr John Fagg, John Griffith, sailor, Henry Corles, and John Higinson for the like offence, 6d apiece

Gilbert Coote for using the faculty of a freeman, not being free, 3s 4d

Gabriel Pymington, Thomas Birch, James Bradshawe, Richard Holland, shoemaker, and Thomas Fazakerley, for working unlawful leather, 2s 6d apiece

Roger Rose and John Boulton for neglecting office of leavelooker, 3s 4d apiece

William Mosse and William Midleton for neglecting office of surveyor, 12d apiece

Henry Corles for not making the way sufficient in Sickman's Lane as his predecessor, James Southerne, was ordered, and to be done before 1 May on pain of 13s 4d

p. 479
We find upon view:

That the wall between the garden of Edward Formby and the garden of Nicholas Nicholson too far on the land of Nicholson

The watercourse annoying Elizabeth Seddon from John Quark's house to be returned to its former course on pain of 5s

The ancient cartway from Sarjants Common by the Short Butts towards the lower end of the Heavy Lands has been diverted by recent ploughing; it should be left as large as formerly

All fences and headbolts to be made up, and ditches scoured within 15 days on pain of every offender 3s 4d

We agree to all ancient orders and laudable customs.

p. 480
LIVERPOOL. PORTMOOT COURT OR SESSION OF THE PEACE, 22 JULY 1650, before Thomas Hodgson, the mayor, and Gilbert Formby and Evan Marsh, bailiffs.[8]

Inquest taken on the oath of John Chantrell, Edward Alcock, Richard Williamson, John Sturzaker, Richard Washington senior, Richard Crompton, William Sutton, Richard Lunte, William Toping, Thomas Carr, Thomas Coppull, Thomas Nicholson, William Mosse, Thomas Roe, William Chorley[9]

8   Latin.
9   Latin.

We present:

George Prescott for stopping watercourse between him and Cecily Roughley, 1s

Gilbert Coote using faculty of freeman, not being free, 3s 4d

Richard Taylor, Richard Rymmer, Thomas Jumper, Peter Halle, Elizabeth Barker, Robert Cowborne, William Leece, Robert Warmingham, Thomas Abram, John Poultney, Archibald Lindley, Thomas Parker, Edward Fazakerley, Cuthbert Harrington, James Hoult and John Heyes, hatter of Derby, for the like offence, 3s 4d apiece

Thomas Lancellott, James Williamson, John Eccleston, John Higinson, Edward Ashton, Mr Blackmore, for keeping their swine unrung, 1s apiece

Elinor Gognell and her two children for robbing Richard Rymer's garden, to be set in the stocks

Thomas Browne, James Boulton, Thomas Birch, Thomas Fazakerley, James Bradshawe, John Slack, Gabriel Pinington, Thomas Nicholson and Peter Layford, for working unlawful leather, 2s 6d apiece

Mr Richard Johnson, William Seacome, Thomas Pemberton, John Henshawe, William Platt, for cutting grass in the field, 2s 6d apiece

Edward Ryding for drawing blood on Richard Coppull, 6s 8d

Robert Halle for buying coal to send into Cheshire, 3s 4d

Edward Chambers, Thomas Raineford, Mr John Chandler, Mr Thomas Bicksteth, Dorothy Bicksteth, John Owen, John Higinson, for ploughing up part of town's common, 1s apiece

p. 481

William Jumpper, Darby Caton, Richard Williams, William Seddon, William Sutton, Richard Washington junior, Henry Craine, Mrs Ellen Eccleston, William Darwen, Isabel Moore, John Lurting, smith, John Royle, John Higinson, Richard Rose, Richard Higinson, cutler, Thomas Burton, Margery Williamson, Richard Higinson, butcher, John Lurting, mariner, Peter Farrer, Robert Eccles, John Johnson, Richard Kenion, mariner, John Cook, Anthony Hunt, Thomas Seale, William Chantrell, Michael Barker, Thomas Lancellott and Elizabeth Barker, William Leece, Elizabeth Heapey, widow, Archibald Findley, for keeping unlicensed alehouses, 3s 4d apiece

For keeping inmates and not having given security to the town:

John Higinson, Mr Strangwais, James Greene, Ellen Blevin, Robert Cornell, Elizabeth Barker, Ralph Massam, James Burton, John Royle, Richard Higinson, butcher, John Higinson, William Lurting, Jane Haskaine, Henry Craine, Thomas Duke, Mawdline Quark, John Chandler, William Middleton, Richard Turner, John Almond, Edward Winstanley, Mr Moore, Robert Clark, Ellen Smith, Thomas Lancellott, Mr Bird, John Quark, Peter Lurting, Dorothy Bicksteth, the landlords of Cook's house, Widow Shepheard, according to the note given to Mr Mayor, 6s 8d apiece.

We order:

Dorothy Bicksteth to make the gutter and wall up between her and Richard Crompton before Michaelmas next, and Richard Crompton to do the same so one does not annoy the other on pain of 5s apiece

The bailiffs, at the town's charge, to have 12 leather buckets and 4 or 6 hooks made for pulling down any house on fire, which God defend

The bailiffs forthwith to have an iron standard for measuring cloth yards and weights according to the statute made on pain of 20s

Mr Alcock's gift of Barker's house to the town to be recorded in the town's book on pain of 10s

We agree to all ancient orders and laudable customs

We order that 2 indifferent men be chosen by the mayor for measuring land in the town field between the town's land and William Carter's land.

p. 482

FREEMEN

29 October 1649:

Robert Halle, locksmith, admitted a free burgess with the consent of the mayor and aldermen because he married Margaram, once wife of Geoffrey Halle, late freeman, and gave £3

29 November:

Thomas Pryde, colonel of foot, admitted a free burgess, free

Charles Walley, gentleman, alderman of Chester, admitted, free

Thomas Fazakerley, miller, admitted, 3s 4d

9 January 1649:

Cuthbert Holland, shoemaker, £3

Abraham West, feltmaker, apprentice of John Tompson, through his indenture, 6s 8d

23 February 1649:

Richard Barrowclough, clothier, son of Richard Barrowclough once a freeman, 3s 4d

14 February:

William Rydeing, cooper, 40s

Thomas Roe, shoemaker, £4 10s

Robert Balle, apprentice to Gilbert Formby, 6s 8d

Gregory Formby, apprentice to Edward Formby, 6s 8d

7 March 1649:

William Higinson, blacksmith, son of William Higinson late freeman, 3s 4d

18 June 1650:

George Glover, schoolmaster, free

8 August 1650:

John Smith, shoemaker, apprentice of Evan Marsh, admitted through his indenture, 6s 8d

Peter Brooke, knight, free

p. 483

11 October 1650:

Gilbert Coote, tailor, 40s

John Tennant, tailor, 40s

Edward Lea, tailor, married to daughter of a freeman, 20s
William Newis admitted at instance of Edward Alcock, 20s
George Tarleton, son of James Tarleton, once a freeman, 3s 4d

All sworn[10]

p. 484
29 OCTOBER 1649: COMPOSITIONS
For 120 tuns of Danzig rye brought in by Mr Curtos and consigned to Mr Horton, voted to pay £4
For 126 maze of herrings in bulk brought in for Thomas Sandiford in the *Prudence*, to pay 12s and William Davies, master and owner 40 maze, 4s
For 48 barrels of herring in bulk by Henry Key and Abraham Ellis, merchants, in the *Michael*, to pay 9s
For 48 barrels and 4 hogsheads of Mrs Whyte and John Gregorie brought in the *Samuel*, to pay 10s[11]
For 10 barrels more in the *Samuel* for John Sturzaker, 3s
More undertaken by the same John Sturzaker, 6s 8d
Peter Jumper for 4 barrels, 1s
Christopher Marshall for 8 barrels of beef, 3s
Richard Simpkins for Blevine, 10s
For Blevine 30 maze more, 3s 4d
Thomas Ambrose for 3 parcels of 26 barrels, 8s
Mr Bayley for Mr Horton for 50 barrels, 16s
Richard Norris for his part and 100 maze more, 20s
John Marsh for his part, 12s 8d
John Johnson in the *Gift* for 28 barrels, 9s
Gilbert Richardson in the *Katherine* for – barrels, 2s
Thomas Scarisbrick in the *Charity*, 5s 6d, debt
Mrs Fowler for 37 barrels of beef, 16s
John Dowgall for 16 barrels of beef, 6s 8d
For 600 of butter at 2s
Richard Johnson for 80 barrels for Mr Blackmoore, herrings, 26s 8d
William Houlmes for 68 barrels, 22s 8d
William Bushell 50 barrels herring for Mr Horton, 16s 8d
Mr Johnson a Scottish man for 16 last. 12 barrels in the last to be viewed for a town's bargain, or else the composition to be paid by mayor and aldermen. Went to Chester.

15 JULY 1650
At an Assembly it was ordered:

10   Latin.
11   Entry is crossed out, with note, 'twice'.

That Nicholas Newis and Thomas Bayley pay for composition of their corn brought in the *Judith* of Plymouth, 30s

Composition for 88 barrels of herrings for Mr Blackmoore and Gilbert Formby, to pay 26s 8d[12]

Mr Grene for ten tuns of iron in the *Hopewell* last May for licence money for Chester men, to be paid by him 25s

And for 6 butts of sack for butlerage, to pay 6s

For butlerage for 12 tuns of his own and the Chester men's, 24s

For licence money for 4 tuns thereof being Chester men's, 10s

p. 485

p. 486
5 NOVEMBER 1649
At an Assembly before the worshipful Mr Mayor, the aldermen, bailiffs and common council:

It was agreed, concerning the leasing of Mr Dobson's house, town's land and built by Mr Robert Dobson, his father, that £70 should be the fine for 3 lives, or £40 for Mr Dobson's own use, and the old rent of 13s 6d. Otherwise he is to enjoy it for £6 13s 4d rent per annum for 6 years, and afterwards to compound with the town as he can agree, provided he does not let or assign it without the town's consent nor otherwise to the use of himself, his wife and children, and that not above 3 years. This assembly appoints Mr Thomas Tarleton and Mr John Sandiford to treat with him about it, and, as a result, he now enjoys it at £6 13s 4d rent.

Memorandum: it was also referred to Mr John Walker, Mr William Williamson, Mr John Winstanley and Mr Edward Williamson to treat with Mr Henry Burscough about his title in Susan Eccleston's house, which is the town's land, and to compound with him for his term of about – years yet in being, but nothing concluded. Afterwards there was a bargain between him and the said Susan, with the town's consent, whereupon the said Susan paid in the £16 mortgage money due to the town and is to enjoy it for his term.

19 NOVEMBER 1649
At an Assembly before Mr Mayor, the aldermen, bailiffs and most of the common council:

It was ordered that the corner shop now in the possession of Roger Harrison shall be rented at 40s per annum from year to year, and the rent to be received by the bailiffs and accounted for at every audit, to commence at Christmas next, 1649.

The former order of this house concerning Mr John Sandiford's fine of 20 marks for buying goods contrary to order is suspended until Mr Girling come, upon whose information the said order is either to be confirmed or repealed.

12   Entry is crossed out, with note, 'twice'.

The leys and taxations for raising money for the monthly assessment are to be collected and paid, and a letter written to Mr Massey concerning the same.

p. 487
29 NOVEMBER 1650
Upon reading the Governor's letter concerning the preferring of a petition to Parliament for the renewing of the Charter and confirmation of the ancient privileges of this town, it was resolved that we should consult with the recorder about it, and have his assistance in the drawing up of the petition.

And the like petition concerning the demolishing of the works which are so much prejudicial to the town, but suspended until the Governor should come hence.

9 JANUARY 1650
At an Assembly it was propounded by Mr Mayor concerning Mr Bicksteth his long stay at London, and resolved that enquiry be made to know how much money will discharge his engagements there, and that he shall forthwith come down if his health will permit.

25 JANUARY 1649
Upon reading of a warrant from the high constables for 3 months' assessments beginning the 25 December 1649 for £1,200 per month in Derby hundred, whereof Liverpool's proportion is £17 6s 7½d per month for the army, it was resolved that the same should be forthwith assessed and collected.

p. 488
Whereas there are diverse debts due unto the town which are like to prove desperate unless they be looked for in time, and the town having great occasion to use money, it is ordered that the said debts shall be examined and set down by the mayor and the aldermen, and the note of them delivered to the bailiffs to be called for and paid in, and they are to sue for them as they shall think fit, and the bailiffs are to disburse the charges to recover them.

It was ordered by Mr Mayor, the aldermen, bailiffs and common council assembled that Mr Thomas Bicksteth, alderman, who has long time lain at London at a great charge to the town, and the great grief and trouble of his friends, shall speedily come down and give in his account. Whereupon Mr Wainewright was written to who took much pains in the business and sent down a note of his debts and judgements contracted upon him by his long stay there which amounts to about £90. Whereupon Mr Washington being questioned by the house concerning the £50 taken up of one Mr Weston for which Mr Way is engaged confessed that money all came to his hands.

11 MARCH 1649
Received the 29 January 1649 of Colonel Birch the order of parliament that concerns the towns of Liverpool, Lancaster and Manchester, which are filed with

the commissioners for compounding and are numbered 6,7,8, and are to be read and determined according to their numbers. John Leech.

A lease being drawn up between the town and Mr Poole on behalf of Mr Dobson was denied. And ordered that the said house shall not be otherwise let than according to former order.

p. 489

Whereas violent suits have been and are persecuted in the upper bench against Mr Walker by Mr Edward Johnson and Mr Nicholas Hawett of Manchester for certain goods of Irish rebels which by him were seized on behalf of the town in the time of his mayoralty, the proceeds whereof were violently taken away by the Earl of Derby, whereupon he has been outlawed, and after reversals and special bail entered at London the issues are ready for trial at Derby assizes where the accusations are laid, it is therefore ordered that Mr Mayor and Mr Winstanley shall go to Derby to attend those proceedings, the town being concerned therein, and shall have their charges borne, and are to be there the 22nd instant, where they attended accordingly but the plaintiffs did put in the records.

p. 490

18 MARCH 1649

Memorandum: that the audit of account for 4 years past being held with much trouble, and all arrears of the receipts of the several late bailiffs appeared to remain in their hands and due to the town, which were ordered to be paid over to the now bailiffs this day. These several sums were now this day paid in:

By Mr Edward Williamson and Robert Cornell	56s		
By Mr Hodgson, now mayor, and Mr Sandiford	£12	18s	4d
By Richard Williamson and John Sturzaker	£15	4s	
By Edward Lyon and Thomas Storie besides the 40s abated by Richard Williamson	£94	1s	2d

2 APRIL 1650

At an Assembly held before Mr Hodgson, mayor, John Walker, senior alderman, and the most part of the common council:

It was propounded concerning the purchasing and contracting with the trustees at Worcester House for the fee farm rents of this borough, and ordered that the governor, being a burgess, be consulted about what course is to be taken, and to prevent Lord Mollineux or any others in looking for it the town will endeavour to contract for it themselves with the said trustees for the town's use.

A letter from Mr William Langton, the recorder, was read whereby he resigns his place of recordership with much expressions of love and thankfulness to the town, which office is for the present suspended and no new election as yet to be made.

p. 491

Upon reading of a warrant from the high constable for payment of £11 11s 1d charged upon this town towards the payment of £90,000 per month for maintenance of the army in England and Ireland, due for 3 months' assessments beginning 5 March 1650, it was ordered by this assembly that a ley of £12 shall be laid throughout the town proportionately.

Whereas Edward Alcock, late bailiff of this borough and one of the common council, having obtained a lease for 40 years to commence from the death of Elizabeth Barker, widow who died about 12 years since, from Richard Barker in consideration of £10 long since paid, which said messuage and tenement being in the possession of Elizabeth Barker, wife of the said Richard, the said Edward Alcock hath freely bestowed upon the town, it is ordered that the assignment be drawn up accordingly and the rent and proceeds thereof be yearly received by the bailiffs to increase the town's revenues. And the said Elizabeth, detaining possession, is to be cast out unless she compound with the town.

p. 492

It was ordered that Richard Higginson, cutler, shall be discharged from his office of clock keeper. And that William Higginson shall serve in his stead, and shall receive the wages due, 26s 8d per annum, during the pleasure of the town.

It is also agreed that Cook's house and lands, so much as belong to the town, shall be let by Mr Thomas Blackmoore and Mr Thomas Tarleton, aldermen, for the town's use, and accounted for at every audit.

16 APRIL 1650

Memorandum: that this day, being Easter Monday, according to ancient custom by consent of the worshipful Mr Mayor and the aldermen of this borough, George Potter and Thomas Lurting were elected churchwardens for the year ensuing, whereupon the old ones, having made their account, were discharged from their said office.

Whereas it is certainly reported that the Sickness is in Dublin, which by reason of the intercourse from thence may prove dangerous to this town, it is ordered that all owners and passengers coming from thence shall be restrained from coming into this town unless they can make oath that they have not been in any infected place, nor bring over any infected goods or passengers from thence, and be allowed of by Mr Mayor. And a warrant to be drawn up for the guard to examine all passengers coming from thence until they be sworn and examined, which was done accordingly.

p. 493
18 JUNE 1650

Forasmuch as the town's charters have long been in London and are to be sent down, remaining in the hands of Thomas Wareing, it is ordered that if Mr John Winstanley happens to go up this term he shall have half of his expenses for the despatch of the business, vizt. to search for judgements against Colonel Moore and his surety for the £100 due to the town and sued for by Mr Wells; to enquire after and send down the town's books and charters; to enquire about the purchase of the fee farm rents. Which was done and £3 allowed him.

Ordered by the same assembly, that, on Friday next, Mr Mayor and the persons underwritten, shall pass throughout the town to take notice of all inmates as are or like to be prejudicial to the town: Edward Chambers and Roger Jones for Water Street; Thomas Williamson and Thomas Andoe, Chapel Street; John Chantrell and Richard Williamson, Castle Street; Edward Alcock, Juglars Street; which was done, and their names presented and their landlords fined.

p. 494
18 JUNE 1650
At an Assembly before Mr Mayor, the aldermen and bailiffs and most of the Common Council:

Ordered that that part of the Common which lies between the sea and the way leading to the Park Gate westward, unto the New Bridge or the Bowling Green, shall be improved and enclosed at the town's charge next winter, and managed for the benefit of the town. The mayor and bailiffs shall disburse money to see the same fenced.

Ordered that speedy course shall be taken to recover £100 and interest from Colonel Moore and Mr James Sotherne, both deceased, and search be made in London for the judgment thereupon by Mr Wells, late town clerk, at the town's charge, according to former order.

15 JULY 1650
Ordered that the former order against Mr John Sandiford shall stay until he returns or until Michaelmas Day, and if he then does not clear himself the estreat of his last fine to be due.

11 OCTOBER 1650
On further debate of this fine, and on reading of Gurling's certificate, that the same bark and goods were bought in Wirral before their coming to this harbour, the business was suspended because of the absence of Mr William Williamson.

Memorandum of December 1652: on reading Mr Gurling's certificate it was voted by the 40 that he be discharged of his fine.[13]

p. 495
18 JUNE 1650
Whereas 16 barrels of tallow bought by Mr Richard Parsivalle are subject to licence money which, not being known, is likely to be lost to the town, this assembly, noting that he bought them contrary to order before 14 days had passed or the mayor acquainted with it, holds it to be a great offence and imposes a fine of 20s, and for the next offence, £10.

The same offence and fine levied on Roger Jones, Edward Formby, Adam Leathes and George Potter.

---

13   Memorandum is added in different ink.

Agreed that the persons restrained are to admitted to the town, and if hereafter any shall go to Dublin or any other infected place they shall be restrained from coming on shore.

15 JULY 1650

Forasmuch as Mr Johnson and Mr Hanett have last term taken out the records in the upper bench for the trial at Derby against Mr John Walker in the business concerning the rebels' goods, it is ordered by this assembly that letters be written to Mr Greene, the counsellors and Mr Halley, and that Mr Edward Chambers shall go to Derby to attend the trial, and have his expenses paid.

p. 496

11 OCTOBER 1650

At an Assembly in the common hall before the Worshipful Mr Mayor, the aldermen, bailiffs and common council:

Mr Mayor proposed the rent to be paid by Elizabeth Barker for the house given to the town by Mr Bailiff Alcock. After debate it was ordered that she pay 50s 6d for a year's rent to Michaelmas 1651, and shall pay 25s 3d, the half year's rent due since the death of old Elizabeth Barker, for repairs. And she shall continue to be tenant on her good behaviour at a rent to be set by this assembly.

Susan's rent: The rent of 6s 8d for Burscough's house was debated, formerly paid to Colonel Moore and his ancestors who were entrusted to receive the rent for the town's use. Ordered that henceforth the rent shall be paid by the immediate tenants to the bailiffs.

p. 497

p. 498

p. 499

JAMES WILLIAMSON, GENTLEMAN, MAYOR, 1650 [1650–51]

p. 500

LIVERPOOL. COURT OF ELECTION, 18 OCTOBER 1650, before Thomas Hodgson, gentleman, mayor, and Gilbert Formby and Evan Marsh, bailiffs, by virtue of letters patent of Charles, late king.[14]

James Williamson, gentleman, is elected mayor, sworn

Thomas Ayndoe is elected bailiff for the republic and mayor, sworn

14   Latin.

William Lurting is elected the other bailiff for the town, sworn. (He died the 16 June 1651 and 23 June 1651 his brother, Peter Lurting, was elected and sworn.)[15]

Officers elected by the Common Council:
Minister suspended
John Winstanley, town clerk
John Kirk, serjeant at mace
Richard Dwarrihouse, water bailiff[16]
George Glover, schoolmaster
Church clerk suspended
John Williamson, hallkeeper
Edward Ashton, town customer, upon his fair demeanour
Richard Poultney, subcustomer
Richard Lewesley, Christopher Brookbank, stewards of the hall, sworn
Robert Halle, William Newis, supervisors of the highways
Heyward suspended
John Sharples, William Eccleston, churchwardens, 1651

p. 501
Officers chosen by grand jury at the portmoot, 4 November 1650:
Merchant appraisers, John Chantrell (dead; John Walles elected last of June),[17]
John Higinson, Robert Lurting, Edward Lyon, sworn
Registers of leather, John Birchall, Thomas Roe, sworn
Alefounders, Edward Lea, William Higinson, sworn
Barley men, William Midleton, Anthony Hunte, Thomas Rainford, Thomas Fazakerley
Murenger, John Cooke
Scavengers, Gilbert Coote, William Ryding, cooper, George Tarleton, John Tennant, sworn
Leavelooker, —
Porters, John Barton, Edward Rycrofte
Boardsetter, John Formby, Edward Rycrofte
Boothsetters, John Ryce, Richard Widdowes
Swineherd, —

p. 502
21 NOVEMBER 1650
At an Assembly before Mr Mayor, John Walker, Thomas Blackmoore, Thomas Tarleton and Thomas Hodgson, aldermen, the bailiffs and most part of the

15   Latin; note about death of William Lurting is added in different hand.
16   Latin.
17   Note on death of John Chantrell is added in different hand.

Common Council it was resolved that the fee farm rents of this borough, which are £14 6s 8d per annum, shall be bought and contracted for with the trustees of parliament for the use and benefit of this corporation. £100 shall be raised towards prospecting of the purchase, and whoever stands security for the same shall be saved harmless by this house, and be secured out of the said rents, which shall be purchased in the name of the mayor, bailiffs and burgesses of this town. It is also agreed that the butlerage rent of 20s per annum shall be bought from the same or other trustees of parliament that have power to sell the same: James Williamson, mayor, Jo. Walker, Tho. Blackmor, Thomas Tarleton, T A (sign. Thome Ayndoe), William Lurting, bailiffs, Jo. Winstanley, town clerk, Jo. Chantrell, R L (sign. Robti. Lurting), Edward Chambers, Roger Joane, Edward Alcock, John Williamson, Edward Formby, Tho. Williamson, Edw. Williamson, Robert Cornell, Jo. Sandiford, Tho. Story, John Walls, Peter Larting, John Kirke, Ri. Dwarihouse, Richard Williamson, Richard Peircivalle, John Sturzaker, Edward Lyon, Even Marshe, John Higginsonn[18]

p. 503

p. 504
GREAT PORTMOOT COURT OR SESSION OF THE PEACE, 4 NOVEMBER 1650, before the mayor, and Thomas Ayndoe and William Lurting bailiffs.[19]

Inquest held on the oath of Gilbert Formby, John Higinson, Ralph Massam, Robert Cornell, Thomas Storie, John Sharples, Peter Lurting, John Walles, Richard Turner, William Sutton, Thomas Hanckcok, Gilbert Tarleton, Thomas Coppull, Richard Holland, Thomas Leaver, Thomas Nicholsonn, Henry Kilshawe, William Mosse, Robert Halle, Richard Kenion, cooper, John Johnson of Everton, William Darrwen, John Henshalle and William Sympson.[20]

We present:
John Lurting, mariner, for abusing Mr Thomas Tarleton, alderman, calling him a cheating rogue, 20s
    The same for a tussle on Thomas Ayndoe, 3s 4d
    Thomas Ayndoe for a tussle on John Lurting, 3s 4d
    Richard Coppull, smith, 3s 4d
    Richard Coppull for a tussle on Peter Boulton, 3s 4d
    William Chorley for a blood wipe on Thomas Nicholson, shoemaker, 6s 8d
    Margery Martine for a tussle on him also, 3s 4d
    Thomas Nicholson for the like on William Chorley, 3s 4d

18   These names are signatures, and the original spelling and abbreviations are retained; henceforth such lists are noted simply as signatures.
19   Latin.
20   Latin.

William Seacome of Everton for a tussle on Elizabeth, 3s 4d

Thomas Fazakerley, miller, for a tussle on Robert Hill, ferryman, 3s 4d.

Robert Hill for the like on Thomas Fazakerley, 3s 4d

Robert Sympson for abusing John Higinson, a bailiff's peer, saying in open market he was an idle fellow and blamed this town for electing him bailiff, 2s 6d

Mr Thomas Blackmore, alderman, for tethering in the town field, 3s 4d

Edward Chambers, John Higinson, Ralph Massam, Edward Williamson, Henry Moore, John Owen, John Bankes of Liverpool, Henry Rydeing, James Burton and William Fazakerley for the like, 3s 4d apiece

Thomas Fazakerley for cutting grass in the town field, 3s 4d

Richard Johnson of Everton, James Topping, William Platt of Liverpool for the like, severally 3s 4d

Mr Edward Chambers, Mrs Elizabeth Heapie, Jane Haskaine, Margery Tarleton, widow, John Williamson junior, John Cook, Thomas Burton and Richard Turner for keeping their swine unrung, 12d apiece

Elizabeth Mosse, Thomas Glover and Ellen Asline the market, 3s 4d apiece

Edward Lyon, Thomas Burton, Robert Houghton, John Birch, Thomas Roe, Thomas Nicholson, Richard Blevine, Peter Laford, Richard Holland, Henry Radcliffe and Henry Cooper for working unlawful leather, 3s 4d apiece

p. 505

Thomas Abram, Humphrey Mercer, Thomas Parker, Robert Crowborne, Archibald Finley, John Poultney, Richard Rimer, Robert Tipping and Peter Halle for using the faculty of freemen, not being free, 3s 4d apiece

Susan Eccleston, widow, Elinor Sharples, widow, Mrs Elizabeth Heapey, widow, Richard Washington junior, Ralph Winstanley, Peter Halle, Mr Edward Plumer, Mr John Chandler and Thomas Burton for selling beer and ale by unlawful measures, 3s 4d apiece

Thomas Whitfield, Serjeant Warmisham, Hamlett Deane, James Hoult, Adam Huchinson, Robert Marsh, Thomas Brumvell, William Norres and John Robinson for using the faculty of freemen, 3s 4d apiece

John Higinson, John Yong, Dorothy Bicksteth, William Gardner, Thomas Lancellott, George Tarleton for keeping inmates and not giving security to the town, 3s 4d apiece

Mr Edward Chambers for not keeping the street clean, 6d

Edward Ashton, William Chorley, Robert Halle and William Bushell, late scavengers, for neglecting their office, 3s 4d apiece

All free burgesses as have not made their appearance and not essoyned or excused: Nehemiah Brettargh esq., William Bell, clerk, William Ward, clerk, Thomas Sheppard, Edward Stockley, Thomas Blackburne, Edward Dicconson, Edmund Smoult, Peares Gearrard, Ralph Shorrock, Robert Wingreene, Edward Starkey, Edward Ogle, James Massey, John Fox esq., John Waide, Henry Webster, Robert Bicksteth junior, Henry Birchall, Richard Barker, Thomas Gardner, Robert Farrington, Richard Morecroft, John Bate, William Smithelles and Derby Caton, 3s 4d apiece

We order:

That all who have land along the sea bank shall make up their fence before 25 March next on pain of 5s apiece

The sexton to ring curfew every night at 8 o'clock, and 4 in the morning from the 1 November till Candlemas according to custom

We agree to all ancient orders and laudable customs.

p. 506

LIVERPOOL. PORTMOOT COURT OR SESSION OF THE PEACE, 31 MARCH 1651, before the mayor and Thomas Ayndoe and William Lurting, bailiffs.[21]

Inquest held on the oath of Roger Jones, Thomas Williamson, John Sturzaker, John Sharples, John Owen, Thomas Ploumb, Gilbert Tarleton, Thomas Carr, Robert Lyon, William Toping, Richard Lunte, William Eccleston, Robert Clark, Richard Holland and Edward Lea, jurors.[22]

We present:

William Mee of the Lowe, butcher, for publically cursing in open court, saying the devil go with you and all your actions, pointing at the jury, 33s 4d

The same for cursing in open court and pointing his finger at Mr Mayor and the jury, saying the devil go with you and all the acts that you have done, £5

Thomas Hoskins, gentleman, for a tussle on Thomas Lurting, smith, 3s 4d

The same for a tussle on William Lurting, one of the bailiffs, 3s 4d

The same for a blood wipe on William Lurting, 6s 8d

Thomas Lurting for a tussle on Thomas Hoskins, 3s 4d

Thomas Storie for allowing his fence to lie down to the annoyance of Adam Leigh, 1s

p. 507

John Eccleston, John Chandler, Thomas Lancelot and William Strangeways for their fences lying down, and James Hey for annoying Gilbert Tarleton, not making up his house end, 1s apiece

Ralph Winstanley for selling his drink with unlawful measure, 2s 6d

Luke Harrison and Nicholas Rideing for the like offence, 6d apiece

Edward Fazakerley, John Webster, Thomas Parker, Peter Hall, Thomas, Abraham Culbert, Mr Walker's tenant, and Hamblet Deane for using the faculty of freemen, not free, 3s 4d apiece

John Lurting, mariner, Richard Holland, Thomas Seale, Michael Barker, Thomas Lancelot, William Chantrell, Margaret Foster, Richard Higinson, Henry Craine, Gregory Formby, Mr Walker's tenant, George Potter, Richard Washington junior, Isabel Moore, widow, William Newis, Peter Lurting, John Lurting, smith,

21   Latin.
22   Latin.

Robert Cowburne, Elizabeth Barker, Robert Hall, Henry Rydeing, Edward Rycrofte, George Prescot, Anne Mason, widow, Robert Johnsonne, tailor, John Poultney, Thomas Nicholson, for not appearing to be licensed to brew and sell ale and beer for the year following, 3s 4d apiece

John Arven, William Bushell, James Burton for the like offence, 3s 4d

John Tirer of Litherland for a tussle on John Jameson, 3s 4d

Thomas Tarleton, alderman, for keeping his swine unrung, 6d

Thomas Ambrose, servant to John Eccleston, for a tussle on Henry Darbishire, 3s 4d

Thomas Tarleton, alderman, for letting his timber lie in the street to annoyance of neighbours, 1s

John Poultney for not cleansing his part of the street, 1s

p. 508

Thomas Bicksteth, alderman, for the like offence, 1s

We order:

That the streets about this town of Liverpool be amended before 1 June next

That there be a coal barrel made for the use of the town, provided by Richard Dwarihouse, water bailiff, before 12 April next

We agree to all ancient orders and laudable customs.

p. 509

p. 510

PORTMOOT COURT OR QUARTER SESSIONS, MONDAY 30 JUNE 1651, for the borough and port town of Liverpool in the county of Lancaster, before James Williamson, gentleman, mayor, Thomas Andoe and Peter Lurting, bailiffs, according to ancient custom.

Inquest taken on the oaths of Edward Alcock, Ralph Massam, Robert Cornell, Richard Washington, Henry Rydeing, Richard Higinson, cutler, Oliver Fairehurst, John Sutton, William Rydeing, cooper, Thomas Leaver, Thomas Roe, William Mosse, Thomas Fazakerley, Thomas Coppull, Richard Widdowes.

We present:

Edmund Whalley for a blood wipe on Robert Leavies, 6s 8d

Robert Halle and William Newis, supervisors of the highways, for neglecting their office before 1 June last, according to order made at portmoot court held 31 March

Thomas Abram, James Hollinsworth, Thomas Kellie, Peter Halle, Robert Sympson for retailing beer and ale, not being free, 3s 4d

Peter Halle selling ale by small measures, 2s 6d

James Boulton, gunsmith, and William Mee for taking turf from the common out of the liberties of the town, 6s 8d

Dorothy Bicksteth, Thomas Nicholson, Margery Tarleton, John Higinson, John Eccleston, William Newis, John Owen, Richard Washington junior, Gilbert Formby, Thomas Lancellot, William Gardiner, Mrs Bicksteth and Mrs Sharples for like offence, 1s apiece

Thomas Woods for selling unlawful leather, 3s 4d

p. 511

Peter Leyforth selling shoes in market made of unlawful leather, 3s 4d

James Boulton for like offence, 3s 4d

Mr Edward Moore for letting dung lie in Castle Street to annoyance of neighbours, 1s

Mr Thomas Tarleton for letting timber lie in Chapel Street

Mr Chambers for letting dung lie in Water Street, 1s

Margery Martine for letting dung lie in Dale Street, 1s apiece

John Whytestones, Katherine Samon and John Higinson for the like —,

George Tarleton, one of the scavengers, for neglecting his office, and peremptorily denying its execution, —

Alderman Blackmoore, for leasowing horses in the town field, contrary to order, —

Mr Richard Johnson for cutting growing grass in the townfield, 1s

John Henshawe and John Owen for the like —,

Mr Thomas Blackmoore, John Higinson, butcher, William Moss and Dorothy Bicksteth for not repairing the fence by the land they hold by the sea bank according to order of 4 November last, 6d apiece

James Moorcroft of Lunte in Sefton parish, Peter Smith of Derby, Thomas Aspe of Kirkby, Thomas Robinson of Ormskirk for buying skins in the market before the hour appointed, 3s 4d

Richard Dwarrihouse, water bailiff, for not providing a coal barrel for the town, according to an order made 31 March last, 2s 6d.

We elect:

John Walles to be merchant appraiser in stead of John Chantrell, deceased.

We order:

That the present possessors of the Moor Croft make up their fences, now open to the town field, within 10 days, on penalty of 20s apiece

We agree to all ancient orders and laudable customs.

p. 512

31 OCTOBER 1650

Forasmuch as £50, part of a year's tithe, remains in the hands of Mr Tompson since preferred to Sefton, which Mr Fogg, our present minister has claimed as his, now, having relinquished the same, it is due to the mayor and bailiffs for the use of such minister as is appointed hereafter. Ordered without dissent.

Whereas Mr Henry Burscow is in debt to this corporation of £16, long since due for his interest in the messuage now in possession of Susan Eccleston, widow, now she has contracted with him for his little interest in the same, and, with the consent of the mayor, bailiffs and common council, has paid the bailiffs the £16, who are to receive it without further interest since it had been formerly tendered.

p. 513
CORONER'S INQUEST, 12 NOVEMBER 1650

Before Thomas Hodgson, alderman, coroner, and Richard Washington junior, Peter Bennett, Thomas Hancock, Thomas Potter, William Sutton, John Evans, Thomas Seddon, Thomas Gorsich, John Dyke, John Wilson, John Rachdall, Richard Greaves.[23] Who, upon oath, presented that Ralph Heton of Hindley was accidentally killed on Monday 11 November from a wound in the forehead by the bursting of a firelock piece discharged by John Hollingworth from a window in the house of Roger Rose in Tithebarn Street where he was quartered.

p. 514
19 DECEMBER 1650

Whereas it was formerly agreed to purchase the fee farm rent of the town, it is ordered by this assembly that a letter of attorney be drawn up, naming Mr John Walker, Mr William Williamson, Mr Edward Chambers and Richard Williamson as trustees and purchasers on behalf of the town, which was sent up accordingly, and the purchase prospected, and a special grant obtained by the solicitations on Mr William Williamson.

Considering the abuse done to the town by divers freemen who use divers stalls and standings, the benefit of which should accrue to the town and not to any private person, and having spent much money in purchasing the fee farm rent of £14 6s 8d per annum, to clear their title, tolls and customs, it is ordered that Mr Mayor, Mr Bailiff Andoe and Mr Edward Williamson survey the stalls and standings in the market, and that every one shall pay 2d per day and no other rent, and one of the bailiffs shall collect this every day. This ordinance confirmed on 7 May, and the toll to be collected until the recorder shall be informed about it.

p. 515
COMPOSITIONS

19 December 1650:

Mr Denman for 160 barrels of herring aboard *John Millan* of Dunough a Dee, 40s
John Marsh and two William Rymers for 60 barrels, 15s
Richard Norris of Formby in his bark for 100 barrels, 25s
Mr Wilcock of Dublin for 200 barrels of herring, £5 2s 10d
Henry Darbisheire for 60 barrels, 16s
Mr Sand for 18 barrels, 4s 9d
Philip Harrison for 12 barrels, 3s 4d
Mr Waterhouse for 24 barrels herring, Mr Chambers, 7s 8d

23 Latin.

William Goore for 10 barrels, 3s 4d
  5 February 1650:
Captain Whitworth for beef and tallow, 25s 8d
Thomas Parsifall for the like goods, 19s
Captain Sherrwin and others for the same[24]
John Waterhouse for 34 barrels of herrings for Richard Williamson in the *Michael*, for Mr Chambers, 10s 4d
Christopher Waller for 9 barrels herrings in the same vessel, 3s 4d

p. 516
10 JANUARY 1650

On producing a lease from the town to Thomas Tickle and Margaret, his daughter, of a messuage in Dale Street at 3s 2d rent for 100 years, if Tickle, Margaret and Robert Kenion live so long, with one life remaining, Robert Kenion petitions the town for a new lease to him and his two children. Ordered by the mayor, bailiffs and common council that he may have a new lease for the lives of him, Thomas and Jane Kenion, paying a £24 fine and the old rent, and to keep it in good and tenantable repair and not to dispose of it for above a year without the consent of the town. Burgage rent 6d.

Concerning Cook's house, part of which is claimed by Mr Tarleton, the same is suspended until the recorder gives advice, and meanwhile the profits are to be received and accounted for by the bailiffs.

William Halsall of Harleton, esq., was elected recorder in place of Mr Langton who, refusing to subscribe the judgement, freely resigns his place. Mr Halsall was sworn on 23 January a free burgess, one of the common council and the recorder by general consent and is to have the stipend due.

p. 517

p. 518
5 FEBRUARY 1650

Concerning the common formerly ordered to be enclosed, Mr Mayor, with the consent of this house is willing to take 2 acres next to the Pool and offers to give 30s per acre fine for 21 years, and 12d per acre rent, and not to let the same unless to freemen inhabitants. On 10 April following, in full debate, the fine was agreed to be too high, considering the cost of fencing and improving the closes. And on a vote of the last mentioned assembly it was resolved that the tenants of the said new enclosures shall have them for 31 years for a fine of 30s per acre, and 12d rent, and that 2 acres of the common where the best marl is should be left unenclosed where everyone might have liberty to dig marl for improving the enclosures, and no one should let the same to any foreigner, but only freemen, on pain of forfeiting their estates.

---

24   'Sum' is crossed out.

p. 519

Memorandum: That Thomas Ayndoe, bailiff, and James Hey have agreed with the town for one large close of 3 acres and 46 falls of ground, part of the common lying next to the park gate, westward towards the sea side, jointly for 31 years for a fine of 30s per acre and 12d per acre rent.

Richard Washington senior and Richard Washington junior have also agreed for one other close or new enclosure next to the abovementioned, northwards, and adjoining John Sturzaker's Limekiln Close, containing – acres, according to the aforesaid order.

p. 520
12 MAY 1651

On reading a warrant from the high constable for the £12,000 assessment charged on England and Wales for the maintenance of the forces raised by authority of parliament for 6 months, to begin 25 March last, of which sum £1,600 per month is charged on the county of Lancaster, of which £42 13s 7d is charged on this town, to be paid in May, July and September next to Mr John Sorrocold, receiver and treasurer, it is ordered that the merchant appraisers shall assess the said sum in an equal and proportional way, according the the act of parliament and the custom of this borough. And in the absence of Edward Lyon, one of the appraisers, Mr Bailiff Storie is appointed to assist.

The assembly was informed by Mr Mayor that the stone house in the churchyard is out of lease, and hath been held and kept from the town by Thomas Tarleton, alderman. Resolved that since Mr Tarleton had held the same from the town for the space of 9 years the mayor and bailiffs shall cause an entry to be made on behalf of the town, having noted that his estate is long since settled, and that the rents hereafter arising from the same shall be received by them for the use of the town.

p. 521
1 APRIL 1651

The accounts of the churchwardens were examined before Mr Mayor, the aldermen and bailiffs, and 3s 4d found remaining, paid to the bailiffs.

23 JUNE 1651

Peter Lurting was elected bailiff for the rest of this year.

7 MAY 1651

John Sharples, son of Cuthbert Sharples, is elected to the common council, and sworn.

30 JUNE 1651

Ordered by Mr Mayor and the council that, because there is not a full number to be at the council because of death and removal, Mr John Bird, Mr Thomas Sandiford, Henry Moore, John Eccleston, Adam Leathes, William Rymer and George Potter be admitted of the common council, the forty of this town, whereof the last six were sworn.

p. 522
30 JUNE 1651

At an Assembly in the common hall, before the mayor, bailiffs and common council, the mayor proposed the election of a minister, who by ancient custom is chosen by the said assembly, and upon debate it was ordered that two orthodox ministers should be elected to officiate here since there is hope of better maintenance than formerly, it being the chief port and only garrison in these parts, and a place of great resort. Mr Peter Stanynough and Mr Michael Briscowe are proposed and approved jointly to officiate and serve the cure here, dividing the allowances equally, and for precedence as they can agree, during their good demeanour.

10 SEPTEMBER 1651
At an Assembly:

The mayor proposed the election of another minister to replace Mr Peter Stanynough who has resigned. Mr James Rigbie is elected to join Mr Briscowe. James Williamson, mayor.

Memorandum: that Mr Briscowe has resigned, being engaged in the place he formerly lived, and because of the sickness. Being disappointed, the town has invited Mr Fogg to return if he, by subscribing the judgement, agrees to officiate in the garrison which the town is very desirous of.

p. 523
8 OCTOBER 1651

At an Assembly of the Common Council it is agreed that the bailiffs shall be freed from the collecting of fines because of the present condition of the town due to the infection, and for future collection they are to follow ancient orders. Ja. Williamson, mayor.

APPRENTICES

Memorandum that John Birch, son of John Birch of Okenshawe, was apprenticed to Mr Robert Greene and Mr Alexander Greene, merchants, from the 1 March 1649 for 5 years.

Memo. that John Walsh, son of Cuthbert Walsh of Ainsdale, has by consent of his father put himself apprentice to William Rymmer, mariner, for 7 years from 24 June 1651. His master is to provide clothes and necessities, and after his term to make him free.

Memo. that William Fazakerley, son of Richard Fazakerley of Fazakerley, was with the consent of his father apprenticed to Thomas Nicholson, shoemaker, for 7 years, from the said day, and was made free 18 October 1658.

p. 524

p. 525

p. 526
INDENTURE, 14 OCTOBER 1651
Between the mayor and bailiffs on one part and Robert Kenion of Altcar, husbandman, on the other. Witness that the mayor, bailiffs and burgesses, on the surrender of one indenture of lease made to Thomas and Margaret Tickle, deceased, whereas the life of Kenion is still in being, and for the sum of £24 paid by Robert Kenion, demise and lease to Robert Kenion the dwelling house situated in Dale Street, the inheritance of the borough, now occupied by Edward Williamson or his undertenants, a part in the tenure of Dorothy Mather, widow, usually let with all appurtenances to the said Robert Kenion, for 100 years, if he, and his children, Thomas and Jane, live so long, paying to the town 3s 2d per annum at Michaelmas, and all other ancient burgage and chantry rents as shall be due. Robert Kenion agrees to maintain the property in good and tenantable repair, and the mayor, bailiffs and burgeses grant Robert Kenion the tenancy without hindrance.

p. 527

p. 528
FREEMEN
   25 October 1650
Jeremy Berstow, merchant, late apprentice of Mr Beck, admitted a free burgess by the consent of the mayor, aldermen and common council, paying for his composition, £3
   31 December 1650
William Olive, mariner, £3
Richard Rymer, sailor, 50s
Humphrey Mercer, slater, 50s
   23 January 1650
Henry Ogle, gentleman, free
Michael Tarleton, gentleman, free
   8 February 1650
Robert Barrow, colonel of foot, free
   13th
John Sutton, pumpmaker, £3
Edward Sutton, blacksmith, £3
   22 September 1651
Henry Corles, £5
John Eccles, £5
William Reynold, mariner, £5
   7 March 1650
Richard Galloway, 40s
Thomas Chapman, son Thomas Chapman, gentleman, 40s

p. 529
James Barton, mariner, apprentice of Thomas Ayndoe, 6s 8d

10 April 1651

John Corker, merchant, £10

Thomas Sandiford, son of Ralph Sandiford, late alderman, admitted according to custom, 3s 4d

James Hey, milliner, £3

   12 May 1651

Thomas Parcivall, merchant, admitted and sworn 24 May, £6 13s 4d

Robert Swifte, cutler, £6 13s 4d

All sworn.

Memo: paid to the bailiffs by the old churchwardens on making of their accounts, 3s 4d.

p. 530

THE AUDIT OF THOMAS HODGSON, MAYOR, 25 JANUARY 1651 by Gilbert Formbie and Evan Marsh, late bailiffs, before Thomas Williamson, mayor, for receipts and disbursements from 28 October 1649 to 28 October 1650.

Receipts:

From town's customer, ingates	£7	6s	9½d
outgates £5 0s 7d Total	£12	7s	4½d
John Williamson, hall keeper, ingates and outgates	4	2	7
Richard Poultney, subcustomer, tolls and stalls	10	0	10
For freemen	23	0	4
For composition, licence and butlerage	19	16	6
Town's rents, besides Barker's owing	13	3	4
Rent for ferry boats	14	0	0
From Susan Eccleston, for a debt	16	0	0
For a horse and stray bullock	7	13	5
For pedlars' and butchers' stalls		38s	
For the schoolmaster, allowing charges	5	0	4
Fines	7	16	7
The overplus of 6 leys collected	13	7	10
Elizabeth Barker's rent, besides repair		20s	
For the arrears of several audits, and now paid over	124	19	6

The total receipts	£273	6s	8d
Total disbursements allowed	19	3	1
The remainder to be paid to the present bailiffs, deducting town's burgage rent, £3 9s 11d	80	13	8

Signed and allowed by the aldermen.

p. 531

THOMAS WILLIAMSON, GENTLEMAN, MAYOR, 1652[25] [1651–52]

p. 532
Liverpool. Election Court, Saturday 18 October 1651, before James Williamson, gentleman, mayor, Thomas Aindoe and Peter Lurting, bailiffs, by virtue of several letters patent and according to the ancient custom of the borough.

Thomas Williamson is elected mayor, and sworn
Richard Parsivalle is elected bailiff for the mayor and the commonwealth of England, and sworn
John Ecleston is elected bailiff for the borough, and sworn.

Ministers, Michael Briscowe and Rigbie
John Winstanley, town clerk
John Kirks, serjeant at mace
Richard Dwarrihouse, water bailiff

Officers chosen by the common council on Friday following according to custom:
Minister —
Schoolmaster, George Glover
Church clerk, Richard Poultney
Hall keeper —
Town's customer, Edward Ashton
Subcustomer, Richard Poultney
Steward of the hall, Edmund Leivesley, Thomas Roe, sworn
Supervisors, John Sutton, Thomas Fazakerley
Heyward, Thomas Coppull, sworn
Churchwardens, Thomas Burton, William Eccleston

p. 533
Officers elected by the jury:
Merchant appraisers, Thomas Ayndoe, John Sturzaker, Evan Marsh, George Potter, sworn
Registers of leather, John Birchall, Thomas Nicholson, sworn
Ale founders, Gilbert Coote, William Litherland, sworn
Barleymen, James Hey, Thomas Leaver, Thomas Lancellot, John Tennant, sworn
Scavengers, Richard Coppull, Humphrey Mercer, Edward Sutton, Abraham West, sworn
Porters, John Barton, Edward Rycroft

25   The year is given as 1652, even though the mayoral year began in 1651. In most years the calendar year in which the mayoral year began is recorded.

Boardsetters, John Formby, Edward Rycrofte
Boothsetters, John Ryce, Richard Widdowes
Swineherd, Richard Samme
Churchwardens elected 2 April 1652, Richard Leivesey, Edward Winstanley.

p. 534
PORTMOOT COURT OR QUARTER SESSIONS, MONDAY 12 JANUARY
1651, for the borough and port town of Liverpool, before the mayor and Richard
Peircevall and John Eccleston, bailiffs.

Inquest of the jurors on the oaths of Thomas Andoe, John Sturzaker, Evan
Marsh, George Potter, Robert Lurting, Richard Williamson, Thomas Sandiford,
Henry Corles, Adam Leathes, Richard Washington junior, Richard Blevine,
Richard Leivsey, William Higinson, smith, Anthony Hunt, John Cook, William
Ryding, cooper, Richard Widdow, Edward Rycroft, Thomas Nicholson, William
Mosse, Robert Halle, Thomas Coppull, William Litherland, Oliver Fairehurst,
Thomas Lurting, Christopher Brookbank, Thomas Hancok.

We present:
    Richard Williamson for a tussle on William Sedon
    William Seddon for tussle on Richard Williamson
    Peter Halle, Robert Sympson, John Webster for retailing beer, not being free
    Robert Williamson, the Dutchman, for using faculty of a freeman, not being free
    John Stanley for the like
    Thomas Rowell for getting turf on the common, not being free
    Edward Lyon, Thomas Burton, Thomas Nicholson, Richard Blevine, John
Birchall, Thomas Roe, Henry Cooper, Henry Radcliffe, Thomas Fazakerly, James
Bradshawe, Thomas Birchall, James Boulton, John Woodward, shoemaker, John
Corley for working unlawful leather
    John Poultney and William Mosse for keeping muck and an unclean channel
between their houses
    Edward Richardson for neglecting to sweep the street before his house, whereby
there is much annoyance
    Gilbert Coote and George Tarleton, scavengers, for denying assistance to fellow
officers
    Gilbert Coote, William Ryding, cooper, George Tarleton and John Tennant,
scavengers, for neglecting their office
    Mr Thomas Blackmoore, Ralph Massam, Edward Chambers, John Higinson,
butcher, John Banks, William Platt, Richard Boden, James Boulton, Jane Lurting,
Richard Henshawe, Thomas Whitfield, William Seacome for tethering in the
townfield
    Richard Crompton, William Fazakerley for breaking the pound
    Thomas Fazakerley, Robert Mollineux for cutting growning in the town field
    Anthony Hunt, William Midleton, Thomas Raineford, Thomas Fazakerley,
barleymen, for neglecting their office

p. 535

Mr Thomas Tarleton for letting his wall lie down between Alderman Williamson and him to his annoyance of swine

Mr Strangwaise for allowing his fences to lie down in Dale Street between Anne Smyth and him

John Higinson for doing unfitting work on the sabbath

Richard Poultney, sexton, for neglecting to ring curfew.

We order:

Thomas Lancellot to make up his fence between him and Richard Coppull before Candlemas, on pain of 20s

Richard.

p. 536

25 OCTOBER 1651

William Fleetewood, glasier, admitted a free burgess by consent of the mayor, aldermen and common council, paying £3 6s 8d.

At the same assembly it was ordered that Mr Chambers and Bailiff Sturzaker, who have been confined for seven weeks on suspicion of the Sickness, may have liberty to walk to the water side, but are to sequester themselves from company, and on the 2 or 3 January they are to be free if nothing but well happens in the meantime. Bailiff Sturzaker may have liberty to go to his shop at night to cleanse it. And John Lunte to continue in his house for a fortnight.

14 JANUARY 1651

At an Assembly before the mayor, aldermen, bailiffs and common council:

By general consent John Fogg, clerk, was nominated as minister, provided that he subscribe the engagement, and declare his submission to the present government, which afterwards he did accordingly, and is established.

Concerning Mr Dobson's house, it is ordered that the last order shall stand, and he may take it for three lives, or enjoy it as now.

That the schoolmaster shall have his whole quarter's wages in spite of the discontinuance of teaching because of the sickness.

Ordered that Mr Tarleton's house in the churchyard, being out of lease, be forthwith taken into the town's hands and let to best advantage.

p. 537

Ordered that Mr Chambers go to Warrington to attend the audit and receive the ancient allowance from the auditors which belongs to the minister and schoolmaster.

Ordered that Mr William Williamson go to Wigan about the leys to be collected for the poor and infected, and solicit the Justices of the Peace for the furtherance of the payment.

Whereas there is a writ brought from London against Mr Corles and his wife in order to revive the judgment for £100 debt owing by Mr Moore to the town, ordered that the same be put under the county palatine's seal, and the sheriff asked for a devastavit.

The close belonging to Thomas Andoe and others is to be made meet acres, and fine and rent paid accordingly, and the rest to be left to a lane.

That the stalls and standings in possession of Mr Corles and Widow Haskaine be seized as being the town's standings.

William Whalley is admitted a free burgess by the consent of the mayor, aldermen and common council, and Ralph Massam undertakes to free the town from charge, and paid 50s

John Stanley, wettower, also admitted by like consent, and Richard Holland undertakes that he nor his shall be chargeable to the town, and paid 50s.

p. 538

Received for the 9 months' assessments several warrants, with £2 13s 8d for the poor of Prescot and Whiston, £37 8s 1d. Ordered that a ley be laid for this sum, and the same be paid accordingly.

p. 539

p. 540

Rental

Mr Dobson's house and land by Mr Washington and Mr Chambers, £11, of which the town is to receive	£6	13s	4d
Susan Eccleston's rent		6s	8d
Roger Harrison for the corner shop		40s	
Edward Moore esq. for the town common steel		4s	
Richard Poultney for his house		13s	4d
William Boats for his house		13s	4d
Margaret Lay for her house		4s	
Mr Thomas Tarleton for Church Steel house		8s	
more for Alexander Tarleton's house			2d
Mr Strangwas for Seacom's rent		6s	8d
more for his new erected cottage		5s	
Mr Robert Cornell for Browne's Croft		1s	8d
John Vece of Garston, his ancient rent		8s	
Edward Williamson for Kenion's house		3s	2d
Mr Edward Aspinwall for a little enclosure		1s	
Rose, his daughter, for the house in Castle Street		2s	
Widow Jane Lurting for her house		12s	5d
Mr Corles for Sickman's Lane and the town's common slack enclosed, per annum		2s	1d
Ellen Blevine for the Mill Dale and damesteed		2s	6d
Edward Tatlock's children for the town's common		1s	
Elizabeth Barker's house to pay as the council shall agree; for 1 year		50s	6d

Thomas Cook's house, half a garden and close called
Hoggs Hey, and 4 lands in town field worth £4 or £5
per annum

Shops to be let:
Edmund Raphson's next to Jane Haskaine	3s
Edward Williamson for Richard Rose's	6s
John Higinson for his shop	6s
Richard Higinson's butcher's shop	3s
Edward Horrobin's shop by John Sturzaker	
John Sturzaker's shop	6s

If these be not burgage rents.[26]

p. 541

RALPH MASSAM, GENTLEMAN, MAYOR, 1652 [1652–53]

p. 542
LIVERPOOL. ELECTION COURT, MONDAY 18 OCTOBER 1652, before
Thomas Williamson, mayor, Richard Peirceavall and John Eccleston, bailiffs,
according to several charters heretofore granted and custom.

Ralph Massam is elected mayor, sworn
Peter Lurting elected bailiff for the mayor and commonwealth of England, sworn
William Rymer elected bailiff for the borough, sworn.

John Fogge, clerk, minister
William Halsall esq., recorder
John Winstanley, town clerk
John Kirke, serjeant at mace

   Officers chosen by the council:
George Glover, schoolmaster,
Richard Poultney, church clerk
John Williamson, hall keeper
William Whalley, town's customer, sworn
Richard Poultney, subcustomer
John Eccles and Thomas Leaver, stewards of the hall, sworn
John Sutton and John Lunte, supervisors of the highways
Thomas Coppull, heyward, sworn

---

26   Six shops are crossed out.

p. 543

Officers elected by the grand jury at the portmoot court, 15 November 1652:
Merchant appraisers, Mr John Sandiford, Mr Robert Greene, John Eccleston, Robert Lyon, sworn
Registers of leather, Thomas Burton, Thomas Roe, sworn
Alefounders, William Litherland, William Neweis, sworn
Barleymen, Thomas Lancellott, William Daintieth, Humphrey Mercer, sworn
Scavengers, John Stanley, Thomas Bankes, William Rydeing, sworn
Murenger, Thomas Croper
Porters, John Barton, John Sanderson
Board setters, Thomas Bankes, Widow Rycrofte
Booth setters, John Ryce, Peter Walker
Beadle and bell man, Edward Rydeing
Churchwardens, Henry Corles, Edmund Leivsey, chosen at Easter

Memo. Thomas Chapman is admitted and sworn an attorney of the borough court, 15 November 1552
Richard Washington the younger, the like, 8 July 1653.

p. 544

LIVERPOOL. PORTMOOT COURT OR QUARTER SESSIONS, MONDAY 15 NOVEMBER 1652, for the borough and port town of Liverpool, before the mayor and Peter Lurting and William Rymmer, bailiffs.

Inquest of the jurors on the oaths of Richard Peirceavall, John Higinson, John Sandiford, Gilbert Formbie, Robert Greene, Richard Washington, John Chandler, John Owen, Henry Rydeing, Robert Lyon, George Potter, Thomas Hancock, Thomas Lurting, John Banks junior, James Heyes, Thomas Roe, William Litherland, Robert Eccles, Robert Fleetwood, Thomas Leaver, William Mosse, Thomas Coppull, William Newis, Thomas Carr, good and lawful men of the borough.

We present:
Henry Craine for a tussle on John Brownebill, 3s 4d
John Brownebill for the like on Henry Craine, 3s 4d
Peter Boulton the like on Edward Ryding, 3s 4d
Edward Ryding the like on Peter Boulton, 3s 4d
Richard Reeves for using the faculty of a freeman, not being free, 3s 4d
Robert Sutton, the like, 3s 4d, since free
Mr Bicksteth, John Griffiths junior, Richard Atherton, Thomas Tarleton alderman, Mr Sandiford, George Tarleton, Edward Williamson, Darby Caton, for letting timber lie to the annoyance of others, 6d apiece
James Bradshawe, James Boulton, Richard Holland, Peter Leaford, John Slack, Thomas Birch, John Corles, Thomas Roe, Thomas Burton, for working unlawful leather, 2s 6d apiece

Thomas Lancellott, John Tenant for neglecting office of barleyman, 2s 6d apiece

John Fogge, minister, Roger Jones, William Middleton for tethering in the town field, nil

Thomas Harrison of Kirkdale for breaking town pound and rescuing impounded cattle, 6s 8d

Henry Rogerson, servant to John Owen, for the like, 6s 8d

Richard Crosse esq., for not making up his fence in Morecroft according to order made by the jury in June 1651, 3s 4d

Robert Mollineux for keeping a horse and cows on the Town Common, not being free, 3s 4d

Mrs Elizabeth Chambers for neglecting to scour a ditch by the Hogshey Common before the 30 November 1649 on pain of 5s, 3s 4d

John Eccleston for not removing his timber and ashlars in Dale Street before his garden, according to order in October 1649 on pain of 5s, 3s 4d

Mr William Strangewais for erecting a cottage on the Town Common without consent, 5s

Mr Thomas Tarleton, alderman, and other freemen who have not appeared this day to perform their duty and have not essoyned:

p. 545

Thomas Storie, Nehemiah Brettargh esq., William Bell, clerk, William Ward, clerk, Edward Stockley, Thomas Blackburne, Thomas Mossock, Edward Dicconson, Hugh Cooper, Edmund Smoult, Peers Gerrard, Ralph Shorrock, Robert Wingreene, Jeffrey Birchall, Edward Starkey, Edward Ogle, John Fox esq., John Fox, Thomas Horton, Henry Rolline, John Barrowe, William Hawkeshead, Thomas Haskaine, Henry Radcliffe, Thomas Taylor, Richard Parr, Robert Farrington, John Lurting, smith, Richard Morecrofte, Henry Ambrose, John Everett, Edmund Lyon, maltster, William Chorley, Thomas Morecroft, Henry Kilshawe, Thomas Croft, John Burges, Edmund Tyrer, John Haskaine, William Wray, Thomas Darbisheire, Robert Fairehurst, Thomas Gallaway, Richard Tyrer, Thomas Cooper, John Lyon, Cuthbert Holland, John Smith, Richard Rymer, Henry Ogle, gent., Michael Tarleton, Robert Swift, 3s 4d apiece[27]

Orders:

Richard Dwarrihouse, water bailiff, for not having a coal barrel, according to former order, 2d

Mrs Sharples to make up her wall, lying to annoyance of Thomas Hancock, on pain of —

The headbolts shooting to the Breck be made up and ditched by people holding land abutting the hedge before 1 February next, on pain of 10s apiece

27 Three of these names not appearing and fined are crossed out: Nehemiah Brettargh esq., William Bell, clerk, and John Fox, esq.

John Johnson to scour his ditch against Hogshey Common before 2 February next, on pain of 20s

Mrs Chambers to scour the same ditch, 20s

All with any land lying along the sea bank shall make up fence before 25 March, on pain 20s apiece

The sexton to ring curfew according to custom

All who have tenants shall give in their names to the mayor before 2 February next. Mr Mayor to set down on pain of every one presented by the following jury, 50s

All dung lying in the street shall be removed before Candlemas next by people in houses adjacent, and no inhabitant shall make any dunghill or allow dung to lie in the street for more than three days, on penalty of 5s apiece, on being presented by a jury, this being a public nuisance and to be rectified

Officers named

Agreed to all ancient orders and laudable customs.

p. 546

LIVERPOOL. PORTMOOT COURT OR QUARTER SESSIONS, MONDAY 4 APRIL 1653, for the borough and port town of Liverpool in the county of Lancaster, before the mayor and Peter Lurting and William Rymer, bailiffs.

Inquest before the mayor on the oaths of John Eccleston, Richard Williamson, Evan Marsh, Richard Washington junior, Edward Winstanley, Adam Leathes, William Bushell, Thomas Raineford, Henry Moore, Oliver Fairehurst, Robert Swifte, William Rydeing, cooper, Thomas Banks, Richard Holland and Thomas Coppull.

We present:

William Seddon for a blood wipe on Thomas Lurting

Thomas Lurting the like on William Seddon

John Eccleston for offensive language to Mr Ralph Massam in the time of his mayoralty

Thomas Andoe for very uncivil language to Mr Ralph Massam in the time of his mayoralty

Thomas Ley, Richard Strange, John Webster, Robert Simpson, Robert Tipping for using the faculty of freemen, not being free

Mr Edward Moore for not cleansing the street in his liberties

John Higinson, John Eccleston, Henry Craine, Mrs Margaret Bicksteth, Edward Rydeing for the like

Mrs Elizabeth Chambers for not removing the dunghill by the cellar door of the house where she lives, facing the street, in Slatter Street before Candlemas past, in contempt of an order of 25 November 1652

Marie, wife of John Lunacox, for abusing William Williamson, alderman, in language and otherwise, he being an alderman

Ellen, wife of John Linet, for calling Mr Edward Alcocke a rogue, he being a bailiff's peer

Thomas Lancelot for not coming to be licensed to sell ale

John Andoe, Michael Barker, Anthony Carre, William Gardner, Thomas Seale, Margery Kenyon, widow, Richard Rymer, William Chantrell, John Sutton, Richard Browne, William Cliffe, Edward Winstanley, Isabel Moore, Robert Johnson, Jane Lurting, Robert Hall, James Burton, Anne Young, widow, junior, George Prescot, John Webster, Robert Sympson, George Tarleton, William Litherland, William Jumpe, Richard Williams, Humphrey Mercer, Robert Lyon, Jane Haskine, John Eccles, Gregory Formbie, Thomas Nicholson, Richard Higinson, butcher, Edward Sutton, Margaret Gilberthrop, widow, Timothie Holt, widow, Robert Eccles, John Stanley, Peter Forer, William Rydeing, Margaret Granger, widow, Richard Washington, for the like

Anne Smith for not keeping her fences and headbolts up

Mr Fogge for letting his back fence lie down

George Tarleton for the like, and Dorothy Bicksteth for letting the fence at Tithe Barn Gate lie down to annoyance of William Litherland

Edmund Ralphson for letting his fence lie down on the back of Cook's house to annoyance of Mrs Bicksteth

Richard Lunt for cutting sods in the close in Tithebarn Street commonly called Mr Walker's field

Dorothy Bicksteth, Anne Chantrell, Jane Gerrard, Richard Turner, Gregory Formby for keeping swine unrung

p. 547

Thomas Storie for letting his back fence lie down to annoyance of Adam Leathes

Thomas Lancelot for neglecting office of barleyman

John Johnson for not scouring ditch by Hogshey Common according to order of 25 November 1652 on penalty of 20s

John Barker, Mr John Bird, Edward Banckes for ploughing up the town's common in Town Field

Robert Molineux for getting gorse and keeping a horse and cow on Town Common, not being free

William Seacome for not making up his headbolts in Breckside, according to order of 25 November for making them up by 2 February on pain of 10s

Thomas Roe, Thomas Burton, registers of leather, for neglecting duties

Thomas Roe, Thomas Burton for working unlawful leather

Thomas Tarleton for casting stones from his vessel, the *Seaflower*, between half flood and low water to the danger of other shipping

Dorothy Bicksteth, Mr Richard Johnson, Mr Ralph Massam, Jane Lurting, widow, Mrs Walker, John Higginson, Thomas Brookbanck, Mr Richard Crosse, John Johnson of Everton, John Williamson, John Lurting, John Sturzaker, Mr Robert Moore, Thomas Coppull, Mr Strangwaye, Mr Chandler, Robert Cornell, Mr John Bird, John Barker, Mrs Elizabeth Chambers, Edward Banckes of Kirkdale, and all others that have lands abutting the sea bank, and sufficient fences not made up before 25 March past in contempt of order of 25 March 1652 on penalty of 20s

Ralph Winstanley, Margaret Banister, Ellen Greene, widow, Ellen Blevine, Thomas Hodgson, alderman, Dorothy Bicksteth, John Querke, Thomas Williamson, Mrs Godson, Darby Caton, Mrs Margaret Bryster for having tenants and giving in their names in writing to Mr Mayor before 2 February past in contempt of order of 25 November 1652 on penalty of 40s, to be paid by the parties presented by this jury

Richard Turner, John Cooke, Margery Kenyon, widow, William Rymer, Thomas Lancelot, Abraham Ellis, Thomas Linacker, William Chantrell, for letting dunghills lie in the open street before their houses, a public nuisance, in contempt of order of 25 November last on penalty of 5s

Richard Livesley, Henry Rydeing, John Boyle for not attending the portmoot court and neglecting to give information of tussles and abuses in this borough

Ellen Houline for abusing bailiff Alcocke in very bad words and calling him a rogue in the presence of many people[28]

Mary, wife of Thomas Linocker, for abusing William Williamson, alderman[29]

We order:

Those said fences be made up before 1 May on penalty of 40s apiece

Thomas Tarleton, alderman, to clear all the stones cast out of his vessel, so there will be no danger to shipping, before 6 April on penalty of £10

p. 548

John Higinson to scour the ditch between Castle Hey belonging to John Eccleston, and his field on the north side thereof, before Mayday

The supervisors to cause the streets and highways of the town to be sufficiently paved and amended, on penalty of 40s

The persons above named, and all others who have tenants shall before midsummer give Mr Mayor in writing the names of such inmates and the names and number of their families, and shall perform such order as the mayor shall set down, on penalty of £5 apiece.

All dunghills to be cleared by midsummer, and no more made in the street, on pain of 40s

We agree to all ancient and laudable customs.

p. 549
DEEDS
1. 5 Edward IV: Charles Gillibrond and Ellen, his wife, release their title to James Harebron, mayor of Liverpool, and the commonalty, of lands and tenements in the town and field of Gerston, then in the mayor's possession.
2. 19 Henry VII: David Griffith, mayor of Liverpool, grants to Richard Beswick, merchant, the fourth part of a burgage in Bank Street, late in the tenure of John

28   Ellen Houline presentment is crossed out.
29   Mary Linocker presentment is crossed out.

Ines, between the land of Stanley on the west, and William Harbron on the east, for 60 years, paying for the first twenty 3s 4d per annum, and the third twenty, 6s 8d.

3. 21 Henry VI: Robert del More, mayor of Liverpool, grants to James Harbron a half burgage in Bank Street between land of William Brand on the east, and Richard Brerewood on the west, for 65 years, paying 5s 6d; by the same deed the mayor grants to James Harbron two pieces of land in Moregreen at the end of the Aprestreet, one between the chantry land of Sir Nicholas the priest of Liverpool on the west, and the highway on the east, and the other between two highways, for 65 years, paying 6s per annum.

4. Henry VIII: William More, esq., and David Griffiths, mayor of Liverpool, agree about the ways up the Milne Street and north into the field.

5. 22 Henry VIII: Thomas Rose grants to Roger Fazakerley, mayor of Liverpool, a rent of 2s per annum for a minister for ever to say divine service in Our Lady and St Nicholas at the rood altar.

6. 15 Henry VIII: William More, esq., mayor, grants in fee farm to William Mollineux, knight, land by the side of the Moregreen opposite to a croft of William Fazakerley of Kirkby, containing 4 roods by 24 foot to the rood, at 6d per annum and the repair of St Nicholas's chapel.

7. 14 Henry VII: Evan Haghton, mayor, grants to William Harebrowne, half a burgage in Bank Street in fee farm for ever, paying 6s 8d per annum.

8. 10 Edward IV: Robert Taylor and Margaret his daughter, if Margaret dies without issue, grant to Edmund Crosse, mayor, and William Brand, priest, a half burgage of land in Chapel Street for maintenance of a priest at Our Lady's altar in Liverpool.

9. 24 Henry VIII: Edward Noris, mayor, grants to Roger Nelson, half a burgage in Bank Street, a barn in Chapel Street, and lands in the field for 61 years at 15s 8d per annum.

10. An ancient release without date from John, son of John the priest of Gerston, to John son of Robert of Gerston, his wife, and Robert his son, of his right to lands which John his father and Eida his mother had given him.

11. An ancient deed without date, from John, son of Robert of Gerston to Robert his son, of several parcels of land which he had bought in several fields: Cleyfield, Humblebadle, Hungarralle, Ruthrake, Hecindalimore, Haldifield, Sandifield, and Highforlonge.

12. 5 Edward IV 10 October: Charles Gelibrond and Ellen his wife, grant to James Harebron, mayor, all the lands and tenements which they had of John Gerston lying in the town and several fields in Gerston for the maintenance of a priest in the chapel of St Mary of the Key.

15 September 1653. These deeds were viewed and this note taken by Ralph Massam, mayor, Thomas Berwik, William Williamson.

p. 550

PORTMOOT COURT OR QUARTER SESSION, MONDAY 8 AUGUST 1653, for the borough and port town of Liverpool in the county of Lancaster, before the mayor, Peter Lurting and William Rymmer, bailiffs.

Inquest on the oaths of Edward Alcock, Edward Formby, William Gardner, Thomas Sandiford, William Olliffe, William Reynard, Richard Lunte, Thomas Lancellott, John Lunte, William Newis, Thomas Banks, Thomas Copull, Richard Lewesley, James Johnson, John Lurting, Richard Tyrer, Robert Harvey, honest and lawful men.

We present:

John Bidle for a blood wipe on William Litherland, 6s 8d

William Litherland for the like on John Bidle, 6s 8d

Thomas Goodine for the same on James Goore, 6s 8d

James Goore for a tussle on Thomas Goodine, 3s 4d

Thomas Lancellott for a tussle on Thomas Johnson, 3s 4d

Thomas Johnson for a blood wipe on Thomas Lancellott, 6s 8d

Margaret Farrer, wife of Peter Farrer, for a tussle on Margery Lurting, 3s 4d

William Jump for a tussle on Thomas Ambrose, 3s 4d

Jeanette Whytehead for calling Mr Alcock an old arrant knave, he being a bailiff's peer, 3s 4d

Richard Washington senior for getting turf on the common on this side of the hills contrary to order, 3s 4d

Edward Winstanley, Anthony Hunte, Jane Lurting, widow, William Reynold, William Gardner, for the like, 3s 4d

Thomas Tarleton, alderman, Richard Holland, Edward Horrobine, Richard Higinson, butcher, Ralph Winstanley, Mrs Heapey, John Royle, Anne Higinson, widow, John Eccleston, Henry Craine, for keeping swine unrung, 2s apiece

John Higinson, butcher, for not making his fence in Tithebarn Street, 2s

John Royle for the like in Dale Street, 2s

Timothy Hoult, Widow Rying for selling unwholesome drink, 1s apiece

John Eccleston, Margaret Bicksteth, widow, William Mosse, John Higinson, Robert Clark, Richard Turner, Robert Sutton, Oliver Fairehurst, Evan Marsh, Edward Ryding, Elizabeth Harrison, William Chantrell, William Rymmer, John Cook, Margery Kenion, Elizabeth Rycroft, Robert Swifte, John Royle, Dorothie Bicksteth, Thomas Marrow, William Daintieth, Robert Fleetwood, Edward Cognell, John Orrer, Anne Boulton, Widow Johnson, Giles Mercer, for not cleansing their streets, 1s apiece

Edward Moore, esq., for a dunghill in Castle Street, 2s 6d

Peter Halle for keeping unjust measures for ale and beer, 3s 4d

John Chandler for keeping inmates, not giving security to the town, 6s 8d

Mary Corker, Richard Turner, Dorothy Bicksteth and Roger Harrison for the like, 6s 8d apiece

p. 551

Dorothy Sandiford, widow, for the like, 6s 8d

Roger Hey, Robert Rose, Anthony Johnson, William Mee, William Henshaw for bringing cattle to the commons, 3s 4d

Mr Richard Johnson of Everton for cutting other men's grass in the town field, 1s

Thomas Rowe, Thomas Burton, registers of leather, for not bringing in their presentments, 3s 4d

Ralph Burges for cutting other men's grass, 1s

James Toping for tethering his horse in the town field on other men's grass, 3s 4d

John Higinson for not repairing his fence at the sea bank according to former order, 2s

Richard Crosse, esq., alderman, John Johnson of Everton, John Williamson, John Lurting, clothier, Thomas Plumb, Mr Richard Johnson, Mr John Bird for the like neglect, 2s apiece

John Johnson of Everton for not scouring the ditch in Halls Hey, 2s 6d

Evan Marsh for the like, 2s 6d

John Johnson, mariner, for laying limestones at half flood, 5s

All freemen who neglected attendance at this court

We order:

The ditch between Dorothy Bicksteth and John Eccleston be scoured so that water may pass through the old water course before Michaelmas next on pain of 10s

The water course between William Garner and Alderman Thomas Tarleton's houses be scoured by Garner within ten days, 5s

The water course at John Lurting's house in Dale Street be scoured in eight days, 5s

The gunes and limestones under the schoolhouse end within full sea be removed and all the scattered stones be gathered by the water bailiffs within eight days, 10s

John Eccleston to remove his mast from the channel at Mr Oliffe's house end so that the water may have its free course, 10s

Agreed to all ancient orders and laudable customs

The pool at the bridge end be mended within ten days

That the millers bring in their toll ditches within ten days, 10s apiece.

p. 552
AUDIT OF MR THOMAS WILLIAMSON, LATE MAYOR, 2 DECEMBER 1652, Richard Pearceavall and John Eccleston, bailiffs, taken in the town hall.

Edward Ashton, town customer, receipts for ingates and outgates	£7	11s	3d
Mr John Williamson, hall keeper, for ingates, 14s 7d, and outgates, 38s 3d, in total		52s	10
Richard Poultney, subcustomer for boards and tolls	4	8	8
Freemen admitted, only three paid in	8	6	8
Composition money, £7 5s 3d}			
Licence money, £6 15s 10d}	27	11	1
Butlerage of Mr Greene, £13 10s 0d}			
Town's rents for houses and shops	19	9	8

Rents of ferry boats £5, which is £13 but because of restraint of passage due to the sickness this year £5			
From the old churchwardens		5s	
Fines		21	8
Schoolmaster's allowance from chantry rents, not yet paid nil			
For straw and corn since last audit	48	16	
Burgage rents, besides shops and such in town's hands	11	2	10
Overplus of one ley of £43 5s 5d	3	2	5
Rent for new enclosures at 12d per acre nil			
Of the old bailiffs, Thomas Ayndoe and William Lurting, paid over	124	17	3
Of the poor's account, allowed them by the country for the sickness		8s	3
Total of receipts	£264	13s	9d
Total disbursements	109	10	2
Remaining	155	3	7

Which sum was paid over by the old bailiffs to Peter Lurting and William Rymmer, the new bailiffs, whereof £9 10s is in clipped money and £1 10s 7½d base money, £3 5s in pieces of eight, and the remainder in good money, whereupon they are discharged.

Also paid in for the poor as appears by that book, 18 January 1652	£22	15s	9d

Examined by John Winstanley, town clerk

Ralph Massam, mayor
Thomas Hodgson
Thomas Williamson.

p. 553
29 OCTOBER 1652
    At an Assembly before the mayor, the aldermen and common council, the following were elected to be of the common council because of the death of others, formerly aldermen, and of the council, being many dead: John Bird, Alexander Greene, John Owen, Henry Ryding, Richard Leivesley, Thomas Burton, William Gardner, Robert Lyon, all sworn.

11 DECEMBER 1652
    At an Assembly before the mayor, etc. regarding £11 4s claimed by Mrs Walker as due to her late husband, Mr John Walker, alderman, as money paid by him to

Mr Lawley, the town solicitor, it was voted that it not be paid unless she make it appear to be a real debt. But 20s which was sent by him to Mr Leivsey of Staple Inn shall be paid to her.

p. 554
22 NOVEMBER 1652
At an Assembly before the mayor, aldermen, bailiffs and common council:

A letter from Colonel Birch, the governor, was read, whereby it appears that the £10,000 to be allowed by parliament for repair of the losses of the town from delinquents' estates is now to be paid from lands in Ireland. A letter was written that the allotment might be as near Dublin as possible.

It was ordered that the order made in Mr Blackmoor's mayoralty concerning the limitation for the buying of goods within 14 days be annulled, it being found prejudicial to the town. Any freeman may buy goods at will.

A ley of £58 be assessed by the merchant appraisers and collected by the bailiffs, and accounted for at audit.

9 DECEMBER 1652
At an Assembly in the common hall before Ralph Massam, gentleman, mayor, the aldermen, bailiffs and common council:

On reading of a certificate from Mr Gurling concerning the buying of pink and certain goods against former orders of the town, it was ordered that Mr John Sandiford shall be discharged of the alleged contempt and his fine of 20 marks.

A special letter was written to the governor about Chester men's prejudicing this port by seeking liberty to land goods on the Wirral side and pay customs there, which is against our privileges and charter.

p. 556
21 JANUARY 1652
At an Assembly in the town hall before the mayor, aldermen, bailiffs and common council, the payment of town customs and compositions for all kinds of provisions imported was raised, in particular herrings brought in by Formby men to Ault river without breaking bulk, who refuse any town customs. It is ordered that even though they do not break bulk but only make their entry in the customs house and pass on to another place or creek belonging to this port, nevertheless they shall pay half duty and composition for their goods at the discretion of the mayor and alderman. And because Bailiff Andoe has paid 45s for such Formby men he is to receive 22s back.

COMPOSITIONS
At half rate by Richard Norris for 5 score and 12 barrels of herring in the *Elizabeth* of Formby, 13s 4d

For 26 barrels of herrings of Mayor Swift brought in by Thomas Preeston, half dues, 3s 1d

Herrings by Richard Fisher, 3s 3d

Butlerage for 4 tuns of wine brought in by Mr Greene, voted to pay 4s per ton, 16s
Butlerage for 8½ tuns of wine in the *Mayflower* from Dublin at 4s per tun, 32s.

p. 557
FREEMEN
   22 November 1653
John Blundell, late apprentice with Mr Edward Williamson, admitted and sworn a free burgess by consent of the council, paid 6s 8d
Pearcivalle Crosse, apprentice with Roger Harrison, sworn, 6s 8d
John Lurting, son of Robert Lurting, deceased, late a free burgess and bailiff's peer, sworn, 3s 4d
Robert Sutton, ship carpenter, sworn by the consent of Mr Mayor and the Common Council, £4
   4 February 1652
Richard Sympkine of Ormskirk, merchant, sworn by the consent of the mayor, aldermen and council, £6 13s 4d
   22 February
Robert Harvey, grocer, sworn by the like consent, £5
   8 July 1653
Robert Kenion, husbandman, sworn by like consent, 40s

21 JANUARY 1652
   A ley of £60 ordered to be assessed by the merchant appraisers and collected by the bailiffs for the discharging of the following:
For the six months' assessment by warrant, £44 9s
For the poor of Prescot and Whiston by warrant, £5 6s 8d
For relief of maimed soldiers and widows, £4 12s 7d

p. 558
4 FEBRUARY 1652
   Ordered that no allowance be given towards the repair of Walton church as demanded.

p. 559
4 FEBRUARY 1652
At an Assembly before the mayor and common council:
   A disagreement between Thomas Tarleton, alderman, and the town, concerning a lease of the house at Church Steel, and whether the life named was Thomas Tarleton the father, who was the lessee, or Thomas the son, who now enjoys it, is referred to a trial at law and a copy of old Thomas Tarleton's will is to be searched for.
   Cook's land, also in dispute, was referred to Mr Recorder who gave the opinion that neither the town nor Mr Tarleton have good title to the same because of the confiscation or escheat, he never appearing to the indictment of felony or being convicted. The same belongs not to Mr Tarleton in regard it fell not out in his time, but 18 years before, so that Cook forfeits nothing but his provisional estate.

17 FEBRUARY 1652

At an Assembly before the mayor, aldermen and greatest part of the common council:

Whereas there are several former orders that forfeitures and confiscations of felons' goods, lands and tenements in this town belonged to the mayor and bailiffs for the time being, and that a share of these should belong to the town, and the other share to the mayor and bailiffs, and the charges of all suits should be paid by the town, now it appears that the said forfeitures do, of right, wholly belong to the corporation and not to the mayor and bailiffs. It is ordered that the former orders be null and void, and henceforth the said escheats, confiscations and forfeitures, wrack of the sea, and such other incidents, shall belong to the corporation, and not the mayor and bailiffs, and shall be seized by the bailiffs for the use and benefit of this corporation, and the charges of suits shall be paid for by the town from the public stock.

Ordered that the oath of a freeman be drawn up according to the ancient rule and form, with a change of some sentences for the commonwealth, which being done was at another assembly read, and confirmed, and the same now entered.

p. 560

6 JUNE 1653

Persons fined for not appearing at an assembly of the forty according to warning: Thomas Blackmore, Thomas Tarleton, alderman, Gilbert Formby, John Walles, John Bird, John Sandiford, Henry Ryding, 3s 4d apiece, to be collected by the bailiffs.

8 JULY 1653

At an Assembly before Thomas Blackmoore, Thomas Tarleton, William Williamson, Thomas Williamson, alderman, Peter Lurtinge, one of the bailiffs, and the greater part of the common council:

Consideration was given to a pipe and chimney of stone begun to be built by Edward Williamson on the town's waste and market place, which he at first claimed was on his own land, a claim immediately afterwards relinquished, and a request made for a license from the town to erect the same, and for a rent to be fixed. Whereupon this assembly voted on whether he should continue the work. By the greater number it was resolved that the said chimney shall not go on.

See another order in this business made 10 January 1653.

p. 561

22 FEBRUARY 1652

On the death of Mr John Williamson, late hall keeper, Mr Mayor proposed the election of a new hall keeper. John Sturzaker voted to fill the office during the pleasure of this house and ordered to give security to the mayor for the time being for the true execution of the office, and to save the mayor harmless. And, concerning his fees, it is ordered that he shall take a penny for every draught under 400 pounds weight, and 2d for over 400 pounds weight from freemen. And for foreigners, 2d for every draught, as formerly.

Whereas it was formerly ordered that the house in the churchyard late in the possession of Thomas Tarleton, alderman, should be disposed of by the mayor and bailiffs, it is now ordered that it shall be disposed of by the mayor and any two of the aldermen for the best advantage of the town, to Edward Tarleton or any other, and they shall be saved harmless by this assembly for what they do. The yearly rent to be paid to the bailiffs, and accounted for.

8 JULY 1653

Whereas many exceptions are taken to the old oath of a freeman which, because of the change of government, needs to be amended, it is ordered that the new oath be entered as drawn up by the clerk of the town, and publically read and approved by this assembly.

p. 562

p. 563

THE OATH OF A FREEMAN

You shall be true and faithful unto the Commonwealth of England. And in order thereunto you shall be obedient unto the instant good government of this borough and port town of Liverpool you shall aid, assist and obey the mayor of this town or his deputy as also all other the officers within the same in the due and lawful execution of their several offices, and especially concerning the preservation of the public peace, the observation of good order and the maintenance of the ancient and laudable privileges, franchises, liberties and customs of the corporation. Which said privileges you shall further and increase to the best of your endeavour. You shall not by covine colour or deceipt free any foreigner or the goods chattels or merchandise of any foreigner or other person not free within this town in the name of your own proper goods, chattels or merchandise, whereby the town's duties or customs may be impeached, impaired, hindered, delayed or embezzled. You shall be liable and contributory at all times convenient to all reasonable leys and taxations which shall be imposed and assessed upon you amongst others the freemen, burgesses and inhabitants of this town, as well for the maintenance of all its just privileges as also towards the repair of the chapel within the same, being lawfully demanded. And, furthermore, you shall not sue nor implead any freeman inhabitant of this borough for any matter, cause or thing, whereof the mayor's court may hold pleas out of the jurisdiction of this court, unless it be for want of justice there to be ministered. And lastly, if you shall know or hear of any unlawful tumults, riots, routs or unlawful assemblies to be had or made within this town you shall forthwith give notice thereof unto the mayor, his deputy or bailiffs as occasion shall require, and shall do and perform all such other things as are fit to be done and performed by a good and honest burgess and freeman of the same borough, according to your power, skill and wit, so help you God.

p. 564

EDWARD WILLIAMSON, GENTLEMAN, MAYOR [1653–54]

p. 565
LIVERPOOL. ELECTION COURT, TUESDAY 18 OCTOBER 1653, before Ralph Massam, gentleman, mayor, Peter Lurting and William Rymer, bailiffs, according to several charters and customs.

Edward Williamson elected mayor and sworn
John Blundell, chief bailiff for the mayor and commonwealth
John Lurting junior, bailiff for the borough and corporation.

William Halsall esq., recorder
John Fogg, minister
John Winstanley, town clerk
Richard Dwarrihouse, serjeant at mace
Thomas Leaver, water bailiff, all sworn.

   Officers chosen by the Common Council:
George Glover, schoolmaster
Richard Poultney, subcustomer and church clerk, sworn
William Walleyn, town customer, sworn
John Sturzaker, hallkeeper, sworn
James Johnson, Robert Harvey, stewards of the hall, sworn
Thomas Coppull, heyward.

p. 566
   Officers chosen by the jury:
Robert Cornell, William Rymer, Adam Leathes, Richard Leivsey, merchant appraisers, sworn
Thomas Nicholsonn, Edward Horrobine, registers of leather, sworn
Thomas Cropper, Humfrey Mercer, alefounders, sworn
Robert Sutton, Robert Kenion, Richard Tyrer, Edward Sutton, barleymen or moss reeves, sworn
Richard Rymer, John Sanderson, Peter Walker, Peter Boulton, scavengers, sworn
Anthony Hunte, murenger
John Sanderson, Peter Walker, porters
Richard Farrer, John Carr, leavelookers, sworn
William Chorley, Elizabeth Rycraft, boardsetters
Richard Farrer, Richard Widoes, boothsetters
Edward Ryding, beadle and bellman
— churchwardens.

p. 567
LIVERPOOL. PORTMOOT COURT OR QUARTER SESSION, MONDAY 24 OCTOBER 1653, for the borough and corporation of Liverpool, before mayor and bailiffs.

Inquisition of the jurors on the oaths of Peter Lurting, Roger Jones, Evan Marsh, Richard Parce, John Chandler, Roger Harrison, Thomas Nicholson, Robert Kenion, Thomas Carr, John Banks junior, William Ryding, Edward Winstanley, William Litherland, Edward Tarleton senior, Edward Tarleton junior, Thomas Roe, John Johnson, James Hey, Richard Turner, William Mosse, Humfrey Mercer, Thomas Coppull, Robert Fleetwood, Thomas Cropper, good and lawful men of the borough.

We present:

John Burton for tussle on Richard Rogerson

Richard Rogerson for tussle on Burton

John Kenion, Peter Halle, James Hoult, Edward Barton for using faculty of freemen, not being free

Williamson of Dale Street, widow, William Gardner, Elinor Loy, Nicholas Rydeinge, Richard Blevine, Robert Johnson, Isabel Fells, Ralph Winstanley, George Tarleton, James Williamson, Alderman Thomas Nicholson, William Brewer, Mrs Bicksteth for keeping swine unrung

Thomas Nicholson for making unlawful leather

Mr Edward More for allowing muck to lie before his horse mill and stopping of the channel

Robert Mullinex for annoying Richard Widowes

Ralph Winstanley, Mr William Mee, John Lurtinge, Richard Turner for the like

John Fogg, minister, James Burton, Robert Mollinex, Randle Walley, Margaret Durninge, John Litherland, William Trantham, Thomas Watmowe for tethering in the town field

Thomas Christian, Robert Langsdell for breaking the pinfold

William Fazakerley, Robert Simson, Mr Richard Johnson of Everton, Michael Rumley for making use of the town common

William Strangweas for erecting a cottage on the town's common without consent of the town and not paying rent for it

All freemen who have not made appearance this day to perform their homage and duty.

We order:

Mr Greene to take away the door and make up the stone wall between him and John Sturziker before 2 February

All those with land on the sea bank to make up their fences before 26 March

All within the town who have tenants to give their names to the mayor before 1 January, and obey such orders as he shall set down

A swineherd to be chosen before 20 January, and all who have swine to pay for every head, according to former orders

Richard Poultney to ring curfew acording to former custom.

p. 568
8TH DAY 1653[30]
Memorandum: that John Ecles was sworn an attorney of this court for a year.

p. 569
LIVERPOOL. PORTMOOT COURT OR QUARTER SESSION, MONDAY 10 APRIL 1654, for the borough and corporation of Liverpool, before the mayor and bailiffs.

Inquisition of the jury taken on the oaths of Edward Alcock, Robert Cornell, Thomas Storie, Henry Ryding, Robert Lyon, Edmund Leivsley, Richard Lunt, Thomas Radcliffe, James Burton, Richard Crompton, John Loy, William Eccleston, Robert Sutton, John Tompson, John Sanderson, Peter Farrer, Thomas Coppull, honest and lawful men of the borough.

We present:
   Peter Boulton for tussle on William Singleton, 3s 4d
   William Singleton for tussle on Peter Boulton, 3s 4d
   Richard Atherton for striking and abusing Widow Boulton, 3s 4d
   Peter Hall for using faculty of a freeman, not being free, 6s 8d
   Edward Boulton, Henry Atherton, Philip Cork, Margaret Granger, Timothy Hoult, Henry Potter, Dorothy Houghton for the like, 3s 4d apiece
   William Darbisheire for working unlawful leather, 2s 6d
   John Cowley, John Dunnbovine for the like, 2s 6d apiece
   Mr Michael Tarleton, Mr John Chandler for neglecting office of churchwardens for present year
   Jane Haskeine, Thomas Lurting for building on town's waste, 6s 8d apiece
   Edward Winstanley, Isabel Rennalds, David Hall, Robert Johnson for letting fences lie down, 1s apiece
   John Higinson for fence lying down between Boer Croft and the town's land, 1s
   John Chandler and Margaret Gilberthrop for the like, 1s
   William Olife, William Gardner for keeping swine unrung, 6d apiece
   Margaret Gilberthrop, widow, for setting boards and stopping up of lights of Edward Alcock's house, 6d
   John Orrens for not cleansing street where stall stands, 1s
   Thomas Marrowe, George Harrison, Thomas Gorton, Elizabeth Rycroft, John Woodbrough, Robert Harrison, John Chaddick, Anthony Hunt, Richard Chantrell, Humfrey Harrison, Michael Harrison, for not cleansing street where their stalls stand, 1s apiece
   Elinor Gognall, William Choreley, John Higinson, Jane Eccleston for not cleansing corn market, 1s 6d apiece

---

30   No month is given.

p. 570

Richard Washington the younger, Michael Barker, Thomas Lancelot, Robert Eccles, Jane Eccleston, Peter Halle, John Chandler, Robert Kenion, John Lurting, smith, Humfrey Mercer, George Prescot, John Higinson, William Chantrell, Thomas Fell, Jane Rydeing, Anne Chantrell, Robert Clarke, Isabel Fells, Jane Parkinson, Darby Caton, Gregory Formby, Margaret Banister, John Chambers for selling ale and beer, not being licensed, 3s 4d apiece

John Lurting, bailiff, for not cleansing his water course to annoyance of his neighbours, 1s

Peter Parr for freeing former goods contrary to oath, £3

Memo: the defendant 22 April pleads not guilty, and is found not guilty

We order:

Henry Craine to clear his part of the gutter before 1 May

The bailiffs to see the town's part done by the same time

The stalls in the street annoying Oliver Fayrehurst and Thomas Astbrooke to be removed by 1 May

Jane Eccleston to fill up ditch between the Castle Field and Dorothy Bicksteth's ground, and make a fence before 1 May on penalty of 40s

John Higinson to hedge and scour his ditch between his ground and Evan Marsh before 20 April on pain of 40s

John Johnson of Everton to ditch between Henry Craine and him before 20 April on pain of 40s

The two lands of Mr Massam and two lands of John Higinson be made all one breadth before 1 May

Two lands of Mr Fazakerley and John Higinson, and land of Thomas Ploumbe be made all of one breadth before 1 May

Dorothy Robinson to make up her fence according to the quickwood row by 1 May

Mr John Winstanley to fill up gutter at Widow Tarleton's house before 1 May

We agree to all ancient laws and laudable customs.

p. 571

LIVERPOOL. PORTMOOT COURT OR QUARTER SESSION, MONDAY 7 AUGUST 1654, before the mayor and bailiffs.

Inquisition of the jury on the oaths of William Rymmer, Edward Formeby, Richard Williamson, Evan Marsh, John Chandler, Richard Blevine, George Petter, Roger Harrison, Bryan Mercer, Edward Winstanley, Thomas Carr, Thomas Leaver, William Mosse, John Royle, Thomas Nicholson, Edward Sutton, Thomas Coppull, honest and lawful men of the borough.

We present:

William Glover for tussle on John Darbisheire

John Darbisheire for tussle on Glover

William Goore for tussle on Richard Blevine

Richard Blevine for tussle on William Goore

Richard Glover for tussle on John Hyton

John Hyton for tussle on Richard Glover

Thomas Marrowe for not keeping the street clean where his stall stands

John Orrell, Gabriel Houghton, John Dobson, John Dobson his son, Richard Knowles, William Chorley, Henry Atherton for the like

William Raineford, Timothy Hoult, Margaret Granger, Edward Barton, James Blevine, Peter Halle for using the faculty of freeman, not being free

Jane Gerrard for selling unwholesome drink

William Daintieth for selling drink by unlawful measure

Edward Barton for getting turves on common, not being free, and John Everett, Randle Whalley, Thomas Marsh for the like

John Chandler for keeping swine unrung

Mr Richard Johnson and Ralph Burges for cutting grass in town field, not being their own

Mr Michael Tarleton and Mr John Chandler for neglecting office of churchwarden

We find Peter Parr not guilty of the presentment of freeing of foreigner's goods, £3

We order:

The town's pinfold to be repaired and built half a yard higher before end of August

We agree to all ancient orders and laudable customs.

p. 572

CATALOGUE OF NAMES OF FREE BURGESSES OF LIVERPOOL,[31] OCTOBER 1653

Edward Williamson, mayor, Sir Thomas Stanley, bart. ald., John Holcroft esq. ald., William Halsall esq. recorder, James Williamson, ald., Thomas Blackmoore, ald., Thomas Tarleton, ald., William Williamson, ald., Thomas Williamson, Ralph Massam, ald.

Knights: Sir Francis Willahbie, Sir Walsingham Cook, Sir Ralph Assheton, bart.

Esquires: Richard Shuttleworth, Henry Brook, John Braddill, John Bradshawe, William Banks, John Leightbourne, Thomas Longworth, William Morgell, Bartholomew Hesketh, William Langford, James Chantrell, William Langton, Jeffrey Holcroft, Nehemyah Brettargh, Richard Holland, John Booth, Gilbert Ireland, Peter Egerton, Richard Crosse, Thomas Fell, Edward Butterworth, John Fox esq.

---

31   As with the list of freemen in 1649 this list has many later emendations. Only the original names and occupations have been transcribed.

George Ireland, Mathew Aluread, Thomas Birch senior, Thomas Birch junior, Thomas Pryde, col., George Key, lt.col., Michael Richardson, Thomas Worsley, George Smithson, Thomas Talbott, Ralph Ashton esq., William Ashurst esq., Charles Walley esq., John Jackson, lt col., Peter Brook esq., John Hewetson, James Pitson, William Duckenfeild, Henry Ogle, gent.

Ministers: James Hyatt, Nevill Kay, Peter Shaw, Henry Shaw, Joseph Tompson, Edward Lapach, Thomas Walworth, John Coe, Richard Lyon, William Bell, John Fogg, David Ellison, William Ward, Henry Naylor, William Dunne, Henry Boulton, Richard Pickering

p. 573

Bailiffs' peers: John Blundell, John Lurting, draper, bailiffs, John Winstanley, town clerk, John Higinson, Roger Jones, Edward Alcock, John Woods, Edward Formeby, Robert Cornell, Gilbert Formby, Evan Marsh, John Sandiford, Richard Williamson, John Sturzaker, Thomas Storie, Thomas Ayndoe, Richard Percevall, John Eccleston, Peter Lurting, William Rymer

Common Council: Mr Robert Moore, Mr John Bird, Mr Robert Greene, Mr Alexander Greene, Thomas Shephard, Richard Dwarrihouse, John Walles, Richard Blevine (at sea), Thomas Sandiford, Henrie Moore, Adam Leathes, Henry Rydeing, Thomas Clayton, Richard Duckenfield, Thomas Warburton, Henry Blundell, Richard Fleetwood, Edward Stockley, Thomas Blackburne, John Brookes, Richard Hockenhall, George Halley, Alan Walley, Arthur Burron, Edward Moore, William Rigbie, Thomas Mossock, Edward Dicconson, William West esq., William Patten, Richard Sankey, John Sharples, Hamlet Holcroft, Peter Stanley, Hugh Cooper, Nicholas Sherburne, Edmund Smoult, Peares Gerard, John Bexwick, John Greene, mariner, Robert Ireland, Edward Garret, Alexander Greene senior, Robert Clark, capt., Thomas Morgan, Robert Philpot, Leonard Rollinson, William Swanley, John Sorrocold, William Carrington, John Birch, John Atherton esq., Henry Stanley, Robert Wingreene, William Lea, George Crammage, Andrew Asheton, Jeffery Birchall, John Eaton, Peter Flitecroft, John Newton, John Daniell, Edward Ogle, Richard Ratcliffe, William Mossey, William Fyffe, Alexander Bomer, Henry Asheton esq., Gregory Holcroft, Robert Gardner, William Edwards, Thomas Baxter, Edward Manne, William Toxtethe, John Ashurst, gent., John Fox esq., Thomas Horton, Henry Porter, James Johnson, Richard Washington senior, John Chandler, John Goore, John Bancks, Richard Brookes, Thomas Higinson, Henry Rolline, John Sympson, Thomas Coppull, Ralph Winstanley, Henry Johnson alias Nichson, Edward Fumeby, Thomas Seale, Giles Mercer, Thomas Ploumbe, John Lurting, mariner, Thomas Chapman, Thomas Leivesey, Richard Higinson, capt., Richard Higinson, cutler, Robert David alias Macatere, Richard Turner, John Barrowe, Humphrey Webster, Edmund Ogden, John Waid, Richard Holland, Bryan Mercer, Richard Lunte, Richard Poltney, Robert Johnson, Henry Webster, Richard Martine, Thomas Ballive, John Henshawe, Henry Goore, Samuel Halle, Edward Winstanley, Robert Clarke, Thomas Ratcliffe, John Tompson, Robert Bicksteth, Henry Burchall, Robert Fleetwood, Richard Higinson, butcher, George Prescot, Francis Waleworth, William Lurting senior, Robert Seacome, William Henshawe,

William Eccleston senior, John Knape, Thomas Haskaine, John Harrison, William Gardner, John Mathew, Robert Eccles, Thomas Duk, Robert Taylor, Richard Keawic,

p. 574

Robert Fidler, Richard Walker, smith, James Burton, Roger Harrison, Richard Browne, Henry Ratcliffe, Thomas Taylor, Thomas Preeston, William Daintieth, Thomas Carre, John Lunte, John Bancks, Edmund Lyon, Richard Parr, William Widnes, Peter Parr, Henry Fearnehead, Thomas Banckes, Richard Barker, Thomas Gardner, Michael Barker, Robert Farrington, William Webster, John Lurting, smith, Richard Fazakerley, William Horrocks, Edward Horobine, Joseph Dixon, Richard Moorecroft, John Bate, Edward Taylor, Henry Ambrose, Richard Farer, James Patterick, Henry Cooper, John Hussie, William Smithies, Thomas Burton, Richard Leivesey, Thomas Cheaney, Thomas Rainford, John Everard, Edmund Lyon, maltster, John Lyon, tanner, John Johnson of Everton, Richard Williams, Thomas Lurting, Peter Bolton, Robert Lyon, William Chantrell, Thomas Hancock, William Choreley, John Carr, Richard Widoes, Thomas Nicholson, John Ryce, Abel Lyon, John —, Henry Wilcock, William Jumper, John Cook, Rowland Asheton, Thomas Moorecroft, William Gardner, Henry Kilshawe, sadler, William Midleton, William Litherland, James Ainsedalle, Henry Craine, John Royle, Edward Plumer, Anthony Hunt, Thomas Cropper, John Halles, Thomas Croft, John Burges, William Mosse, Edmund Tyrer, John Hoskins, William Wroy, Oliver Fayrehurst, William Eccleston, Darby Caton, Thomas Lancelot, Thomas Darbishire, Robert Fairehurst, Alexander Moore, gent., Peter Farer, Edward Tarleton, Thomas Galloway, Gilbert Tarleton, John Dichfield, John Manwareing, Christopher Brookbanck, William Marshall, Richard Tyrer, Edmund Leivesey, Richard Washington, Richard Crompton, William Seddon, Richard Williamson,[32] Edward Tarleton junior, Anthony Carr, John Lyon, tanner, Christopher Bennett, Thomas Leaver, Robert Halle, Cuthbert Holland, Richard Baroclough, William Rydeing, cooper, Thomas Roe, Robert Baltesole, Gregory Formby, William —, George Glover, John Smith, shoemaker, Gilbert Coote, John Tennant, tailor, Edward Lea, William Newis, George Tarleton, Jeremy Berstowe, William Olliffe, Richard Rymer, Humphrey Mercer, Michael Tarleton, Henry Ogle, gent., Robert Barrowe, John Sutton, Edward Sutton, Henry Corles, bailiff, John Eccles, William Reynald, Richard Galloway, Thomas Chapman junior, James Hey, James Barton, Thomas Sandiford, Thomas Percivall, Parcival Crosse, Robert Sutton, Richard Simpkine, Robert Harvey, Robert Kenion, Thomas Parcivall, Robert Swift, William Fleetwood, Cuthbert Holland, William Whalley, John Stanley, John Sanderson, Peter Walker, Thomas Asbrook, Thomas Witter, James Hoult, Anoch Boulton, John Loy, John Kenion, John Chambers, Ralph Higinson, Henry Ashton, William Moore, William Accars, Anthony Moyer, Richard Atherton, James Blevine, John Moneley, Walter Mathewes, John Melling, Richard Scarisbrick, John Heyes, Ralph Carr, William Finch, Robert Kenion, cooper, John Holland, Robert Sympson,

32   Richard Williamson's name is partly obscured by crossing out.

Edward Bankes, Andrew Over, Ralph Belline, Hugh Renald, John Crane, Jonathan Geraw, Thomas Christian, Mr Andoe, Thomas Johnson, George Smith, Lawrence Jumper, Richard Brown, John Cary, Randle Danson, Thomas Andoe, Mathew Heyes, Ralph Halle, William Parker, John Pemberton, William Mallmey, Thomas Mosse, Edward Ryding, Richard Halliwell, John Poultney, John Simpson,[33] Thomas Farrer, Robert Eaton, Henry Gregson, Thomas Bridge, Richard Goore, James Litherland, Richard Rogerson, John Griffith, Edward Carr, Philip Peircie, Henry Tarbock, Samuel Sandiford, William Poultney, William Lewis, Thomas Crompton, John Williamson, George Thorp, Jonathan Gleve, John Rymer, Roger James[34]

p. 575
INDENTURE, 8 NOVEMBER 1653
Between Edward Williamson, gentleman, mayor of Liverpool, John Blundell and John Lurting the younger, bailiffs on the one part, and John Lurting of Liverpool, blacksmith on the other part. The mayor, bailiffs and burgesses grant to John Lurting and his assigns, for the sum of £40, the half burgage in Dale Street late in the tenure of William Lurting, late brother of John, with all buildings and advantages of the premises, lying between the land of John Moore esq., on the east, and the land of the late John Williamson, alderman, on the west; and also three lands and a half and the fourth part of a piece of ground in the townfield, vizt. two lands called the Higher and Lower Heavy Lands lying between the land of Richard Viscount Molyneux now in the tenure of John and Sarah Chandler on the north, and the land of Edward Moore esq., now in the possession of Thomas Warton on the north;[35] the other land lying in the Higher Heavy Land between the land of Robert Burton now in the possession of Thomas Tarleton, alderman, sometime chantry land, on the south, and the land of Richard Crosse, esq., in the possession of Edward Ryce on the north; and the half land lying in Liverpool field in a part called the Whittakers between the land of Nicholas Nicholson on the south, and the land of Margery Barker, widow, and Robert Barker, her son, on the north; and the fourth part of ground lying in Whittakers between the land of John Moore, esq., on the south, and land of John Warren, esq., late in the possession of John Walker, alderman deceased, on the north; to have and to hold the said half burgage for 99 years if Ann, wife of John Lurting, Nicholas, his eldest son, and Alice, his eldest daughter, shall live so long, paying yearly to the mayor, bailiffs and burgages 12s 5d in two parts at the Annunciation and feast of St Michael; if these payments fall behind by 20 days the property can be repossessed.

p. 576
John Lurting promises to keep the half burgage in repair, and not to assign property to anyone for longer than a year, unless for the use of his wife and children, without the agreement of the mayor, bailiffs and burgesses. And they agree to

---

33   John Simpson's name is partly obscured by crossing out.
34   The last name on the list is indecipherable.
35   The boundary is given as butting on to the north twice.

allow peaceful possession of the property. In witness the mayor and bailiffs have set their hands and put the common seal to the same.

p. 577
INDENTURE, 28 JUNE 1654
Between Peter Bold, esq., high sheriff of the county of Lancaster on the one part, and James Williamson, Thomas Blackmore, Thomas Tarleton, William Williamson, Thomas Williamson, Ralph Massam, Robert Moore, John Winstanley, John Higinson, Roger Jones, Edward Alcock, Edward Formeby, Robert Cornell, John Sandiford, John Sturzaker, Thomas Storie, Richard Pearcivall, Gilbert Formeby, Evan Marsh, John Fogge, clerk, Thomas Ayndoe and Peter Lurting, with other burgesses and inhabitants of the borough of Liverpool on the other part; witnesseth that by a warrant to Edward Williamson, gentleman, mayor of Liverpool, John Blundell and John Lurting, bailiffs, and the burgesses of the borough from the high sheriff for electing one burgess of good understanding, knowledge and discretion for causes concerning the public good of this commonwealth to be at his highness's parliament at Westminster on 3 September, we have elected Thomas Birch the elder, esq., to attend, who for himself and all the people of the borough has full power to do and consent to those things there ordained, provided that he shall not have power to alter the government as it is now settled in one single person and a parliament; in witness whereof the parties above set their hands and seals. Peter Bold, sheriff.

p. 578

p. 579
FRIDAY 10 DECEMBER
At an Assembly in the town hall before the mayor, aldermen, bailiffs and greatest part of the common council:
It was ordered and agreed that £10 be given to Widow Alice Mercer and Edward Formeby towards the money paid by them to Mr Hartley which was for Mr Malone's money left in Lawrence Mercer's hands on the town's order. Giving a general acquittance to the town they were paid the said sum by the bailiffs.
Ordered that two lanterns with candles burning be set at the High Cross and at White Cross, and places prepared to set them, each dark moon night till 8 o'clock by the serjeant and water bailiff, from All Saints to Candlemas.
The ferry boats to be let for the best advantage of the town by the mayor and bailiffs.
A lease of a messuage, stone house and garden in the churchyard be made by the mayor, bailiffs and burgesses to Edward Tarleton junior for 99 years, if he, Margaret his wife, and John his eldest son shall live so long, for a £16 fine and 2d a year rent, payable at Michaelmas only, with a covenant not to let the property without the town's consent.
Another lease to John Lurting, smith, son of Nicholas Lurting, late tenant to the corporation, for 99 years, if three lives live so long, for £40 fine, and 12s 5d. rent payable at Michaelmas, with covenant to repair property and not let it without consent.

30 MARCH 1654

Memorandum: ordered by an assembly of the common council in the town hall that the three lands and three farthings of land lately belonging to Cook's house be leased to Mr Evan Marsh by the mayor and bailiffs for three years to commence from 2 February last.

p. 580
TUESDAY 10 JANUARY 1653

At an assembly in the town hall before Edward Williamson, gentleman, mayor, the recorder, aldermen, bailiffs and most part of the common council:

Mr Mayor raised the matter of the building up of his cellar chimney adjoining the market place, formerly begun, but stopped by the vote of this house. It was voted that he could build it, notwithstanding the former order, and he undertakes to pay 2d. a year to the town at Michaelmas so long as the chimney remains.

On reading several letters from Dublin concerning the sending over of solicitors about the allotment of £10,000 in lands in Ireland, it was voted and ordered that Alderman Thomas Blackmoore and John Winstanley, town clerk, shall go as soon as convenient, and be authorised under the seal of this corporation to solicit and act on behalf of the town, and have all charges born. And a petition is referred to the Lord Protector that this be settled before the adventurers and soldiers be satisfied.

Whereas the mayor and bailiffs by consent of this house have lately leased to Evan Marsh and John Sturzaker three lands and three farthings of land lately belonging to Thomas Cook, which being forfeited fell to the town by escheat, this assembly approves the lease, and further orders that the mayor and bailiffs shall let the rest of Cook's estate for the benefit of the town, and if any suits result the same shall be defended by the town.

Ordered that the mayor, bailiffs and minister shall speedily endeavour to obtain satisfaction of the £20 left by Richard Houlmes's will to the town, from which 20s per year should be paid to the minister of Liverpool by Thomas Tarleton, alderman, and the executor of Mr John Williamson, deceased.

p. 581
FREEMEN 1653

John Carr, on his petition to be admitted a freeman, and promising to furnish all freemen with unslaked lime at 6d a bushel during his life, which if he fails, loses his freedom, is admitted and sworn without composition.

John Sanderson is elected and admitted a free burgess, paying for his composition, 40s, sworn. Memo. that 10s is remitted.

Peter Walker admitted, paying £3, and sworn. The same two persons are allowed to be town porters.

9 October 1653:

Thomas Asbrook, son of Thomas Asbrook, late burgess, admitted paying 3s 4d and sworn.

Thomas Witter, spurrier, son of Witter, late freeman, admitted, 3s 4d, sworn.

James Holt, shoemaker, son of a freeman, admitted, 3s 4d, sworn.

Enoch Boulton, gunsmith, son of James Boulton, late freeman, admitted, 3s 4d, sworn.

John Loy, sailor, son of a freeman, admitted, 3s 4d, sworn.

John Kenion, cooper, son of a freeman, admitted, 3s 4d, sworn.

30 March 1654:

John Chambers, son of Edward Chambers, late freeman, admitted and sworn, 3s 4d.

6 April 1654:

Ralph Higinson, mariner, son of William Higinson, a freeman, admitted, 3s 4d, sworn.

12 August 1654:

Henry Ashton of Whiston, gentleman, admitted and sworn, by consent of the mayor, aldermen and common council, £3, with 6s 8d over and above this remitted.

20 June 1654:

William Moore, son of Mr Anthony Moore, late a freeman, admitted and sworn, 3s 4d.

11 August 1654:

William Accars, currier, admitted and sworn, paying and giving security to Mr Mayor to save harmless the town, 50s.

Anthony Moyer, joiner, admitted and sworn, 50s.

Richard Atherton, tobacco pipe maker, admitted and sworn, 50s.

James Blevine, son of Richard Blevine, admitted and sworn, 3s 4d.

John Moneley, son of Thomas Moneley, admitted and sworn, 3s 4d.

Walter Mathewes, apprentice of Thomas Storie, admitted and sworn, 6s 8d.

John Melling, apprentice of Thomas Burton, shoemaker, sworn, 6s 8d.

9 October 1654:

John Heys, feltmaker, voted free, paying £3 and security, not free.

John Sellers, compass maker, also voted, paying £3 6s 8d, not free.

Thomas Marow proposed, to pay £5, not admitted[36]

13 October 1654:

Richard Scarisbrick of Formby, butcher, admitted and sworn, £3.

p. 582

2 NOVEMBER 1653

Ordered and agreed that a letter be written to Mr Randle Beckett in Dublin about the allocation of £10,000 in lands in Ireland, to take advice from him and other friends what can best be done to send a solicitor to negotiate the business.

There shall be a chimney built in the schoolmaster's chamber at the charge of the town, paid for by bailiffs.

That an answer to the commissioners' letter be sent, concerning the relief of the order to send poor prisoners to Preston, there being only one, William Wareing, for

---

36 Thomas Marrow entry is crossed out.

£51 damages recovered from him in the borough court at the suit of George Parker, and one, Richard Jerman, who escaped.

Ordered that Mr Fogg shall pay the accustomed dues for his wife's burial to the churchwardens of the town.

Ordered that James Chorleton and Jonas Horrocks shall be paid for their work surveying the new enclosures on the town common at the discretion of the mayor.

Ordered and agreed that the roof of the town hall be latted and teered over with lime and hair, and made handsome above at the charge of the town.

Memo: Nehemiah Mercer, son of Robert Mercer, gent., was apprenticed to Mr John Sandiford, merchant, 1 December 1653, to serve after the custom of the town, for 7 years from 1 May last, for £40 according to an indenture whereby £35 is to be repaid him or preferred to as good a master within three months.

13 OCTOBER 1654

Alexander Greene, merchant, formerly nominated one of the common council, was sworn.

Memo. Several fines imposed on Thomas Ayndoe and others for not attending council meetings.

p. 583
TUESDAY 31 JANUARY 1653

At an Assembly before the mayor, aldermen, bailiffs and common council:

Mr John Fogg, minister of the corporation proposed that he: 1. have the surplus of a year's profit in his absence, and of the £50 paid by Mr Joseph Tompson; 2. be freed of all leys and taxation which he alleges was promised at his coming; 3. have all the church dues and the town's assistance in collecting them, and the arrears of the £10 per annum due to the minister from Mr Ward, parson of Walton; 4. have six months warning of his removal. These propositions were made with a long apology, and after he departed they were considered, and answered as follows: first, there is no surplus left, the money being all used for ministers supplied in his absence, and in the beginning of the time of the visitation; second, it was ordered before by the assembly that he should pay his proportion of all leys; third, it is readily granted that all church dues shall be paid him, and the town's officers will assist in collecting them if they be withheld, and if any be in arrears it is his own fault for not calling for them; fourth, they will not be bound to give any notice but in courtesy.

Whereas a petition was presented at the last assizes[37] sessions by the register of this parish against the mayor about the delivery of the register book to him, and an order was given by the justices, it is ordered that he may take a copy of the book kept by the church clerk, but the church clerk will register all burials, births and marriages within the town as before, as the town's record, and shall have the fees due him for the service.

---

37   Assizes is crossed out.

Memo. That it was ordered by consent that the bailiffs shall pay £8 to Mr Robert Cornell for his portion of the ferry boat and two stone of oakum and some pitch. The ferry to be let at £12 per annum or above, and the fare to be 1d for a person, 2d for a horse and rider.

Regarding the newly erected cottage and several fines and presentments against Mr Strangwais, it was ordered that he pay 10 shillings to the bailiffs in lieu of all arrears of the 5 shillings per annum rent formerly ordered, and 2 shillings a year for the future, the first payment to commence at Michaelmas next. And Mr Strangwais to give security to the town for any cost arising from tenants. If he refuses the bailiffs are to enforce the former order for pulling it down after distraining for the whole arrears of several years past.

p. 584
A COPY OF ORDER OF JUSTICES OF THE PEACE FOR THE ELECTING OF A REGISTER, 1654
At a sessions of the peace at Ormskirk in the county of Lancaster on Monday 10 April 1654, on hearing of the difference between William Ellison and the clerk of Liverpool concerning the execution of the office of parish register, for registering births and burials according to a late act of parliament, it is ordered by this court that the inhabitants of Liverpool shall elect an able man to be parish register within the corporation of Liverpool, and have him sworn. Examined by Joseph Rigbye.

Afterwards, on public notice and a full meeting of the freemen in the church before the mayor, Robert Seacom was elected as register and sworn.

9 JUNE 1654, BUTLERAGE
For 22 tuns of wine called Jackalynne, £10 or three full hogsheads ordered to be paid for butlerage. Mr Greene. At an assembly on 13 October 40 shillings of this sum was ordered to be remitted in regard of the badness of the wine.
For 10 tuns of wine brought in by Tristram Fooler, 40s.
4 hogsheads in the *Alexander*, at 4s per tun, 16s.
6 hogsheads in the *Goodspeed*, William Gardner, 4s per tun, 6s.

Memo:
Ordered that Captain Thomas Croft be paid £3 by the bailiffs from the town's stock because his house and lands were spoiled by infected people being put there in the time of God's visitation of the sickness.

Ordered that 10 shillings each be restored to Peter Walker and John Sanderson from their composition money for being admitted freemen.

Mr John Sandiford to pay 5 shillings for composition money of a parcel of tallow brought in by Tristram Fooler.

p. 585
THE AUDIT OF RALPH MASSAM, GENT., MAYOR, 5 DECEMBER 1653, Peter Lurting and William Rymer, late bailiffs

Receipts of the hallkeepers ingates and outgates	£6	19s	2d
Town's customer's ingates and outgates	13	5	
Subcustomer's receipts for tolls, stalls and standings	14	13	4
Composition for freemen admitted	18	10	
Received for town rents, ferry boats and churchwardens	30	11	2
For the fine of Mr Dobson's house £70 and for boards and poles sold 27s 3d	71	7	3
Burgage rents, allowing deductions	12	3	7
Surplus of 4 leys		41	11
Composition money, licence money and butlerage	10	6	9
Received for the use of the poor	3		
Fines and amercements compounded for by bailiffs	10		
Minister and schoolmaster, 2 years arrears nil			
Received from the old bailiffs with poor's money, clipped and brass money	177	19	4

Receipts total	£370	17s	6d
Disbursed in all	242	14	1
To be paid over	128	3	5

28 December 1654. Which sum being paid in, the abovesaid bailiffs are discharged.

> Robert Cornell, mayor
> Thomas Blackmore
> Edward Williamson.[38]

p. 586

ROBERT CORNELL, GENTLEMAN, MAYOR [1654–55]

p. 587

ELECTION COURT WEDNESDAY 18 OCTOBER 1654, before Edward Williamson, gentleman, mayor, John Blundell and John Lurting, bailiffs, according to charter and custom.

Robert Cornell is elected mayor and sworn
Robert Corles elected chief bailiff for the mayor and lord protector of the commonwealth and sworn

---

38   Signatures.

Richard Leivsey elected bailiff for the town of Liverpool by the votes of the freeman, and sworn.

William Halsall, esq., recorder
John Winstanley town clerk
Richard Dwarrihouse serjeant at mace, sworn
Robert Seacome water bailiff, sworn.

By the Common Council:
John Fogg, clerk, minister
George Glover, schoolmaster
John Sturzaker, hallkeeper, sworn
William Whalley, town customer; Robert Seacome chosen, Whalley refusing to serve, sworn
Richard Poultney, subcustomer, sworn
Thomas Asbrook and Robert Sutton, stewards of hall, sworn
Thomas Coppull, heyward, sworn.

Chosen by the jury:
Edward Formeby, John Lurting, draper, Alexander Greene, Henry Rydeing, merchant appraisers, sworn
William Accars, James Hoult, registers of leather, sworn
Thomas Seale, John Cooke, alefounders, sworn
Richard Atherton, Peter Walker, Robert Halle, Anthony Hunt, barleymen or mossreeves, sworn

p. 589[39]
Ralph Higginson, deceased, and John Holland in his place, John Moneley, Thomas Witter, John Kenion, scavengers, sworn
Richard Tyrer, murenger
Robert Kenion, Edward Sutton, overseers of the highways
John Sanderson, Peter Walker, porters
Richard Farrer, John Carr, leavelookers, sworn
William Chorley, Elizabeth Rycroft, boardsetters
Richard Farrer, Richard Widdowes, boothsetters
John Carr, bellman

Thomas Roe, churchwarden
Robert Harvy, sidesman.

Memo. that Richard Poultney has paid to the current bailiffs for the churchwardens' receipts of last year, they refusing to serve, 27s., which they are to acount for at the next audit.

39   Page 588 does not appear in the manuscript.

Attorney. Richard Washington the elder admitted and sworn an attorney of the borough court for a year by consent of Mr Mayor and the aldermen.

p. 590

LIVERPOOL. PORTMOOT OR QUARTER SESSIONS OF THE PEACE, MONDAY 23 OCTOBER 1654, before mayor and bailiffs according to custom.

Inquisition by the oaths of John Blundell, Thomas Storie, Thomas Ayndoe, Peter Lurting, John Walles, Henry Moore, Henry Ryding, Thomas Nicholson, Robert Harvie, Edward Sutton, John Lurting, smith, John Cooke, Richard Crompton, Thomas Seale, Richard Lunte, Thomas Croper, John Lunte, William Accars, Thomas Copull, John Banks, Brian Mercer, John Henshawe, Thomas Asbrook, James Hoult, honest freemen.

We present:

John Syers for a tussle on Henry Southwell, 3s 4d

Henry Southwell for tussle on John Syers, 3s 4d

Margaret Granger and Edward Barton for using faculty of freemen, not being free, 1s against Barton

James Paterick for pulling fence down and breaking flag stones of James Burton, 2s 6d

Anthony Moyers and Dorothy Hodgson for not cleansing their streets to annoyance of neighbours, 6d apiece

James Burton, Margaret Fazakerley, Randle Whalley, Edward Whalley, Richard Buckley, Robert Hughson of Bootle, for tethering in the town field, nil

Thomas Nicholson, Peter Laithwait, John Cawdey, James Hoult, for working unlawful leather, 2s 6d apiece

Thomas Roe for the like, 2s 6d

Michael Tarleton and John Chandler for neglect of office of churchwardens, nil

All freemen who have not appeared at this court nor essoyned, viz. Mr Bird, Mr Thomas Shepard, Thomas Clayton, Edward Stockley, Thomas Blackburne, George Halley, William Rigbie, Edward Dicconson, William Patten, Hugh Cooper, Peirs Gerrard, John Sorrocold, William Lea, Andrew Ashton, Edward Ogle, Thomas Baxter, Richard Brook, Richard Martin, Henry Birchall, Robert Fleetwood, William Henshaw, Robert Fleetwood, Henry Radcliffe, Edmund Lyon, Thomas Gardner, Henry Fearnehead, Richard Fazakerley, John Bate, Edward Taylor, Henry Ambrose, Henry Cooper, John Hussie, Thomas Cheaney, John Everard, Peter Boulton, Rowland Ashton, Edward Lea, Thomas Moir, Henry Kilshawe, Thomas Croft, John Burgess, John Haskins, Thomas Darbisheire, Robert Farehust, John Dichfield, Gilbert Coote, John Tennant, Parcivall Crosse, Thomas Parcivall, William Fleetwood, John Stanley, William Moore, Walter Matthew, 3s 4d apiece

We order:

All who have any inmates to appear before Mr Mayor before 28 January next and give security to town, on pain of 10s apiece

Richard Poultney to ring curfew according to ancient custom on pain of 10s

Mrs Bicksteth to set up door to her swineyard and chains to it wyneging to Robert Seacome's house, on pain of 3s 4d

John Lurting, smith, to cut his hedge which hangs over Widow Hacking's garden before 2 February on pain of 5s

John Raphson or his overseers to make chimney to the house where Elizabeth Winstanley lives before 10 November next on pain of 10s

We agree to all ancient laws and laudable customs.

p. 591
20 OCTOBER 1654

An Assembly in the common hall before Robert Cornell, mayor, Thomas Blackmoore, William Williamson, Thomas Williamson, Ralph Massam, Edward Williamson, aldermen, Henry Corles and Richard Leivsey bailiffs and the greater part of the common council assembled. Since many inconveniences have been done by swine wandering in the streets instead of being kept in their styes, prejudicing the market and other people, it is ordered that from 9 November owners of swine keep them shut up on sabbath days and Saturdays. The heyward should impound any wandering swine in a pinfold, from where owners can redeem them for 4d each, and he is to impound all unrung swine found trespassing in the town, and keep them until redeemed for a similar sum. All offices and freemen are required to assist in executing this order. If the heyward neglects the order he is to be discharged.

p. 592
LIVERPOOL. PORTMOOT COURT OR QUARTER SESSIONS OF THE PEACE, MONDAY 8 JANUARY 1654, in presence of mayor and bailiffs according to custom.

Inquisition by the oaths of John Lurting, Evan Marsh, John Sandiford, John Owen, Richard Turner, Richard Holland, William Daintie, William Eccleston, William Whalley, Anthony Hunt, Robert Halle, Robert Kenion, Thomas Coppull, Richard Widdowes, John Kenion, lawful and honest men of the town.

We present:
John Bird for bloodwipe on Michael Tarleton, 6s 8d
Michael Tarleton for tussle on Mr Bird, 3s 4d
Jane Williamson for using faculty of freeman, 3s 4d
Peter Halle for the like, 6s 8d
Henry Atherton for the like, 3s 4d
Robert Johnson, Mrs Margaret Bicksteth, Mrs Olliffe, Henry Craine, Jane Haskaine, John Chandler, George Tarleton, Richard Crosse esq., Thomas Lancelot, Isabel Fells for keeping swine unrung, 6d apiece
Mr Mayor, Mrs Tarleton, widow, Mrs Hodgson, Darby Caton, Mr John Chandler, Christopher Broockbanck, Mrs Bicksteth, Robert Haughton, William

Rydeing, Elizabeth Rycroft, Robert Swifte, Thomas Widdowes, John Orrell, Jane Morse for not cleansing the street, 6d apiece

Gilbert Tarleton, John Widdowson, butchers, for not bringing their tallow and sheepskins to market, 2s apiece

Richard Crosse esq., for ploughing up town's land near the pinfold gate, 12d

John Eccles for not appearing the court of trials, 6s 4d

We order:

12 leather buckets to be made for quenching fire, 6 hooks, and two ladders, one of 30 pins and the other of 25 pins, to be ready in three months time, and the bailiffs to see this done on penalty of £5

Mr Crosse to set a dowe stone on the north side of his Nine Lands and not encroach on the town's land by 8 February on pain of 10s.

The bailiffs to see the wall made up between Cooke's house and Mrs Bicksteth within 20 days, on pain of 5s

Mr Strangwayes or his tenant to make up the fence between Mr Winstanley and his house in Dale Street on pain of 5s

A stone bridge to be made in Dale Street at the end of Mr bailiff Lurting's house and George Tarleton to see to the making of the wall by the backside of Lurting's by the water course within three months

Robert Tyrer to make up his fence between Moore and himself before the end of January

We agree to all ancient laws and laudable customs.

p. 593

p. 594

INDENTURE, 24 FEBRUARY 1654

Between Robert Cornell, gentleman, mayor, and the bailiffs and burgesses of the corporation on the one part, and Edward Tarleton son of John Tarleton of Liverpool on the other. Witnessing that the mayor bailiffs and burgesses for £35 paid by Edward Tarleton have granted to him, his executors and assigns the messuage, dwelling house and garden in Liverpool at the Church Steele, late in the tenure of Thomas Tarleton, and all houses, edifices, buildings, yards, orchards, gardens, barns, stables, backsides, ways, commodities and easements belonging, to have and hold for 99 years if he, or Margaret his wife, or Edward his son shall live so long, paying to the mayor, bailiffs and burgesses 8 shillings per annum on the feast of St Michael. And if the rent fall behind by twenty days the mayor and bailiffs may repossess the house. And Edward Tarleton agrees to keep the property in tenantable repair, and not to let or dispose of the messuage without the consent of the mayor and bailiffs other than for the term of one year, or for the benefit of his wife and children. And the mayor and bailiffs agree to allow Edward Tarleton, his heirs and assigns to hold the messuage without

p. 595
hindrance. And the mayor and bailiffs have full legal title to dispose of the property and assure it against other claimants. In witness whereof the parties have set their hands and seals.

p. 596
26 JANUARY 4 CHARLES
At court held in the manor of West Derby before Lord Molineux, John Williamson of Liverpool, beer brewer, surrenders a messuage and eight acres in West Derby, with all appurtenances, to the use of William Fox of Toxteth Park, gentleman, Robert Williamson of Liverpool, mariner, Ralph Sandiford of Liverpool, sadler, and Thomas Tarleton of Liverpool, cooper, and their heirs, to hold the land according the customs and service due to the king, to the use of such persons and intentions as are set out in the indenture of 4 June 1628 between John Williamson on the one part and William Fox, Robert Williamson, Ralph Sandiforth and Thomas Tarleton on the other part. And, no one contesting it, John Williamson asks that the indenture be enrolled here in the court of record, and the said indenture follows in his own words.[40]

This indenture of 4 June 1628 provides that the said William Fox, Robert Williamson, Ralph Sandifort and Thomas Tarleton and their heirs shall, after the death of John Williamson, occupying the two closes called the Two Far Heys containing five acres, shall pay from them £4 per year, at the feast of the Nativity and St John the Baptist by equal portions, to an able and preaching minister who shall every sabbath preach the word of God in the chapel of Liverpool, and shall be approved of by the mayor of Liverpool and five of the frequent communicants living in Liverpool. If this payment be unpaid it shall be lawful for the minister to enter the said two closes and enjoy the profits, paying to the king the yearly rent and services due. And in the absence of such a preaching minister the said yearly payment shall cease. In witness, James Winstanley, 1655.

p. 597

p. 598
LIVERPOOL. PORTMOOT COURT OR QUARTER SESSIONS OF THE PEACE, MONDAY 23 APRIL 1655, before the mayor and bailiffs according to custom.

Inquisition taken on the oaths of John Higinson, Thomas Storie, William Rymer, John Eccles, Robert Eccles, William Mosse, Thomas Seale, William Accars, John Tompson, Richard Lunte, Peter Walker, Thomas Coppull, Thomas Witter, Richard Atherton, Richard Scarsbrick, honest and lawful men of the borough.

40   Latin.

We present:

Edward Rydinge for a tussle on Richard Eccleston and Richard Eccleston for a tussle on him, 3s 4d

Edward Rydinge for a tussle on Ralph Mercer and Ralph Mercer for tussle on him, 3s 4d

James Patricke for striking Thomas Coppull, 3s 4d

John Darbie for a bloodwipe on Edward Henshall and Edward Henshall a bloodwipe on him, 6s 8d

Edward Ridinge for a bloodwipe on Ellen Waide and Ellen Waide for a bloodwipe on him, 6s 8d

John Chandler for refusing to bring his quarts and pints to Mr Mayor and selling unlawful measure, 6s 8d

Richard Williams for the like, 6s 8d

Robert Kenion, cooper, for selling beer by unlawful measure, 1s

Margaret Granger for selling beer, not being free, 2s

Davie Halle for selling bread not being free, 1s

Jane Wilson for the like, 1s

Dorothy Bickerstaffe for her swine spoiling the mayor's ground, 1s

Anne Chantrell for swine unrung, 1s

John Chambers for the like, 1s

Evan March, Robert Kenion, Mr John Chandler, George Potter, Mr John Buird, Margaret Granger, Mrs Elizabeth Tarleton, widow, John Royle, William Gardner, Mrs Margaret Williamson, widow, Dorothy Robinson, Davie Halle, for the like, 1s apiece

Mr Alexander Greene for keeping a mastiff dog unmuzzled, 6d

Mr John Chanler for the like, 6d

Dorothy Bickerstaffe for fence lying down to annoyance of Mr Rumley, 6d

James Glover for fence lying down, 6d

Alice Pollard alias Lee for garden wall lying down to annoyance of Mrs Heapie, 6d

Mr Henry Corles, Mr Richard Livesley for not causing the fence between Mr Robert Seacom and the town's land to be made up, 6d apiece

Mr John Chandler for fence lying down at the Castle Hill, 6d

Jane Williamson for fence lying down to annoyance of James Skinde, 6d

Jonney Tarleton, widow, for her fence lying down, 6d

Greggson for getting clay at the Tithe Barn near the highway, 5s

John Burton for the like, 5s

James Glover for not cleaning the street at his croft end, 6d

William Gardner for laying timber in street, 6d

Thomas Andowe for not clearing the street by his field in Old Hall Street, 6d

Richard Widdowes for not cleaning market staie, 1s

Thomas Aspinall for working unlawful leather, John Candowe, James Bradshawe for the like, 2s a piece

Mr Richard Crosse for letting muck lie in the street

p. 599

Edward Edmunds for not giving his outvoice to the town's customer, 40s

Mrs Elizabeth Heapy for keeping her fence down to annoyance of William Rimmer, 6d

We order:

John Chambers not to put any tenant in his cottage built on the heath without the consent of Mr Mayor

All the inhabitants who have cellars open to the street to make rails or doors on the top or sides of the steps, to keep people from falling down in the night, 5s apiece

Robert Harvie and Dorothy Bickerstaffe to make up the gutter between their houses and share the cost, by 7 May

Everyone who has ploughed up town's waste or common to shovel it up and leave the common according to the ancient dole stone by 10 June, on pain 40s

The ditch of the Parlor Field next to the lane to be scoured by the 1 June by the present possessors, on pain of 40s

John Lurting to scour the gutter between him and Widow Tarleton and make it deeper so that water may have free passage, by 12 June

All those that have land on either side of Ackers Lane to scour their ditches by last of May, on pain of 40s

We present Peter Mason, cooper, for using the faculty of a freeman, 3s 4d

We present John Griffie for annoyance to Mr Thomas Williamson by abuse of office

We choose John Holland scavenger in place of Ralph Higginson

We order the bailiffs or those whom they employ to acquaint several parties concerned in the former order in time convenient

We present Mr Henry Corles and Mr Richard Livesley, bailiffs, for buying a parcel of herring by order of the town and converting them for their own use

We present all the inhabitants of the town that sell ale or beer and came not to be licensed.

We agree to all ancient laws and laudable customs.

p. 600

LIVERPOOL. PORTMOOT COURT OR QUARTER SESSIONS OF THE PEACE, MONDAY 30 JULY 1655, before the mayor and bailiffs, according to custom.

Inquisition taken before the mayor and bailiffs on the oaths of Edward Formby, Gilbert Formby, John Lurting, draper, Thomas Sandiford, Thomas Preeson, William Gardner, Henry Moore, Roger Harrison, James Hoult, Thomas Seale, Thomas Carr, Robert Halle, Thomas Coppull, John Holland, and Edward Horrobine, honest and lawful men of the borough.

We present:

Philip Tooke, chirurgeon of the *Satisfaction*, frigate, for reproachful and abusive language to Mr Mayor and the whole corporation

Lawrence Jumper, Margaret Granger and Abigail Martin for selling ale and beer not being free, 2s

Parcivalle Houline for evesdropping under Ellen Higginson's window on 16 June last, 1s

Henry Cooper, Peter Laithwaite, William Bradshaw, Thomas Nicholson and James Hoult for working unlawful leather, 10s

Isabel Rennald, widow, for her fence lying down; Edward Winstanley, Robert Johnson, Dorothy Bicksteth, Richard Scarsbrick, Robert Kenion, John Chandler, John Owen, Philip Cock and Brian Mercer for the like, 8s

Mr Richard Crosse for not cleansing his water course in Dale Street; James Glover for the like, 2s apiece

Alderman William Williamson for not cleansing before his croft in Tithebarn Street; James Glover and Margaret Bicksteth for the like, 6d apiece

John Mason for letting dung lie at the pillory; Richard Farrer, Richard Widdowes, Richard Chantrell, William Chorley, Elizabeth Rycroft, Edward Teasdalle, and bailiff John Higinson for not cleansing the market place and corn market, nil

Joanne Tarleton for not cleansing the street against her house; and Mr William Strangewais, John Owen, John Chandler, Richard Scarisbrick, Ellen Wade and bailiff John Lurting for the like, 6d apiece

Jane Eccleston, widow, for keeping her swine unrung; Lawrence Jumper, Robert Sutton, Mr Gilbert Formeby, John Chandler, Thomas Nicholson, Richard Holland, Margaret Fazakerley, Ralph Winstanley, Richard Scarsbrick, Anne Brookbank, Henry Craine, Jane Haskaine, John Higinson, Dorothy Bicksteth, Richard Crosse esq., Dorothy Robinson, John Royle, Widow Chantrell, Widow Browne, Roger Jones, Robert Clark, John Chambers, John Lunte, Thomas Lynnaker, Richard Rymmer, Widdow Kenion, Mrs Tarleton, Matilda Johnson, Edward Sutton, Margaret Bicksteth, Henry Moore for the like, 1s apiece

p. 601

John Londsdalle and Richard Buckley for getting clay at the Tithe Barn, nil

Thomas Pombton for his horse's trespass on John Owen, nil

Richard Tyrer for the like, nil

William Gardner for his swine's trespass on Brian Mercer, nil

Ralph Higinson, John Moneley, Thomas Witter and John Kenion, scavengers, for letting dung lie in the streets, nil

William Gardner for letting his dunghill lie above the fence so that his swine run over, 1s

William Seacome for carrying turf from the common to Everton, nil

Richard Poultney and William Poultney, his son, for a tussle on a country man, nil

We order:

Mr Strangwais to scour the watercourse at the Two Lands ends near Mr Crosse's field

Mr Bailiff Corles to scour the watercourse at the end of the common adjoining to Mr Crosse's field, and make a plat for the carts to pass over within fourteen days, that the highway may suffer no more

The Fall Well be cleansed before the end of August

We agree to all ancient laws and laudable customs

John Owen for not appearing at a court of trial to serve on the jury according to summons, 3s 4d

p. 602

11 JULY 1655

At an Assembly in the common hall before the mayor, the aldermen, bailiffs and common council:

On the petition of Mr John Fogg, minister of Liverpool, that the house called Cooke's House in Tithebarn Street, lately fallen into the town's hands by escheat, may be set apart for him and succeeding ministers, this was agreed provided that he and they shall dwell there and keep it in repair at their own expense. This gift is to be in satisfaction of all legacies heretofore given to the minister by Mr Darbie or Mr Robert Williamson or Sammell, his wife, deceased.

Same date. On the petition of Richard Williams to build a wall at the entrance to his newly repaired house to defend it from the violence of the sea breaking on it, offering a small rent if required, and promising to leave the said ground in as good a condition as it now is, it is ordered that he can erect a wall at a rent of 4d per year, provided that he does not build on it hereafter without consent.

Same date. It was ordered, at the request of Captain Edward Tarleton, that he shall have liberty to build a porch adjoining his house in the churchyard, not to exceed six foot square, to be placed at the sight and discretion of the mayor and bailiffs.

It is also ordered that every freeman may have the benefit of the town's seal to any certificate, freely, provided that the certificate be drawn up by the town clerk or his deputy; foreigners to pay 3s 4d for the same use of the seal.

p. 603

Names of those who contracted for the Common to be enclosed:

James Williamson, alderman, for 4 acres

Thomas Williamson, alderman, for — acres, fine paid

Edward Williamson, alderman, for — acres, fine paid

Roger Jones for 2 acres, fine £3

Evan Marsh for 2 acres, fine £3

Richard Williamson 1 acre

Richard Parceavall, 3 acres, fine paid

Dorothy Sandiford, widow, Mr John Sandiford, 4 acres, fine paid

John Sturzaker, 1 acre, fine paid

John Chambers, 1 acre, fine paid

Richard Washington, — acres, fine paid

Thomas Ayndoe and James Hey

Memo. That the wines brought in by Mr James Williamson in the *Marie* for Mr Greene and Mr Aynesworth rated at 16 tuns are to pay by consent £5 butlerage, in regard it amounts not to 20 tuns for which butlerage is due, and therefore it is put to composition for licence money only.

Ordered that Mr Greene is rated to pay for the cargo of dale boards[41] after the rate of 80 tuns, at 8d per tun, £2 13s 4d, 12d per tun formerly paid for the like. No custom is due because the goods were bought in Chester water, and brought in on his own adventure.

p. 604
17 NOVEMBER 1654
At an Assembly held in the common hall before the mayor, aldermen, bailiffs and most of the common council:

It was proposed that in regard this town is endowed with all the privileges of a parish, having time out of mind had the nomination of its minister, clerk and churchwardens, that a petition be drawn up and sent to the Governor to make this town a parish of itself, distinct from Walton, especially in view of demands for an allowance toward the repair of their church which this town is not willing to pay unless compelled to by law.

Whereas Richard Houlmes by his noncupative will gave £20 for the use of the minister of Liverpool, yearly, if John Houlmes, his son, should die in his minority, and left Thomas Tarleton, alderman, and John Williamson executors, who, as is conceived, ought to have paid the same since John Houlmes is long absent and supposed dead, it is ordered that a petition be sent to the commissioners for pious uses, and that Mr Washington be asked to give his information concerning the business at Prescot. This was done, but the commissioners have declared it is not within their jusrisdiction since it appears that John Houlmes is living.

It is ordered by the same assembly that the mayor and bailiffs shall cause the ferry boats to be employed to the best advantage of the town until they can be farmed at a good rent, or be otherwise disposed of.

Whereas Cook's house is let to a soldier for one year from May day last for a rent of 26s 8d, the tenant to keep it in repair, and there is 13s 4d of the rent in arrears, to be called for by the bailiffs, the house is to be let to some better tenant. And the lands in the town field are to be let to bailiff Marsh and bailiff Sturzaker for 20s per annum rent, to be collected by the bailiffs and accounted for at every audit.

Ordered that the bailiffs shall provide a bushel measure, a brass quarter or gallon, and an iron rod for standards, to remain in the town.

p. 605
19 DECEMBER 1654
At an Assembly:

41   Dale boards are possibly deal boards, or wooden troughs for drawing off water: OED.

It is ordered that, whereas several sums of money have been heretofore given to the use of the poor of this town by Mrs Derby, Mr Robert Williamson, being £17 10s, the present bailiffs shall pay 20s yearly to the overseers of the poor to be given where most need is, and the interest of all bonds now owing is likewise to be distributed, whereof there is received on Lynnaker's bond, 37s.

It was proposed that a weekly lecture be held in the town, and every one to be asked what they will pay.

Ordered that Mr Sandiford shall pay 30s for 12 tuns of wine in Mr Brere's vessel, the *Marie*, from San Sebastian, rated at 2s 6d per tun, and 7s for 7 hogsheads more at 4s the tun, in total 37s. Afterwards, on 24 January, ordered that Mr Sandiford pay for 7 tuns of decayed wines at the rate of 2s 6d per tun, which is 17s 6d.

Also ordered at same assembly that the mayor and bailiffs shall bargain and pay for the rebuilding of Eastham Mill, and sell materials left over, and get Mrs Bicksteth to deliver to them the old mill stones which Mr John Williamson borrowed.

p. 606
24 JANUARY 1654
At an Assembly held in the town hall before the mayor, the aldermen and bailiffs and the greater part of the common council:

It was ordered that Mr John Winstanley, town clerk, shall again go to Dublin about the delivery of the Lord Protector's letter to the Deputy there, to enquire of the forfeited lands in Ireland appointed by act of parliament for the use of this corporation, which his Highness' letter directs to be in Wicklow, to the value of £10,000, in lieu of their great loss. He is to have his charges paid, and an allowance of £10 from the town's stock for his two former voyages, and more if his stay shall be long and the voyage troublesome, and for his loss of time and practice. This was referred to the judges of the court for adjudication of claims, and by them reported that the adventurers and soldiers must be first satisfied, and this allotment to be set out in course.

At the same assembly the house at Church Steele, town's land and out of lease, was discussed. It was petitioned for by Captain Edward Tarleton as having been his father's and built by him, and also sought by Thomas Tarleton, son of Alderman Thomas Tarleton, deceased. A decision was deferred till the Recorder gave his opinion which of them ought to have the right of tenancy. Memo. It was afterwards ordered to be leased to Captain Edward Tarleton, as appears by the indenture entered on page 594, and by the following order.

At an assembly on 23 February 1654, it was ordered that the mayor and bailiffs shall lease the house at Church Steele to Captain Edward Tarleton for £35, for 99 years if the said Edward, Margaret, his wife, and Edward, his son, shall live so long, paying a rent of 8s, and to keep the same in good repair.

p. 607
COMPOSITIONS
For 60 barrels and ten mace of herring by William Raineford and others in the *Unitie*, 21s

For 60 barrels and 20 mace of herring in the *Elizabeth* by Richard Norres and Thomas Dobb, 22s 6d

10 barrels and 40 mace of herring in the *Margaret* by Philip Harrison and John Sutton, 6s 4d

40 barrels in the *Gift* by Mr Picton, merchant, 12s 6d

600 Dalles[42] by Captain Whitworth, 10s

p. 608
FREEMEN
    19 December 1654
John Heyes, feltmaker admitted by consent of mayor, alderman and common council assembled, giving security to the town and paying for his composition, £4
Ralph Carr, shoemaker, John Carr his father engaging for his security, 50s
William Fynch, clerk, vicar of Walton, free
Robert Kenion, cooper, son of Richard Kenion late a freemen, 3s 4d
John Holland, beerbrewer, son of Richard Holland, 3s 4d
Robert Sympson on petition that he keeps Robinson's child so that it shall not be burdensome to the town, free
    23 February 1654
Edward Banks, 50s
Andrew Over, sadler, £3
Ralph Belling, £4
    13 September 1655
Hugh Rennald on the petition of Thomas Preeson, £3
All sworn

Memo. Proposed by mayor at meeting of the 40 on 9 May 1655 that William Henshaw be admitted free, to pay 50s
John Craine, son of a freeman, also to be admitted but came not
Memo. 11 July 1655 Henry Atkinson, whitesmith or jackmaker, also proposed, to pay £3, but he has since gone to Ireland
Samuel Postlethwait of Warrington, 22 August 1655 also proposed, to pay £6, but refused
Jonathan Glave, whitesmith, also voted, to pay £4, but came not.

p. 609
23 FEBRUARY 1654
    It is ordered by the consent of the mayor, the aldermen, bailiffs and common council that the church, being in decay, shall be repaired, and that the bailiffs issue money to pay for the same.
    Memo. The same day, it was ordered that John Blundell and John Lurting shall be defended against any trouble arising from Robert Clark's complaint for being taken in execution on the sabbath day, as is pretended at the town's charge, and

42   Deals: see fn. 41.

neither they nor any other officer is to be damnified thereby. Memo. This order was afterwards taken into consideration at another meeting, and respited.

9 MAY 1655

Gilbert Coot's child, which has hitherto been kept at the town's charge, was considered. A letter of attorney was sent to London to get him apprehended. Afterwards he was discovered living in Southwark, and on his letter to Mr Mayor it is ordered that his child be sent up to John Evans, a shoemaker in Aldersgate Street, to Trinity Court, having promised to receive it, and so the town may be discharged.[43]

Memo. This day several papers concerning the lands in Ireland were read and the judges' report, whereupon it was resolved that a new address be made to the Lord Protector, and that Colonel Ireland and Colonel Birch be again solicited for a more absolute and authentic order, and that we should consult Mr Recorder about it.

p. 610
9 MAY 1655

It is ordered by the mayor, aldermen, bailiffs and most part of the common council assembled that all the ashlar stones lying in Water Street end shall be pulled up, and employed for making up the old way to the church by the Tower foot, and also that the gates at Dale Street end and all other street ends shall be pulled up, taken away, and the ways and works levelled, and causeways made as formerly they were.

The town's interest in Cook's house, agreed to be allowed to the minister of the town as a vicarage, was discussed and deferred to another time.

It is ordered that the barleymen and scavengers make their presentments once a month to Mr Mayor for the better keeping up of fences and cleaning of streets.

On reading of a warrant for payment of £2 13s 4d of £12 levied on all of Walton parish towards the repair of the church of Walton, under the hands of Mr Moore, the parson, vicar and one churchwarden, it is conceived that this town is not therewith to be charged, nor is the warrant well grounded or legally issued. Therefore it is referred to the recorder for his opinion, and in the meantime it is not to be paid.

22 AUGUST 1655

At an Assembly in the town hall before Mr Mayor, the most part of the aldermen and common council:

It is again ordered that Mr Mayor and the bailiffs shall treat with Richard Whytehead or any other about the setting up of Eastham Mills, with power to contract for a certain term and rent for the best advantage of the corporation, and to

---

43   Note about Coot discovered living in Southwark is added in a different hand.

reserve the ancient rent of 20 shillings per annum and what more they can agree. See former order.

Upon reading of Richard Ralphson's petition concerning the little shop late in the possession of Heaton Dyer. It is ordered that the shop shall be let for a yearly rent to the petitioner before any other at such a rent as he or any other can agree with the mayor and bailiffs for the town's best advantage.

p. 611

Memo. That I Robert Cornell, mayor of the town, have demised to Richard Ralphson of Ince Blundell, yeoman, one shop in the market place in Liverpool, late in the possession of Edmund Ralphson or his assigns, to hold from the feast of St Michael last for one year for 16 shillings yearly rent payable to the bailiffs, providing that he shall keep the shop in good repair and permit old Thomas Higinson, the cobbler, to work in the shop in the weekdays at 4s 2d per year rent, according to an order of the common council lately made concerning the disposal of the said shop. In witness I have put my hand, 17 October 1655.

> Robert Cornell, mayor
> Witness, John Winstanley

To be added to the town's rental this 16s a year, and for a standing near the High Crosse let to Jane Witter and Elizabeth Mosse, widows, 2s a year.

p. 612

AUDIT OF EDWARD WILLIAMSON, GENTLEMAN, MAYOR, John Blundell and John Lurting, bailiffs.

Total receipts	£312	2s	9d
Total disbursements	163	7	6
Remaining to be paid to Henry Corles and Richard Leivsey, bailiffs	148	15	3

Accounted for 28 December and the audit signed

> Robert Cornell, mayor
> Thomas Blackmoore
> Edward Willinson, aldermen

p. 613

THOMAS AYNDOE, GENTLEMAN, MAYOR [1655–56]

p. 614

LIVERPOOL. ELECTION COURT, THURSDAY 18 OCTOBER 1655, before the mayor and bailiffs, according to the form of several charters.

Thomas Ayndoe, gentleman, elected mayor by the votes of the major part of the burgesses and sworn

Robert Sutton elected chief bailiff for the mayor and his highness the Lord
Protector of the Commonwealth and sworn
Henry Moore elected bailiff for the town by the votes of all the freemen, and sworn.

William Halsall nominated recorder
John Winstanley allowed clerk
— nominated serjeant at mace
Robert Seacome nominated water bailiff, and sworn.

    Officers chosen by the Common Council on Friday following:
John Fogg, clerk, allowed minister
George Glover allowed schoolmaster
John Sturzaker allowed hallkeeper, sworn
Robert Seacome allowed town's customer, sworn
Richard Poultney allowed subcustomer and church clerk
John Chambers, James Hoult chosen steward of the hall, sworn
Thomas Coppull chosen heyward.

    Officers chosen by the jury on Monday 22 October:
John Higinson, Richard Percivall, John Blundell, Richard Leivsley, merchant
appraisers, sworn
Edward Horrobine, John Mellinge, registers of leather, sworn
John Heyes, John Holland, alefounders, sworn

p. 615
Richard Holland, William Midleton, Robert Clarke, Robert Sympson, barleymen, sworn
Richard Scarsbrick, William Fleetwoode, Robert Kenion, cooper, Enoch Boulton,
scavengers, sworn
William Ryding, murenger
William Mosse, Robert Halle, overseers of the highways
John Sanderson, Peter Walker, porters
John Carr, Richard Farrer, leavelookers, sworn
William Chorley, Elizabeth Rycroft, boardsetters
Richard Farrer, Thomas Witter, boothsetters
John Carr,[44] beadle and bellman, Thomas Witter
— churchwardens

f. 616[45]
PORTMOOT COURT OR QUARTER SESSIONS OF THE PEACE, MONDAY
22 OCTOBER 1655, for the town and borough of Liverpool, in the common hall
before the mayor and bailiffs.

44   John Carr's name is crossed out.
45   Pagination is replaced by foliation for five folios.

Inquisition taken by the oaths of Henry Corles, Peter Lurting, William Rymer, John Blundell, John Chandler, John Walles, John Owen, Richard Turner, Thomas Nicholson, John Chambers, Thomas Radcliffe, Robert Eccles, Richard Lunte, Michael Barker, James Burton, Anthony Carr, James Hoult, Thomas Coppull, John Henshawe, John Johnson, John Heyes, John Melling, Edward Banks, honest and lawful men of the borough.

We present:

Thomas Fazakerley and Richard Atherton for working unlawful leather, 2s 6d apiece

Thomas Bridge, Ralph Halle, Margaret Granger, William Brettan for using the faculty of freemen, not free, 1s apiece

Richard Scarisbrick, Richard Crompton for keeping swine unrung, 1s apiece

Robert Henshawe of Everton and Adam Leathes for tethering in the townfield, 3s 4d apiece

Thomas Andoe, mayor, for not cleaning the street before his croft in the Halle Street, 6d

William Williamson, alderman, for the like in Tithebarn Street

Jane Eccleston, widow, for not cleaning the street at her parlour end, 6d

Mr William Strangwais for not cleaning the street before his door in Castle Street, 6d

Mr John Winstanley for letting muck lie before his garden wall in Dale Street, 6d

Richard Dwarrihouse for not making clean before his door, 6d

Richard Widdowes, Richard Farrer, not making clean the market place, 6d apiece

Anne Charnock for laying muck before her door, 6d

James Glover for not cleaning in Dale Street, 6d

Anthony Hunt for not cleaning street before his croft in Tithebarn Street, 6d

James Apleton for not cleansing the street before his door, 6d

Robert Bancroft for the like, 6d

John Higinson for letting his cart be in the highway, 1s

Robert Aughton for not cleansing his street against the hall, 1s

All such as did not appear or essoyne at this court and were not excused, 3s 4d apiece

Orders by the Jury:

Richard Scarsbrick, Anthony Garrard, William Raineford make up their fences that are annoying William Chantrell and Robert Johnson by 11 November on pain of 5s

John Rose under the hill to clear his ditch from the Netherfield Steele as far as his ground reaches, to the townfield, 5s

f. 616d

The cart way going up to Everton near the little stone bridge be widened that a cart may pass with a load, 3s 4d

After 21 December any man's swine in the street on Saturdays or sabbath days shall pay 3s 4d, and that inhabitants shall have present notice hereof by the bellman

Mrs Ellen Eccleston take away her runnage from her back and lay the ground even and make a paved gutter so that the watercourse may pass as formerly through her entry, by the last of November, 5s

James Hey and Thomas Roe to do the like in their backsides, 5s apiece

The mayor and bailiffs cause the wall on the backside of Margaret Loyes, Richard Poultney, Margaret Boots to be made up by 2 February, 5s

Richard Rymmer raise up his backside that the watercourse pass through his entry within ten days, 5s

Henry Moore, bailiff, cleanse his gutter between Mr Henry Corles and him within ten days, 5s

Any with dead swine or cattle to bury them, 5s apiece

Richard Poultney shall ring Coverlesne according to ancient custom

We agree to all ancient laws and laudable customs.

f. 617

PORTMOOT COURT OR QUARTER SESSIONS OF THE PEACE FOR THE TOWN AND BOROUGH OF LIVERPOOL, MONDAY 21 JANUARY 1655, before the mayor and bailiffs.

Inquisition taken by the oaths of Richard Pearcivall, Edward Alcock, John Higinson, John Lurting, William Bushell, Anthony Moyer, Edmund Leivsey, William Litherland, Gregory Formeby, John Melling, John Cary, Robert Clark, Richard Scarsbrick, William Ryding, Thomas Coppull, honest and lawful men of the borough.

We present:

John Woodward, Richard Holland, William Bradshaw, Ralph Stock, John Johnson, John Bullock, John Houghton, James Hoult for working unlawful leather, 2s 6d apiece

William Accars for cutting and selling unlawful leather, Thomas Burscoe for the like, 2s 6d apiece

Thomas Bride, Owen Morgaine, John Tompson, sailor, Philip Cock, Margaret Granger, William Greton, William Parker,[46] for selling ale and not being free, 3s 4d apiece

Mr Ralph Massame, Joany Tarleton, John Royle, Mr Lawrence Brears, Mrs Manarainge, Anthoney Moyer, John Williamson senior, James Glover, for not cleaning the street, 6d apiece

Mr Edward Moore, Mr Thomas Andoe, Jane Williamson for the like in Old Hall Street, John Higginson for the like in Tithebarn Street, John Walles, Robert Bancroft for the like, 6d apiece

---

46 Names of John Tompson, sailor, Philip Cock, Margaret Granger and William Parker are crossed out.

Marie Williamson, wife of Mr Thomas Williamson, for buying corn in the market before the bell rings, and Marie Jameson near Prescot for the like, 3s 4d apiece

Widow Johnson of Everton for cutting gorse on the common and leading it away, not being free, 3s 4d

James Apleton, Thomas Bridge, Richard Browne, Lawrence Jumper, Robert Johnson, John Owen, Robert Lyon, Richard Livesley, Mr John Chandler, Richard Crompton, John Sturzaker, Thomas Seale, Henry Moore, John Lunt, Elizabeth Tarleton, Dorothy Bicksteth, for having their swine unrung, 12d apiece

William Richardson for letting the wreck of a vessel lie below the full sea mark to the endangering and great annoyance of shipping in the harbour, 40s

Mr John Sandiford for suing Mr Richard Williamson out of this court contrary to the custom of the town, traversed

Edward Blanchett for tussle on Thomas Ballard, and Thomas Ballard for tussle on Edward Blanchett, 3s 4d apiece

We order:

William Ackers and Widow Blevine to clear the water course on the west end of their house by 1 March on pain of 5s

Mr John Winstanley to clear the water course in his garden that annoys John Heyes, 5s

All that have lands lying to the Breckside to make up their fences by last of February, 5s apiece

All others to make up their fences within the liberties, by the said time, 5s apiece

f. 617d

f. 618
THE AUDIT OF ROBERT CORNELL, LATE MAYOR, Henry Corles and Richard Leivsey, bailiffs, taken Tuesday 11 December 1655, from 18 October 1654.

John Sturzaker, hallkeeper, receipts for ingates		26s	9d
outgates		56	9
Robert Seacome, his outgates and ingates	£7	18s	2d
Richard Poultney, subcustomer, receipts for tolls stalls and standings	11	12	
Received for compositions for freemen	19	6	8
Town's rents, including Cook's house	14	3	4
Burgage rents, allowing deductions for shops, Millme hall chantry	12	1	4
Received from chantry rents for use of minister and schoolmaster for two years past, there being two years yet arrears	21	1	4
Butlerage licence and compositions	10	13	2

Received from rent of ferry boat at 5s per week	12	5	
Receipts for leys and taxation nil			
Received from the old churchwardens		27s	
A fine for Captain Tarleton's lease	£35		
For herring sold, bought by bailiffs	56	14	3
For boards, lime and other necessaries sold	3	1	8
Fines and amercements from four portmoots	7	12	10
From old bailiffs, part clipped money	148	15	3

f. 618d

f. 619
PORTMOOT COURT OR QUARTER SESSIONS OF THE PEACE, MONDAY 17 APRIL 1656, before the mayor and bailiffs.

Inquisition taken by the oaths of Richard Leivesley, Edward Formby, Thomas Story, Roger Harrinson, James Burton, John Johnson, Robert Kenion, William Middleton, Thomas Seale, William Mosse, Edward Horrobine, John Holland, Thomas Coppull, William Fletwoode, John Poultney, honest and lawful men of the borough.

We present:
William Lambe for a bloodwipe on Richard Dwarrihouse, being then servant, 6s 8d
Henry Cowper John Shlack for working unlawful leather, 2s 6d apiece
Richard Washington, William Mosse for keeping unlawful quarts, 6d apiece
Ralph Burges, Janet Johnson for getting gorse on the common, 6s 8d
William Turner for fence lying down to annoyance of Robert Kenion; Mr Thomas Blackmore and Dorothy Bicksteth for the like, 6d
Mr John Fogg, minister, for his fence lying down to the annoyance neighbours in Dale Street, 6d
John Owen, Alexander Harracks, Richard Rymer, Matilda Ellis, Margery Burton, Lawrence Jumper, Margery Tarleton, John Sutton, Olive Fairehurst, for swine unrung, 6d apiece
Mr Richard Crosse, Mr John Winstanley, Mr William Strangwaies, for not cleaning their streets, 6d apiece
John Lurtinge, Elizabeth Rycroft, John Royle, Thomas Bridge, Susan Eccleston, Dorothy Bicksteth, Peter Lurtinge, Robert Clarke, William Mosse, Mr John Sandiford, Mr John Chandler, Mr James Williamson, Mr William Williamson, John Leyes, William Rymer, Evan March, Margaret Bicksteth, Mrs Dorothy Sandiford, Edward Edmaines, John Higinson, Mr Edward Moore, William Raineford, all for the like, 6d apiece
Philip Cocke for using faculty of a freemen; Margaret Granger, Owen Morgan, William Gretten, Nicholas Curren, Alexander Harrox, for the like, 6d
Those that sell ale and beer without licence: John Poultney, James Burton, William Chantrell, William Litherland, William Parker, John Chambers, William Mosse, Owen Morgan, Philip Cocke, 2s apiece

We order:

Mr Henry Corleys to mend the footway on the town's common between Hodgshey and Halls Hey before 1 August, on pain, nil

The Pool Lane and the cowsey on the same to be mended, and all other ways and pavements about the town before 1 August, nil

We agree to all ancient laws and laudable customs.

f. 619d

f. 620

PORTMOOT COURT OR QUARTER SESSIONS OF THE PEACE, MONDAY 30 JUNE 1656, before mayor and bailiffs.

Inquisition taken on the oaths of Roger Jones, Evan Marsh, Peter Lurting, John Owen, John Walles, Richard Crompton, Thomas Roe, Edmund Leivsey, Richard Holland, Robert Simpson, John Melling, John Sutton, Thomas Copull, Thomas Carr, Hugh Reynold, honest and lawful men of the borough.

We present:

John Bullock, John Johnson for working unlawful leather, 2s 6d apiece

Mr Bailiff Sutton for keeping swine unrung; John Owen, Robert Lyon, Gilbert Formeby, Robert Kenion, carter, Mr John Chandler, Robert Johnson, Thomas Lancellott, Margaret Granger, Brian Mercer, William Gardner, Richard Rymmer, Gregory Formbie, Susan Eccleston, Edward Barton, Maudline Johnson, John Lunte, George Seddon, 6d apiece

William Turner for letting his fence lie down, Mrs Elizabeth Heapey, Robert Harvey, John Lurting, draper, for the like, 6d apiece

Thomas Coppull for leasowing his cattle on Mr William Strangwais' ground, 2s 6d

John Williamson junior for his muck lying before his door, John Higinson, Mr John Chandler, William Mosse, Mrs Bicksteth, for the like, 6d apiece

William Chorley, Anne Rycroft for not making clean the market street, 6d apiece

William Fleetwood for neglect of office, 1s 6d

James Burton for selling ale and beer, not being licensed; William Chantrell, William Litherland, John Parker, John Poultney, William Mosse, Owen Murgan, for the like, 2s apiece

Mrs Lyme for buying corn in the market before bell ring, 6s 8d

Mr William Williamson for tussle on Mr John Chandler, 3s 4d

Mr John Chandler for tussle on Mr William Williamson, 3s 4d

Marie Hunt for calling Thomas Roe, his wife, and Ellen Lurting, wife of Peter Lurting, dogs, in the presence of Mr Mayor after she was bound to the peace, nil

Edward Tysdall and Elizabeth Henshawe for getting growning in the town field, 6d apiece

Esther Hardman for using faculty of a freeman, Jane Wilson for the like, nil

Ellen Blevine for keeping inmates and not giving security to Mr Mayor, 1s

We order:

Jane Garrard to remove her rubbish between Mr Corless's garden wall, and the end of her kiln within ten days

Robert Fleetwood to cleanse gutter betwen him and Mr Massome, that the water current may run the ancient way, within five weeks

We agree to all ancient laws and laudable customs.

f. 620d

p. 621[47]

Swine. Forasmuch as divers orders have been formerly agreed by this assembly about keeping swine which are a general nuisance, which are not observed, it is ordered and agreed by Mr Mayor, James Williamson, Thomas Blackmore, Ralph Massam, Edward Williamson, Robert Cornell, aldermen, and the bailiffs and most part of the Common Council, that after 1 March next all inhabitants shall keep their swine in their own backsides or in styes, so that no swine be found in the streets, or trespassing in other men's grounds or gardens, on pain of every owner forfeiting to the use of the poor 12d for every swine, immediately to be levied by distress and sale of their goods, at the sight and discretion of the mayor and bailiffs.

Middings. It is likewise ordered that all middingsteads in the streets shall be removed and the places paved, or else every owner to wall them, four foot high at least, before 1 June, so they will not be a nuisance as they have been, on pain of 20s to the use of the poor to be levied as above. Thomas TA[48] Andoe, mayor, James Williamson, Thomas Blackmore, Ralph Massam, Edward Williamson, Robert Cornell, aldermen; Robert Sutton, Henry Moore, bailiffs; John Winstanley, town clerk[49]

Carrion. Whereas there are many dead swine found at the waterside, and other carrion and laystalls to the annoyance of people, it is ordered that the mayor and bailiffs shall cause them to be buried, and that hereafter if anyone shall not bury such swine or carrion they shall forfeit 3s 4d, to be levied and disposed as above.

p. 622

20 NOVEMBER 1655

Ferry Boats. At an assembly before Mr Mayor, the aldermen and common council, it was ordered that the ferry boats be farmed to Mr Edward Formeby for seven years from Christmas next at £10 a year rent payable every Michaelmas, and he is to give security by bond for — for the safe keeping and restoring of the two boats, the new one valued at £22 5s, and the old boat with cables, anchors, at £16. The bond was drawn up, and security given for payment of the rent, duly attending the ferry, and taking no more than the due and accustomed fare.

47   Pagination resumes.
48   Andoe made a mark, TA.
49   Signatures.

Memo. That Mr James Williamson paid in the money due by him to the use of the minister and schoolmaster, £10, and bond is given for the same by Mr Sturzaker and others.

Ordered that Mrs Bicksteth shall restore a millstone taken from Eastham Mill, or give satisfaction to the bailiffs for it.

James Hey is ordered to pay his fine and rent for — acres of the new enclosures, according to his contract.

23 JANUARY 1655

Pool Bridge. It is ordered by the mayor, aldermen and common council that the Pool Bridge, which is in decay, shall be repaired at the town's charge, at the sight and discretion of the mayor and bailiffs.

Sea Wreck. It is also ordered that the old wreck of a ship lying towards the Pool shall be taken up and valued, and converted to the use of the town, being adjudged a lawful wreck. viz. Mrs Windell's ship.

p. 623[50]
12 FEBRUARY 1655

Serjeant at mace. William Mulliney is chosen serjeant at mace and sworn, by the consent of Mr Mayor and the common council, and he was contented to give Mr Richard Dwarrihouse 40s as a gratuity. This assembly, taking into consideration the service done by Mr Dwarrihouse, now he is removed from that employment freely give him, his wife and children, for their maintenance the £4 given by William Mulliney for his freedom.

BUTLERAGE

Ordered that Mr Greene pay a tun of wine for 22 tuns brought in by Mr Gold for which he is to pay £10.

11 April 1656

Ordered that Mr Alexander Greene, merchant, shall pay for the pryzage of 55 tuns of wine in the *Fortune*.

Thomas Wilson, master, five full hogsheads, £25.

Memo.[51] That on second consideration he is to have an abatement of £9 because the quantity of the wine is less than reported, and by order of the assembly, 17 July 1656, he is to pay £16.

Mr Horton, merchant, for 16 tuns of wine in the *Thomas and William* from France by William Rymmer, master. Butlerage was paid at Beaumaris.

COMPOSITIONS

Gilbert Formeby for 20 barrels of herring, 6s 8d

---

50   Folio 622 is written and erased in favour of page 623.
51   The memo is written in a lighter hand.

Thomas Asbrook for 22 barrels of herring, 7s

Thomas Harrwood for 50 barrels of herring in Mathew Heyes, 16s, or else the owner to pay for 60 barrels

William Bushell for Arthur Harvie and Peter Leigh for 250 mace of herring in bulk, 43s 4d

William Gardner for Brian Ayres, 20 barrels in the *Mary Cach*, 6s 4d

Seal. Anthony Lovly for the town's seal to a certificate, 3s 4d; Thomas Christian for the seal paid to the bailiffs, 1s

Butlerage. The butlerage for Mr Sandiford's wines suspended till next assembly, and afterwards, 23 January, ordered that he pay for 22 tuns of French wine, £10, or a tun of wine in kind, £10.

p. 624
JANUARY 1655

Assessments. Ordered that Mr Alexander Greene and Mr Winstanley go to Chester to petition the major-general about this town being oppressed in the monthly assessments.

Mr Corles' business. At an assembly before the mayor, James Williamson, Thomas Blackmoore, Thomas Williamson, Ralph Massam, Edward Williamson, Robert Cornell, the bailiffs and most part of the common council, the suit against Mr Henry Corles and Margaret, his wife, executrix of James Southerne, at the suit of Thomas Blackmore and Edward Alcock, for £202 of town money loaned to Colonel John Moore, was reviewed. For this debt they have been prosecuted and are now in the bailiffs' custody. It is ordered that unless they satisfy the whole sum they are to be sent to Lancaster, and are to bear the bailiffs' charges while they stay at home. And the business be further prosecuted at the town's charge.

11 April 1656.[52] The same business was again reviewed, when they had made an escape, and the suit is ordered to be prosecuted in London and Mr Winstanley, who is served with an order from the duchy for a pretended disobeying of an injunction, shall go and have his charges borne, and shall solicit to get the injunction dissolved, and proceed at common law as requisite.

John Lunt's order for 30s. On the petition of John Lunte concerning his losses in the sickness time, shut up for many weeks, for which he has recorded 14s in an action of trespass for coals taken by Mr James Williamson, mayor, and by the cleanser, the bailiffs are ordered to give him 30s and he is to acquit Mr Williamson of that verdict.

Beadle and bellman. It is also ordered that Edward Ryding, admitted a freeman, gratis, shall be bellman or crier of this corporation, and shall perform all services of that office, and also to be beadle to keep out beggars who are foreign, and shall

---

52   This entry is written in smaller and lighter hand.

have 26s 8d wages and also a grey or blue coat yearly, and for all such wanderers or rogues whipped he is to receive 6d apiece from the bailiffs.

p. 625
FREEMEN
   19 October 1655:
Thomas Christian, merchant, apprentice to Mr Greene, having performed time according to indenture, sworn, 6s 8d
Thomas Johnson, grocer, apprentice to Alderman Hodgson, sworn, 6s 8d
George Smith, shoemaker, having served his apprenticeship, sworn, 6s 8d not free[53]
Lawrence Jumper, sailor, paying composition, 40s
Richard Browne, admitted, sworn, 40s
   1 January 1655
John Cary, victualler, late servant to Mr Windas, sworn, paying for composition, £3
Randle Dawson, mariner, late apprentice to Thomas Andoe, mayor, sworn, 6s 8d
Thomas Andoe, mariner, also apprentice to Mr Mayor, sworn, 6s 8d
Mathew Heyes, mariner, sworn, composition, 40s
Ralph Halle, one of the waiters in this port, admitted by consent of the mayor, aldermen and common council, gratis
   23 January 1655:
William Parker, mariner, on petition to assembly, sworn, composition, 40s
John Pemberton, apothecary, sworn, composition, £6 13s 4d
William Mulliney admitted, sworn, £4, which composition was given to Richard Dwarrihouse when he replaced Dwarrihouse as serjeant at mace
Thomas Mosse, blacksmith, apprentice to William Higinson, sworn, 6s 8d
Edward Rydeing, son of Nicholas Ryding, admitted on undertaking to be beadle and bellman, and is to have allowances and wages as settled, gratis
   27 February 1655:
Mr Richard Halliwell of Manchester, innkeeper, admitted and sworn by consent of mayor, aldermen and common council, composition, £4
John Poultney, mariner, son of Richard Poultney, a freeman, sworn, 3s 4d
John Thompson, mariner, apprentice to Thomas Andoe, mayor, sworn, 6s 8d
   9 August 1656:
Thomas Farrer of Ormskirk, woollen draper, admitted by former votes, sworn, composition £10
Robert Eaton, clerk, parson of Walton, admitted by vote, sworn, gratis
Henry Gregson, husbandman, sworn, composition, 50s
Thomas Brige, innholder, admitted by vote, sworn, composition, 40s
Richard Gore of Formby, blockmaker, sworn, composition, £3
James Litherland, webster, sworn, composition, £3

---

53   Entry for George Smith is scored through and marginal note added, not free.

Richard Rogerson, husbandman, sworn, paying 40s
John Griffith, carpenter, having been apprentice to William Rymmer, sworn, 6s 8d

p. 626
ASSEMBLY, TUESDAY 12 FEBRUARY 1655
Chantry. Whereas there is some obstruction in the allowance of the minister's and schoolmaster's wages received yearly from chantry rents purchased by Captain Holt, being about £11 a year, letters are to be written to Colonel Birch for his assistance.

27 FEBRUARY 1655
Ireland. Ordered that a petition be sent to His Highness the Lord Protector about our lands in Ireland which Captain Browne, now bound for London, is desired to press. This was left with Mr Sandford who has been since solicited, but nothing can be done it being referred to Lord Deputy Fleetwood with whom another petition now remains.
That a letter be sent to Lieut. Newcomen in answer to his relating to our lands in Ireland.
Apprentice. Memo. that Caesar Paten was put apprentice to Andrew Over, sadler, for — years according to indenture.

p. 627
INDENTURE, 14 AUGUST 1656
Between John Starkey, esq., sheriff of the county of Lancaster on the one part, and Thomas Andoe, gent., mayor of the town of Liverpool, Robert Sutton and Henry Moore, bailiffs, and the burgesses and inhabitants of the town on the other. Witnesseth by virtue of a warrant to the mayor, bailiffs and burgesses from the said sheriff for the electing of one burgess of good understanding, knowledge and discretion for causes concerning the public good of this commonwealth, to be at his highness' parliament at Westminster on 17 September next, we the mayor, bailiffs, burgesses and inhabitants have elected Thomas Birch esq., the elder, of Birch Hall in the county of Lancaster, to be the burgess of the borough of Liverpool to attend the said parliament, to have full power to do and consent to those things which in the parliament shall be ordained, provided there is no power to alter the government as it is now settled in a single person and parliament. In witness whereof the parties above have put their hands and seals. Thomas Andoe, mayor.

17 SEPTEMBER 1656
At an Assembly before the mayor, Thomas Blackmore, James Williamson, William Williamson, Ralph Massam, Thomas Williamson and Robert Cornell, the bailiffs and most part of the common council, a letter from the late governor, Colonel Birch, was read, whereby he desires to have the heads of our desires, which are reduced to three:
1. To endeavour to get our lands in Ireland established according the the late act of parliament to the value of £1,000

2. To labour that the town be made a parish of itself, distinct from Walton, in regard it is the only port in Lancaster and has always had all parochial privileges
3. To have it made a free and independent port of itself so as to have a surveyor resident, and that they of Chester may be restrained from entering here which tends to the prejudice of trade
4. To enquire concerning the butlerage, and make it certain, and have a full grant of it to the corporation.

Tradesmen. To inform him that the tradesmen desire there might be a restraint against pedlars and foreign tradesmen that are not free from selling in stalls on market days.

Recorder. Memo. That Mr William Halsall, late recorder, being dead, a letter to Mr Langton about his acceptance of the office which he formerly had was read, and his answer was that he was willing to accept it. It was therefore put to a vote in the assembly, and unanimously carried that Mr Langton be recorder, elected during pleasure, who was afterwards sworn, 16 October 1656.

p. 628
Common Councilmen added: Roger Harrison, Thomas Asbrook, Robert Seacome, William Mulliney, sworn to be of the common council. Richard Williams also nominated but not sworn.

9 AUGUST 1656
Ordered and voted at this assembly that Mr Greeneshall have £9 of the £25 lately charged him for butlerage, in regard the quantity of 55 tuns was mistaken.

Philip Peircie, shipcarpenter, voted to be a free burgess of this corporation and pay composition, £3, but not yet sworn.

p. 629
THURSDAY 9 OCTOBER 1656
At an Assembly before the mayor, aldermen, bailiffs and greatest part of the common council, Mr Moore proposed that new security for Mr Corles' debt be accepted. On full debate, considering the present condition of Mr Corles and his wife, and at the instance of Mr Moore, it was resolved that £160 should be accepted in full satisfaction of the debt, and that Mr Moore should give such security as the town should approve of for payment by Christmas next, and that thereupon Mr Corles should be discharged of the debt of £202. Whereupon afterwards proposals were made concerning the security, by acknowledging a statute merchant, confessing judgement or by bond with surety, but, choosing the first a statute merchant, was accordingly entered for payment of £160 by 26 December next, and enrolled accordingly.

p. 630

GILBERT FORMBY, GENTLEMAN, MAYOR [1656–57]

p. 631
LIVERPOOL. ELECTION COURT SATURDAY 18 OCTOBER 1656, the feast of St Luke the Evangelist, before Thomas Andoe, mayor, Robert Sutton and Henry Moore, bailiffs, according to several charters.

Gilbert Formby, gentleman, elected mayor by votes of mayor, bailiffs and burgesses present, sworn
Thomas Sandiford nominated and elected chief bailiff for said mayor and his highness the Lord Protector, sworn
William Bushell, mariner, elected bailiff for the town, sworn.

William Langton, esquire, counsellor at law, nominated recorder
John Winstanley, gent., allowed town clerk
William Mulliney nominated serjeant at mace
Robert Seacome nominated water bailiff

   Officers chosen by the common council:
John Fogg, minister
George Glover, schoolmaster
John Sturzaker, hall keeper, sw.
Robert Seacome, town customer, sw.
Richard Pultney, sub-customer
Same Richard, church clerk
John Heyes, William Accars, stewards of the hall
Thomas Coppull, heyward

p. 632
   Officers chosen by the grand jury:
Thomas Storie, Henry Moore, William Gardner, Roger Harrison, merchant appraisers
Thomas Roe, Thomas Nicholson, registers of leather
John Pemberton, Andrew Over, alefounders
John Griffiths, John Lunte, Robert Kenion senior, Richard Tyrer, barleymen
Thomas Andoe junior, Thomas Mosse, Henry Gregson, Richard Browne, scavengers
Humphrey Mercer, murenger
Thomas Bridge, Robert Sympson, overseers
John Sanderson, Peter Walker, porters
Thomas Banks, Richard Rogerson, leavelookers
William Chorley, Elizabeth Rycroft, boardsetters
Thomas Banks, Thomas Witter, boothsetters
Edward Rydeing, beadle and bellman.

p. 633

LIVERPOOL. PORTMOOT COURT OR QUARTER SESSIONS OF THE PEACE, MONDAY 27 OCTOBER 1656, before mayor and bailiffs.

Inquisition taken by the oaths of Robert Sutton, Thomas Storie, William Rymer, John Blundell, John Lurting, Henry Rydeing, Thomas Lurting, John Johnson, Robert Eccles, James Hoult, Thomas Nicholson, Richard Lunte, John Heyes, Robert Clark, John Banks, William Middleton, Thomas Coppull, William Ryding, John Melling, Robert Halle, John Wade, John Henshawe, John Tompson, Robert Fleetewood, honest and lawful men of the borough.

We present:
  John Stringer for a tussle on Edward Taylor, Richard Walley pledge for fine, 3s 4d
  Edward Taylor for tussle on John Stringer, 3s 4d
  John Slack, John Bullock, James Mather, Lawrence Perrine, James Hoult, working unlawful leather, each 2s 6d
  Owen Morgan, Jane Martine, widow, William Cretton, for using faculty of freeman, not being free, 3s 4d each
  Phillip Dey, Rowland Pouthton, Esther Hardman, Ellen Harkine, widow, John Lurtinge, Edward Horrobine, Edward Sutton, Elizabeth Birchall, Ellen Skinner, Jane Burton, widow, Jane Wilson, Thomas Carr for making bread too light, £3
  William Gardner, Anthony Carr, John Chandler, Thomas Galloway keeping swine unrung, 6d each
  James Toppinge for leading turf from the town common out of the liberties, 6d
  Richard Whytehead, Robert Whytehead for watering hemp on common, out of liberties, 6d
  John Hill for getting turf on common, not free, 6d
  Roger Jones, John Lurting, bailiff, Adam Leathes, John Tompson, Andrew Over, John Borton, Robert Simpson, Thomas Bennett, Robert Seacome, Edward Rydinge, Richard Crompton, Thomas Roe, Robert Eccles, Richard Lansdell, Richard Buckley, William Secome, James Topinge, John Heyes of Everton, Edmund Walley, Randell Walley, William Wainewright, Robert Henshaw, Thomas Pemberton, Robert Hughson, William Throughton for tethering in town field, 12d each
  Mrs Margaret Bicksteth for letting muck lie before her barn door, 6d
  Mr Edward Moore for letting muck lie in Old Hall Street, 6d
  Joane Tarleton, William Mosse, John Chandler for the like, 6d each
  The scavengers, Robert Kenion, Robert Fleetwood, Richard Scarsbrick, Enoch Boulton for neglect of their office, 6d each
  All those who did not appear at this court and have not essoyned.

p. 634

p. 635

PORTMOOT COURT, 12 JANUARY 1656, OR QUARTER SESSIONS OF THE PEACE before mayor and bailiffs, according to custom.

Inquisition taken on the oaths of Henry Moore, Edward Formeby, Richard Peircevall, Henry Corles, John Owen, Roger Harrison, Richard Crompton, John Pemberton, Thomas Gallaway, William Accars, Thomas Roe, John Griffith, Thomas Mosse, Thomas Coppull, John Poultney, honest freemen.

We present:
  William Midleton for bloodwipe on John Burton, 6s 8d
  John Burton for bloodwipe on William Midleton, 6s 8d
  Jane Wilson for bloodwipe on Ellen Storie, 6s 8d
  Ellen Storie for bloodwipe on Jane Wilson, 6s 8d
  Mr Robert Moore for tussle on Robert Harvey, 3s 4d
  Robert Harvey for tussle on Mr Robert Moore, 3s 4d
  George Thorpe for using faculty of freeman, not free, 1s
  Thomas Justice, Owen Morgan, Esther Hardman, William Creaton, James Cleyton, all 1s, and Jane Wilson, 6s 8d
  Henry Cooper, Ralph Stock, James Walker, Abraham Dyson, James Tatlock, Thomas Roe, working unlawful leather, 2s 6d each, 1s for Roe
  William Bushell, Susan Eccleston, Mrs Margaret Bicksteth, Richard Crompton, Gregory Formby, for keeping swine unrung, 1s each
  William Rymer, mariner, for speaking abusive and reproachful words against Mr William Williamson, alderman, vizt. thou art a cheating knave and I will prove thee that and more too. Traversed and pleaded not guilty.

Orders:
  Richard Crosse, esq. and Robert Kenion to scour ditches on both sides Sickmans Lane by last of February, on pain 10s each
  All with any tenants in town to give names to mayor, and to observe his orders about the giving of security, before 1 March, 6s 8d
  All headbolts to be made up, fences cut, ditches scoured, and water courses cleansed by 12 February, 6s 8d
  All inhabitants to be married to be asked and published by the appointed register, and Thomas Asbrook to pay all duties to the town as if he had been here published, 40s
  We agree all ancient orders and laudable customs.

p. 636

p. 637
PORTMOOT COURT, MONDAY 20 APRIL 1657, OR QUARTER SESSIONS OF THE PEACE before mayor and bailiffs.

Inquisition on the oaths of Thomas Storie, Peter Lurting, John Owen, Henry Rydeing, John Lurting, smith, Robert Eccles, Robert Sympson, Thomas Nicholson, Andrew Over, Robert Kenion, carter, Richard Lunt, Thomas Coppull, Edward Carr, William Poultney, Edward Horrobine, honest and lawful freemen.

We present:

William Strangwais for taking tenant strangers into his houses and not giving security to mayor, 3s 4d

Mr John Chandler, Margaret Bannester, Richard Higinson, cutler, Margery Tarleton, for the like, 3s 4d each

Jonathan Cleave, Owen Morgan, James Conon, Henry Mosse, William Gretton, for using faculty of freemen, not free, 3s 4d

Richard Holland for working unlawful leather, 2s 6d

William Bushell, John Royle, Ellen Higinson widow, Mrs Margaret Bicksteth, William Gardner, Samuel Cook, Dorothy Brookbank, Margaret Granger, Mr John Chandler for not ringing swine, 6d each

John Higinson for getting clay at the tithe barn, 3s 4d

Nicholas Gallamoore for getting clay near the pool, 2d

Ellen Hacking for not making bread to be weight, 1s 6d

Ellen Winstanley for keeping small quarts, 6d

John Lurting, smith, Jane Burton, widow, Owen Morgan, Jane Tarleton, John Lunt, Margaret Granger, William Gretton, Thomas Nicholson, Andrew Over, Elizabeth Heapey, Robert Clark, Widow Washington, for not coming to be licensed, 2d each

Thomas Darrwen for butchering meat meane, with John Widowson, 3s 4d

John Widdowson for same, 3s 4d

Anne Andoe for unseemly words spoken against Mr Mayor, 10s

Jane Haskaine for not cleansing her gutter behind Mr Corles, 1s

The scavengers, Thomas Andoe junior, Thomas Mosse, Henry Gregson, Richard Browne for neglect of office, 2s each

Orders:

p. 638

The dow stone to be set on the town common, now in occupation of Peter Lurtinge, and likewise dowstones be set in the common now in hands of Edward Horrobine, and that all who have ploughed up the common to make it even with the dowstones before end of April

The old cartway to Everton be mended before 1 May

The Fall Well be repaired and highway mended before end of May

Cartway and pavement in Sickman Lane be mended before 20 July

No muck to be laid near the bridge at end of the town, and a good causeway be made over the bridge to the field gate

A watering pool be made near the end of the town

A pavement be made in Tithebarn Lane

William Bushell to make up his fence between Edward Horrobine and him before end of May

The highway to Bolton's Moore be kept open as formerly

Swine be kept up every Saturday and Sunday according to former orders

We agree all ancient laws and laudable customs.

p. 639

PORTMOOT COURT OR QUARTER SESSIONS OF THE PEACE, MONDAY 14 JULY 1657, before mayor and bailiffs according to custom.

Inquisition on the oaths of Roger Jones, Richard Williamson, Richard Percivall, Robert Sutton, Robert Harvie, Richard Crompton, John Pemberton, Mathew Heyes, John Griffith, Thomas Gallaway, William Accars, John Johnson, Thomas Radcliffe, Thomas Seale, Richard Scarsbrick, honest and lawful freemen.

We present:
    William Gretton for tussle on Mr John Wareing, 1s 8d
    Mr John Wareing for tussle on William Gretton, 1s 8d
    George Smith for tussle on John Dale, 3s 4d
    John Dale for tussle on George Smith, 3s 4d
    George Thorpe for using faculty of freemen, 6d
    Thomas Justice 1s, Owen Morgan 3s 4d, Esther Hardman, William Gretton, Roger James, each 6d, Henry Robinson, Henry Hey, John Mulliney, Thomas Dobb each 2s, for like offence
    William Bushell, bailiff, having 6 swine unrung, 2s
    Mrs Sandiford for keeping 2 swine unrung, 8d
    Mrs Bicksteth for 2 swine unrung, 8d
    Richard Eccleston, Margaret Grange for the like, 4d each
    Richard Widowes for getting turf and selling it, 2s 6d
    Matthew Gleave for the like, 2s
    Edward Banks, John Everett for the like, 6d each
    Roger Johnes for taking slush out of the pool, 6d
    Mr Richard Crosse for not walling in his midding stead according to former orders, 20s.

Orders:
    Widow Andoe to clear gutter between Richard Holland and herself before 25 July
    The way between the two stones which we conceive to be dow stones, shall be the way to the highway to the common stile on Salton's Moor.
    Gabriel Barton, hosier, by consent, to have his standing on the town's waste in the market place, paying town duties
    We agree to all ancient orders and laudable customs.

p. 640

p. 641

ASSEMBLY OF COMMON COUNCIL, 22 OCTOBER 1656
    Moore's debt. It was resolved that Edward Moore esq. having undertaken the payment of Mr Corles' debt to the town, which was his father's, and for which Mr James Southerne was engaged, entered into a statute merchant for payment of £160 due 26 October 1656.

Repair of church. Ordered that the church, being in decay, be repaired in roof and walls.

Town's plate. Ordered that divers pieces of plate of the town, much decayed, and some cups broken and not fashionable, shall be exchanged for new plate, with the town's arms engraved on them. Bailiffs to pay for the same.

19 NOVEMBER 1656

At an Assembly held in town hall before mayor, Thomas Blackmore, Thomas Williamson, Thomas Andoe, aldermen, the bailiffs and most of the common council:

Walton church. Ordered, that because of the losses of this corporation in the late war, and because the late parliament has settled on the minister of this place all the tithes remaining in the liberties, it is presumed that we, having formerly been a parish, enjoying all parochial privileges, ought not to contribute to the repair of Walton church, and this be told to Walton churchwardens when they shall demand leys. And if any suit result then the town is to bear the charge.

Swine. Ordered that a man be hired to impound swine in the streets or trespassing on men's grounds or gardens, to be detained until the owners pay 12d for each case, from which 6d should go to the official, 6d to the poor of this corporation, notwithstanding any former orders.

Hallkeeper. Ordered that Mr John Sturzaker, hallkeeper, shall find a porter to attend all merchandise and in lieu shall have a third part of all portage fees and allowances as the hall keepers have always had.

Rates of goods imported. Ordered that the mayor with the advice and assistance of — or more of the aldermen may agree what rates or composition shall be received for any goods imported and not mentioned in any ancient table.

p. 642
COMPOSITION LICENSES, 19 NOVEMBER 1656
Mr William Kitchine, merchant, for 50 barrels of herring, 12s
Henry Lyon for 160 barrel of herring, 47s
Thomas Harrwood for 66 barrels, 20s
William Corles for 106 barrels, 33s 4d
John Marsh for 82 barrels, 25s 4d but 16s
John Rymmer for 80 barrels, 25s, are but 16s
Henry Key and Richard Rymmer for 17 barrels, 5s 4d
Richard Norris for 80 barrels, 25s
Joseph Witter for 47 barrels, 14s 8d

11 DECEMBER 1656

Concerning the Poor. Ordered that town shall keep its own poor and the poor of other places shall be kept from begging here, and the old custom that the churchwardens be overseers of the poor in the year ensuing be observed, and the minister and overseers shall keep a book of the names of such as are most poor and necessitated if they be aged persons or infants, and all others to be excluded. The number of the poor are computed at 60 odd. A monthly ley of £3 is to be levied by the merchant appraisers to be distributed to those in most necessity by the overseers, and the rest of the country poor are to be kept out by the beadle under pain of losing his wages.

Colonel Birch. It is also ordered that in regard Colonel Thomas Birch goes not to London to attend parliament as was expected, that Mr Thomas Sandiford, town's bailiff, shall go to Birch to advise with him about it, and a letter be written to him about the affairs of the town.

Audit account. Memo: that the balance of the account of the last audit is £99 16s 11d, which Robert Sutton and Henry Moore are ordered to pay over to the present bailiffs before 2 March.

p. 643

Apprentice of Andrew Over. Because a complaint has been made for Cesar Pattern, apprentice of Andrew Over, late of Liverpool, sadler, that Andrew is indebted and sued in several actions in this borough court, having removed his goods from hence at night and fled to Ireland, and has neglected to provide for his apprentice, it is ordered that Cesar Patten, surrendering his indenture, shall be freed from his master to serve his time with any other master of the same trade, according to statute. In witness the mayor and aldermen of Liverpool put hands and seals, 31 July 1657. Gilbert Formby, mayor, Thomas Blackmore, William Williamson, Ralph Massam, Thomas Andoe.

BUTLERAGE
9 January 1656:
Mr Thomas Horton, merchant, ordered to pay butlerage on 20 tuns of wine imported from Bordeaux in the *Hope*, £15, to the bailiffs for the use of this corporation, or five full hogsheads of wine.
Mr Alexander Greene to pay for above 20 tuns of Bordeaux wine imported in the *Judith*, £18 or five full hogsheads.
9 April 1657:
Mr Horton for 7 tuns of French wine in the *Swan* of Liverpool, 28s
Mr Thomas Drinkwater for 7 tuns at 6s the tun, 42s
Captain James Browne for 14 tuns of wine imported in the *Fortune*, £4 4s, and for license money for 40 barrels of herring, 6s 8d, remitted by consent.

Apprentice. Ordered that mayor and bailiffs agree with Thomas Mosse, smith, for taking as apprentice one of Edward Rycroft's sons, a poor boy, and shall pay money from the town's stock for his apprenticeship.

p. 644
14 MAY 1657
Church Clerk. Concerning the church clerk's place which Mr Newton solicits, it was ordered by the mayor, aldermen, bailiffs and greater part of the common council that Richard Poultney, sexton, shall continue in the position, by himself or his son, and have fees as formerly, by reason of his age and infirmity.

Composition. Mr Thomas Horton for Mr Francis Davies for 5 tuns of small decayed French wines, 16s.

Walton parish. Proposed by mayor that the suit begun against him by Nicholas Valentine for the churchwardens of Walton, be defended at the town's charge, and that Mr Winstanley try, on his visit to London, to have this town severed from the parish of Walton and made a parish of itself. And he is to confer with Mr Humphrey Kelshall for the benefit of his discovery about butlerage, and try to compound with him and the trustees for the same for the use to be established for the benefit of the town.

Court day. Mr Winstanley proposed to the assembly that the court day be changed to Friday as more convenient for market day here and at Ormskirk, but the business was suspended till the recorder was present to advise.

FREEMEN
Philip Percie, ship's carpenter voted to be admitted free, 50s

p. 645
    19 November 1656:
Henry Tarbock, nailer, voted to be admitted, £3 10s, sworn
    9 April 1657
Samuel Sandiford, gentleman, sworn, gratis
William Poultney, son of Richard Poultney, sworn, 3s 4d
William Lewis, gentleman, sworn, gratis
    13 August 1657
Roger James, 50s, sworn
John Rymer, 40s, sworn
Jonathan Cleave, 50s, sworn
George Thorpe, 40s, sworn
Philip Peircie, ship's carpenter, 50s, sworn
    16 October 1657
Thomas Crompton, minister at Toxteth, free, sworn
John Williamson, son of John Williamson, free burgess of corporation, admitted according to custom, sworn, 3s 4d

14 MAY 1657[54]
    Church Clerk. Ordered by consent of mayor, aldermen, bailiffs and common council assembled, that Richard Poultney by himself, or some other, shall serve in the office of church clerk till further order, and Mr Newton be discharged.
    Ordered that Mr Thomas Horton, merchant, pay butlerage for 5 tuns of small decayed wines on the account of Francis Davies, 16s.

---

54   The entry for 14 May 1657 repeats decisions noted on the previous page, in a slightly different form.

Ordered that Mr Winstanley on going to London shall try to have town made a parish distinct from Walton with all parochial privileges. And that butlerage may be purchased from the trustees or Mr Humphrey Kelsall, as before ordered.

p. 646

p. 647
13 AUGUST 1657
Butlerage. Ordered that Mr Alexander Greene pay for 7 tuns of wine imported in the *Margaret* of Rochelle, 28s
Ordered that Captain James Browne pay town dues for — tuns of wine and — barrels of herrings imported in the *Constant Joane*, and if he refuses the bailiffs are to seize his goods and be secured by the corporation if any suit arises.
Composition. Mr Thomas Christiane to pay 10s composition for town's custom for 600 dale boards.

16 OCTOBER 1657
Town solicitor. At an assembly before the mayor, aldermen, bailiffs and the greatest part of the common council, concerning the town being made a parish of itself, and the lands in Ireland, it was ordered that Mr John Winstanley, town clerk, shall be solicitor for the corporation and go to London in this and the next term, to try to get the business effected, and any other of concern to the town, and shall have £5 a quarter to his pains and expenses.
Barker's house. Ordered that William Houlme, in possession of Barker's house, who refuses to pay rent of 50s a year, shall pay 50s for the past year, but may enjoy it at 30s 6d a year for the future, and discharge the town of all chantry rents and other charges, and shall keep the premises in good repair, and he should continue as tenant during his and his wife's good carriage towards the town, according to former order.

p. 648

p. 649
TOWN PLATE
Memo. that the town's plate delivered to the succeeding mayor, was inventoried on 23 October 1657 as follows:

The bottom of a great salt gilded
One great cup gilded with harts and cover
One great cup gilded with a half moon and cover; disposed of to church use 1667
One lesser cup gilded without cover, 9oz 1d weight, also to church 1667
One wine bowl gilded
One silver bowl of Mr Edward's gift
One gilded can of Mr Seacom's gift
12 silver spoons
2 silver beakers

One escrutcheon with town's arms; this the town's wait has
One cawdell cup with a top, exchanged for the top of a salt and marshal's cup
2 silver wine cups, bought 25 June 1657
Statute seal, the greater part

Books:
The statutes at large
The country justice
The complete justice
The collection of several acts of parliament
Statutes at large from Pulton to 1664, in two books bought in Mr Peter Lurting's mayoralty
Jewell and Harding, a great volume in folio, bought in Mr Corley's time
A large blank paper book in folio bought in Mr Stanley's time

In the town hall:
2 great fire hooks
11 buckets
One piece of timber and a piece of a fir dale,[55] used
One brass gallon and 2 brass toll dishes
One iron cloth yard for a standard
One white box and brass scales and a case of brass troy weight

A note of the weights remaining with the hallkeeper, 1658:
    Old weights:
One new iron beam and scales
One old iron beam
8 half hundredweights of lead
2 quarter hundredweights of lead
1 twenty pounds weight
Small weights: 1,7,6,5,4,3,2 pounds
    In Mr Blackmore's mayoralty 1658:
8 half hundredweights more
2 quarter weights of 30 pounds with a piece
3 half quarter weights of 15 pound with a piece
1 four pounds weight of lead
2 two pounds weight of lead
4 single pounds with a piece
4 single half pounds
4 quarter pounds

9 cushions, one new carpet, one old carpet, a bridle.

---

55   Fir dale is probably a wooden trough: OED.

p. 650

p. 651
A RENTAL OF BURGAGE RENTS, lately purchased from the trustees according to act of parliament

James late earl of Derby for his lands in Liverpool, 19s 8d
Edward Moore esq. the Town's End Mill, the Horse Mill, and certain parcels of land, £4 1s 5d; for the land late Humphrey, 6d, and the Pool House, 6d; Total £4 2s
Richard Crosse esq. for his lands, 25s 7d; and for Brook's house, and for the — 12d; total 26s 7d
John Higinson for his part of Mr Bower's land, 3s 6d; John Rose, Underhill 7d; John Chandler, 20d; John Tatlock 11d; Total 7s 8d
Thomas Leigh esq. for Mr Warren's lands, 12s
William Singleton for Mr Percivall's house, 3s; more for John Barton's house, 8d
Mr Robert Moore for his house
Mrs Sarah Walker, widow, for two houses
Richard Lord Mullineux , Viscount Mariburgh, by John Chandler
Mr John Bird for Rose's house
Robert Barker for his house and lands
Mr Thomas Sorocold for Sutton's house
Thomas Storie for John Crane's house and for messe room
Mr Edward Dobson for Mr Washington's
James Williamson, alderman, for his two houses
Mr William Johnson by John Walls
Mr Henry Hockenhall in Juglers Street
Henry Corles for Mr Fazakerley
Ellen Eccleston, widow, for Alderman Eccleston's house
Ellen Raphson and her sister
Alice Morris, widow, by Mr Aspinall
Isabel Moore, widow, for her house in Castle Street
Richard Washington the elder
Mr William Strangewase for the heirs of Ralph Seacome for the houses in Dale Street and Castle Street
John Eccleston for Mr Tarleton's lands
Henry Moore for Mr Balshaw's house in Castle Street
William Blundell esq. by Mr Greene for Pool house
Susan Almond for Ralph Worr's house
Mr William Moore his heirs by Thomas Ashbrooke
Robert Blundell esq. by John Higinson
Mr Robert Mercer by Widow Higinson
Mr Burscowe by Susan Eccleston for the town's land
Thomas Blackmoore, alderman, for William Blundell esq.
Jane Lurtinge widow for town's land
John Lurtinge for Mr Gerrard of Aughton

Edward Williamson for Huberstall's house
George Prescott for Mr Sorocold
Anne Younge widow for the same

p. 652
Mr William Fazakerley by Widow Bose
Alice Marcer, widow, for Mr Gerrard
Ralph Massam, alderman, for Potter's house
Richard Barker by Elizabeth wife of William Houlme
Mr Ogle by Thomas Ditchfield for a croft
Robert Dornell for Browne's croft and the house
Richard Naris for Mr Lathom of Erlam
Widow Widdowes for Mr Hockenhull
Jane Eccleston for Henry Cooke's house
Thomas Tarleton, alderman, for Dale Street house
Christopher Brookebanke for his in Dale Street
Elizabeth Tarleton, widow, for Seacome's lands
Henry Corles for Mr Mossocke's lands
Dorothy Bixteth, widow, for Richard Higinson's
Elinor Sharples, widow, for her house and Needham Hall
Edward Alcocke for his house
Richard Bloom for Mr Norris of Derby
Thomas Burton for Thomas Carter
John Williamson for the house in Dale Street
Margaret Bixteth, widow, for the house late Mr Williamson, and more for her barn
John Williamson for James Higinson's lands
Rachel Bixteth and John Williamson for Mosse's house and two lands
Dorothy Sandiford, widow, for the lands late of Roger Rose, and more for lands in Milne Street
Elizabeth Anderton, widow, by Richard Anderton
Mr Thomas Sorrocold by Robert Eccles for bridges
Cooke's house and land now belonging to the town
Richard Lunt for his house in Tithebarn Street
John Higinson for Mr Blundel's land in same street
William Mee for John Lurting's land
Thomas Coppull for Edmund Tyrer's house and Arnehill
Peter Lurtinge
Robert Sutton for Pickavance house
Thomas Tarleton, alderman, for Mr Blancharts
Matilda Johnson or the heirs of Thomas Denton for a barn and lands
John Higinson for Thomas Car's house
The heirs of Mr Balshaw for the house and barn of Sorocold
John Woods by Thomas Nicholson.

p. 653

p. 654

THOMAS BLACKMORE MAYOR 1657 [1657–58]

p. 655
LIVERPOOL. ELECTION COURT, MONDAY 19 OCTOBER 1657, before Gilbert Formby, gentleman, mayor, Thomas Sandiford and William Bushell, bailiffs, as by charters.

Thomas Blackmore elected mayor by the major votes of the freemen and burgesses then present, sworn
Alexander Greene nominated and elected chief bailiff for the mayor and lord highness the Lord Protector, sworn
Thomas Ashbrooke, innholder, nominated and elected bailiff by the burgesses according to custom, sworn.

William Langton, esq., recorder
John Winstanley, town clerk
William Mulliney, serjeant at mace
Robert Seacome, water bailiff.

   Officers chosen Friday following by the council:
John Fogg, clerk, minister
George Glover, schoolmaster
John Sturzaker, hallkeeper
Robert Seacome, town customer
Richard Rogerson, subcustomer
Richard Poultney, church clerk and sexton
John Williamson, Robert Halle, stewards of the hall
John Hollande, heyward, sworn.

p. 656
   Officers chosen by the jury, 2 November 1657:
William Bushell, Peter Lurting, Robert Sutton, Robert Lyon, merchant appraisers, sworn
William Accars, Edward Horrobine, registers of leather, sworn
Ralph Beling, Thomas Mosse, alefounders, sworn
Thomas Copull, William Poultney, John Sutton, William Fleetwood, barleymen, sworn
Jonathan Gleave, George Thorpe, Henry Tarbock, Roger James, scavengers, sworn
Edward Banks, murenger
William Litherland, Edward Sutton, overseers of the highway
John Sanderson, Peter Walker, porters
Thomas Banks, Richard Rogerson, leavelookers, sworn
William Chorley, Elizabeth Rycroft, boardsetters
Thomas Banks, Thomas Nutter, boothsetters
Edward Ryding, beadle and bellman.

LIVERPOOL. PORTMOOT COURT OR QUARTER SESSIONS FOR THE PEACE, MONDAY 2 NOVEMBER 1657, before the mayor and Thomas Ashbrook, one of the bailiffs.

Inquisition taken by the oaths of Thomas Sandiford, John Higinson, Evan Marshe, William Rymer, Henry Corles, Henry Ryding, George Potter, Robert Lyon, Anthony Mayries, William Cliffe, William Poultney, John Lurting, smith, Richard Lunt, Thomas Mosse, Robert Sympson, Randle Dawson, William Mosse, Henry Gregson, Gregory Formby, James Litherland, Robert Halle, John Johnson, John Henshawe, Edward Carr, honest and lawful freemen.

We present:
    Robert Williamson, son of Richard Williamson for a tussle on Thomas Mosse, 3s 4d
    John Robinson of Raby, yeoman, for a tussle on William Mulliney, serjeant at mace, 3s 4d
    Thomas Nicholson, James Hoult for working unlawful leather, 1s apiece
    Thomas Goulding, Henry Cooper, Edmund Whalley, for like offence, 2s apiece
    Thomas Burscough, William Accars for selling unsealed leather, 1s apiece
    Owen Morgan for using faculty of a freeman, 3s 4d
    Alexander Horrocks for like offence, 1s
    Esther Hardman, Ellen Skinner, Thomas Dicconson, William Lich, Margaret Grange, Jane Martine, Philip Dey, Thomas Darrwine, William Gretton, 6d each, Dorothy Robinson nil
    William Fazakerley, gentleman, for not cleansing the steet against John Lunt's door, nil
    James Williamson, alderman, for the like offence, nil
    Elizabeth Rycroft and William Chorley for neglecting to sweep the street at the butchers' shambles, 1s apiece
    John Lunte, John Griffith, Robert Kenion, carter, and Richard Tyrer for neglect of office of barleymen, 6d apiece
    William Bushell for his swine being unrung, 1s
    John Higinson for the like, 1s
    John Chandler and Thomas Lurting for keeping small quarts in breaking the assize, 1s apiece
    Richard Crosse esq. for not walling in his midding stead according to order, nil
    Richard Widowes for calling Robert Sympson a forsworn man because he informed the jury that Widowes sold turves to foreigners, 1s
    Mr Alexander Greene the younger, elected bailiff of this borough, for neglect of his office, 3s 4d
    All who did not appear at this court and have not essoyned, 3s 4d each: Edward Stockley, Thomas Blackburne, William Lea, Andrew Ashton, Edward Ogle, John Gore, Richard Brookes, Henry Webster, Robert Fleetwood, Henry Ratcliffe, Edmund Lyon, William Widnes, Thomas Gardner, Henry Cooper, Robert Fairehurst, Edward Lea, Thomas Percivall, William More, Andrew Over, William Lewis, John Williamson.

p. 658

Orders made by the Grand Jury:

That the bailiffs cause new sufficient hipingstones in the market footway over the common between Hogsehey and Halls Field before the 20th of this month

That a new cook stool be erected at the watering pool at the lower end of Mr Cross's field

That the sextons ring curfew every night at 8, and at 4 in the morning till 2 February next

We agree to all ancient orders and laudable customs.

p. 659

PORTMOOT COURT OR QUARTER SESSIONS FOR THE PEACE, MONDAY 11 JANUARY 1657, before the mayor and Thomas Ashbrook, one of the bailiffs.

Inquisition taken by the oaths of William Bushell, Edward Formby, Thomas Storie, Robert Sutton, Roger Harrison, John Walles, Thomas Carr, Robert Eccles, Thomas Roe, William Litherland, John Royle, Jonathan Gleave, Henry Tarbuck, Edward Horobine, William Fleetewood, honest and lawful freemen.

We present:

Alexander Horrocks for using the faculty of a freeman, not free, 6d

William Lath, Esther Hardman, Jane Martin, for the like, 6d

Thomas Kelly for setting Thomas Dey, a tailor, at work and not being free, 1s

Edward Ryding for letting his muck lie in the street, nil

Judith Anderton, for the like, nil

Elinor Loy for the like, nil.

Orders:

That all headbolts be made up, hedges cut, ditches scoured before 23 February next, 3s 4d

That Edward Alcock make up his fence before 1 March, between him and Robert Kenion, 3s 4d

We present all freemen who did not appear at this court

We agree all ancient orders and laudable customs.

p. 660

p. 661

PORTMOOT COURT OR QUARTER SESSIONS OF THE PEACE, MONDAY 19 MARCH 1656,[56] before the mayor and Alexander Greene and Thomas Ashbrook, bailiffs.

---

56   The year is given as 1656, presumably a mistake for 1657.

Inquisition taken on the oaths of Evan Marsh, John Blundell, John Lurting, draper, John Chambers, John Lurting, smith, Peter Farrer, William Pultney, Ralph Beling, John Heyes, William Accars, George Thorpe, John Holland, Robert Kenion, cooper, William Daintie, John Kenion, honest and lawful freemen.

We present:
Thomas Rose of Low Hill for a bloodwipe on Edward Henshawe, 6s 8d
Edward Henshawe for a tussle on Thomas Rose, 3s 4d
Thomas Banks for a tussle on Thomas Witter, 3s 4d
Thomas Witter for the like on Thomas Bankes, 3s 4d
Richard Holland of Upholland for working unlawful leather, 2s 6d
Owen Morgan for using the faculty of a freeman, not free, suspend.
Alexander Horrocks, Esther Hardman, Dorothy Robinson, Jane Martine, Thomas Darrwine, Ellen Skinner, William Leech, Margaret Granger, William Gretton, Thomas Davies, a stranger, for the like offence, 3s 4d apiece
William Bushell, Esther Hardman, John Chandler, Gilbert Formby, alderman, Henry Moore, Thomas Hancock, Thomas Ashbrook, Thomas Roe, for keeping swine unrung, 1s apiece
Thomas Bridge for keeping small quart, 2s 6d
Lawrence Wetherby for buying meat and selling it same day, 2s 6d
Mr John Chandler for selling drink, not licensed, 3s 4d
Christian Manwaring, Margery Burton, James Blevine, Robert Halle, Henry Craine, William Daintie, John Chambers, Henry Moore, Thomas Hancock, Margaret Granger, William Gretton, Edward Sutton, John Lunte, John Sturzaker, for the like, 3s 4d
Mr Alexander Greene and Mr Thomas Ashbrook, bailiffs, for not causing hiping stones to be set between Hogsehey and Hall Field and for not causing a new cook stool to be set up according to former order.
John Sutton for not taking oath and neglecting office of barleyman, 3s 4d
John Chandler for ploughing up the town common at the end of Barker's Field, 3s 4d
Mr John Bird and Edward Banks for the like, like fines

Orders:
Edward Alcock to clear the water course behind him and Mrs Heapey before 10 April next, on pain of 5s
Ellen Eccleston to clear the watercourse at the end of her house before 10 May, 5s
Richard Browne to make wall between Susan Eccleston's house and the smithy, as formerly made, before 5 May, 5s
A cartway to be left at both ends of the Pyke Acres, and that the green soil be laid down again by those who have ploughed it up before April next, 5s
Margaret Gilbtthrop make up the fence between her and John Blundell, 5s
Edward Alcock to bury his cow lately dead, 5s
We agree to all ancient orders and laudable customs.

p. 662

p. 663
PORTMOOT, not held.

AUDIT OF GILBERT FORMBY, GENTLEMAN, MAYOR, 1656, Thomas
Sandiford and William Bushell, bailiffs.

Received by the bailiffs	£392	7s	3d
Disbursements	191	3	8
Rest to bailiffs	201	3	7
and rest of assessment money		50s	

23 July 1658
Memorandum that security is given by Robert Sutton for £30 to be paid in six years with
interest to the town, and £10 he paid in hand, whereupon the bailiffs are discharged.

p. 664
13 JANUARY 1657, COMPOSITION
    At an Assembly in the town hall, ordered that there shall be paid for the
composition for herrings, 6s 8d for every score of barrels, and so rateably for any
quantity imported.

The *Mathew* of Liverpool for — barrels of herring bought
The *Bonaventure*
The *Elizabeth* of Formby
The *Vintie* of
The *Elizabeth* of Liverpool
The *Mary Cath*
The *Prymrose*

p. 665
24 NOVEMBER 1657, COMPOSITION
John Hignett, merchant, to pay composition for 52 barrels of herring imported in
the *Thomas and Katherine* from Wexford, 18s 2d, which was afterwards remitted
on his certificate to be a freeman of Wexford.
Captain Lathom to pay for 26 barrels of herring imported in the same vessel, 8s 6d.

    Ordered by Thomas Blackmore, mayor, Ralph Massam and Thomas Andoe,
aldermen, Thomas Ashbrook, bailiff, and the greater part of the common council,
that Mr Alexander Greene, the younger, pay £10 for his neglect of the office of
bailiff, and on default the bailiff is authorised to distrain for the same unless
Mr Greene come and accept the office and take oath before 3 December next.
    Memo. That Mr Greene did come in and took his oath, whereupon the fine is
suspended.

23 DECEMBER 1657

At an Assembly of the common council, whereas Mr Alexander Greene the younger still fails to appear as bailiff, it is ordered by mayor Thomas Blackmore, Thomas Williamson, Edward Wilson, Ralph Massam, Thomas Andoe and Gilbert Formby, aldermen, Thomas Ashbrook, bailiff and the general consent of the council, that Mr Greene shall pay the sum of £10, and the bailiff is required to levy the same unless Mr Greene come and take the oath before 1 January next.

13 JANUARY 1657

Whereas several orders have been made that Mr Alexander Greene should take on the office of bailiff, but he does not appear or execute the office for which he has been fined, it is now ordered by the mayor and greater part of the common council that the fine of £30 be imposed on Mr Greene for his contempt, to be forthwith levied on his goods, and that the former fines of £10 apiece be remitted.

Alexander Greene, merchant, is fined £30 for not taking on the office of bailiff acording to the order above, which the other bailiff is ordered to levy of the goods, chattels, merchandise of the said Alexander for the use of the corporation, by virtue of several charters, £30.

p. 666
23 OCTOBER 1657

Ordered that the church wall on the north shall be surveyed and repaired at the discretion of the mayor and bailiffs, at the town's charge.

Ordered that John Higinson, John Blundell, John Lurting, William Bushell be fined 3s 4d apiece for not appearing at this assembly.

Ordered that a letter be written to Colonel Birch, burgess, that the business of this corporation requires his personal attendance in parliament, and to know his resolution concerning his going to the next parliament, and meanwhile to please come here to consult about the town's affairs.

Whereas a church ley for Walton of £2 13s 4d is demanded by the churchwardens by warrant from Edward Moore, esq., the vicar of Walton, being a proportion of £12 charged on Walton parish, it is ordered that the ley shall be not paid, being unduly taxed, and that the plate and goods of Mr Gilbert Formby which are distrained, shall be restored, and the suit defended at the town's charge.

Ordered that there shall be more weights made for the town to make them complete, one thousand weight, and hundred, half hundred, and quarters, and the hall keeper to stand chargeable with them for the use of the corporation.

9 NOVEMBER 1658[57]

Ordered that an action be brought in the borough court by the bailiffs against James Standish, gentleman, for taking a silver can from Mr Gilbert Formby as a distress for the church leys of Walton and the charge of the suit to be born by the town.

---

57   The year should be 1657.

p. 667

Whereas by an act of parliament of 26 September 1653 it was enacted that in consideration of the great losses of the town the commissioners of parliament in Ireland should appoint lands to the value of £10,000 at the rate that the public debts are to be satisfied, for the use of the town, in pursuance of which great efforts and money have been expended, and notwithstanding his highness's letter of recommendation, the lands have not been procured because the judges in Ireland to which the case was referred have opined to the Lord Protector that the adventurers should first be satisfied from the said lands, and it was alleged that they are not enough to pay both, it was agreed at an assembly of the common council in the common hall before the mayor, Thomas Williamson, Ralph Massam, Edward Williamson, and Thomas Andoe, aldermen, Thomas Ashbrook, one of the bailiffs and the greater part of the common council, that the effecting of this business will be very difficult and expensive unless it is undertaken by some particular persons interested therein. It is therefore ordered that Mr John Winstanley, town clerk, and such other persons as he shall agree with, shall have a lease and grant of the one full moitie of the said lands in Ireland, and that he and such others shall have the said one moitie and half part thereof to them and their heirs and assigns, paying to the said corporation the yearly rent of 20 shillings, after possession of the lands shall be obtained. And that John Winstanley and the others give security to try to use all their power speedily to procure the said lands to be surveyed at their own charge without further charge to the corporation, to be given as council learned in this behalf shall advise. And the said survey shall be made at the charge of John Winstanley and his partners, and the whole lands to be divided between then and the corporation. Thomas Blackmore, mayor, Thomas Williamson, Ralph Massam, Edward Williamson, Tho T A Andoe, Robert Moore, Thomas Ashbrook, Roger Jones, Edward Formby, Richard Williamson, John Sturzaker, Thomas Storie, Evan Marsh, Peter Lurting, John Lurting, William Rymer, John Blundell, Henry Corles, Robert Sutton, Thomas Sandiford, William Bushell.

13 JANUARY 1658

At an Assembly in the common hall before Mr Thomas Blackmore, mayor, the aldermen, one of the bailiffs and greater part of the common council, it was ordered, concerning the making of this town into a parish, that the business be prosecuted at the town's charge, and that the order already obtained be prosecuted, and that Mr Winstanley shall go to London as solicitor, according to a former order, and an allowance of £5 a quarter be given to him for his expenses on his return. And it is agreed that Mr Fogg, the minister here, may go at his own charge if he please, which is afterwards to be considered by this house on his return. And care is to be taken to get the £10 augmentation already allowed to be continued for the future if it may be had. Afterwards, at an assembly on 21 May 1658 it was voted that Mr Fogg shall have the allowance of the charge of his London journey, £4 3s.

26 JANUARY 1658

Ordered concerning the church leys from Walton still demanded that Mr Mayor and any three of the aldermen shall treat with and allow what they think fit to the churchwardens of Walton for the repair of the church.

p. 668
FRIDAY 9 JULY 1658

At an assembly held in the town hall it was ordered, concerning the business of Ireland, that Alderman Gilbert Formby and Mr Thomas Sandiford shall go to Dublin in answer to Captain Browne's desires, and if necessary to Galway, at the charge of the corporation, and shall act according to such orders as from time to time shall be agreed by this house.

27 JANUARY 1657

Ordered that the void place under the hall window shall be railed for a place to set the stalls and boards so they may be removed out of the trouble of others, and there shall not be any more rent paid to Jane Haskaine for the same stalls.

Ordered that at the first opportunity Major Ellotson be treated with concerning the purchase of the chantry rents if they may be purchased from him or Captain Hoult at a reasonable value.

p. 669
2 AUGUST 1658

At an Assembly of the common council held in the common hall before Mr Mayor, Thomas Williamson, Ralph Massam, Edward Williamson, Thomas Andoe, the bailiffs and greater part of the common council, it was ordered concerning the business of Ireland, that Alderman Gilbert Formby and Mr Thomas Sandiford shall at the first opportunity go to Ireland according to former order, and that all patents, writings and assurances of the said portion of houses and lands in Ireland shall first be obtained for the corporation, and that they be established in possession before any division be made between the town and Mr John Winstanley and his partner, Captain James Browne, and then their leases of their moitie are to be made according to order and as council learned in this behalf shall advise, and that Mr Formby and Mr Sandiford shall be satisfied for their charges in pursuance of this order. Thomas Blackmore, mayor, Tho Williamson, Ralph Massam, Edward Williamson, Thomas Andoe, Robart Moore, Alexandr Greene, Thomas Ashbrooke, John Higginsonn, Edward Formby, John Winstanley, John Sturzaker, Thos Storey, Richard Pecivall, Evan Marsh, Peter Lurting, John Blundell, John Lurting, Henry Corles, Robert Sutton, John Walls, Henry Rydinge, Robert R L Lyon, Rodger Harrison, Robert Seacome, Will Mulliney.[58]

p. 670
18 JUNE 1658

At an Assembly in the common hall before the mayor, aldermen, bailiffs and greater part of the common council, it was ordered that Mr John Winstanley shall go to London to solicit the purchase of the butlerage, and shall give to

58   Signatures.

Mr Humphrey Kelsall, in whose name the discovery is entered, the sum of £6 and shall agree with him for the altering of the same discovery for the use of the corporation and shall compound for the same or such part as may be obtained for the town, and shall have certificates for the completing of a survey of the value thereof, and shall have liberty to alter the same as he has occasion. Whereupon £6 was paid to Mr Kelsall, and the discovery amended and entered in his and Mr Winstanley's name.

Ordered that Mr Nathaniel Overton shall be paid £4 7s due to him for money disbursed in the perfecting of the instrument for dividing this town from the parish of Walton and making it a parish of itself which is accordingly to commence from the decease of Mr Robert Eaton, the present incumbent, and Mr Finch, the present vicar.

Letter from Captain Browne concerning the houses in Galloway given to this town, read, but nothing ordered.

p. 671
24 SEPTEMBER 1658

At an Assembly of the common council in the town hall before the mayor, Thomas Williamson, Ralph Massam, Edward Williamson, Thomas Andoe, aldermen, the bailiffs and major part of the common council, on reading several queries made to William Langdon, esq. recorder, for his advice in the busines concerning the lands in Ireland, it is ordered that the undertakers, Mr John Winstanley and his partners who have not yet perfected that business, shall first procure letters patent for the houses and lands in Galway mentioned in the order of the Lord Deputy and Council, so the town may be legally invested in possession of the premises before any division is made from the town to the undertakers. Thomas Blackmore, mayor, Tho Williamson, Ralph Massam, Edw Williamson, Thomas Andoe, Robart Moore, Alexandr Greene, Thomas Ashbrooke, Edward Formby, John Sturzaker, Tho Story, Evan Marsh, Richard Peircivall, Peter Lurting, John Blundell, John Lurting, Thomas Sandiford, Henry Corles, Henry Moore, Robert Lyon, Richard Blevin, Ri Dwarihouse, Henry Rydinge, Roger Hareson, Robert Seacome, William Mulliney, John Winstanley, 1658.[59]

p. 672
12 MARCH 1657

Butlerage. Ordered that Mr Peircivall and Mr Sandiford shall go to Colonel Birch for the note concerning the butlerage from Mr Kelsall and that Colonel Shutleworth shall be solicited to resign his interest in the discovery thereof to the use of the town, which note was procured accordingly.

Church Repair. Ordered that the church shall be repaired as required, being in much ruin and decay, and that a ley shall be set to which all foreign burgesses shall contribute.

59   Signatures.

Town hall. Ordered that the town hall shall be boarded new at the town's charge.

Arrears. Ordered that Robert Sutton and Henry Moore, late bailiffs, give security by bonds for the payment of £40 which they owe the town, whereof they are to pay £10 in hand and the rest at £5 a year with interest, which bonds are made ready but not sealed.

BUTLERAGE

It is ordered that Mr Alexander Greene for 8 tuns of French wine brought in by Israel Thomas rated to 26s 8d.

Mr Greene to pay for 31 hogsheads and 19 more for Mr Chapman, 40s

Mr Horton to pay for 2 tuns of French wine, 6s 8d

21 May 58

The same merchants for over 20 tuns of wine in the ship *Fortune*, ordered that they pay £15 or 3 hogsheads of wine, £15

Mr John Sandiford for 4 tuns of wine in the *Love's Increase*, 16s and more to be paid for butlerage, 4s.

APPRENTICES

Ordered that certain poor children of the town shall be apprenticed and clothed at the discretion of the mayor, aldermen and bailiffs; John Lurting, smith, shall take the daughter of John Ryce for three years at such allowance as by a note of agreement appears.

p. 673

FREEMEN

12 March 1657:

Henry Neild, late apprentice to Mr John Sandiford, merchant, admitted free, 6s 8d, sworn

2 August 1658:

Thomas Coventrie, late apprentice of Mr Blackmore, 6s 8d, sworn

John Walker, tailor, admitted, £3, sworn

Thomas Steedman, tailor, admitted, £3, sworn

William Nicholls, wine cooper, servant to Mr Greene for 5 years, composition 40s, but only 20s, sworn

William Gretton, porter, voted to be admitted, ordered to pay 40s, but for some reasons is to have 20s restored, 20s, sworn

8 October 1658:

Thomas Tatlock, wettower, admitted as apprenticed, 6s 8d, sworn

18 October 1658:

William Fazakerley, son of Richard Fazakerley, late apprentice of Thomas Nicholson, 6s 8d, sworn

2 September 1658:

Thomas Litherland, butcher, admitted, 40s, sworn

Robert Fleetwood, skinner, served apprenticeship, 6s 8d, sworn

Thomas Scarisbrick, sailor, 40s, sworn

Thomas Dobb, sailor, 40s, sworn

John Minnley, mariner, 40s, sworn.

p. 674
21 MAY 1658

At an Assembly of the Common Council in the town hall before the mayor, Thomas Williamson, Ralph Massam, Edward Williamson, Thomas Andoe, aldermen, the bailiffs and most of the common council, it was ordered that a certificate concerning the yearly value of the butlerage be drawn up and certified to the trustees at Worcester House, at the rate of £5 per annum, and two others blank which are to be returned according to advice with Mr Kelsall, and that Mr Winstanley shall solicit that business and complete the purchase thereof at the charge of the town, and to work out an agreement with Mr Kelsall concerning the same discovery for the benefit of this corporation.

p. 675
2 AUGUST 1658

Suit in Chancery. Whereas a suit is commenced in the high court of Chancery against Gilbert Formby and others of this town by Edward Moore esq. concerning the walking of the liberties last year, it is ordered that the same shall be answered at the public charge of the town, and a commission sued for the taking of the answers of Mr Thomas Williamson and the rest according to the recorder's advice, whereto two of the defendants have answered; Mr Formby, being then at sea, and Mr Sandiford, whose name was mistaken, have not answered.

Walton church ley. Ordered that the suit be prosecuted and brought to trial against Mr Standish of West Derby for the taking of Mr Gilbert Formby's silver can by way of distress for leys to Walton church, which was done accordingly, whereupon the leys were recovered and the plate by order of the court restored at the town's charge.

2 SEPTEMBER 1658

At an Assembly in the common hall before Mr Mayor, the aldermen and most part of the Common Council it was ordered that Mr Henry Corles and Mr Thomas Sandiford shall with the first wind go to Galway in Ireland and there enter the houses and lands given and now belonging to this town by act of parliament and order of the Lord Deputy and Council in Ireland, and take seisin of the premises for the town and corporation. And they shall take a perfect survey of the same, with tenants' names and rents, and the value of the houses, and further do whatever is necessary for the receipt of the present rents by the town according to a letter of attorney and instructions given to them.

It is also ordered that Mr Thomas Williamson and Mr Greene shall go to Preston and take advice of the recorder concerning the present business in Ireland, and view all the papers and proceedings. Accordingly done.

p. 676
24 SEPTEMBER 1658

Concerning Ireland. At an Assembly of the mayor, aldermen and common council of the town and on reading of the several queries made to Mr Langton, the recorder of the town, in the business concerning the lands in Ireland, it is ordered that Mr John Winstanley and his partners, the undertakers in that business, have not as yet perfected their work, and therefore they are to procure a further act of parliament or letters patent for confirmation of the houses in Galway to this corporation according to the order of the lord deputy and council, so the said town may be legally in possession thereof before any division is made to the undertakers.

8 OCTOBER 1658

The same. At an assembly it is ordered that Mr Henry Corles and Mr Thomas Sandiford as agents for this corporation shall repair to Dublin and so to Galway, and there act according to the power given them by a letter of attorney and instructions, and shall have the sum of £20 for their pains and charges, and be saved harmless by this town for their acting therein, and to survey the houses.

Walton leys. Concerning the church leys to be paid to Walton the Justices of the Peace shall be spoken with and if they sign warrants for the same to be paid then the bailiffs for the time being are to pay the same.

p. 677

AUDIT OF THOMAS BLACKMORE LATE MAYOR, HELD ON 22 DECEMBER 1658 before Richard Percivall, gentleman, mayor.

Town customer ingates,	£8	6s	1d
outgates	2	19	10
Subcustomer ingates	8	17	11
outgates	4	13	0½
Hallkeeper ingates	2	8	4
outgates	2	0	0
Freemen compositions			
Ferry boat rents by			
Mr Edward Formby			
Town's rents			
Burgage rents lately			
purchased for minister			
and schoolmaster			
Licence money			
Butlerage and prysage			
wines			
Churchwardens' accounts			
Debts of Robert Sutton &			
Lynaker			
Received for timber			
Received for fines at			
3 portmoots			
Received the old bailiffs			
accounts balanced			

p. 678

RICHARD PEIRCIVALL, MAYOR, 1658 [1658–59]

p. 679
LIVERPOOL. ELECTION COURT, MONDAY 18 OCTOBER 1658, the feast of
St Luke the Evangelist, before Thomas Blackmore, gent. mayor, Alexander Greene
and Thomas Ashbrook, bailiffs.

Richard Peircivall, gent., is elected mayor by the votes of the freemen and
burgesses and sworn
John Sturzaker, sadler, nominated by Mr Mayor as chief bailiff for the mayor and
his highness the Lord Protector and sworn
John Owen, mariner, elected sub-bailiff by the freemen and sworn, and also sworn
to be of the common council.

William Langton esq., recorder
John Winstanley, town clerk
William Mulliney, serjeant at mace, sworn
Robert Seacome, water bailiff, sworn.

   Officers chosen by the common council on Friday after the election:
John Fogg, minister
Mr George Glover, schoolmaster
John Sturzaker, hallkeeper, sworn
Robert Seacome, town customer, sworn
Roger Rogerson, subcustomer, sworn
Richard Poultney, church clerk & sexton
Thomas Johnson & William Fleetwood, stewards of the hall and leygatherers,
sworn
John Holland, heyward, sworn

p. 680
   Officers chosen by the jury:
Thomas Ashbrook, Evan Marsh, Henry Corles, John Walles, merchant appraisers,
sworn
Thomas Nicholson, Henry Cooper, registers of leather, sworn
Jonathan Gleave, Alexander Horrocks, alefounders, sworn
Edward Banks, George Thorpe, Thomas Litherland, Henry Tarbock, barleymen,
three sworn
William Gretton, William Nicholls, Thomas Tatlock, Robert Johnson, scavengers,
sworn
Robert Sympson, murenger
John Banks, Robert Fleetwood, overseers of the highways

John Saunderson, Peter Walker, porters
Thomas Banks, Richard Rogerson, leavelookers, sworn
William Chorley, Elizabeth Rycroft, boardsetters
Thomas Witter, Thomas Banks, boothsetters
Edward Ryding, beadle and bellman.

Churchwardens chosen at Easter:
John Tompson, John Pemberton for 1659.

p. 681
PORTMOOT COURT OR QUARTER SESSIONS, 25 OCTOBER 1658.
Inquisition at Liverpool in county of Lancaster before the mayor and bailiffs.

The jurors sworn: Alexander Greene, Thomas Storie, John Blundell, Robert Sutton, Edmund Leivsey, Robert Swifte, Thomas Hancock, Thomas Preeson, Richard Lunte, Thomas Roe, Thomas Bridge, John Banks, John Holland, Edward Horrobine, John Johnson, Thomas Copull, William Litherland, Thomas Mosse, Jonathan Gleave, Edward Sutton, Edward Banks, John Henshawe, Henry Webster, Alexander Horrocks.

We present:
Richard Widowes for a tussle on Edward Ryding, 3s 4d
Edward Ryding for the like on Richard Widowes, 3s 4d
Edward Holland, William Preston, Edward Buckley, William Accars, Edward Horrobine, for working unlawful leather, amerced
James Chapman, Thomas Davies, Ellen Skinner, Richard Bowar, Esther Hardman, Margaret Granger, Thomas Dicconson, William Leech, John Williamson, Dorothy Robinson, George Nagbor, Jane Martine, Richard Strange, Thomas Darwine, Robert Ballard, all for using the faculty of a freemen
Edward Alcock for not cleansing his street in Dale Street
Mrs Dorothy Sandiford for the like by the White Cross
John Rosonn for not cleansing his street, amerced
Thomas Banks and Thomas Witter for not cleansing the market place, it being their office of boothsetter
William Accars, John Higinson, Thomas Ashbrook, John Lurting, draper, Mr John Fogg, minister, for not cleansing Dale Street, Tithebarn
Robert Cornell, alderman, for refusing to mend the highway on lawful warning; Ralph Massam, alderman, Mrs Elizabeth Tarleton, widow, John Sturzaker, John Williamson the younger, Peter Lurting, Richard Crompton, Thomas Plombe, William Mosse, for the like offence
Roger Hey of Everton for cutting grass in the town field, not his own; Robert Henshawe and Anne his wife for the like
Richard Boar for making his bread too light; Ellen Hacking, widow, for the like

John Chandler for keeping unlawful quarts; Mrs Christian Mannwaring for the like

William Gardner for keeping his swine unrung; Richard Rymmer, Michael Barker for the like

Richard Widowes for selling turves of the town's common to those not free

The same Richard Widdowes for loitering on the sabbath

The same Richard Widdowes for being drunk on the sabbath

Mrs Heapey for entertaining loitering persons on the sabbath

p. 682
Orders:

That Thomas Andoe, alderman, make his wall from the old gate on the east side of Old Hall Lane from the ancient stock to the south end of the wall to be lineable with the Quickwood Roe if it appears to be the town's waste by 25 March next on pain of 40s

Alderman Massam to allow Simon Arowsmith to have the compass of one end of a well turn of ground as formerly, forthwith, 5s

William Bushell to make up his fence between Edward Horrobine and him by 2 February, 20s

Margaret Gilbtthrop to make up her fence between John Blundell and her by 2 February, 5s

Elizabeth Bushell to make up her wall between Simon Arowsmith and her by 2 February, 5s

Henry Moore to make up his wall between Henry Corles and him by 2 February, 10s

Ellen Blevine to scour ditch at her house by 11 November, 5s

Mr John Winstanley to do the like that the water may have free passage, 5s

Ellen Hacking to allow John Lurting, smith, to come on her back side to repair his house and cleanse the watercourse between them at times convenient, 10s

Mrs Margaret Williamson to make up her wall fallen down between her and Mr John Chandler, by 2 February, 20s

The said Mrs Williamson to cleanse the watercourse between her and Mr Chandler, on her back side, by 10 November, 5s

Any carrion laid at the waterside or elsewhere, shall be buried, 6s 8d

We approve of Thomas Johnson and William Fleetwood as stewards of the hall, and ley gatherers

We present all who sell beer, unlicensed by Mr Mayor

We present all freemen who did not appear at this court

We order all swine to be kept out of the street on Saturdays and Sabbath days according to former order

The poor of town to be provided for and all wanderers and beggars to be taken up by the beadle of this town

A cook stool be made and set up according to former order

A curfew shall ring as formerly

The bailiffs to see these orders executed, 20s

We agree to all ancient orders and laudable customs.

p. 683

PORTMOOT COURT OR QUARTER SESSIONS, MONDAY 10 JANUARY
1658. Inquisition taken at Liverpool in county of Lancaster before the mayor and
bailiffs.

Jury sworn: Thomas Ashbrooke, Peter Lurting, Thomas Sandiford, Robert Lyon,
Richard Crompton, William Gardner, Robert Eccles, Thomas Nicholson, James
Hoult, William Fleetwood, William Nicholls, Thomas Tatlock, Thomas Litherland,
John Griffith, John Holland.

We present:
Samuel Postlethwaite, Stephen Platt, Robert Houghton for using the faculty of
freemen, not free, 6s 8d apiece, remitted
Edmund Ryding, cooper, Henry Mercer of Crosby, cooper, Edward Kenion,
Thomas Hoult, William Blackmore, Henry Robinson, James Chapman, John
Pearle, William Mills, Robert Leadbeater, John Cooke, Thomas Birch, Jane Martin,
widow, Esther Hardman, widow, Thomas Davis, Henry Charnock, Ellen Robinson,
widow, Thomas Dicconson, John Williamson, seaman, William Harrison, glasier,
William Holland, glasier, William Leech, Ellen Skinner, James Apleton, for the
like, 3s 4d apiece
Peter Smith, Henry Goore, Thomas Aspe, Edward Stockeley, James Moorecroft
for buying skins before the market, 2s 6d apiece
James Hoult, Thomas Nicholson, Henry Cooper, Thomas Gooding the younger
for working unlawful leather, 6d each for two, 1d each for other two
Mrs Heapey and Elinor Winstanley, widow, for keeping swine unrung,
6d apiece
Edward Ryding, Anne Higginson, widow, Elinor Loye, Isabel Anderton for
making midding steads streetwards, and not walling them according to former
orders, 0s 0d
Jonathan Gleave, Alexander Hancock for neglecting their office, 6d apiece

We order:
The ancient watercourse at the back of John Raphson's houses be scoured before
the last of day of February, on pain of 5s
Mrs Ellen Eccleston, widow, to remove earth and rubbish which lies at Edward
Formby's house side by the last day of February, 3s 4d
The dung and rubbish which lies alongside Mr Chandler's house in
Mrs Margaret Williamson's back side to be removed and the water course cleansed,
and the encroachments made in several parts of the wall adjoining to
Mr Chandler's garden and croft which lately fell down and was repaired by
Mrs Williamson be removed and built on the old foundation stones, 20s
Mrs Margaret Williamson to build up the wall between her and William
Middleton before the last day of February, 5s
Isabel Livesley, widow, to build up the wall between her and William Middleton
before the last day of February, 5s

Alderman Massam to cleanse the old watercourse through Dichfield's croft before the last day of February, 5s

Edward Alcock to cleanse the ancient watercourse in Tithebarn Lane which runs along his croft before the last day of February, 5s

Margaret Gilberthorpe, widow, to make up the fence between her and John Blundell before the last day of February, 5s

The bailiffs to cause the old water course which crosses Tithebarn Street into William Rynd's croft to be opened before 25 March, 10s

A new cook stool to be made and erected at the watering pool at Mr Cross's field before the last day of February, 20s, to be paid by the bailiffs

The bridge at Dale Street end to be repaired, and a new flag to be laid on the watercourse at John Lurting's house before the last day of February, 0s 0d

All headbolts to be made up, hedges cut and ditches scoured before the last day of February, 3s 4d

We agree to all ancient orders and laudable customs.

p. 684

p. 685

INQUISITION TAKEN AT THE PORTMOOT COURT OR QUARTER SESSIONS AT LIVERPOOL IN COUNTY OF LANCASTER, ON MONDAY 4 JULY 1659, before the mayor and bailiffs.

The jurors for the keepers of the liberties of England by authority of parliament: Edward Formby, William Rymmer, Henry Corles, Thomas Preeson, Richard Blevine, Robert Harvie, John Heyes, Richard Holland, Robert Leadbeater, Robert Johnson, Robert Sympson, John Williamson, Robert Halle, Alexander Horrocks, John Holland.

We present:

William Leach, George Naylor, John Ashton, William Harison, Henry Chapman, John Williamson, mariner, Edward Clarkson, Jane Martine, widow, Esther Hardman, Dorothy Robinson, William Walsh, Thomas Davies, William Mills, John Cooke, William Blackmore, Thomas Tarleton, for using the faculty of a freeman, not free, 3s 4d apiece

Bryan Fleetwood for a bloodwipe on Richard Rogerson, subcustomer, 6s 8d

Richard Crompton for keeping a tenant in his house and not giving security to the town, 2s 6d

Nicholas Banks for the like, 2s 6d

Edward Alcock for getting clay where the old tithe barn stood, and John Lurting, draper, for the like, 1s apiece

William Leach for a tussle on William Litherland, 3s 4d

William Litherland for a tussle on William Leach, 3s 4d

Henry Shill for selling shoes out of the market, 2s 6d

The bailiffs for neglecting to build a cook stool according to former order, amerced, suspended.

We order:

Mrs Aspinwall to let the ancient watercourse be opened between her and John Roson by 1 August, on pain of 5s

John Lurting to make up wall between him and Peter Lurting before said day, 5s

Captaine Browne to make up wall between him and Richard Crompton before said time, 5s

The Merestones for the liberties to be set up by the advice of the mayor and aldermen and other knowing persons they think fit

The swinecote adjoining the church wall to be pulled down, and nobody to keep any swine loose in the churchyard, 5s

The shoemakers who come to market begin to sell at 11.0 a.m. and leave off at 5.0 p.m., 5s

The streets and highways to be repaired

The subcustomer to receive tolls of such as buy cattle and sheep according to ancient custom

A line to be drawn betwixt the town's common and those that have trespassed upon it with their corn and shall be mown as far as the Dowe stones reach, on pain of

We agree to all ancient orders and laudable customs

p. 686

22 OCTOBER 1658

Stewards of the hall. Ordered at an assembly of the mayor, aldermen, bailiffs and common council that Thomas Johnson and William Fleetwood, stewards of the hall, for the present year, and those elected hereafter, shall also be ley gatherers, and shall collect all leys, taxes and assessments, and that the bailiffs shall assist them on occasion to distrain, and shall receive money from them, and give an account at the audit.

Apprentice. Ordered that William Rycroft, a poor boy of the town, shall be apprenticed to Edward Sutton for seven years, and that the money for his apprenticeship be paid out of the town's stock.

COMPOSITION

Thomas Ashbrook for Mr Harvie ordered to pay for 40 barrels herrings, 11s
Daniel Mather for 20 barrels of herrings, 5s 6d
Richard Williamson for Captain Joseph Witter for 200 barrels, 55s
Mr William Kiching for 30 barrels, 8s 3d

p. 687

20 DECEMBER 1658

Ireland. At an assembly it was ordered concerning the lands in Ireland that no division shall be made with the undertakers till the corporation be settled in full possession of the whole premises, and then the grants are to be made according to the first agreement with Mr Winstanley, notwithstanding any importunity or pretence.

17 JANUARY 1658

At an assembly of the common council it was by general consent approved that Colonel Gilbert Ireland should be one of the burgesses for this town to serve in parliament.

Ordered that all burgesses that are not free who have on market days or week days sold goods in houses, shops or pentice, to the prejudice of freemen and contrary to ancient custom, shall henceforth be restrained and those who refuse shall be presented at the next quarter sessions and fined.

Ordered that Mr Thomas Storie and his partners shall have liberty to make bricks on the common in the place where formerly Mr Eccleston made brick.

Samuel Postlethwait voted a freeman, paying £7.

p. 688

CORONER'S INQUESTS

An inquisition taken 25 August 1659 before Thomas Blackmore, alderman, coroner within the borough, on the oaths of Edmund Leivesley, Henry Ryding, Thomas Chapman, Robert Harvy, Thomas Roe, Thomas Johnson, John Heyes, John Pemberton, Thomas Bridge, Thomas Hancock, Thomas Galway, Robert Leadbeater, lawful and honest freemen, who say that Rachel, the late wife of Simon Arrowsmith, being in the house of Gilbert Formby, alderman, on 24 August about 4 o'clock, was slain by accident and misfortune by the discharge of a flint lock piece, which Thomas Hudson, a soldier under the command of Major Edward Hoore, had in his hands. As he was screwing on the lock in the open street, a bullet broke through a wall and wainscot of the same house and pierced the body of the said Rachel, making a wound from her left pap to her back whereby she immediately died, there being no malice at which to us may appear.

An inquisition taken 1 July 1659 before Thomas Blackmore, alderman, coroner, on the oaths of Thomas Storie, Peter Lurting, John Blundell, John Lurting, smith, Roger Harrison, William Litherland, Thomas Mosse, Hugh Bennett, John Lunt, John Mulliney, William Parker, Robert Lyon, Edward Horrobine, Robert Kenion, Edward Sutton, who say that John Craine, son of John Craine of Liverpool, mariner, on 1 July 1659 was found dead on the sea shore at Liverpool, drowned by accident and we know of no one guilty of his death.

Inquisition taken at Liverpool on Friday 7 October 1659 before Thomas Blackmore, alderman and coroner, after the death of Robert Greene, corporal of Major Boulton's troop. The jury on their oaths present that Robert Greene on 6 October 1659 about 10 a.m., being on horseback and going towards Chester at Birkett Pool on the Cheshire side of the Mersey, entered the pool at deep water. His horse lost its footing and turned over several times. The horse landed on the further side, but Robert Greene was by misfortune drowned and found lying there dead as the tide ebbed, near the place where he entered the pool. Thomas Blackmore, coroner. Sworn: Henry Corles, William Jameson, Thomas Hewett, Richard Crompton, Randle Dawson, Richard, Thomas Nicholson, Henry Robinson, Edward Horrobine, Thomas Andoe, Thomas Chapman, Thomas Mosse.

p. 689
7 MARCH 1658
At an assembly of the mayor, aldermen, bailiffs and greater part of the common council:

It was ordered that the church walls and roof shall be repaired at the discretion of Mr Mayor and the aldermen, and the money will be raised as this house shall hereafter agree.

Ordered that no persons shall be permitted to set any locks on the pews and seats in the church without leave of this house.

Ordered that Mr Mayor and the aldermen with such other burgesses as they shall call shall treat with Mr Smith, vicar of Walton, concerning the glebe and church dues which he claims, and shall compound with him at the easiest rate they can for the years passed, and that for the future a yearly sum should be paid him from the public stock. This was afterwards done, viz. £5 to be paid him in lieu of all arrears, and 40s a year for the future.

Also ordered that Michael Barker shall have reasonable satisfaction given him from the town stock for the maintenance of James Williamson, son of Matthew Williamson, deceased, since the death of Alderman James Williamson.

COMPOSITION
Alexander Greene to pay £9 for wines imported in the *Ruth* of Liverpool, and to be received by the bailiffs
Gilbert Formby, alderman, shall pay 6s composition for 6 hogsheads of wine imported in the *Anne Pink*
Mr William Kichine to pay 6s composition for 6 hogsheads of wine in the same vessel
Mr Thomas Sandiford to pay 6s for the like in the *Charitie* of Chester
Mr Thomas Chapman jnr. to pay 8s composition for 8 hogsheads of wine imported in the same vessel

BUTLERAGE
Mr Greene to pay for 10 pipes of sack and 8 tuns of wine, 52s
Mr Thomas Sandiford to pay composition for – tuns 4s
In the *Fortune* of Liverpool for 22 tuns of wine, leak and damnified, Mr Greene to pay for 10 tuns, Mr Thomas Christian for 4 tuns, Mr Horton for 4 tuns, in all, £10

p. 690
29 OCTOBER 1658
Port customs. Be it remembered that on a difference arising betwixt Mayor Henry Ogle, Mr Brett, Mr Michael Tarleton and Mr Harware, officers for collecting customs at the several ports of Chester and Liverpool, concerning the taking of duties on goods imported on this side of the place called the Red Stones in Wirral which is within the limits of the said port of Liverpool, it was debated and resolved as follows. That Mayor Ogle affirmed that the Red Stones is the place which divides this port and Chester, and that from thence all along the sea side and up to Sankey

Bridge as far as the tide flows all customs duties are payable to the officers of Liverpool, on both sides of the river Mersey. Mr Brett alleged that he knows not how far the liberties reach but that Liverpool had been a member of Chester, and that it is to the advantage of the state that the officers of Hilbre should remain there near to them. Mayor Ogle replied that it is to the advantage of the state if the service is done for a lesser charge by Liverpool, it being but six miles distant from Liverpool, and 16 from Chester. So that it was concluded and resolved by the said officers that all goods landing within the same places shall pay custom at Liverpool and Mr Dormett is required to give notice and stay all goods so landed to be entered in the custom house of Liverpool and that Owner Wright who has herein miscarried be no more employed by them of Chester, but that William Harrison be employed as deputy for both officers, and shall be paid by Mayor Ogle for his service to Liverpool, and by Mr Brett for Chester, and the payments are to be certified each to the other so his wages are not double. Samuel Sandiford, Henry Ogle, John Brett.

Whereas a difference arose between the officers of the customs in Chester and Liverpool as abovesaid in that they of Chester interrupted them of Liverpool in their ancient liberties on the Cheshire side, the whole matter was referred by both of them on 29 November 1658 to Mr Samuel Sandiford, surveyor general of the customs and excise, and he declared that the liberties of Liverpool reach to the accustomed place on the further side of the Red Stones and advised that the corporation of Liverpool should set a Mere stone there to divide the liberties, and that all goods there landed shall pay customs to the offices of the custom house of Liverpool, and so consequently town dues. Samuel Sandiford

p. 691
7 OCTOBER 1659
Ordered by the mayor and major part of the common council that no middingsteads shall be in the streets, but that they shall be removed, paved and kept clear, and every one is to pave their said midingsteeds before 20 May next on pain of 20s. And that all men keep swine according to former orders.

Ordered that Colonel Birch be moved to return speedily to London to exercise his trust as burgess for the parliament, and that he be moved to cause the walls of the castle to be demolished and the trench filled according to votes and order of parliament.

Common Council. Edmund Leivsey, Henry Robinson, Thomas Johnson, John Tompson, nominated and elected and sworn to be of the common council.

Ordered that interrogatories be drawn up and preparation made for executing of the commission against Edward Moore, esq. concerning the liberties of this town, according to notice given, and that Richard Holland be sworn and examined. He can depose that the liberties extend round about the Beacon Heyes and over the Beacon Gutter within the field. And that Mrs Crosse be sent for to produce the boundaries and depositions taken long since in the court of wards. And that in the meantime, Alderman Blackmore, Alderman Massam, and Alderman Andoe do treat with Mr Moore about the composing of those differences in the suit in the high court of Chancery against Mr Thomas Williamson, Mr Gilbert Formby and other defendants.

A warrant was received commanding every one to bring in a note of their arms to Mr Richard Williamson, Mr Marsh, Mr Bushell, Robert Seacome and John Tompson, who are appointed to receive and return the same notes.

p. 692

p. 693
22 OCTOBER 1658. FREEMEN
    28 January 1658
Alexander Horrocks, tailor, late apprentice of Robert Woodward, admitted and sworn a freeman, paying 6s 8d
Thomas Birch admitted by free consent, 40s
John Sadler of Prescot, sworn, 50s
Robert Houghton, collarmaker, sworn, 50s
Henry Robinson, mariner, late apprentice of his father, sworn, 6s 8d
Robert Leadbeater, mariner, sworn, 40s
George Bennett, late apprentice of Roger Harrsion, sworn, 6s 8d
Thomas Holt, son of Gilbert Holt, sworn, 3s 4d
Thomas Dicconson, joiner, 40s, sworn
Richard Jones, son of Roger Jones deceased, sworn, 3s 4d
    14 July 1659
Thomas Wilson, mariner, late apprentice of John Walles, sworn, 6s 8d
William Marshall, late apprentice of Adam Leathes deceased, sworn, 6s 8d
    13 October 1659
William Blackmore, son of Thomas Blackmore, alderman, sworn, 3s 4d
William Mills, mariner, sworn, 40s
John Williamson, mariner, sworn, 20s, 20s refunded
Edward Clarkson, gratis, sworn
    17 January 1658
Samuel Postlethwaite, ironmonger, £7, sworn
    7 March 1658
Josiah Ambrose, clerk, gratis, sworn
John Wareing, gentleman, sworn, gratis
John Stirrup, £6 13s 4d, sworn
Stephen Platt, tallow chandler, £5, sworn
34 16 8[60]

p. 694
28 JANUARY 1658
    Ordered, concerning the town's affairs in London, that a horse and £10 be paid to Alderman Blackmore, burgess for the town, and what more he spends is to be allowed during his attendance in parliament with Colonel Ireland.

---

60   This is the total of freemen fines.

That enquiry be made and search at Drury House to know whether the late Lord Mollineux compounded for Liverpool lordship, it being in his particular. Also, whether Mr James Wainewright purchased any part of the commons within Liverpool and how much he gave for the same.

To advise whether it be requisite to have a confirmation of the making of this town into a parish by parliament.

To cause a reference to the masters of Chancery to have the depositions taken on Mr Moore's part against Gilbert Formby concerning our liberties to be suppressed in Chancery, it being surreptitiously obtained and his sole common illegally issued in a new common name. Commissioners for the town, John Fox esq., Michael Tarleton, Richard Mercer.

That Mr Henry Corles and Mr Sandiford, having made their accounts for the Galway voyage, be discharged and indemnified, the remainder of the rents, being £9 1s 5d, now paid to the bailiffs for the town's use.

Ordered that Captain James Browne shall be accountable to the town for all the money he receives in rents at Galway, and that he shall resign possession of the house there to the mayor and bailiffs, which he took receipt of in July 1658 as agent for this town, and leave it to the corporation.

p. 695
7 OCTOBER 1659, 14 JUNE 1659[61]

At an assembly of the common council held before the mayor, aldermen, bailiffs and major part of the council it was ordered that the present bailiffs shall cause merestones set in the most convenient places about the liberties of this town at the town's charge in such manner as the jury of the next portmoot court shall direct.

Likewise ordered that Mr Mayor and the aldermen shall treat with Mr Moore concerning the present differences between him and the town in relation to the liberties, and shall endeavour to compose the same.

p. 696

THOMAS WILLIAMSON, GENTLEMAN, MAYOR, 1659 [1659–60]

p. 697
ELECTION COURT, TUESDAY 18 OCTOBER 1659, feast of St Luke the Evangelist, for the town and borough of Liverpool, before Richard Peircivall, mayor, John Sturzaker and John Owen, bailiffs.

Thomas Williamson, gentleman, is elected mayor and sworn, by the vote of the burgesses

---

61   Both dates are given.

Thomas Storie is elected chief bailiff for the said mayor and sworn
Edmund Leivsley elected sub-bailiff and sworn.

William Langton, esq., recorder
John Winstanley, town clerk
William Mulliney, serjeant at mace
Robert Seacome, water bailiff

Officers chosen by the common council on Friday after the election according to custom:
John Fogg, minister
George Glover, schoolmaster
John Sturzaker, hall keeper, sworn
Robert Seacome, town customer, sworn
Richard Rogerson, subcustomer, sworn
William Poulton, church clerk and sexton
Thomas Birch, Robert Fleetwood, stewards of the hall and ley gatherers, sworn
Thomas Litherland, heyward, sworn

Officers chosen by the jury, 24 October 1659:
John Owen, Thomas Sandiford, Alexander Greene, Richard Blevine, merchant appraisers
Thomas Roe, James Holte, registers of leather

p. 698
Henry Tarbock, Thomas Tatlock, alefounders, sworn
John Johnson of Everton, Robert Kenion, Richard Scarisbrick, William Ryding, barleymen, sworn 2
Thomas Dicconson, John Williamson, Edward Clarkson, William Millnes, scavengers, sworn 3
James Heyes, William Mosse, overseers of the highways
Humphrey Mercer, murenger
John Sanderson, Peter Walker, porters
Thomas Banks, Richard Rogerson, leavelookers, sworn
William Chorley, Elizabeth Rycroft, boardsetters
Thomas Witter, Thomas Banks, boothsetters
Edward Rydeing, beadle and bellman

Churchwardens elected at Easter:
Thomas Preeson, Thomas Johnson, for 1660

p. 699
INQUISITION TAKEN AT THE PORTMOOT OR QUARTER SESSIONS COURT, MONDAY 24 OCTOBER 1659, before the mayor and bailiffs according to custom.

The jurors for the liberties of England by authority of parliament: John Sturzacre, Henry Corles, John Blundel, Thomas Ashbrooke, Richard Holland, Henry Robinson, Robert Lyon, John Heyes, Thomas Nicholson, John Bancks, Robert Kenion, husbandman, Edward Bancks, Robert Hall, William Midleton, Richard Jones, James Hey, Thomas Tatlocke, Thomas Mosse, John Henshawe, William Fleetwood, Jonathan Gleave, Robert Houghton, Edward Sutton, Richard Rymer.

We present:

Henry Chapman for using the faculty of freeman, not free, 3s 4d

Jane Martin, widow, 3s 4d, William Holland, nil, William Welsh, 3s 4d, for the like

Thomas Aspe, Peter Smyth, Edward Stockley, Edward Fleetcroft, Thomas Barton, Thomas Norland, Richard Edwardson, Thomas Greaves, Edward Greaves, James Morecroft, for buying skins before the market, 2s 6d

James Holt, 6d, Thomas Nicholson, 6d, Henry Cooper, 2s 6d, for working unlawful leather

William Bushell for ten swine unrung, 5s

Mrs Elizabeth Tarleton for one swine unrung, 6d

Margaret Granger for two swine unrung, 1s

John Moneley, tailor, for one swine unrung, 6d

Thomas Storie, Anthony Mayres, Thomas Ashbrooke, Lawrence Breeres, Thomas Andoe, alderman, James Browne, for letting rubbish and muck lie in the streets, 6d

John Sadler for letting a barrel of stinking herring lie in the streets, 1s

Ralph Massam, alderman, William Accars, 1s, Robert Henshawe, 1s, Thomas Bennet, 1s, John Sturzacre, 1s, Thomas Henshawe, 6s, John Bullock, 1s, for tethering in the town field

John Owen for having his beasts and swine in the town field, not on his own, 3s 6d

Orders:

There shall be a cartway by Thomas Preeson's door to the other houses on the west side of the castle, on pain of —s

Mr Edward Alcock to remove his gate which stands on the town's waste near the Castle and set it where it formerly stood within his own fence, and the nook of the wall that stands on the town's waste next to Thomas Preeson's be removed to his own land, 10d

The watercourse on the back side of Robert Barker's house shall pass between that and William Middleton's into the street as formerly, 10s

Dorothy Bicksteth to scour her ditch between her and Anthony Mares in Dale Street, and that she do the like in Tithebarn Street between her and Robert Fleetwood, 10s

William Rymer to make a gutter in Tithebarn Street that the water may drain out of the street, 10s

Robert Fleetwood to make his watercourse on the back of his house in Old Hall Street, and that Thomas Alcock shall do the like next to it, 10s

John Lurtinge, draper, shall make a sough through his chamber for the water to issue down Thomas Andoe's entry in Chapel Street, 10s

The surveyors chosen to see that Tithebarn Lane be mended and the water course pass as formerly at Spring, 10s

Mrs Crosse and Thomas Birch to make a gate for a cart to pass between Middle Mill and Town's Common as formerly, by 1 March, 5s

John Lurting, smith, shall build up the wall between him and Peter Lurting, lineable from the ancient wall to the corner of his house as formerly by the last day of November, 10s

Nehemyah Warton to scour his ditch and lay a plat at his close within the liberties in Kirkdale Lane by 28 February, 5s.

p. 700

No middingsteads to be in the streets, but that they be removed and kept clean and everyone to pave the places before 20 May on pain of 20s apiece levied by the bailiffs on the offenders

All swine to be kept up on Saturdays and Sabbath days according to former order

All carrion found lying on the waterside to be buried at the charge of the owners, and there shall be 2s 6d paid to the informer, 2s 6d to the town, and 20d to those who bury it, to be levied on the goods of the offender

A curfew to be rung according to former order

The bailiffs to see these orders executed on pain of 20s

p. 701

INQUISITION TAKEN AT PORTMOOT COURT OR QUARTER SESSIONS, MONDAY 9 JANUARY 1659, before the mayor and bailiffs according to custom.

Jurors for the keepers of the liberties of England by authority of parliament: Edward Formby, John Lurting, draper, Robert Sutton, William Bushell, William Oliffe, Richard Crompton, John Chambers, Henry Tarbock, William Mills, William Parker, Robert Leadbetter, William Litherland, James Hoult, John Williamson, Thomas Litherland.

We present:

William Leach for using the faculty of a freeman, not free; William Newport, John Cook, Lawrence Williamson, Robert Birt, William Rainforth, William Welsh, William Mallison, Thomas Bicksteth, John Ashton, William Harrison, Thomas Davies, for the like offence, 3s 4d

Captain James Browne for not making up his wall between Richard Crompton and him according to order, nil

Edmund Alcock for not removing his gate and corner of his wall from off the town's waste according to order, notice

John Chandler for having swine unrung, 6d

The barleymen for neglect of office, nil

Alderman Thomas Blackmore for getting clay where the old tithe barn stood, 7d

We order:

All head bolts to be made up and watercourses cleansed and that hedges be cut by 10th of next month, 3s 4d apiece

We present all freemen who did not appear at this portmoot and are not at sea, essoined or excused, 3s 4d

We agree to all ancient orders and laudable customs.

3 NOVEMBER 1659

At an assembly held in the town hall before Mr Mayor, the aldermen, bailiffs and the major part of the common council the election of someone learned in the law was proposed to be recorder of this borough after the death of William Langton esq. On full debate it was resolved and voted that John Leightbourne esq. shall be nominated and appointed recorder of the same town during the pleasure of the same assembly. 2 February 1659 the said Mr Leightbourne was sworn.

p. 702

14 DECEMBER 1659

At an assembly of the common council it is ordered that all merchants and others who shall import herring shall pay for town's custom at the rate of 6 shillings a score.

Ordered that letters be written to friends in Galway to make it known that this corporation is willing to sell or let the houses there before any division is made.

27 MARCH 1660

Apprentice. Memo. that John Christian, son of William Christian, puts himself apprentice to Thomas Christian of Liverpool, merchant, to serve seven years from 1 May 1659 by indenture in that behalf.

Memo. that Thomas Preeson and Thomas Johnson are chosen churchwardens and have received 28s 6d, the balance of the old churchwarden's accounts.

24 AUGUST 1660

Apprentice. Memo. that Francis Meadowcroft, son of Richard Meadowcroft of Brighton was put apprentice to Richard Peircivall of Liverpool, alderman, for seven years by indenture to commence 1 August 1660.

Memo. that Michael Heyes, son of Ellen Heyes, widow, put himself apprentice to Robert Blevine, tailor, for seven years from the date of the indenture, 29 September 1660.

p. 703

CORONER'S INQUEST

Inquisition taken at Liverpool 6 April 1660 before Richard Peircivall, gentleman, mayor and now alderman and coroner for the town, by the oaths of Henry Corles,

Robert Kenion, Robert Lyon, Robert Sympson, William Poultney, Richard Rymer, Richard Jones, James Hoult, Robert Harvey, William Gardner, Edward Suton, Humphrey Mercer, honest and lawful freeman, being a jury sworn to inquire of the death of Henry Halsall. They find that the said Henry being in the stable at Mrs Sandiford's, an inn and hostler there, on 1 April instant about 8 o'clock in the evening, was stricken on the left side of his head by a grey mare of Mrs Alice Eaton of Chester, widow, and part of his brains came forth, whereupon the said Henry Halsall immediately died, which was by misfortune and misadventure.

19 APRIL 1660
Burgesses. Memo. that at an election court for burgesses of parliament the honorable William Stanley esq. and Gilbert Ireland esq. were chosen burgesses to serve in parliament for the borough of Liverpool, George Chetham esq. being then sheriff of this county, 1660.

p. 704
16 FEBRUARY 1659
Concerning lands in Ireland. At an assembly in the town hall before the mayor, Thomas Blackmore, Ralph Massam, Thomas Andoe, Gilbert Formby, Richard Peircivall, the bailiffs and greater part of the common council, it is ordered that Mr Thomas Sandiford, merchant, shall go to Ireland with full power to sell or let any of the houses and lands in Galway which are allotted to this corporation at such rents and rates as he and the undertakers, Mr John Winstanley and his son and Captain James Browne, shall agree to, which shall be confirmed by the mayor and bailiffs accordingly. And they are empowered to receive fines, rents and purchase money arising, and shall pay over a moitie to the said undertakers. And what part remains unsold for the space of a year shall be divided between the corporation and the undertakers, and that Captain Browne should deliver possession of the premises and the papers and the moitie of the money by him received for rents for the same houses in Galway. Thomas Williamson, mayor, Thomas Blackmore, Ralph Massam, Edward Williamson, Thomas Andoe, Gilbert Formbie, Richard Peircivall, Thomas Storie, Edmund Leivsley, bailiffs, John Winstanley, William Mulliney, John Higinson, Richard Williamson, John Sturzaker, Evan Marsh, Peter Lurting, William Rymer, John Blundell, John Lurting, Thomas Ashbrook, Henry Ryding, Henry Robinson, Robert Lyon, Robert Seacome.

p. 705
INQUISITION AT LIVERPOOL IN COUNTY OF LANCASTER, AT THE PORTMOOT COURT OR QUARTER SESSIONS, MONDAY 13 AUGUST, in the 12th year of the reign of King Charles II, according to custom.

The jury for our sovereign lord the king: Edward Formby, John Blundell, Robert Sutton, John Owen, Thomas Chapman junior, George Bennett, Thomas Tatlock, Brian Mercer, John Heyes, Thomas Dicconson, Thomas Roe, Robert Sympson, William Eccleston, John Walker, Thomas Litherland.

We present:

Robert Halle for affronting Mr Mayor in going contrary to his order to shut up Widow Mosse's window, 40s

Thomas Nicholson and Ellen his wife for abusing Mr Bailiff Storie, calling him a cheating knave, 10s

Mr William Kitchins for using the faculty of a freeman, 3s 4d;

Mr John Starkey, Lawrence Williamson, both made free, Edward Bulshawe, 3s 4d, William Harrison, 3s 4d, James Scarisbrick, made free, Thomas Darwine, 3s 4d, all for the like

The barleymen, John Higginson, Robert Kenion, Richard Scarisbrick, William Ryding for neglect of their office, presenting a false bill to this jury, 6d apiece

John Williamson in Castle Street for refusing the office of scavenger, 3s 4d

William Seacome for letting his fence lie down from the Breck into the town field, 1s

William Henshawe, John Rose, William Gorsuch for the like, 1s apiece

Thomas Henshawe for growning other men's grass in the town field, 1s

Thomas Plombe the younger and Roger Part's wife for leaving the townfield gate open, 6d apiece

John Williamson of Castle Street for letting muck lie in the street, 6d; Richard Rymer for the like, 6d; Mrs Margaret Williamson, Hugh Turner, Mrs Elizabeth Tarleton, Lawrence Jumper, Margery Tarleton, widow, John Lurting, draper, all for the like, 6d apiece

William Mosse for his cart standing in the street, 1s

Richard Holland for bringing unlawful leather to the town, and Henry Cooper for the like offence, 2s apiece

All those who sell ale or beer not licensed by mayor: John Higginson, Mrs Williams, widow, Robert Kenion, husbandman, Robert Kenion, cooper, John Sutton, Richard Browne, Richard Rymer, Edward Sutton, Thomas Scale, Thomas Andoe, 2s apiece

We order:

That all freemen that have inmates shall give bond to save the town harmless from any charge, before the 29 September, on pain of 10s, and that some of Mr Mayor's officers give them notice

The plat in Tithebarn Lane be amended by the same time, 10s

Dorothy Bicksteth to cleanse her water course between her and the old joiner, 5s

We agree to all ancient laws and laudable customs.

p. 706
COMPOSITIONS

Memo. Ordered that Mr Alexander Greene, merchant, pay for 18½ tuns of wine at 4s the tun, in the *Ruth*, £3 14s

Memo. Mr Breeres for Spanish wines, 7½ tuns, 30s, 7 of which tuns came from Bristol and paid duty there, 16s due

Mr Thomas Sandiford to pay for 2 hogsheads of decayed wines, 2s

20 AUGUST 1660

Memo. At an Assembly in the town hall before the mayor, aldermen and greater part of the common council, it was ordered that the fee farm rent of £14 6s 8d lately purchased by the town shall be granted to the kings majesty by a grant under the town's seal, with a humble address, and that Gilbert Formby, alderman, shall go to London about it and proceed therein as our burgesses shall advise.

p. 707
FREEMEN
    20 April 1660:
Charles Stanley, earl of Derby was admitted a freeman, sworn
James Lord Murrey, earl of Athol, sworn
William Stanley, esq., sworn, and also elected a burgess of parliament for the borough
Edward Moore, esq., sworn
John Murrey, esq., sworn
John Greenhalgh, clerk, sworn
John Breeres, gentleman, sworn
Fardinando Calcott, gratis, sworn
    16 February 1659:
John Cook, sailor, sworn, 40s
    1 May 1660:
Thomas Alcock, late apprentice to Edward Alcock, sworn, 6s 8d
William Williamson, mariner, son of John Williamson, sworn, 3s 4d
Thomas Sharpe, late apprentice of Edward Williamson, alderman, sworn, 6s 8d
    14 May 1660:
George Prenton, mariner, late apprentice of Gilbert Formby, alderman, sworn, 6s 8d
John Rymer, sailor, late apprentice of Richard Williamson, 6s 8d
    20 August 1660:
John Starkey, gent., sworn, gratis
Richard Williamson, chirurgeon, sworn, 40s
Lawrence Williamson, mariner, sworn, 40s
William Welsh, mariner, sworn, 40s
William Rainford, late apprentice of Edward Tarleton, deceased, sworn, 6s 8d
Edward Flitcroft, skinner, sworn, £3
James Scarisbrick, blockmaker, apprentice of John Sutton, sworn 6s 8d
    17 October 1660:
John Rymer, ropemaker, apprentice of Richard Leivsey, deceased, sworn, 6s 8d
    25 September 1660:
Cuthbert Ogle, esq., sworn
    12 October 1660:
John Case, gent., gratis, sworn
John Bramhall, doctor of theology, Bishop of Derry, nominated primate of Armagh, sworn, gratis

Sir James Graham, knight, sworn, gratis
Thomas Bramhalle, doctor in physick, sworn, gratis
Matthew Didsworth, gent., and John Goghill, gent, sworn, gratis
Henry Byrom sworn, £4
William Watnough, sworn, £4

p. 708

ALEXANDER GREENE, MAYOR, [1660–61]

p. 709
ELECTION COURT FOR THE TOWN AND BOROUGH OF LIVERPOOL IN COUNTY OF LANCASTER, 18 OCTOBER 12 CHARLES II, on the feast of St Luke the Evangelist, before Thomas Williamson, mayor, Thomas Storie, Edmund Leivsley, bailiffs, according to custom, 1660.

Alexander Greene, gentleman, is elected mayor by the freemen, sworn
Evan Marsh chosen by Mr Mayor to be chief bailiff, sworn
John Pemberton elected sub-bailiff, sworn. John Pemberton on 19 October elected and sworn one of the common council.

John Winstanley, town clerk
William Mulliney, serjeant at mace
Robert Seacome, water bailiff

   Officers chosen at common council on Friday next following:
John Leightbourne esq., recorder
John Fogg, minister
George Glover, schoolmaster
William Poultney, church clerk
John Sturzaker, hall keeper, sworn
Robert Seacome, town customer, sworn
Richard Rogerson, subcustomer, sworn
Richard Jones and George Bennett, stewards of the hall and ley gatherers, sworn

   Officers elected by the grand jury:
John Sturzaker, John Lurting, Edmund Leivsley, John Tompson, merchant appraisers, sworn

p. 710
Thomas Nicholson, Edward Horrobine, registers of leather
Samuel Postlethwaite, John Griffiths, alefounders, sworn
William Watmough, Edward Flitcrofte, James Scarisbrick, John Rymer, sailor, scavengers

John Holland, John Henshawe, William Gretton, John Mullney, tailor, barleymen, sworn

Thomas Banks, Richard Rogerson, leavelookers, sworn

Edward Tyrer, John Kenion, overseers of the highways

Robert Johnson, murenger

John Sanderson, Peter Walker, porters

William Chorley, Elizabeth Rycroft, boardsetters

Thomas Witter, Thomas Banks, boothsetters

Edward Ryding, beadle and bellman

Churchwardens, Ralph Hall, William Fleetwood

p. 711

INQUISITION AT LIVERPOOL IN COUNTY OF LANCASTER, MONDAY 22 OCTOBER, 12 CHARLES II, AT THE GREAT PORTMOOT COURT OR QUARTER SESSIONS, before the mayor and bailiffs according to custom.

The jury for our sovereign lord the King: Thomas Storie, Thomas Sandiford, William Bushell, Robert Lyon, John Walles, John Tompson, James Hoult, John Johnson, William Eccleston, Robert Harvie, Edward Banks, William Parker, John Poultney, Thomas Birch, Thomas Andoe, Jonathan Gleave, Thomas Tatlock, Thomas Litherland, Samuel Postlethwaite, Thomas Dicconson, Alexander Horrocks, Thomas Seale, Henry Tarbock, Humphrey Mercer, honest and lawful freemen.

We present:

Cuthbert Culshawe for a tussle on John Kenion

John Kenion for a tussle on Cuthbert Culshawe

William Kerbie, William Robinson, Richard Bushell, Timothy Tarleton, Edward Barton, William Leech, Edward Balshawe, Esther Hardman, Thomas Robinson, Thomas Bicksteth, Robert Blevine, William Harrison, John Roson, for using the faculty of freemen, not free

Thomas Asp, Edward Stockley, John Glover, Henry Dey, Peter Smith, James Morecrofte, for buying skins before the market

Henry Cooper, James Hoult, Thomas Nicholson, Thomas Roe, for working unlawful leather

Edward Alcock, Lawrence Williamson, John Williamson, Robert Halle, William Accars, John Heyes, Thomas Coppull, Henry Tarbock, John Lunte, Peter Walker, John Higinson, Alexander Horrocks, John Williamson, Dorothie Bicksteth, Margaret Bicksteth, Elinor Loy, Elizabeth Tarleton, John Starkey, for keeping swine unwrung

John Williamson, Edward Clarkson, William Millnes, scavengers, for neglect of their office

Thomas Dey for breaking open the pinfold

All freemen that have not appeared nor essoyned nor are excused by the court, 3s 4d apiece:

p. 712
Thomas Shepard, Henry Moore, Henry Ogle, Edward Stockley, Thomas Blackburne, Richard Hockenhull, Robert Ireland, Edward Gerrard, John Sorrocold, Andrew Ashton, Edward Ogle, John Ashurst, Henry Rolline, Humphrey Webster, Henry Webster, Thomas Radcliffe, Henry Radcliffe, Richard Walker, Thomas Gardner, Henry Ambrose, Henry Kilshawe, Darbie Caton, Thomas Lancellott, Alexander Moore, Edward Lea, James Hey, Henry Ashton, Hugh Revinghead, Richard Halliwell, William Fazakerley, John Breeres, William Williamson, for the like.

We order:
Edward Alcock to cause the ditch alongside his croft in Tithebarn Lane to be scoured so that the ancient watercourse have free passage, and the overseers to cause the middle of the highway in that lane to be filled and paved at the town's charge before the 1 May on paid of 10s

John Higinson to cleanse his watercourse between his barn and John Lurting's house in Old Hall Street before 10 November, 10s

Thomas Alcock to remove his coals and cleanse the ancient watercourse in his back side between him and Robert Fleetwood's house before 15 November, 10s

John Lurting to lay a gutterstone between his two houses in Chapel Street to carry the water to Thomas Andoe's entry so that it may not be any further annoyance to him, before 1 November, 10s

The sexton to cause the church to be clean and kept in good and decent order, and to brush down the cobwebs and windows, and to ring curfew at the accustomed time.

We agree to all ancient orders and laudable customs.

p. 713
INQUISITION TAKEN AT PORTMOOT COURT OR QUARTER SESSIONS AT LIVERPOOL IN COUNTY OF LANCASTER, 28 JANUARY 12 CHARLES II, 1660, before the mayor and bailiffs, according to custom.

Jury for our sovereign lord the King: Edmund Leivsley, John Blundell, Thomas Ashbrook, John Wareing, Robert Harvie, Richard Crompton, Robert Eccles, Richard Holland, John Sadler, Thomas Nicholson, William Chantrell, Thomas Coppull, John Holland, William Watmough, John Griffith.

We present:
Richard Widdowes for offering to take away the lives of Alice the wife of Thomas Bancks, Dorothy Kenion, wife of Robert Kenion, Elizabeth Aspinwall, spinster, and for casting a coal of fire into a cartload of hay coming to the market

Elinor Loy for threatening to take the life of her son, Thomas, his wife, and for cursing her son, wishing him to perish at sea, which is a hindrance to his lawful calling, and other harm done to them

William Litherland for abusing William Leach on the sabbath about 1 or 2 o'clock in the morning and for being drunk at the time

Percivall Holme for being drunk in William Litherland's house at the same time

John Williamson of Castle Street for a tussle on John Craine

John Craine for a tussle on John Williamson

William Leach, Robert Blevine, Esther Hardman, John Roson, Margaret Granger, Richard Bushell, Timothy Tarleton, Thomas Bicksteth, Edward Balshawe, Mrs Alice Chatterton, William Robinson, Edward Barton, William Harrison, Thomas Robinson, Ellen Pearle, Thomas Taylor, Jeffrey Clarkson, Susan Chapman, Henry Hardman, for using the faculty of freemen, not being free

John Owen, Thomas Story, Margaret Granger, Edward Alcock, Elizabeth Clark, William Bushell, John Higginson, Dorothy Sandiford, John Sutton, for swine being unrung

Edward Alcock for not removing the corner of his wall and his gate at the Castle according to former order

Samuel Postlethwaite for denying assistance to his partner in the office of aletaster

Margaret Williamson, widow, and Elizabeth Tarleton, for letting rubbish lie in the streets

Mr John Winstanley for stopping the highway with clay and stones in Tithebarn Lane

p. 714

We order:

That all who have any inmates shall come before 25 March to give bond to the town and that Mr Mayor appoint two of his officers to go through the town to give them notice, on pain of 20s

Bailiff Marsh to open his ditch that the water may pass into Bailiff Higginson's ditch in Tithebarn Street before 24 February, 3s 4d

Bailiff Higginson to make up his fence and cleanse his ditch falling from Bailiff Marsh's ditch in Tithebarn Street before 1 March, 3s 4d

Dorothy Bicksteth to scour her ditch in Tithebarn Street before 1 March, 3s 4d

Robert Sutton to scour his ditch on the other side of Tithebarn Street before 1 March, 3s 4d

A water course to be made at the end of Dorothy Brockbank's house as formerly

Mrs Margaret Williamson to remove her principles between her and Dorothy Brookbank, six inches from Brookbank's gable

The stoop of Thomas Birch's gate, next to Mr Winstanley's land in Tithebarn Lane, to be moved nearer Thomas Birche's land before 1 March, 5s

Ellen Blevine to make up her fence between her and John Heyes before 25 March, 3s 4d

Robert Henshawe to make a gutter over Crosse Butts at Sickman's Lane end by Thursday next

All fences and headbolts to be made up by 14 February, 3s 4d

The mayor, aldermen and bailiffs, town clerk and serjeant at mace have gowns made by Easter Day, £5 apiece

We agree to all ancient laws and laudable customs

Herrings. Ordered that all herrings imported in the ensuing year shall pay for licences or composition, for every score, 6s 8d

p. 715
22 NOVEMBER 1660
At an Assembly before the lord mayor, Mr Alderman Blackmore, the aldermen, bailiffs and greater number of the common council:

It was ordered concerning the suit in the duchy commenced against the mayor, bailiffs and some others: (1) that Mr John Case, Michael Tarleton, Thomas Sandiford, and John Winstanley shall be named commissioners for taking the defendants' answers if need require; (2) that Mr Mayor and the alderman or any three of more of them may meet with Lord Mollineux or his commissioners to treat with them on the town's behalf; (3) that the duty of butlerage shall be demanded from merchants and owners who are chargeable to pay the same for the use of the town and Colonel Shuttleworth and Mr Humphrey Kelshall who has the deed of purchase.

Memo. January 31 an order was agreed for making an agreement with Lord Mollineux as followeth.

Memo. that John Harrison, son of William Harrison, was apprenticed to William Harrison of Liverpool, glasier, for 7 years to commence from 1 May 1660.

p. 716
FREEMEN
31 January 1660:
Samuel Birch admitted free, paying £10, sworn
13 February 1660:
William Bailie, carpenter, 40s, sworn
William Travis, gunsmith, 40s, sworn
William Sympson, 40s, sworn
James Collier, gent., gratis, sworn
Thomas Hoghton, gent., gratis, sworn
21 February 1660:
Richard Bradshaw of Manchester, £10, sworn
Thomas Weaver, gent., gratis, sworn
Thomas Greene of Manchester, gratis, sworn, promised a piece of plate to the town
Henry Ambrose, practioner in physick, gratis, sworn
John Melling, son of John Melling late freeman, 3s 4d
Robert Blevine, son — Blevine, once freeman, 3s 4d

Memo. That Evan Marsh, nominated bailiff and refusing to serve was committed to prison in the town hall on 18 October 1660 by warrant signed by mayor, and continued that day, and the same night he consented to take his oath and was released.

Thomas Andoe, alderman, for not appearing at an assembly on 31 February, fined 3s 4d; Edward Alcock, John Owen, William Bushell for the like offence fined 3s 4d apiece.

William Price, cutler, admitted free, £4

Edmund Parr, gent., gratis
John Francis, gent., gratis
Thomas Lathom, gent., gratis

p. 717
21 APRIL 1661
Election court for choosing two burgesses for parliament beginning at Westminster on 8 May next, coming by warrant from Sir George Midleton, knt. and baronet, high sheriff of the county palatine of Lancaster, to serve for the town of Liverpool, according to His Majesty's writ. The honorable William Stanley esq., and the right worshipful Gilbert Ireland of Hutt in the said county, knt., were elected and by indentures certified accordingly.

30 OCTOBER 1660
At an Assembly in the town hall before the mayor, aldermen, bailiffs and greater number of the common council, it was ordered that the two burgesses of parliament, together with Captain James Browne and Mr John Winstanley or his son, shall be authorised to sell all the town's interest in Ireland lately given them by act of parliament, to any persons as they have opportunity to sell, to the town's best advantage, which agreement this assembly will ratify as occasion shall require.

FREEMEN SWORN BEFORE THE MAYOR, 14 OCTOBER 1661
Robert Seacome, gent., admitted, gratis
James Lideate, gratis
James Jerram of Childwall, £6
Nathan Gleave, £4
William Kichins, merchant, paid by plate
Richard Eccleston, son Thomas Eccleston late alderman, 3s 4d
John Roson, tailor, son William Roson, 3s 4d
Anthony Dunbabine, apprentice of John Sturzaker, 6s 8d
Michael Jenkinson, 40s
William Leech, tailor, 40s

p. 718

HENRY CORLES, GENTLEMAN, MAYOR [1661–62]

p. 719
ELECTION COURT FOR BOROUGH OF LIVERPOOL IN COUNTY OF LANCASTER, FRIDAY 18 OCTOBER, 13 CHARLES II, the feast of St Luke the Evangelist, before Alexander Greene, gent., mayor, Evan Marsh and John Pemberton, bailiffs, according to custom and charters, 1661.

Henry Corles, gent., is elected mayor by the freemen and burgeses, sworn
John Chandler is chosen by the said Mr Mayor to be chief bailiff, sworn
William Blakmore is elected by the freemen and burgeses to be the other bailiff, sworn.

John Leightbourne, esq., recorder
John Winstanley, town clerk
William Mulliney, serjeant at mace
Robert Seacome, water bailiff

    Officers chosen by the common council:
John Fogg, clerk, minister
George Glover, schoolmaster
William Poultney, church clerk
John Sturzaker, hallkeeper, sworn
Robert Seacome, town customer, sworn
Richard Rogerson, subcustomer, sworn
Thomas Alcock, Thomas Bridge, stewards of the hall and ley gatherers, sworn
Thomas Coppull, heyward, sworn

p. 720
Thomas Storie, John Blundell, John Pemberton, Henry Ryding, merchant appraisers
Nathan Gleave, William Watmough, alefounders, sworn
William Accars, Cuthbert Holland, registers of leather, sworn
Thomas Dicconson, William Sympson, Edward Banks, Edward Flitcrofte, barleymen, sworn
John Rosonn, sworn, William Leech, sworn, John Rymmer, Anthony Dunbabin, scavengers
John Banks, Kirkdale, Jonathan Gleave, overseers of the highway
Thomas Litherland, murenger
Peter Walker, John Sanderson, porters
Thomas Banks, Richard Rogerson, leavelookers, sworn
William Chorley, Elizabeth Rycroft, boardsetters
Thomas Witter, Thomas Banks, boothsetters
Edward Rydeing, beadle and bellman

28 OCTOBER 1661
    John Chandler, bailiff, is also elected and sworn one of the common council.

p. 721
INQUISITION TAKEN AT LIVERPOOL IN COUNTY OF LANCASTER, MONDAY 28 OCTOBER 13 CHARLES II, AT THE PORTMOOT COURT OR QUARTER SESSIONS OF THE PEACE before the mayor and bailiffs, according to custom.

The jury for our sovereign lord the King: Evan Marsh, John Owen, Thomas Ashbrook, Edmund Leivsley, John Walls, Thomas Preeston, Thomas Alcock, John Johnson, Richard Eccleston, Thomas Roe, John Ecles, Robert Harvie, James Hoult, Samuel Postlethwaite, Thomas Johnson, John Melling, John Sadler, Thomas Nicholson, Edward Flitcroft, John Holland, Robert Houghton, Nathan Gleave, James Hey, Thomas Copull.

We present:
Anne the wife of William Oliffe for a tussle and bloodwipe on Anne Royle, widow
Anne Royle for a tussle on Anne Oliffe
Simon Arrowsmith, William Robinson, Timothy Tarleton, Edward Barton, Edward Balshawe, William Blundell, William Brewrton, Jane Eccleston, widow, Margaret Granger, Thomas Norburie, Esther Hardman, widow, Thomas Bicksteth, William Harrison, Cuthbert Kilshawe, John Alcock, Timothy Houlte, Elline Pearle, widow, Alice Chatterton, John Burton, for using the faculty of freemen not free
Peter Smith, Edward Stockley, James Morecroft, John Glover, Thomas Norland, Thomas Barton, Thomas Aspe, for buying skins before the market
Thomas Nicholson, Edward Horrobine, Thomas Roe, James Hoult, Henry Cooper, Thomas Fazakerley, Richard Tompson, Thomas Goulden, for working unlawful leather
William Accars for cutting leather before it was sealed
Cuthbert Culsheth for calling Richard Rogerson, subcustomer, a knave and a bangbeggar
Richard Crompton for refusing toll for 5 sacks of corn from Cheshire, saying that Richard Rogerson had taken toll who had not
Dorothy Johnson, widow for 3 swine unrung; William Gardner for 4; Thomas Andoe, sailor, for 2; Mr John Fogg for 1; Dorothy Bicksteth for 1; Thomas Gallaway for 6; Richard Rymer for 3; Dorothy Sandiford for 1; William Bushell for 1; Mr John Winstanley for 1; Alice Jones, widow, for 1
David Halle, foreigner, for getting turf on this side of the quarries; John Everard for the like
Dorothy, wife of William Ryding and their daughter for cutting of John Johnson's quickwood on Salton's Moor
The said Dorothy Ryding and her daughter for abusing the said John Johnson, calling him rogue and rascal, and saying he had nothing to do there

p. 722
Alderman Thomas Blakmoore for letting his wood lie in the street; Mr Alexander Greene for the like
Mrs Margaret Williamson, widow, for not dressing the street over against the shop; Captain Edward Tarleton's tenants for the house in Chapel Street for the like; John Lurting, draper, William Halsall, Gregory Formby, Richard Mercer, mariner, George Thorpe, Thomas Scarisbrick for the like offence; John Higginson for the like
William Chorley and Elizabeth Rycroft for not dressing market

Thomas Banks and his partners for not cleaning the corn market place

Samuel Postlethwaite and John Griffith, alefounders, for neglect of office

Mrs Margaret Williamson for contempt of former order concerning a nuisance to Mr Chandler

Robert Hey of Ormskirk for selling his meat and not bringing the skins to the market as by statute

The aldermen and bailiffs for the last year, the town clerk and serjeant at mace, for not wearing gowns

All freemen who have not made appearance at this court, nor essoyned nor excused.

We order:

Mr Mayor and the aldermen and bailiffs, the town clerk and serjeant at mace to provide themselves with gowns before 5 December

William Poultney to make a fence between him and Elizabeth Birchall before 2 February

No carter to go over another man's cable unless he give notice on pain of 3s 4d (for them to lay a bar)

Men allow swine to come into streets on market or sabbath days on pain of 12d for every swine

Edward Ryding, beadle and bellman to ring the yarn market bell every Saturday by 10 o'clock

All who entertain any inmates either to give security for the same inmates, or give their names to Mr Mayor by 25 December on penalty of 20s for each inmate

The bailiffs to give notice of aforesaid order to every one who entertains any strangers before 17th of next month on pain of 40s

The sexton to keep the church in clean and decent order and to ring curfew at the accustomed time

The stewards of the hall to inquire for the fire hooks belonging to the town, and to be provided at the town's charge

We agree to all ancient orders and laudable customs, 1661.

p. 723

INQUISITION AT LIVERPOOL IN COUNTY OF LANCASTER AT PORTMOOT COURT OR QUARTER SESSIONS, MONDAY 13 JANUARY 13 CHARLES II, before mayor and bailiffs, according to ancient custom.

Jury for our sovereign lord the King: John Pemberton, Thomas Storie, John Lurting, Brian Mercer, Thomas Tatlock, William Accars, William Sympson, William Leech, William Mills, Anthony Carr, Edward Banks, Edward Horrobine, John Rymer, Roper, Thomas Copull, Edward Carr, honest and lawful men.

We present:

William Litherland for a tussle on William Leech

William Leech for the like on William Litherland

Edward Harrison, Thomas Paterick, William Harrison, Esther Hardman, Alice Chatterton, William Bruerton for using the faculty of freemen not free

John Johnson of Ormskirk for working unlawful leather

Thomas Scarisbrick for breaking the assize of bread in making it not weight; Edward Horrobine, Mary Buckley, Ellen Hacking for the like offence

John Griffith for laying timber in the street

William Mosse for setting his cart in the street

William Gardner for keeping two swine unrung

Mr John Winstanley for not delivering the orders to the bailiffs made the last court that they might give an account to Mr Mayor of inmates.

We order:

Alderman Blackmore to remove timber and rubbish lying before his door before 1 February, on pain of 3s 4d

Anthony Moyries to remove his rubbish lying in the street by the same time, 3s 4d

Mr Crompton to cause a watercourse to be made according to former order between John Roson and him before 1 May, 10s

Mr John Higinson to cleanse his ditch at Cowpedale and to make a gutter over it as formerly, by 1 February; the same Higinson to scour his ditch in Sickman's Lane by the same time, 6s 8d apiece

All fences and headbolts to be made up by 14 February

We agree to all ancient orders and laudable customs, 1661

p. 724

30 DECEMBER 1661

At an assembly before the mayor, Thomas Blackmore, Thomas Williamson, Ralph Massam, Edward Williamson, Thomas Andoe, Gilbert Formby, Richard Peircevall, Alexander Greene, aldermen, William Blackmore one of the bailiffs and the greater number of the common council, concerning the claim made by the right honourable Lord Mollineux of £20 a year over and above the burgage rents due to his Majesty, out of which £20 it was conceived that the said burgage rent of £14 6s 8d ought to have been paid by him, according to a late agreement between him and some of the aldermen, but which is now denied, it was ordered that Mr Mayor and such of the aldermen as did formerly treat shall go to Lord Mollineux and treat with him further and endeavour to rectify that mistake.

25 SEPTEMBER 1662

At an assembly it was ordered that the burgage rents be collected by the bailiffs and paid to Lord Mollineux all but for one half year, and that the arrears of the tenants who refuse to pay shall be returned to his officers, and a transcript of the town's rental should be made, him paying for the same.

30 DECEMBER 1661

It was ordered that a pump shall be made and placed in the street end near the water side, over against the Tower for the use of shipping if the spring there be found good, and the charge allowed by the town.

It is also ordered that William Houlme, whose widow, now dead, was formerly the relict of Richard Barker, shall compound with the town for the house and premises he is now in possession of, or else the same be seized. And John Williamson who is said to make some claim to the inheritance shall make out his title, if he have any, or be debarred.

It is also ordered that letters be written to Mr Henry Waddington concerning the town's interest in Galway, and that he would inform himself of Captain Browne's receipts of rents and his other proceedings there, that course may be taken to bring him to an account for the whole that the town and his partner, Mr Winstanley, may be satisfied.

p. 725
3 JUNE 1662
At an assembly of the common council:

It was ordered that the mayor and bailiffs make a letter of attorney to some special friends in Ireland to enable them to call Captain James Browne to account for money received , and concerning his other transactions on behalf of this corporation in Galway.

Ordered that Lord Mollineux have a copy of the town's rental of the burgage rents.

Ordered that security, according to the statute, be required from all inmates, their landlords, or proceeded against according to law.

Ordered that goods and debts belonging to Philip Cock, late deceased, be taken into safe custody, and provision made for his children's education and advantage by the mayor and bailiffs, and an account be kept and yearly shown in the town's account.

Ordered that a ley of £60 be assessed on the inhabitants and foreign burgesses for the repair of the chapel in this town, and those who refuse be denied the benefit of their freedom.

Ordered that the streets and highways in the liberties of this corporation be repaired and that country carts be sought for assistance in the work which the overseers are to see done.

22 AUGUST 1662
At an assembly of the mayor, bailiffs and the major part of the common council:

It is ordered that Thomas Storie and John Pemberton shall go to Ormskirk to confer with Mr Heyward.

John Hawney to be admitted free, paying for his composition, £8

28 OCTOBER 1662
A warrant for three month's assessment for the raising of £932 6s 8d, £233 6s 8d for the county, £4 6s 5½d in this town, beginning 10 July 1661.

p. 726
20 JANUARY 1661
At an assembly before the mayor, bailiffs and greater part of the common council:

It was ordered that the yearly rent of £20 agreed by Mr Mayor to Lord Mollineux be duly paid according to the said agreement at or before Michaelmas next, at which time the agreement expires.

Also ordered that those who keep stalls in the market and refuse to pay a penny a day toll shall have goods distrained for the toll.

30 OCTOBER 1662
At an assembly held before the mayor, aldermen, bailiffs and the greater part of the aldermen:

It was ordered that there shall be 20s for every sabbath day allowed to any minister who shall officiate here during the vacancy.

It was also ordered that the Pool Bridge shall be repaired and the way there amended and that the inhabitants of Toxteth Park be asked to assist with their teams and servants.

p. 727
INQUISITION HELD IN LIVERPOOL IN COUNTY OF LANCASTER AT PORTMOOT COURT OR SESSION OF THE PEACE, MONDAY 15 SEPTEMBER 14 CHARLES, before the mayor and bailiffs, according to custom.

Jury for our sovereign lord the King: Edward Formby, William Rymer, John Owen, Thomas Alcock, Thomas Johnson, Robert Fleetwood, Robert Sympson, William Watmough, William Fleetwood, Edward Flitcroft, Jonathan Gleave, William Litherland, Cuthbert Holland, John Roson, Anthony Dunbabine, honest and lawful men.

We present:
   Margaret, wife of Cuthbert Culshaw for a tussle on Ellen Dingle, 3s 4d.
   Ellen Dingle for the like, 3s 4d
   William Williamson for tussle on Timothy Tarleton, 3s 4d
   Timothy Tarleton for the like, 3s 4d
   Elizabeth Walker, wife of Peter Walker, for tussle on Margaret Plomb, 3s 4d
   Margaret Plomb, wife of Thomas Plomb, for the like, 3s 4d
   John Syer of Kirkdale junior, for tussle on Robert Mercer, 3s 4d
   Robert Mercer of Ryce Lane for the like on John Syer, 3s 4d
   Simon Arrowsmith, William Robinson, Edward Barton, Edward Balshawe, William Blundell, William Bruerton, Jane Eccleston, widow, Margaret Granger, Thomas Norburie, Esther Hardman, widow, Thomas Bicksteth, Henry Fazakerley, Arthur Hatton, Joseph Keele, William Harrison, Cuthbert Culshawe, John Alcocke, Timothy Hoult, widow, Ellen Pearle, widow, Mrs Alice Chatterton, John Burton, Robert Burton, Richard Windle, Henry Croste, Richard Lurting, John Hawney, ironmonger, Thomas Patterick, for using the faculty of a freemen, 3s 4d apiece
   Peter Smith for buying skins before the market time, 3s 4d; Edward Stockley, John Glover, Thomas Barton, James Morecroft, Thomas Norland, 2s; Thomas Aspe, 2d; Richard Edwardson, all for the like offence

Thomas Rose of Huyton for working unlawful leather, 2s; John Johnson, Henry Cowper, for the like, 2s apiece

John Poultney for drawing beer without a licence, 2s 6d; Joan Potter, Margaret Granger, Margaret Birch, widow, for the like

Edward Moore esq. for letting a millstone lie in the middle of the street

William Poultney for contempt in not obeying former order

p. 728

Alexander Greene, alderman, for two swine unrung

Margaret Granger for the like

John Cancett for getting turf in the liberties of the town

John Celly for getting turf for his own use, not being free

We present him for selling turf to foreigners

Brian Webster and John Hill for the like

Henry Knowles for getting turf not being free

Thomas Duke for getting five loads of turf on this side of the hill

Henry Ryding for selling beer by unlawful measure; John Rymer and Thomas Holland for the like

Henry Ryding for not cleansing the street before the tithebarn; Joseph Wilson for the like

Nathan Glave for making a midding in the street; Anthony Mearis for the like

William Mosse for setting his cart and a midding in the street

William Chorley for neglecting to cleanse the market place; Elizabeth Rycroft, Thomas Witter, Thomas Banks, Ann Ryding for the like

John Sturzaker for lesowing his horse on other men's ground; John Owen, bailiff, Roger Heyes, John Rose, for the like

We order:

That all who entertain inmates shall bring their names to the mayor by 29 September, on pain of 20s

We present:

All landlords or landladies who entertain inmates for disobeying former order

Margaret Culshawe for a common drunkard and an eavesdropper, and abusing Robert Kenion's wife

George Smith, ferryman, for taking cattle at the park side and hindering the town of the toll

Thomas Pudder and his son, Robert, for taking cattle out of the town over the water, not paying toll

We order:

Joan Carter, widow, to cleanse her water course as far as her land goes

William Gardner to make a channel on his back side after Mrs Tarleton's house side to cast the water of her house side

William Bultney to make up fence between Elizabeth Berchall, widow, on his own land by 29 September 1662, 13s 4d

John Higginson, bailiff, to cleanse his ditch in Sickman's lane by 19 September, 13s 4d

Richard Holland to cleanse his ditch in Sickman's Lane by 19 September, 6s 8d

Peter Lurting to open the water course in Ditchfield's Croft by 19 September, 6s 8d

Anthoney Mearis make a passment at the end of Alice Shourrice's house and a channel and remove all the timber out of the ditch and scour it by 16 October, 13s 4d

Jonathan Hunter make up Mrs Woodsis' wall which he pulled down, and make a gutter as formerly, by 16 October, 6s 8d

All who keep swine to keep them up on market day and sabbath day, 12d for every swine taken on those days

We agree to all ancient and laudable customs.

p. 729
6 JANUARY 13 CHARLES, 1661

At an assembly before the mayor and all the aldermen, bailiffs absent, there being an Admiralty Court intended, and divers freemen of the town summoned to serve on the jury, it was ordered that Mr Mayor and the aldermen treat with the Chester men and offices of the vice admiralty, and tell them that it is an infringement of our charter to raise a jury here.

It is also ordered that a meeting be held on Friday 17 January with Mr Hawarden and Mr Nicholas Fazakerley about the differences between the corporation and Lord Mollineux because he denies the agreement lately made to accept £20 per annum, and out of that to pay the burgage rent, and that Mr Mayor, Mr Greene and Mr Sandiford shall go to settle that affair and rectify the mistake.

3 MARCH 1661

At an assembly before Mr Mayor, Mr Blackmore, Thomas Williamson, Ralph Massam, Edward Williamson, Thomas Andoe, Richard Peircivall, the bailiffs and most of the common council:

A letter from Mr Leightbourne, the recorder of this town, was read, whereby he freely resigns his place because of infirmity, and asks Mr Mayor to proceed to a new election, whereupon this assembly unanimously chose John Entwisle, esq. to be recorder during the pleasure of this house, and he shall receive the accustomed fee, and he was accordingly sworn a freemen and one of the common council and recorder.

Ordered that John Mason pay for composition for 40 maze and 26 barrels of herrings in the ship —, 13s 4d

9 OCTOBER 1662

Whereas it was lately ordered concerning Philip Cock's children, that the mayor and bailiffs should take care to provide for them, on better consideration it is now ordered that the churchwardens and overseers, viz. Ralph Halle and William Fleetwood, shall take care to provide for the children and receive their goods and money from Mr Christian or any other debtor, and dispose the same for their education and maintenance, their parents and friends being all deceased. And they shall account to every other churchwarden and overseer yearly, and they are to be kept harmless and indemnified by this house concerning the same.

Also ordered that Richard Williamson, the chirurgeon, shall be recompensed for the cure of the poor man who was wounded by the fall of the chimney, as the mayor can agree.

Ordered that Robert Sutton be discharged from all interest due the town on the bond given by him for the arrears of Henry Moore.

Ordered that Thomas Norris esq. shall be admitted a freeman, gratis, sworn.

p. 730
FREEMEN ADMITTED AND SWORN IN THE TIME OF HENRY CORLES, MAYOR
  22 August 1662:
Joseph Wilson, £6 13s 4d
Lawrence Brownelowe, gent. gratis
Robert Murrey, gratis
John Mercer, gratis
Daniel Trioche, gratis
Richard Fox, gratis
  25 September 1662:
Thomas Peak, £10
Thomas Worthington, physician, £6 13s 4d
John Alcock, mariner, apprenticed, 6s 8d
  9 October 1662:
Josias Fogg, late apprentice, 6s 8d
Abraham Sanderson, late apprentice, 6s 8d, mort
Thomas Blundell, late apprentice, 6s 8d[62]
Edward Litherland and John Litherland, late apprentices, 6s 8d each
William Robinson, shoemaker, son of a freeman, 3s 4d, fine remitted
Walter Motley of Dublin, merchant, £3
Simon Arrowsmith, 40s
  18 October 1662:
John Heywood, clerk, rector of Walton, gratis
Richard Whitfield, gratis
Timothy Tarleton, son of a freeman, 3s 4d
Edward Prenton, late apprentice, 6s 8d

62   Abraham Sanderson and Thomas Blundell entries are crossed out.

25 September 1662:
Memo. that Isaak Ambrose was voted to be admitted free paying £10 composition which he refused; also Hugh Higson voted to be admitted, paying £4.
9 October 1662:
Memo. that Richard Savill of Nantwich voted to be admitted, paying £13 6s 8d, but refused it.

WILLIAM STANLEY, KNIGHT, MAYOR [1662–63]

p. 731
ELECTION COURT FOR THE TOWN AND BOROUGH OF LIVERPOOL IN COUNTY OF LANCASTER, SATURDAY 18 OCTOBER 14 CHARLES II, the feast of St Luke the Evangelist, before Henry Corles, gent., mayor, John Chandler and William Blackmoore, bailiffs, according to charters and custom.

The honourable William Stanley esq. is elected mayor by the votes of the freemen, sworn
William Kichine, merchant, chosen by the said mayor on Monday following to be chief bailiff, sworn
William Gardner, mariner, elected the other bailiff by the freemen, sworn.

John Entwistle, esq., recorder
John Winstanley, town clerk
William Mulliney, serjeant at mace
Robert Seacome, water bailiff

    Officers chosen by the common council, Friday 24 October 1662:
Minister is deferred
George Glover, schoolmaster
William Poultney, church clerk
John Sturzaker, hall keeper, sworn
Robert Seacome, town customer, sworn
Richard Rogerson, subcustomer, sworn
Richard Williamson junior, Thomas Tatlock, stewards of the hall, sworn

Memo. That Thomas Christian, merchant, having been nominated chief bailiff by the votes of the freemen on St Luke's day in the absence of Mr Mayor who of right ought to have the choice of such bailiff and afterwards nominated the above named William Kichines, was by order of the same court discharged, 20 October 1662.

p. 732
Heyward suspended
William Blackmoore, William Bushell, Robert Sutton, Robert Lyon, merchant appraisers, 3 sworn

Thomas Roe, William Robinson, registers of tanned leather, 2 sworn
William Nicholls, James Heys, alefounders, 2 sworn
James Scarisbrick, William Midleton, Anthony Donbavann, William Leech, barleymen, 4 sworn
Robert Blevine, James Litherland, William Trevis, William Bailie, scavengers, 4 sworn
John Johnson of Everton, Edward Banks, overseers of the highways
Humphrey Mercer, murenger
Peter Walker, John Sanderson, porters
William Chorley, Elizabeth Rycroft, boardsetters
Richard Rogerson, Thomas Banks, leavelookers, 2 sworn
Thomas Witter, Thomas Banks, boothsetters
Richard Widowes, beadle and bellman
Churchwardens.

p. 733
PORTMOOT COURT OR QUARTER SESSIONS OF THE PEACE FOR THE TOWN AND BOROUGH OF LIVERPOOL IN COUNTY OF LANCASTER, 27 OCTOBER 14 CHARLES II, before the mayor and bailiffs according to custom.

Inquisition of jurors for our lord King: John Chandler, Richard Williamson, John Lurting, Thomas Sandiford, William Bushell, James Lideate, John Mulliney, John Tompson, Hugh Renald, John Williamson, Thomas Gallaway, Robert Fleetwood, John Banks, Nathan Gleave, Timothy Tarleton, John Lunte, William Williamson, William Accars, Anthony Carr, Edward Carr, John Roson, Edward Flitcrofte, John Walker, John Alcock, honest and lawful freemen.[63]

p. 734

p. 735

p. 736

p. 737
FREEMEN, 30 OCTOBER 1662
Thomas Bicksteth, son of alderman Bicksteth, admitted free and sworn, 3s 4d
Robert Mercer, John Mercer, sons of Ralph Mercer, deceased, 3s 4d each, sworn
William Daintie, son of William, sworn, 3s 4d
John Burton, son of James, deceased, sworn, 3s 4d
William Blundell, son of Brian, deceased, sworn, 3s 4d
Richard Lurting, son of William, sworn, 3s 4d
John Higinson, son of Richard, sworn, 3s 4d

63   Latin. No presentments follow.

William Dwarrihouse, son of William, deceased, sworn, 3s 4d
John Craine, son of Hugh, sworn, 3s 4d

John Hacking, late apprentice of Henry Tipson, admitted free and sworn, 6s 8d
George Smith, late apprentice, sworn 6s 8d
Richard Dobb, late apprentice, sworn, 6s 8d
Thomas Woolfall, late apprentice, sworn, 6s 8d
William Bruerton, late apprentice, sworn, 6s 8d
Francis Hunter, late apprentice, sworn, 6s 8d
Richard Formby, late apprentice, sworn, 6s 8d
John Erbie, late apprentice, sworn, 6s 8d
Richard Mercer, late apprentice, sworn, 6s 8d

Richard Windle, mariner, paid composition, sworn, £3
Robert Woodside, mariner, sworn, £4
William Ploumbe, bodice-maker, sworn 40s
John Kellie, husbandman, sworn, 40s
Joseph Keele, ship carpenter, sworn £5
John Bamber, ropemaker, sworn, 40s, but council remitted 20s of fine
Thomas Sympson, sworn, 40s, like sum 20s remitted
Edward Barton, husbandman, sworn, 40s, 30s remitted

George Neile voted fit to be admitted but absent
Richard Walles, son of Geoffrey deceased, late a freeman, sworn, 3s 4d
Hugh Higson of Warrington, £4
Anthony Johnson, 20s
Richard Parr of Cronton, £4
Patrick Reynolds, £4

p. 738

p. 739
A COPY OF THE ORDERS AND PROCEEDINGS OF THE COMMISSIONERS FOR REGULATING CORPORATIONS MADE TOUCHING THIS CORPORATION, 10 NOVEMBER 1662

County of Lancaster, Liverpool 10 November 1662.
    Declared by the commissioners in pursuance of the act 13 Charles II, entitled An Act for the well governing and regulating of corporations for the county palatine of Lancaster, that Thomas Blackmore, Thomas Williamson, Ralph Massam, Edward Williamson, Gilbert Formby and Richard Peircivall, who have refused to subscribe to the declaration in the said act being thereunto required, be (ipso facto) removed from the offices of aldermen and all other offices of magistracy or other employment relating to the government of the said corporation, and adjudged to be void of all intents and purposes as if the said persons were naturally dead. And be

it further ordered that Thomas Weaver, John Chandler, John Sturzaker, Thomas Story, Peter Lurting, Ralph Mercer are appointed to aldermen in their place.

Ordered by the commissioners aforesaid that all such officers, magistrates, aldermen and common council men as are now elected and, by reason of their absence could not take their oaths and subscribe to the declaration in the said act, be referred to take the said oaths and subscribe to the said declaration before any three of the commissioners who are desired to take the same in the time limited by the said act.

Declared by the commissioners aforesaid that Thomas Sandiford, Thomas Asbrooke, Edmund Leivsley, John Pemberton, William Blackmore, Evan Marsh and John Tompson who have refused to take the declaration in the act being thereunto required be removed from the offices of common council men, and all other offices of magistracy or other employment concerning the government of the corporation, and that the said offices are hereby adjudged to be void to all intents and purposes as if the said persons were naturally dead.

And it is further declared that 7 persons whose names are hereupon endorsed and have taken the said oaths of obedience and subscribed to the declaration in the act, except John Winstanley, who by a particular order is disabled, shall hold and be vested in the said offices of common council men according to the act.

Winstanley, Richard Kirkby, Thomas Norres, John Lightbourne, Nicholas Mosley, John Entwisle, Thomas Grenehalgh, Henry Hoghton[64]

p. 740
Liverpool 10 November 1662.

According to an act for the well governing and regulating of corporations we the commissioners hereafter named administered the said oaths in the act mentioned and took the subscriptions to the declaration in the act of the persons whose names hereafter follow.

I do declare that I hold there lies no obligation on me or any other person from the oath commonly called the Solemn League and Covenant, and that the same was in itself an unlawful oath and imposed on the subjects of this realm against the known laws and liberties of the kingdom: William Stanley, mayor, John Entwisle, recorder, Henry Corles, alderman, Alexander Greene, alderman, Thomas Andoe, alderman, Thomas Weaver, alderman, John Chandler, alderman, John Sturzaker, alderman, Thomas Story, alderman, Peter Lurting, alderman, William Blundell, town clerk, Richard Jones, George Bennett, Thomas Roe, Ralph Hall, Thomas Alcock, William Kitchin, William Gardner, bailiffs, John Winstanley, William Mulliney, serjeant, John Higginson, Edward Formby, Robert Moore, William Rimmer, John Blundell, John Lurting, Robert Sutton, Edward Alcock, John Owen, Robert Seacom, senior, Richard Blevin, Henry Ryding, Robert Lyon, William Fleetwood, John Heyes, William Ackers.

Commissioners: Winstanley, Richard Kirkby, Thomas Norres, John Lightbourne, Nicholas Mossley, John Entwistle, Thomas Grenehalgh, Henry Hoghton.

64   The seven names are written in the margin.

p. 741

Liverpool 10 November 1662.

Ordered by the commissioners for the well governing and regulating of corporations in the county of Lancaster, that John Winstanley be removed from being town clerk or common council man, and that William Blundell of Liverpool be declared town clerk in his place, the commissioners unanimously deeming it expedient for the public safety and encouragement of loyalty given under our hands and seals. Winstanley, Richard Kirkby, Thomas Norres, John Lightbourne, Nicholas Mosley, John Entwisle.

William Blundell, gent. was admitted a freeman of this town on 13 November 1662, and elected a common councillor, and voted to fill the office of town clerk.[65]

p. 742

FREEMEN ADMISSIONS, 24 NOVEMBER, 14 CHARLES II

Roger Bradshaigh, knt., admitted a free burgess, sworn

John Harrington, esq., sworn

Hugh Dicconson, esq., sworn

Henry Blundell, esq., sworn

Richard Townley of Towneley, esq., sworn

Henry Eccleston of Eccleston, esq., sworn

James Anderton of Birchall, esq., sworn

Thomas Lee of Lyme, esq., sworn

Robert Molyneux of le Wood, esq., sworn

Nicholas Fazakerley of Spellowhouse, esq., sworn

William Woolfall of Woolfall, esq., sworn

James Brettargh of Brettargh Holt, esq., sworn

William Gerard of Brin, esq., sworn

Henry Norres of West Derby, gent., sworn

John Towneley of Towneley, gent., sworn

Charles Towneley of Towneley, gent., sworn

William Fazakerley of Spellowhouse, gent., sworn

Richard Norres of West Derby, gent., sworn

Thomas Hawarden of Croxteth, gent., sworn

Henry Parr of Croxteth, gent., sworn

William Curghew of Haigh, gent., sworn

Thomas Turner of Preston, gent., sworn

George Culcheth of Towneley, gent., sworn

Roger Bryars of Walton, gent., sworn

Lawrence Bryars of Mossborough, gent., sworn

Thomas Butler, servant of Henry Eccleston esq., sworn

John Cooke of Little Woolton gent., sworn

John Lathom, servant of William Gerard, sworn

65   Latin.

Thomas Litherland of Prescot, gent., sworn
Henry Marshall of Prescot, gent., sworn
John Blundell of Prescot, gent., sworn
John Laithwaite of Ince Blundell, gent., sworn
William Tootell of Healey, gent., sworn
John Kirkby, servant of Hugh Dicconson, sworn
William Smith of Snape, gent., sworn
Henry Blundell of West Derby, gent., sworn
John Hodgson, servant of Gilbert Ireland, knt., sworn
William Briggs of Wigan, sworn[66]

9 JANUARY 1662
By the common council:
John Rymmer, owner of the *Vinty* assessed for 10s 4d for the custom of 40 barrels of herring carried in the vessel.
John Pluckington admitted free
James Vernon, esq. admitted free

p. 743
PORTMOOT COURT OR SESSIONS OF THE PEACE FOR THE TOWN OF LIVERPOOL, 23 FEBRUARY 15 CHARLES II 1662, before the mayor and bailiffs according to custom.[67]

Inquisition taken before Evan Marsh, gent., William Rymmer, John Walles, William Olive, Thomas Johnson, Richard Windle, Thomas Roe, James Hey, James Scarisbrick, Lawrence Williamson, John Williamson, Robert Woodside, Thomas Copwell, William Traves, William Litherland, John Litherland, Robert Mercer, jurors, who say in these English words.[68]

We present:
   William Mercer of Garstang for being drunk
   The same for a bloodwipe on Robert Kenion's wife, of this town, cooper, and for abusing her in words, as calling whore and threatening to knock out her brains
   Henry Bushell of this town for tussle on Richard Walles of the same
   Richard Walles for a tussle on Henry Bushell
   John Diches, formerly Mr Blundell of Ince's servant, for a bloodwipe on John Sadler's apprentice boy
   John Higginson, butcher, for not appearing to serve on this jury, and being sold
   John Harrison, Edward Balshaw, Margaret Granger, widow, Mr William Stangwayes, Thomas Norbery, Esther Hardman, widow, William Harrison, glasier,

66   Latin.
67   Latin.
68   Latin.

Cuthbert Kilshaw, Robert Burte, Timothy Houlte, widow, Mrs Alice Chatterton, Thomas Pattricke, Jane Martine, widow, John Harrs of this town, Edward Eccles, William Halsall, for using the faculty of freemen

Thomas Fazakerley, shoemaker, for making unlawful leather; John Johnson for the like

William Halsall for selling beer by unlawful quart

Mr Heawood Parson of Walton for not causing the street before the tithe barn to be made clean

Thomas Ashbrooke for letting rubbish in the street before his house in Dale Street

Edward Alcocke for letting muck before his croft in Dale Street

John Higginson for letting rubbish lie in the street before his door and not keeping the street clean before his barn in Old Hall Street

p. 744

Thomas Pattricke for letting rubbish lie in the street

Thomas Banks and Thomas Witter for not keeping the cornmarket clean and for laying the scales at Jane Jarrott's house end that people cannot pass

Henry Corles, deputy mayor, for keeping 1 swine unrung; William Eccleston for 2; Elinor Winstanley, widow 1; Mr Thomas Blackmore 1; John Higginson 1; Mrs Dorothy Sandiford 4; Richard Scarisbrecke 1; Mrs Margaret Bixteth, widow, 2; Mr Alexander Greene, alderman, 1; John Lurteing 2; Margaret Granger, widow, 2; Robert Lyon 1; Mr Gilbert Formby 2

Jane Garrett for swine being in cornmarket on market day, and pulling sack of corn in pieces

Mrs Dorothy Johnson, Thomas Galloway for the like

William Fleetwood, butcher, for proffering to sell unlawful meat in the market

James Hey and William Nicholls for neglect of their office, and not weighing bread since they were chosen

Robert Seacome, water bailiff, for not setting up two poles at the waterside according to former order[69]

All freemen who entertain inmates in their houses and have not given security to the mayor

We order:

That all those with any lands in the town field in the Breck Shoot shall make a ditch against their own lands five foot broad and two-and-a-half foot deep, and where water lies on their lands they shall make gutters and let the water into the ditch before 15 March, forfeit 10s for default

John Rose, Under Hill, shall cleanse his ditch joining the town field to receive the water that comes from the Breck Shoot that it may have passage before 15 March, 10s

---

69   A hand is drawn in the margin pointing to this entry.

Edward Howrobin shall make a large gutter in the ancient water course at the end of his lands in Srafeakers and Henry Corles, deputy mayor, and Mr William Strangewayes to cleanse the water course at the end of their lands in Srafeakers, before last day of February, 3s 4d

p. 745

That John Johnson and Edward Banks see that the ancient way at the end of Srafeakers be made a passable way, and that they see that the hollow way that goes to Everton in the townfield be made passable for man and cart before 10 March, 3s 4d

John Higginson to open the cundeth[70] at the bottom of Mr Crosse's field over against the Town's End Bridge before the 1 March, 6s 8d

John Higginson and Edward Banks to see that the Pool Bridge be mended before last day of March, 6s 8d

Robert Seacome to set up two poles at the sea side according to a former order before 10 March, 10s

Mrs Margaret Williamson make up the wall fallen down between Mr John Chandler's garden and her croft before 10 March next, 3s 4d

Thomas Coppoole to see that the pinfold be made higher with a new door before the last day of March at the town's charge

Thomas Coppoole to see that the gates into the townfield be repaired and set up before 15 March

All inhabitants to make up their fences, between neighbour and neighbour, before 6 March, 6s 8d

John Johnson and Edward Bankes to see that the shooting butts be repaired before last of March

All freemen entertaining inmates in their houses to give security to Mr Mayor before 10 March, forfeit for default 20s

We agree to all ancient orders and laudable customs

We choose Thomas Copwell heyward of the field, sworn.

p. 746

p. 747
24 APRIL 1663
At an Assembly:

It is ordered by Henry Corles, deputy mayor, the aldermen, and greater part of the common council in the town hall, that the freemen of this town, resident and non resident, shall be assessed for the repair of the chapel and the preserving of it from the storms and flowings of the sea, and that £100 be taxed.

---

70   A conduit: OED.

Ordered that John Blundell and Richard Jones be merchant appraisers in the place of William Blackmore and William Bushell lately removed from office by the commissioners for regulating corporations.

Ordered that the accounts of Mr John Winstanley be put into Mr Recorder's hands to examine for the truth of the said accounts.

Richard Parr of Cronton voted a freeman, playing £4, to be paid by William Bushell, and the said Richard has in further consideration of his freedom undertaken to tend the town clock for all the time he shall live in the town, sworn.

Patrick Reynolds of Liverpool, shoemaker, admitted free, paying £4, sworn.

Ordered that if Anthony Walles satisfies the common council that he has served a full apprenticeship with John Wallis, his brother, he may be admitted a freeman, paying 6s 8d.

18 MAY
John Sadler, John Walles, Richard Rymer, sworn of the council.

23 JUNE
Samuel Fazakerley of Allerton, James Parr of Prescot, admitted free.

13 JULY 1663
At an Assembly in the town hall:

It was ordered by Henry Corles, gent., deputy mayor, the aldermen, bailiffs and the major part of the common council, that £20 shall be taxed and assessed by the merchant appraisers on the inhabitants of the town, and collected by the bailiffs for the necessary use and disbursement of the town.

On reading a letter from Mr John Case certifying that writs of Quo Warranto are to be issued to all corporations, it is ordered that a letter be sent to Mr Case for his further advice touching the renewing of the town charter.

It is ordered that a defence be made at the town's cost to the citation procured from the consistory court by the church clerk of Walton against the deputy mayor and bailiffs, claiming a fee due to him from this town as clerk of Walton, and that the deputy mayor and bailiffs are to take care thereof.

p. 748
It is ordered likewise that Cooke's House, in Teane Barn[71] Street and Barker's two houses in Dale Street, all the land of this corporation and now in their hands, shall be surveyed by Alderman Chandler, Alderman Story, John Lurting, bailiff, Henry Ryding and Robert Seacom, and that an account of the values for lives, condition and repairs of the houses be made before 16 July.

John Fairehurst, son of William Fairehurst, late freeman, voted a free burgess, paying 3s 4d, sworn; same day, Patrick Reynolds admitted.

71   Though spelt Teane Barn this is presumably Tithebarn Street.

6 AUGUST 1663

Common Council. Thomas Andoe, gent., deputy mayor, Henry Corles, alderman, John Chandler, alderman, John Sturzaker, Thomas Story, Peter Lurting, aldermen, William Gardner, bailiff, Robert Moore, gent., William Blundell, John Higginson, John Lurting, Ralph Hall, Thomas Alcock, William Fleetwood, Edward Alcock, bailiff, Henry Ryding, William Molyney, Richard Rimer, John Heyes, Thomas Roe, Robert Seacom, William Ackers:

Upon reading the petition of Elizabeth Tarleton, widow, the relict. of – Tarleton, late alderman, it is ordered that the deputy mayor confer with the recorder or other council on the matter and the same be considered by the common council.

It is likewise ordered that the two houses in Dale Street called Barker's houses be granted out by lease and the now deputy mayor and bailiffs contract for the fines and rents to be secured for the use of the town.

Forasmuch the streets in this town are much decayed and abused by the frequent driving of carts laden with coals and mugs to the waterside to be transported and carried away, when carts with equal convenience can pass over Pool Bridge to the water side or to Water Street, it is ordered that every person, after notice is given in open market, who passes through any of the streets with his cart so laden shall pay 12d for every time, to be levied of the goods of such offending in case of refusal.

It is likewise ordered that no person lay any lime stones or other stones to the south of the pole now fixed below Chapel Street end and the rock above the town on pain of 5s every time stones shall be laid, to be levied on goods in case of refusal.

p. 749
6 AUGUST 1663

At an Assembly in the town hall:

Concerning Cockes' children. It is ordered by Thomas Andoe, gent., deputy mayor, the aldermen and the major part of the common council whose names are underwritten, that Thomas Birtch and Richard Jones, now overseers of the poor in this town, do receive from Nicholas Valentyne, administrator of Philip Cox, deceased, such money as the said Nicholas shall have to account for as administrator, and to give acquittance for the same, and that the said Thomas Birtch and Richard Jones shall be saved harmless at the proper cost of the town from all suits and costs which shall hereafter arise against them by reason of their receipt as aforesaid. And they shall be accountable to the common council for such receipts. Tho. Andoe, deputy mayor, Henry Corles, John Chandler, John Sturzakar, Tho.Story, Peter Lurting, Robert Moore, Will.Gardner, Wm.Blundell, John Higginson, John Lurting, Raph Hall, Thomas Allcock, William Fleetwood, Henry Rydinge, Richard R Rimer, John J Hey, Thom.Roe, Robert Seacome, William Mulliney, Edward Allcock.[72]

72   Signatures.

p. 750

It is ordered that the two houses in Dale Street called Barker's houses be leased for lives or years and the now deputy mayor and bailiffs contract for the fines and rents for the same for the use of the town, and to be made by the mayor, bailiffs and burgesses and pass under the common seal of the town. Thomas Andoe, dep. mayor, Henry Corles, Robart Moore, John Sturzaker, Thomas Story, Peter Lurting, Will.Gardner, Wm.Blundell, John Lorting, Thomas Allcock, John Higinson, William Fleetwood, Thomas Roe, Rich. R Rimer, William Mulliney, William Ackars, Henry Rydinge, Ralph Hall, Edward Allcock.[73]

p. 751

14 SEPTEMBER 1663

At an Assembly in the town hall:

It is ordered that a messuage formerly called Cooke's House be leased for lives or years and that the now deputy mayor and bailiffs contract for fines and rents for the same for the use of the town, and the lease to be made by the mayor, bailiffs, and burgesses and pass under the common seal. Tho.Andoe, dep.mayor, Henry Corles, Robart Moore, Thomas Story, Peter Lurting, William Kitchin, Will.Gardner, Wm.Blundell, Jo.Higginson, Edward Allcock, William Mulliney, John Lorting, Robert Sutton, Robt.Lyon, Henry Rydinge, Ralph Hall, Thomas Allcock, Rich.R Rimer, George Bennett, William Fleetwood, Thomas Roe, William Ackars.[74]

On the same day:

Hugh Higson of Warrington, chapman, admitted free, £4, sworn
Anthony Johnson of Everton admitted, 40s, sworn, 20s remitted
John Leigh of Liverpool admitted, free, sworn.[75]

p. 752

A TAX OF THE FIRST PAYMENT OF THE SECOND SUBSIDY GRANTED 18 JAMES 1621

This is two thirds of one subsidy.

John Crosse, gent., in lands £4 value pays	10s	8d
Ralph Seacom, gent., in lands 40s	5s	4d
Edmund Rose, in goods £6	10s	
William Bannester, in goods £3	5s	
Richard Rose, in goods £3	5s	
Thomas Hockenhull, in goods £5	6s	8d
Richard Melling, in goods £3	5s	

---

73 Signatures.
74 Signatures.
75 Latin.

LOAN MONEY TO BE LENT TO HIS MAJESTY, 17 APRIL, 3 CHARLES, 1627

John Crosse esq., in lands £4	£4		
Ralph Seacom, gent., in lands 40s		40s	
Edmund Rose, gent., in goods £6	£4		
William Bannester, gent., in goods £5	£3	6s	8d
Richard Rose, gent., in goods £5	£3	6s	8d
John Williamson, gent., in goods £4		53s	8d

John Crosse esq., in lands £4		16s	
Ralph Seacom, gent., in lands 40s		8s	
John Walker, gent. in goods £6		16s	
William Bannester, gent., goods £5		13s	4d
John Williamson, in goods £4		10s	8d

John Crosse esq., in lands £4
Ralph Seacom, in lands 40s
William Bannester, in goods £5
Richard Rose, in goods £5
John Walker, in goods £6
John Williamson, in goods £4

LIVERPOOL, 30 SEPTEMBER 15 CHARLES II, 1663

A presentment made by the bailiffs and assessors of the township of Liverpool in the parish of Walton, in obedience to a warrant and instructions from the honourable commissioners for the act of subsidies, of the names of all such persons as are liable either for real or personal estate, according to the said instructions.

Mr Crosse, in lands £4
Mr Robert Seacom and his
mother, in lands £2
Thomas Blackmore, in goods £5
Ralph Massam, in goods £5
William Bushell, in goods £6
John Higginson, in goods £4

And further they have not to certify. William Kitchins, William Gardner, bailiffs; Henry Corles, Peter Lurting, Robert Sutton, Thomas Ashbrooke, assessors.

p. 753
COPY OF WARRANT

In pursuance of an act of parliament entitled an act for granting four entire subsidies to his majesty by the temporality, these are to require you to give warning to all the petty constables and others in the schedule annexed to be assessors, and make certificates in their respective parishes, townships and villages in your division of persons liable payment of subsidies. That the said constables and assessors diligently enquire and make true presentments under their hands, fair engrossed on parchment to us, a true estimate of every person, estate, real or personal according to the instructions hereinafter mentioned, at the house of Margery Walls in Prescot, widow, on 30 September by 8 o'clock in the afternoon, requiring each assessor or constable, after reasonable time for copying of the same for himself, to deliver it to an assessor or constable of the next township in the parish, the time and names to be endorsed, so that everyone may better be instructed how to make their presentment, on pain of 40s for delay or neglect.

First, you are to present the name of every person, guild and commonalty, corporate and not corporate, within your parish, township or village worth £3 in money, plate, merchandise, corn, household stuff, and debts owing to them, deducting debts owed by them, excepting apparel, whereof no jewels are to be part; you are to present the value of every pound they have in fee simple, fee tail or for life or years, of the yearly value of 20s; also of all the names of popish recusants convicted or indicted; and every alien, denizen or not denizen of the age of 7 years or above, and every popish recusant convicted being 17 years old, or 21 years old who has not received communion for one year past; you are not to present tithes due to the clergy, nor servants' wages, nor the goods of churches; you are to present no orphans nor infants under 21 years for goods left to them, nor a person for both lands and goods (only the higher in value), nor of any person's possessions in two places (only the place of residence for the year past), and all parsonages, vicarages, free grammar schools are exempt. Given under our hands at Wigan, 21 September 1663. Gilbert Ireland, Thomas Norres, Roger Bradshaigh, L. Rausthorne, Henry Slater, William Banks, Thomas Hawarden, John Entwisle, Nicholas Fazakerley.

This is a true copy of the original warrant, examined by me, John Lyon, High Constable.

p. 754
FREEMEN
Robert Woodside admitted free, £4, sworn
Richard Windle, £3, sworn
William Plombe, £2, sworn
John Kelly, £2, sworn
John Bamber, ropemaker, £1, sworn
Edward Barton, 10s, sworn
Joseph Keele, £5
William Blundell, 3s 4d
John Mercer, 3s 4d
Thomas Bicksteth, 3s 4d
Robert Mercer, 3s 4d
William Dayntie, 3s 4d
William Dwarrihouse, 3s 4d
John Higginson junior, 3s 4d

John Crane, 3s 4d
John Lurting, 3s 4d
John Burton, 3s 4d
Richard Dobb, 6s 8d
Geoffrey Smyth, 6s 8d
Richard Formbie, 6s 8d
William Bruerton, 6s 8d
John Herbie, 6s 8d
John Hackin, 6s 8d
Richard Mercer, 6s 8d
Thomas Wolfall, 6s 8d
Francis Hunter, 6s 8d
Richard Walles, 6s 8d
Patrick Regadd, shoemaker, £4
John Fairehurst, 3s 4d
Hugh Higson, £4
Anthony Johnson, £1
Thomas Simson, £1
Richard Walles, 3s 4d
Richard Parr of Cronton, £4
John Leigh, clerk, gratis[76]

PETER LURTING, GENTLEMAN, MAYOR, 1663 [1663–64]

p. 755
ELECTION COURT FOR THE TOWN AND BOROUGH OF LIVERPOOL IN
COUNTY OF LANCASTER, SUNDAY 18 OCTOBER 15 CHARLES II,
St Luke's day, before Thomas Andoe, gentleman, deputy mayor authorised by the
honourable William Stanley esq. being then on special attendance of his said
majesty, and Mr William Kitchin and William Garner, bailiffs, according to
charters and custom.

Peter Lurting is elected mayor by the freemen, sworn
Thomas Johnson chosen by the said mayor as chief bailiff, sworn
Thomas Alcocke elected by the freemen the other bailiff, sworn.

John Entwisle, esq., recorder
William Blundell, town clerk
William Mulliney, serjeant at mace, sworn before
Thomas Rowe, water bailiff, sworn

76   Latin.

Officers chosen by the common council on Friday next following:
John Leigh, clerk, minister
George Glover, schoolmaster
William Poultney, church clerk and sexton
John Sturzaker, hallkeeper

18 October 1663. I declare that I hold that there is no obligation on any other person from the oath called the solemn league and covenant, and that it was an unlawful oath imposed on the subjects of this realm, against the known laws and liberties of this kingdom. Thomas Johnson, Thomas Alcock, bailiffs sworn. Thomas Preeson, Edmund Whalley.

p. 756
Thomas Rowe, town customer, sworn
Richard Rogerson, subcustomer, sworn
William Nicholls, William Travers, stewards of the hall and ley gatherers, sworn
Thomas Copple, heyward, sworn

   By the jury, Monday next:
William Garner, John Lurtin, Mr Ralph Hall, Thomas Preeson, merchant appraisers, sworn
Thomas Nicholson, Henry Cooper, registers of leather
William Baylie, William Greyton, aletasters, sworn
John Kellie, Thomas Simpson, John Walker, John Balmer, barleymen, sworn
Edward Litherland, William Dwarihouse, Edward Eccoes, Joseph Keele, scavengers, sworn
William Simpson, James Scarisbrick, overseers of the highways, sworn
John Kenion, cooper, murenger
Peter Walker, John Sanderson, porters
William Chorley, John Higginson, junior, boardsetters
Richard Rogerson, Edmund Whalley, leavelookers
Edmund Whalley, Thomas Wittar, boothsetters
Whalley admitted a free burgess and sworn[77]
Richard Widdowes, beadle and bellman

FRIDAY 23 OCTOBER 1663
Edward Ecclesfield, apprentice of Robert Ettles of Liverpool admitted a freeman, sworn
Thomas Patrick, mariner, admitted a freeman, sworn, 50s

p. 757
INQUISITION TAKEN AT LIVERPOOL IN COUNTY OF LANCASTER, MONDAY 26 OCTOBER 15 CHARLES II AT PORTMOOT COURT OR QUARTER SESSIONS OF THE PEACE, according to custom before the mayor and bailiffs.

---

77   Whalley entry is written in margin.

Jurors for the lord King: William Kitchins, gentleman, John Higginson, John Blundell, Samuel Fazakerley, Thomas Peake, John Sadler, Thomas Preeson, Thomas Birch, Robert Eccles, Thomas Copple, Samuel Postlethwaite, John Mulliney, mariner, Robert Fleetwood, William Williamson, William Robinson, William Nicholson, James Scarisbrick, William Leech, William Traves, William Baylie, John Johnson, Edward Bancks, Hugh Reynolds, Edward Howrobin.[78]

We present:

William Watmough, late of Liverpool, blacksmith, who, on 1 July 15 Charles II, by force of arms broke in and took the house of Jane Haskeine, widow, called the Smithy in Juggler Street, and disturbed her peaceful possession of it against her will, and still holds it. Jane Haskeine, Katherin Haskeine, witnesses. The defendant pleads not guilty.[79]

Other presentments in English:

Robert Bicksteth for great and heinous abuse and injury done to the worshipful Mr Peter Lurtin, mayor, since he was elected, to wit saying that he was a thief and a rogue and had robbed a house in Formby, who, being an ill person, very poor and not able to pay, was only fined £5 on his submission on record of several other punishments.

Thomas Fazakerley, shoemaker, for working unlawful leather; John Johnson of Ormskirk for the like

p. 758

Henry Lyon, shoemaker, for the like

Richard Lathom, esq., for striking at Mr Corleyes, alderman of this town

Richard Williamson, chirurgeon, for a tussle on William Travers

William Travers for a tussle on Richard Williamson

William Greyton for a tussle on Mr Richard Percivall

John Glover, boatman, for a tussle on Cuthbert Culcheth

William Bushell for a tussle on William Granger

Margaret Granger, widow, for using faculty of freeman, not free

John Hill for getting turves within our liberties, not being free; George Seddon for the like

Robert Davie, Thomas Plombe, Robert Ballard, Richard Strange, Robert Robinson, Thomas Gildoes, Thomas Darwin, Edmund Ryding, Edward Buckley, William Harrison, for using the faculty of a freeman, not free

William Garner, John Lunt, William Brereton, Edward Buckley, Mr Alexander Breres, Thomas Rowe for keeping and selling by the quart under the due assize

Elizabeth Mosse, Ellen Holland, Ellen Heyes for forestalling the market, buying up herrings

Abigail Martyn for selling in the market stinking unmarketable beef

78   Latin.
79   Latin.

William Garner, Henry Tarbocke, Charles Fairish, Joan Holt, widow, Robert Kenyon, cooper, Ellen Winstanley, widow, Thomas Patrick, Thomas Asbrooke, William Garner, Mr Gilbert Formby, Robert Lyon, Edward Alcocke, Richard Browne, Mr John Sturzaker, alderman, for keeping swine unrung

William Mosse for setting his carts in the streets towards the night time

William Chorley for not dressing his part of the street and leaving boards and other lumber to hinder passage

p. 759

Thomas Wittar for not dressing his part of the street

Huon Gerard and Thomas Litherland for making a dunghill in the street and not cleansing it in due time

John Poultney for the like

Thomas Henshawe of Everton for cutting grass in the town field

Robert Henshawe for the like

William Nicholls and Robert Sympson for abusive words to the ley gatherers and ley layers

All freemen that entertain inmates in their houses and have not given security to the mayor that they will not be chargeable to the town

We order:

Thomas Asbrooke to cleanse his ditch at the end of Tithebarn Street which he holds from Dorothy Bicksteth, widow, within 10 days, on pain of 3s 4d

All who have any lands in Breck Shoot in the townfield shall make a fair ditch, five foot broad and two-and-a-half foot deep, and where the water lies on the land that they make gutters, slit the coppice and let the water into the ditches before 2 February, 10s; John Rose, Under Hill in West Derby, to cleanse his ditch at Netherfield Steele coming into Liverpool Field from Breck Shoot, that it may have fair passage before 2 February, 10s

Hugh Reynold to set up a coll[80] at the end of the quay before St Martin's day, 6s 8d

All those not free of this borough shall not set any muck on the town's waste, 10s, and that all who have any muck on the waste shall remove it before 1 January, 10s

All freemen who entertain inmates to give security to Mr Mayor that they shall not be chargeable to the town, or else cause them to be removed before 5 November, 20s

The curfew bell to be rung as formerly

Mr Winstanley to make a sufficient gutter in his wall at the end of John Heyes' house and that there may not be a stop to the watercourse at the end of the same house by Mr Winstanley's wall

We agree and order the observance of all ancient and laudable customs of this borough.

---

80 Probably a barrel or tub, a variant of cowl: OED. It is referred to as a stoop at a later portmoot court on 15 January 1663.

p. 760
STATUTE MERCHANT
  Henry Webster of Knowsley, yeoman, and Alice Chadderton of Liverpool, spinster, are held by obligation according to statute merchant to William Belling of the City of London, apothecary, for £3,000 to be paid to him, his attorney or assigns, before the feast of the Purification of the Blessed Virgin Mary, for corn and wool and other merchandise bought from him, in line with the statutes of Acton Burnell and Westminster. This recognition is made in Liverpool in the presence of Peter Lurting, gentleman, mayor, and William Blundell, gentleman, clerk, in due form. We, the aforementioned Henry and Alice, append our seals and the seal of the town of Liverpool. Dated 7 November, 15 Charles II, 1663. Taken at the court of Peter Lurting, mayor, 7 December 1663. Peter Lurting. Seals of Henry Webster, Alice Chadderton.[81]

p. 761
9 NOVEMBER 1663
  At an assembly in the town hall before the mayor and the greater part of the common council it was ordered that Mr Archer, who pretends some title to the houses called Barker's now possessed by Mr Edward Alcock, be admitted to a hearing of what writings concern the same houses.
  Ordered the same day, that strangers, whether butchers, pedlars, shoemakers or other chapmen, occupying stalls belonging to this borough, be summoned to appear before the mayor and assistants to compound and take leases of the stalls for lives or years, and to pay what yearly rent shall be contracted, and Mr Mayor and the aldermen or whom he shall take as assistants are empowered to make leases and cause them to be recorded.

12 NOVEMBER 1663
An assembly of the mayor, aldermen and common council in the common hall at the request of Edward Archer who makes claim to a messuage called Barker's house in Dale Street, on the free promise of the said Archer to refer himself to the worshipful Peter Lurting, gentleman, Mr Thomas Andoe, Mr Henry Corleys, Mr John Chandler, Mr John Sturzaker, Mr Thomas Storie, aldermen, Thomas Johnson and Thomas Alcock, bailiffs, and the major part of the common council, and to their decision what to allow him out of a fine paid by Edward Alcock for a lease made to him of the same messuage. If the said Archer prove himself to be the legitimate son of Dorothy Archer, daughter of John Barker, and the rightful heir of the same, they order that he shall have and enjoy the rent from Alcock's lease and the inheritance thereof so that he, by such legal acts as council may advise, may save harmless the borough from any claims from him, and they shall confirm the lease granted to Edward Alcock. If, hereafter, the said Archer wishes to sell the inheritance this borough might have the presumption of the same

81 Latin.

p. 762

paying the same as another might. Further, they order that, on assurances made by the said Edward Archer given in articles of agreement between the said Archer on the one part and the mayor, aldermen and common council on the other, bearing date 11 December, Edward Archer shall receive £13 13s 4d of the fine taken for Alcock's lease, provided always that if the said Archer does not make one himself to the rightful heir of the premises then the same shall return to the use of the borough.

CORONER'S INQUISITION, 27 DECEMBER 15 CHARLES II 1663

Taken before Thomas Andoe, gentleman, for the honourable William Stanley, esq., coroner of this town, being a sufficient deputy. On the oath of Thomas Asbrooke, Thomas Bridge, Charles Fairish, John Moniley, tailor, Richard Jones, Thomas Birch, Thomas Haslam, Thomas Bancks, Thomas Gildars, Thomas Leakfield, Michael Richardson, John Heyes, Robert Leadbow, Anthony Walles, John Whitestones, who present the following: that about 6 o'clock in the morning Elizabeth, wife of William Ackers of Liverpool, to the dishonour of God, became fels de se,[82] and murdered herself by wilful drowning herself in a well at the back of and belonging to the dwelling house of William Ackers.

p. 763

THE RECANTATION OF ROBERT BICKSTETH

To all christian people I, Robert Bicksteth of Liverpool, send greeting. Know that on the mercy of the magistrates of this borough afforded to me, though undeserved, I make my humble and thankful acknowledgement that I deserve punishment and imprisonment, and I humbly confess to my shame that I have most untruly and unworthily spoken against Mr Peter Lurting, worshipful mayor, to wit that he was a thief and a rogue and had robbed a house in Formby. And I publically declare that I had no cause so to speak of the mayor and therefore, being sensible of the injury I have done him, I promise by God's mercy and goodness never again to offend or misbehave myself in word or deed against the said Mr Mayor or any of his family. In testimony I have put my hand and seal, 22 January 15 Charles, 1663. Robert Bicksteth. Witnesses: Thomas Andoe, alderman, Thomas Storie, alderman, Thomas Johnson, Thomas Alcock, bailiffs, Thomas Asbrook, Thomas Roe, water bailiff, Samuel Fazakerley, town clerk, William Moniley, serjeant.

p. 764

FREEMEN ADMITTED IN THE TIME OF PETER LURTING, GENTLEMAN, mayor
23 October 1663:

Edmund Whalley admitted a freeman, paying 6s 8d, sworn

Edward, son of Robert Eccles, 3s 4d, sworn

---

82   Presumably a variant of the French *fol*, meaning mad.

Thomas Patrick, 50s, sworn
Edmund Whalley, 6s 8d, sworn[83]
    28 January 1663:
Thomas Holland, 6s 8d, sworn
Ralph Johnson, 3s 4d, sworn
Thomas Gildoes, 40s, sworn
Holt, gentleman, gratis, sworn
    25 February 1663:
John Sandiford, £5, sworn
Peter Allen, £5, sworn
Edward Buckley, £4, sworn
James Travers, £4, sworn
Oliver Lyme, £6 13s 4d, sworn
James Bootle, £6 13s 4d, sworn; dead[84]
Henry Knowles, 20s, sworn
    11 March 1663:
William Lord Brabazon
George Collinwood, esq.
Henry Hocknell, gent., all gratis, sworn
    30 May 1664:
James Smoot, £4, sworn
John Storie, son of a freeman, 3s 4d , sworn
Anthony Banister, 3s 4d, sworn
Richard Boare, 40s, sworn
    31 May 1664:
Gilbert Blundel, £2 10s, sworn
James Boates, £2, sworn
Robert Burt, £2 10s, sworn
William Forber, £2 10s, sworn
    22 July:
Matthew Gleave, £3, sworn
    11 June:
Thomas Lurting, £3, sworn
    1 August:
James Smith, gent. seneschal of the royal treasury, free, sworn[85]
    24 September:
Right Hon. William Lord Strange
William Spencer esq.
William Spencer junior, esq.
William Parke of Bradkirk, gent.

---

83   Whalley entry in lighter hand.
84   Note of death is written in margin.
85   James Smith entry in Latin.

Clodius Denis, servant to the right honourable Earl of Derby
Henry Corley, John Storie,[86] 3s 4d
James Bull, £2
Thomas Finlon, 3s 4d
John Moniley, £1
Richard Marsh, 6s 8d
William Williamson, £1
Thames Warrenght, 6s 8d
James Topping, £2 10s
Thomas Derwen, £3
Edward Stockly, £3
Thomas Gregson, 6s 8d
John Allen,[87] £5
Robert Daping, £2; dead[88]

p. 765
28 JANUARY 1663. ELECTION OF S. FAZAKERLEY, TOWN CLERK
Whereas William Blundel of Prescot, gent., was by the commissioners for regulating corporations chosen town clerk in place of Mr John Winstanley, and whereas, now living in Prescot, he cannot answer the full service of the office because of his remoteness he freely resigns on the proposal to elect another clerk. It is, on mature deliberation, ordered by the mayor, aldermen, bailiffs and the rest of the common council that Samuel Fazakerley of this town, gent., shall be town clerk, and he is elected, to perform the office and is to receive the fees due, paying yearly for the said office £5. Samual Fazakerly sworn town clerk. Peter Lurting, mayor, Thomas Andoe, alderman, Robert Moore, Thomas Storie, alderman, Thomas Johnson, Thomas Alcock, bailiffs, William Blundell, lately town clerk, John Higginson, William Kitchin, William Gardner, William Rymer, John Lurting, John Walles, John Heyes, Richard Rymer, William Fleetwood, George Bennet, Ralph Hall, Roger Harrison, Richard Blevin, Richard Jones, Edward Alcock, John Blundel, Thomas Roe, William Morrisey

p. 766

p. 767
PORTMOOT COURT OR SESSIONS OF THE PEACE FOR THE TOWN AND BOROUGH OF LIVERPOOL IN COUNTY OF LANCASTER, 15 JANUARY 15 CHARLES II 1663, before the mayor and bailiffs.[89]

---

86   John Storie crossed out.
87   John Allen crossed out.
88   Note of death is written in margin.
89   Latin.

Inquisition of the jurors for our lord the king: John Lurting, gent., Evan Marsh, William Bushel, Thomas Alcocke, John Owen, John Walles, Richard Rymer, William Ackers, John Heyes, Thomas Nicholson, William Greton, John Bamber, William Simpson, Thomas Tatlock, William Dwarrihouse, honest and legal men, who say in English words.[90]

We present:

Robert Heaton for a tussle and bloodwipe on John Battell

John Battell for a tussle and bloodwipe on Robert Heaton

The wife of John Higginson for a tussle on the wife of William Newport

The wife of William Newport for a tussle on the wife of William Higginson

John Loye and Elinor Loye for a tussle on Thomas Loye, and the abovesaid Elinor for imprecations against Thomas Loy so that he is debarred his trade to the great damage of his wife and children

Samuel Postlethwaite for great and heinous abuse to the present bailiffs (meaning Thomas Johnson), that is to say: I will not go to prison with thee. Where is thy warrant? I will not go with thee. And also for challenging the other bailiff, Thomas Alcock, to fight, saying: I will meet thee when thou will and where thou will or dare

James Heyes for keeping small quarts and selling ale under the assize

Robert Lyon for keeping swine unrung; Widow Haddock, John Chambers, Richard Crompton, Jane Tarbock, William Garner, Edward Buckloe, Thomas Patrick, Mrs Johnson, Edward Alcock, for the like

John Higginson senior, for setting his cart in the street towards the night time; William Mosse, Richard Rogerson, John Holland for the like

John Higginson also for not making the street clean against his ground; John Lurting the like

Captain Thomas Boulton for not removing his muck in Tithebarn Street according to former order

William Vyres, Peter Johnson of Everton, John Heyes, Nehemiah Warton, Jane Horrocks for the like

p. 768

John Boates for using the faculty of freeman, not free; Robert Davie, Robert Robinson, Thomas Gildoes, Thomas Darwin, Edward Backly for the like

Edward Stockley, Peter Smyth, John Glover, Thomas Aspe, James Morecroft, for buying up skins before the market contrary to a former order

Thomas Holland for selling a pair of shoes on a weekday for a foreigner

Edward Buckloe for keeping company in his house drinking on Saturday night and Sunday to the dishonour of God and against former statutes and orders

Hugh Reynolds for not setting up the stoop at the end of the Old Quay according to the order of the last jury.

90   Latin.

We order:

Hugh Reynolds to set up a sufficient stoop at the end of the Old Quay by 1 April on penalty of 13s 4d

Headbolts to be made up and ditches scoured before 23 February, 3s 4d apiece

John Johnson to scour the ditch between his field and the further side of Salter's Moor, by 1 April, 6s 8d

All who are not free of the borough shall not set any muck on the town's waste, 10s apiece; and all who do cast muck on the waste shall remove it before 1 April, 10s apiece

All landlords to give security to the mayor for their tenants by 1 April, 13s 4d for each default

We agree to the observance of all ancient laws and laudable customs.

p. 769

25 FEBRUARY 1664

At an assembly in the town hall before the mayor, aldermen, and greatest part of the common council:

It is ordered that Mr Mayor, with some others whom he thinks fit, shall treat with Captain John Case about his demands for costs expended by him in defending against the bill for making navigable the rivers Mersey and Weaver, and to allow him what the mayor and said assistants think meet.

Also ordered that Mr Hambleton, merchant of Scotland, in the *Margaret* of Glasgow, coming into this port and breaking his bulk of herring here, shall pay for composition at the rate of 8 shillings per score of barrels, the bulk being 120 barrels.

Also ordered that on landing of cattle or other goods on Wirral side against the liberties of this port, the water bailiffs shall distrain the goods, cattle or merchandise for the usual custom due to the town, and shall be indemnified for the distress.

Also ordered that in charity and consideration of the children left by Margaret Tyrer, widow, deceased, 4 shillings per month shall be paid to Hannah Tyrer, one of her children for the maintenance of Thomas Tyrer a young infant, one of the children till further order.

Also ordered that notice being given to the overseers of the poor of this town, that Boates, brother of — Boates, a poor child, who has been maintained at the public charge of this town shall after one month next be not maintained any longer at the public charge. Boates to be bound apprentice.[91]

p. 770

p. 771

AUDIT OF WILLIAM STANLEY, LATE MAYOR, William Kitchin and William Garner, bailiffs, Monday 22 February 1663, before Peter, gent. now mayor.

---

91   Note about Boates to be bound apprentice is written in margin.

Received from Robert Seacome, late water bailiff for ingates and outgates	£28	5s	11d
From Mr Sturzaker, hallkeeper	15	4	4
From Richard Rogerson, leavelooker	12	2	9
Received more	226	6	3
Whole receipt	£281	19s	3d
Total disbursements	260	6	1
Balance	21	13	1

The aforesaid sum of £21 was this day paid to the now bailiffs, Thomas Johnson and Thomas Alcocke, and 13s 1d allowed them for charges, and so this account is cleared.

Memo. £20 more was formerly paid to the now bailiffs.

Signed and allowed by the aldermen: Peter Lurting, mayor, Thomas Andoe, Henry Corles, John Chandler, John Sturzaker, aldermen, Samuel Fazakerley, town clerk

Debts owing to the town by bond delivered to the now bailiffs:
Mr Gilbert Formbie and Edward Formbie, bond of £100
Edward Formbie, bond of £20
Richard Linaker, bond of £5
Robert Sutton, bond of £6 10s, due March '63
Robert Sutton, bond of £60, due January '63
Mr Edward Alcocke note of £20 on demand
Mrs Chandler and Mrs Blackmore note or bill of £2 12s 6d
Robert Sutton bond of £6 16s found and accepted with the other bond on the same sheet.

p. 772
27 JUNE 1664
　　At an assembly in the town hall it is thought fit that Mr Mayor bind William, son of William Boates deceased, apprentice to John Walker, tailor for eight years, giving with the apprentice £3 and one suit of apparel, linen and woollen, and the master to find him necessaries the rest of the time.
　　Voted freeman, Thomas Lyon, £6 13s 4d; George Wright of Croston, mariner, £3
　　Captain Edward Tarleton voted to be tenant of Margaret Lloye's house in the churchyard, and to pay 20s fine, and in building £100, and a yearly rent of 4s and not entrench on any man's land adjoining.
　　Men voted to be of the common council: Captain Edward Tarleton, Mr Thomas Christian, Thomas Birch, Thomas Bridge, William Eccleston; all but Mr Christian

sworn and subscribed their renunciation of the covenant. Robert Fleetwood also then voted to be of the council, and being summoned to take his oath in law in such case prescribed, declared his unwillingness to take on him that charge.

p. 773
LIVERPOOL. PORTMOOT COURT OR SESSIONS OF THE PEACE, 18 APRIL 16 CHARLES II, before mayor and bailiffs.[92]

Inquisition of jurors: John Blundell, Richard Williamson, Richard Crompton, Richard Jones, Thomas Bicksteth, James Blevin, James Travers, John Burton, Richard Windle, Samuel Postlethwaite, William Bayliffe, John Walker, Edward Eccoes, James Scarisbricke, Thomas Copple, honest and legal burgesses, who say in English words.[93]

We present:
John Molliney, tailor, for bloodwipe on Thomas Finloe his journeymen, amerced in —
Henry Livesey of Alker for a bloodwipe and tussle on Richard Mercer
James Farrer of Alker for a tussle and bloodwipe on said Richard Mercer
Edward Reynolds of Alker for a tussle and bloodwipe on said Richard Mercer
Mr — Bradshaw for using the faculty of a freeman, not free; Mr — Tempest, — Nickson, Mr Arthur Hutton, Thomas Lyon, potter, Edmund Bispham, Jeffrey Clerkson, John Harrison, John Hill, John Prescott, James Ball, William Williamson in Dale Street, James Orrell, smith, Widow Martyn, Robert Davie, Robert Robinson, James Boates, Thomas Darwin, for the like
William Mosse for setting his cart in the street towards night; John Holland, Richard Rogerson for the like
Thomas Harrison for selling unlawful meal on the last market day
Mr John Francis for suing Mr John Starkie out of the mayor's court contrary to his oath as freeman of this borough
Jane Gerard for putting her swine out on the market day contrary to former order; Thomas Galloway for the like
Thomas Asbrooke for keeping 3 swine unrung; Gregory Formbie 1; Margery Horrocks 1; William Bushell 3; Edward Sutton 1; Richard Mercer 1; Mrs Sandiford 3; Thomas Andoe 1; Mr Formbie; William Garner 2; Mrs Johnson 2
William Henshaw having land in the Breck Shoot in the town field for not making his ditch according to former order; John Rose of Everton, Margery Henshaw, Margery Heye, John Heyes, for the like

p. 774
John Johnson for not making fence between his field and Salter's Moore
Captain Bolton for not removing his muck at Tithebarn Street according to former order; John Heyes, William Syres, Nehemiah Warton for the like.

92   Latin.
93   Latin.

We order:

That the wall in Tithebarn Street at the end of the Morecroft be made a yard-and-a-half high by 1 June on pain of 10s apiece

The shooting butts to be made up by 10 May

The streets and highways in the liberties of Liverpool to be repaired by the surveyors of the highways by 25 July

We agree to all ancient and laudable customs.

p. 775
INDENTURE, 15 AUGUST 16 CHARLES II

Between Peter Lurting of Liverpool, gentleman, now mayor, Thomas Johnson and Thomas Alcock, bailiffs, on the one part, and Edward Tarleton of Liverpool, gentleman, on the other part. Witnesseth that the mayor, bailiffs and burgesses for the rents and covenants hereafter specified and in consideration of 20 shillings to them paid by Edward Tarleton have demised and let to Edward Tarleton, his executors, administrators and assigns, all that one messuage, dwelling house, garden in Liverpool in the church or chapel yard, late in the tenure of Richard Loye, deceased, now in the occupation of Margaret Loye, daughter of Richard, as tenants at will, and all buildings, yards, gardens, back sides and easements to the same, to have for the term of 99 years, and fully to be complete if the said Edward, Edward and Thomas Tarleton, sons of the said Edward, or any of them shall happen so long to live, paying therefore yearly the rent of 4 shillings at the feasts of St Michael and the Annunciation by equal portions. And if the said rent is in arrears by 20 days, and no sufficient distress can be found on the premises, it shall be lawful for the mayor, bailiffs and burgesses to re-enter the premises and repossess them. And the said Edward Tarleton promises with the mayor, bailiffs and burgesses that he, his executors and assigns shall sufficiently repair and uphold the messuage in good and sufficient tenantable reparations, and shall yield the same at the end of the term, and in the meantime promises not to let or dispose of the same other than for the term of one year, other than to his wife and children to their own use, without the agreement of the mayor and his successors, and, in the event of the death or departure of Margaret Loye

p. 776
that he will within two years build[94]

p. 777
22 AUGUST 16 CHARLES II

At an assembly in the town hall before the mayor and major part of the common council:

Petition against lighthouses: it is ordered that a petition be framed in the name of the merchant owners of ships and seamen of this borough to oppose a bill

94 Sentence breaks off.

intended to be presented in the next parliament, a draft of which is sent us by the honourable member in parliament for this corporation, Sir Gilbert Ireland, now read to us, for the erecting and setting up of lighthouses within the range of the Red Channel, to testify our utter dislike thereof, and disowning our consent thereunto as in the draft is pretended untruly.

It is also ordered that in any suit now or hereafter commenced against the present mayor or Mr Sturzaker, hallkeeper, Thomas Roe, towncustomer, or any of them, concerning any goods distrained for town's custom or hallage so usually called, by Mr Greenwood or any other freeman or inhabitant of the borough of Lancaster, or by Mr Seawell or any freeman or inhabitant of the city of Carlisle, or borough of Wigan, we unanimously agree that the mayor, hall keeper and town customer shall be saved harmless by this borough and all charges concerning the same shall be paid from the treasury of the town.

Edward Stockley of Derby voted to be a freeman.

p. 778

p. 779
10 MAY 1664

At a meeting of the mayor, aldermen and major part of the common council in the common hall it is ordered that our charter be renewed with what speed may be, to make this an absolute free port, and to that end, and likewise towards satisfying what has been expended in opposing the Cutting bill, it is ordered that a ley of £80 shall be assessed in the borough towards paying the charge of the prosecuting thereof. The merchant appraisers shall take to their assistance two or more of the ablest inhabitants that Mr Mayor shall approve, and forthwith assess the said sum. Samuel Fazakerley, the town clerk shall on Thursday next go to London to solicit the renewing of our charter and making this a free port, if it may be obtained. The town clerk is to have such charters and papers belonging to this borough as Mr Mayor and the aldermen think fit. Signed: Peter Lurting, mayor, Thos. Andoe, Henry Corles, Robart Moore, John Sturzaker, Thomas Storey, Tho. Johnson, Thomas Allcock, bailiffs, John Higginson, John Blundell, John Lourting, John Walls, Thomas Preeson, Raph Hall, John Hese, Ric. Blevin, Henry Ryding, Thos. Roe, Robertt Lyon, Richard Jones, George Bennett, William Fleetwood, William Ackers, William Mulliney.

At a meeting on 6 October 1664 the execution of the order above is suspended till further order.

p. 780

p. 781
INDENTURE, 15 SEPTEMBER 16 CHARLES II, 1664

Between William Boates, son of William Boates late of Liverpool deceased, on the one part, and John Moniley of Liverpool, tailor, on the other part, witnessing that the said William Boates by the consent of the worshipful Peter Lurting, gent., mayor, and of the overseers of the poor, has put himself apprentice to John Moniley to serve from the date hereof for seven years, during which term the said apprentice will serve, keep his master's secrets close, do his commands, and not do or allow harm to his master, to the value of 12d per annum, but shall warn his master. He shall not waste the goods of his master, nor lend them, nor play dice or other unlawful games whereby his master may incur hurt, nor commit fornication in his master's house or elsewhere, nor contract marriage, nor frequent taverns or alehouses unless on his master's business. He shall not absent himself from service by day or night but in all things shall behave himself towards his master and mistress as a good and lawful apprentice. And the said John Moniley, for the sum of £3 10s paid to him by the overseers of the poor, shall well and truly teach his trade to the said apprentice in the best way that he can, and will find meat, drink, apparel, lodging, washing and all other necessaries, the apprentice having two suits of apparel at his entrance. In witness whereof the parties have put their hands and seals. Peter Lurting, mayor. Fazakerley, town clerk.

p. 782

JOHN STURZAKER, GENTLEMAN, MAYOR, 1664 [1664–65]

p. 783
LIVERPOOL. ELECTION COURT FOR THE TOWN AND BOROUGH OF LIVERPOOL IN COUNTY OF LANCASTER, TUESDAY 18 OCTOBER 16 CHARLES II, on the feast of St Luke the Evangelist, before Peter Lurting, gentleman, mayor, Thomas Johnson and Thomas Alcocke, bailiffs, according to charters and ancient customs.

John Sturzaker, gentleman, elected mayor by the votes of the freeman and burgesses, sworn
Thomas Birch, nominated by the said mayor and chosen chief bailiff, sworn
James Holt elected by the freemen to be the other bailiff, sworn

John Entwisle, esq., recorder
Samuel Fazakerley, town clerk
William Moniley, serjeant at mace
Thomas Rowe, water bailiff

   Officers chosen by the common council:
John Leigh, minister
George Glover, schoolmaster
John Sturzaker, hallkeeper
Thomas Rowe, town customer
Richard Rogerson, subcustomer
William Dwarihouse, Jonathan Gleave, stewards of the hall and ley gatherers

p. 784

Officers chosen by the jury, 24 November 1664

Mr Thomas Alcocke, Mr William Kitchin, George Bennet, John Heyes, merchant appraisers, sworn

Edward Holrobin, Edward Buckley, registers of leather, sworn

Anthony Banister, Richard Lurting, aletasters, sworn

Peter Allen, John Roson, Richard Parr, John Rymer, roper, barleymen, sworn

Richard Morecroft, Thomas Gildoes, Ralph Johnson, Henry Knowles, scavengers, sworn

Edward Litherland, William Leech, overseers of the highways, sworn

Humphrey Mercer, murenger

Peter Walker, John Sanderson, porters

Thomas Witter, Thomas Banckes, boothsetters

William Chorley, John Higginson, boardsetters

Richard Rogerson, Thomas Banckes, leavelookers

Thomas Witter, beadle and bellman

p. 785

PORTMOOT COURT OR SESSIONS OF THE PEACE AT LIVERPOOL IN COUNTY OF LANCASTER, 24 OCTOBER 16 CHARLES II 1664, before mayor and bailiffs according to custom.[95]

Inquisition of jurors for our lord the king: Thomas Johnson, John Lurting, Robert Lyon, Thomas Beeston, Richard Windle, John Sandiforth, William Dwarihouse, Samuel Postlethwaite, Edward Flitcroft, Richard Jones, John Johnson, William Ackers, Robert Haughton, Richard Parr, John Litherland, Thomas Nicholson, Timothy Tarleton, William Baylie, John Banber, James Scarisbricke, Thomas Coppull, Jonathan Gleave, William Watmough, William Price, who say in English words.[96]

We present:

Edmund Laurenson for abusing Thomas Williamson junior by breaking his head on the stones

The said Edmund Laurenson for driving his horse away and not paying

Peter Walker for giving Alderman Andoe abusive language, saying you understand nothing

William Crompton, Daniel Curtis, William Cookesey for a tussle

Daniel Curtes for a tussle on a Yorkshireman

William Mosse, John Williamson of Castle Street, Edward Williamson, his brother, for a tussle and bloodwipe

Henry Cooper, shoemaker, for working unlawful leather

95   Latin.
96   Latin.

Thomas Lyon of Rainford for using the faculty of a freeman, not being free; Thomas Tyrer, John Widdowson, Robert Robinson, Edmund Bispham, Jeffrey Clerkson, John Erlun, George King for the like

James Morecroft for buying skins before market time; Thomas Norlum for the like

Elinor Winstanley for selling by a quart under the due assize; Nathan Gleave for the like

Margaret Granger for having 2 swine unrung; Isabel Sutton 1; John Roson 3; Thomas Roe 1; Jane Prescott 1

Richard Rogerson for setting his cart in the street in the night; William Mosse, John Roson, Widow Tarleton for the like

John Hacking for having a dunghill before his house in Tithebarn Street

William Chorley and John Higginson for neglect of raking up dirt in the market place

Richard Rogerson for not carrying away muck from the street in due time

p. 786

Joseph Keele for neglect of his office of scavenger

Richard Lansdale of the Lowe in West Derby for breaking up the highway by digging a hole of great breadth in the highway on the heath within the liberties of this borough

For tethering in the town field: John Heyes, John Rose, Thomas Henshaw, James Litherland, Margaret Bolton, William Wainwright, Robert Cleyton, Edmund Carr

Robert Henshaw for cutting grass in the field

Widow Jones for refusing to give a bond for keeping an inmate when asked

All freemen who entertain any inmates who have not given security according to former order

All freemen who have not appeared at this quarter sessions

We order:

Richard Lansdale to make up the hole on the heath before 5 November on pain of 6s 8d

The water bailiff to set up a pole at the end of the quay on the town's account before 10 November

All freemen having any inmates in their houses who have not given security to Mr Mayor according to former order to give in bond for their security before —, 20s apiece

The curfew to be rung as formerly

We agree to the observance of all ancient orders and laudable customs.

A LETTER FROM THE PRIVY COUNCIL TO THE JUSTICES

After our hearty commendations, whereas for the more speedy furnishing of his majesty's fleet from time to time with able and sufficient mariners and seamen we have thought it expedient that a list of the names of all the seamen of this kingdom be exactly taken and presented to us, we hereby require you to give directions to all the headboroughs, constables and tythingmen or such other persons within the county as you shall conceive most fit, commanding them to make exact lists of the names of all such seamen as inhabit within their respective parishes and precincts, with an account of their ages, and to make speedy return thereof to you, which lists we require you forthwith transmit to us, and a duplicate to the admiral of the county or his deputy. And so nothing doubting of your more than ordinary care in his majesty's important service we bid you farewell from the court at Whitehall, 18 November 1664. Your very loving friends: Bath, Hum. London, Na. Berkley, Albemarle, Anglesey, Jo.Berkley, Ormond, Lauderdale, Midleton, Astley.

p. 787
TUESDAY 13 DECEMBER 1664
At an assembly in the town hall by the mayor, aldermen, bailiffs and common council:

It is ordered that Mr Mayor with others he shall take to assist treat with some of the officers of the custom house of this port to receive with his majesty's customs the custom belonging to this town for all cattle, horses and sheep brought hither out of Ireland, for what salary for receiving the same Mr Mayor shall think meet. And if the officer of his majesty's customs refuse, Mr Mayor treat with John Brooks of Birckett, to receive the same for cattle as landed on the Cheshire side within the liberties of the town, and give him such allowance as he thinks meet.

It is also ordered that the arrears of a church ley levied in Mr Stanley's mayoralty on foreign freemen be demanded and on refusal the parties refusing, according to a clause of their oath, are to be disfranchised.

Also ordered that John Higginson the younger shall repair his shop over against the common hall, or the same to be taken into the mayor's hands to the town's use, and repaired at the town's charge.

Also ordered that a new clock for the hall be bought and set up in place of the old one, by Mr Mayor's order and as he shall approve, at the town's charge, and bars and other repairs shall be made in the common hall as Mr Mayor shall think meet at the town's charge.

PORTMOOT COURT OR QUARTER SESSIONS, MONDAY 6 FEBRUARY 17 CHARLES II 1664, before the mayor and bailiffs.

Inquisition of the jurors: Thomas Alcock, John Blundell, John Owen, William Kitchins, William Travers, William Nicholl, George Bennet, Edward Holrobin, John Burton, John Rymer, Henry Knowles, William Leech, Thomas Gildoes, Brian Mercer, Roger Bushell.[97]

97   Latin.

We present:

William Longworth for a bloodwipe on Laurence Sefton, 6s 8d

Laurence Sefton for a tussle on William Longworth, 3s 4d

Thomas Heapie for a tussle on Serjeant Moniley, 3s 4d

Francis Hardman for a tussle on John Taylor, 3s 4d

John Taylor for the like on Francis Hardman, 3s 4d

John Chambers for a tussle on Matthew Gleave, 3s 4d

Matthew Gleave for the like on John Chambers, 3s 4d

Nathan Gleave for abusing Alderman Lurting, 20s

Joseph Peacock for using the faculty of a freeman, not free, 3s 4d

Thomas Lyon, for the like, 6s 8d

Susan Chapman, John Richardson, Robert Robinson, Mr Arthur Hutton, Thomas Plombe, for the like, 3s 4d apiece

Evan Marsh for keeping 2 swine unrung, 1s; Thomas Galloway 1, 6d; Thomas Roe, 3, 1s 6d; Jane Gerard, 3, 1s 6d; Edward Alcock, 1, 6d; John Walles, 1, 6d; John Chambers, 2, 1s; Thomas Holland, 1, 6d; Mr Gilbert Formbie, 2, 1s; John Lunt, 3, 1s 6d; William Baylie, 6d, Mr Thomas Andoe, 1s; Widow Johnson, 1, 6d; William Garner, 2, 1s; Jane Galloway, 2, 1s; Mrs Bicksteth, 2, 1s; Margaret Goore, 1, 6d; Mr Jones, 6d; Widow Winstanley, 6d; Widow Burton, 3, 1s 6d; Thomas Patrick, 5, 2s 6d; William Bushall, 5, 2s 6d; William Ackers, 1, 6d; Anne Moore, 1, 6d

p. 788

Anthony Banister and Richard Lurting, aletasters, for neglect of their duties, 3s 4d apiece

Richard Morecroft, Thomas Gildoes, Ralph Johnson, scavengers, for neglect, 3s 4d apiece

Richard Everard for breaking up the soil of the common getting turves, 2s

We order:

All headbolts and fences to be made up and ditches scoured by 1 March, on pain of 3s 4d apiece

All not free shall not set any muck on the town waste, 10s apiece, and all who have muck remove it by 1 April, 10s apiece

All who have inmates in this borough give security for them by 20 February, 20s apiece

We agree to all ancient orders.

p. 789

MONDAY 6 MARCH 1664

An Assembly of the mayor, aldermen and major part of the common council:

Ordered that the Pool Bridge at the town's end at Dale Street end shall be repaired at the charge of the town at the direction of Mr Mayor and such as he thinks meet, and the inhabitants of Toxteth and other foreigners assist with their teams and servants.

Ordered that – Butler a stone getter and others of that occupation repair to the
mayor for their liberty to get stones for the town's use, and we approve such contracts
as Mr Mayor shall make with them, and we further order that no foreign moss or stone
getter, not free of the town, get any moss or stones from the heath or common.

That the bailiffs demand the year's rent of 1s from Mr Aspinall for a parcel of
land belonging to the town near the Park wall.

That a plank or sough be made before the town hall door to carry the water from
the same lest the wares there laid may take hurt.

That the beadle shall have a suitable staff and daily attend his office in
convenient places to hinder or take up vagabonds, idle, lusty, sturdy beggars whom
it is no charity to relieve, he only permitting to pass such impotent poor people as
are neighbours, and that he have an augmentation of his year's wages as he shall
merit and Mr Mayor thinks meet.

That the town's common in the holding of Mr Peter Lurting shall be surveyed by
Mr Bailiff Higginson and Mr Robert Lyon, and that on their return to Mr Mayor
Mr Lurting shall be admitted tenant for three lives on a fine Mr Mayor thinks meet.

6 March
William Done admitted, paying 50s, sworn

9 March
James Fletcher of Ormskirk, paying £5, sworn
Isaac Ambrose of Ormskirk, £10
Laurence Smith admitted, £8
Mr David Cook, on producing his certificate of freedom of Bristol, £3, otherwise to
pay £5
John Erlin admitted, £3; dead[98]

p. 790
Ordered that the bailiffs distrain for arrears of the town's rents for stalls, and the
town will bear them out and save them harmless.

That all that shall take any apprentice in this borough shall repair to the town
clerk to enrol the indenture according to ancient usage of the town, and on default
not to expect the benefit of freedom by their indentures, and the clerk is to receive
12d for enrolling and no more, and give them copies if they require.

11 JUNE 1665, APPRENTICE
John Hamlett, base son of Edward Hamlett of this town, by indenture made with
Thomas Preeston, shipwright, 11 June 17 Charles II 1665, became bound to serve
as apprentice with Thomas Preeston for seven years.

p. 791
9 JUNE 1665
An Assembly in the town hall before the mayor, aldermen and common council:

98   Note about death is written in margin.

Patrick Reynolds is admitted tenant to a little shop near the Cross, paying rent of 16 shillings yearly during the pleasure of the mayor and council, and is to remove from there at any year's warning.

It is ordered that the woman who keeps Robert Cliffe's child shall have a quarter's pay.

That a lease shall be made to Robert Sutton's children and their trustees to their use for three lives, viz. the lives of his three children, viz. —, upon surrender of the old lease, gratis.

That the former order touching apprentices' enrollments be strictly pursued.

10 JULY 1665

Ordered by the mayor and common council that a watch shall be set at every street end to continue 24 hours: viz. at Water Street end two, at Dale Street end two, two at the end of Castle Street, at the end of Tithebarn Street and Old Hall Street, and two at the end of Chapel Street, to begin at six in the evening and end at six the next evening, to be observed by the householders in their own persons unless Mr Mayor find just cause to spare them.

20 JULY 1665

Ordered that every inhabitant of the town shall before Michaelmas put so much of the street in good repair as is against their dwelling house, barn or wall to the next channel or middle of the street, on payment of 10s apiece.

That Mr Jerome and his partners who load coals shall assist amending the Pool Bridge as Mr Mayor shall appoint.

That the swine in this town be kept up after Monday next and not allowed to go abroad in the street on pain of 12d for every such swine found, and that the bell man shall take notice of every such, and have 2d for every swine found.

p. 792
John Poole admitted free, 30s, sworn; dead[99]
George King admitted, 50s
William Eccoes, 3s 4d
   6 March:
William Done, 50s
   9 March:
James Fletcher, £5
Isaak Ambrose, £10
Laurence Smyth, £8
Nicholas Stones, £3
David Cook, £3; £2 if certificate from Bristol[100]

99 Note about death is written in margin.
100 Note about certificate from Bristol is written in margin.

Thomas Norbury, £3
John Erlin, £3; dead[101]
    1 May:
Robert Breres, merchant, 6s 8d
    9 June:
William Tyler £4
    10 July:
John Widowson, £2 10s
Edward Archer, gratis as freeman's son
Richard Tubman, £2 10s; dead[102]
    20 July:
William Birchall, £4
William Gorsuch, £3
Thomas Preston, knight, gratis
William Sturton, esq., gratis
William Banckes, esq., gratis
Peeres Leigh, esq., gratis
Thomas Atherton, gent. gratis
William Kirkby, esq. gratis
    29 September:
Thomas Lyon senior, £5
William Slaning, knight, gratis
John Mollyneux, servant, gratis[103]
Thomas Lyon junior, £3
Joseph Buckley, £5
Joseph Peacock, £3; dead[104]
Peter Jones, 3s 4d
Hugo Diggle, £3
Silvester Richmond, gratis
William Crompton, £5
Edward Jones, 3s 4d[105]

p. 793
PORTMOOT COURT OR SESSIONS OF THE PEACE, 21 AUGUST 17
CHARLES II, before mayor and bailiffs according to custom.[106]

    Inquisition taken on oaths of John Blundell gent., John Lurting, Ralph Hall,
Anthony Carr, Robert Woodside, John Moniley, Gregory Formeby, William

---

101 Note about death is written in margin.
102 Note about death is written in margin.
103 Entries for William Slaning and John Mollyneux are inserted in a faint hand.
104 Note about death is written in margin.
105 Latin entry.
106 Latin.

Fleetwood, William Travers, Edward Holrobin, Anthony Banister, John Rymer, Richard Morecroft, James Ball, Roger Bushell, honest and legal men, who say in English words.[107]

We present:

Thomas Hughson of Derby for a bloodwipe on the wife of John Blundell

Nathan Gleave for the like on Samuel Postlethwaite

Samuel Postlethwaite for the like on Nathan Gleave

John Owen for a tussle on Richard Maddock

Richard Maddock for the like on John Owen

Richard Jones for uncivil and abusive language, and other uncivil actions to Mr Sturzaker, now mayor

William Rainford for uncivil and abusive language to the mayor

William Mosse for uncivil and abusive language and other uncivil actions to the mayor

Thomas Lyon for using the faculty of a freeman, not free; Thomas Farclough, Jeffrey Clerkson, Joseph Peacocke, Susan Chapman, John Richardson, Robert Robinson for the like

Mr Arthur Hutton, Mr Henry Jones, Captain Nickson, Mr John Tempest for the like

Mr James Carter, John Harrison, John Hill, John Everard, John Prescott, Thomas Hasledeine, William Newport, Hugh Lathom, Peter Martyn for the like

William Hodges, Robert England, Henry Hardman, William Johnson for the like

Samuel Postlethwaite for keeping unlawful weights

Elinor Winstanley for keeping unlawful quarts

Nathan Gleave, James Scarisbrick for the like

Thomas Lurting for working unlawful leather

Nathan Gleave for selling foreigners' goods in the weekday

Thomas Holland for the like

Mr George Smyth for letting his fence lie down to the town field till barley shot

Mr Robert Seacome for letting his fence lie down to Gregory Formbye's back side

Richard Morecroft for letting his fence lie down to the town field

William Mosse for tethering two horses in the town field and abusing the heyward

Mr George Smyth for cutting grass in the town field, not his own

p. 794

Richard Lonsdale for not filling up the hole in the highway to the Low Hill according to former order

Mr Henry Jones for calling an unlawful assembly together on the town common on the sabbath, 30 July last

107 Latin.

Thomas Row, water bailiff, for letting some ballast be unloaded among the shipping and not presenting the offending party

We order that all innkeepers and alehousekeepers forbear to entertain any apprentices or servants after 9 o'clock at night unless excused by their masters

We present William Mosse for a bloodwipe on William Molleney, now servant of this borough

William Leech for revealing the secrets of the last jury

Mr Gilbert Formebie for keeping his swine unrung; Mr John Sturzaker for 1 swine unrung; Margaret Granger for 2, John Lunt 1, Bailiff Rymmer 1, Anthony Andoe 1, Mr Stones 4, Nathan Gleave 3, Thomas Patrick 5, Mr Thomas Birch 3, Mr William Bushell 2, Mr Thomas Asbrooke 2, Richard Boare 1, Roger James 1, Mrs Alcock 1, Robert Kenion 1, John Williamson 1, Thomas Galloway 1

Captain Lathom for flaying up the common ground and carrying it out of the liberty of the borough

Matthew Gleave, James Smolt for the like

Michael Rumley for laying flax in a pit on the common

The executors of John Higginson for their fence lying down on the side of the town field

Richard Windle, James Blevin, William Ackers for the like

John Lurting for laying muck in the steets inconveniently; William Halsall, James Scarisbrick, John Roson, William Mosse

Richard Rymer for laying muck in the street; Elizabeth Harrison, Mr John Chandler for the like

John Wales for laying timber in the street

Richard Walles for laying rubbish in the street and not cleansing the streets; Mrs Tarleton widow, Robert Kenion, Anne Jumper, William Nicholls, Richard Rogerson, Thomas Banckes, Mr Thomas Peake, Anne Ryding, all for the like

Thomas Wolfall for selling ale unlicensed; John Roson, William Newport, Robert Johnson, William Johnson, Roger James, William Mosse, Robert Kenion, Elizabeth Mercer, James Scarisbrick, Edward Barte for the like

Thomas Duke for encroaching on the town common without consent of mayor and council

Mrs Isabel Rose, an inmate of the town in not giving security to town according to order; Robert Blevin, Mark Hebron, Peter Martyn, Philip Harrison, Hugh Lathom for the same offence.

We order the swine of this town to be kept up according to former order till 29 September next.

We agree all ancient orders and laudable customs.

p. 795

INDENTURE, 20 APRIL 17 CHARLES II, 1665

Between John Sturzaker, mayor, and Thomas Birch and James Hall, bailiffs, of the one part, and Peter Lurting, one of the aldermen, of the other part. Witnesseth that the mayor and bailiffs with the consent of the burgesses and commonalty of the borough for divers good causes and considerations and especially for

20 shillings paid by Peter Lurting have demised and let to Peter Lurting and his
assigns all that piece of land within the Town Field, usually called the Town
Common, alias Godcroft, containing half an acre of land, which has been in the
occupation of Peter Lurting and several of his ancestors, together with all ways,
waters, entries and privileges belonging, to have to him, his executors,
administrators and assigns for 99 years, if Peter Lurting, Ellen Lurting and Alice
Lurting, son and daughters of the said Peter, so long shall live, yielding to the
mayor and bailiffs the yearly rent of 12d at the feast of St Michael the Archangel.
And the mayor and bailiffs promise the said Peter Lurting, his executors and
assigns, peaceful possession of the premises, in witness whereof the said parties
have put their hands.

p. 796

p. 797
29 SEPTEMBER 1665
An Assembly in the common hall by the mayor, aldermen and common council:
   It is ordered that all inhabitants of the town shall watch in their own persons,
and on reasonable excuse to be made to Mr Mayor, hire such as he approves of.
   That Richard Parr shall tend the town clock and keep it in order, and for his
pains (notwithstanding his former bargain with the town) to allow him 13s 4d a
year till further order, and the 40s formerly ordered by him to be repaid shall be
suspended.
   That Roger Harrison be remitted all the arrears which he has made of a stall in
the market and not accounted for to the town, and the same stall shall be taken into
the town's hands and the rent of 6s 8d contracted by Mrs Jones for this year shall
be required by the bailiffs to be paid to the town, and all the rents and profits
thereof for the future.
   That all who bring into the town cartloads of mugs or earthenware, which are
now very numerous, and much cut the streets of the town, shall pay to the town's
use 4d for every cart load.

p. 798

p. 799
AUDIT OF PETER LURTING, LATE MAYOR, and Thomas Johnson and Thomas
Alcock, late bailiffs, Monday 8 May 17 Charles II, 1665.

Received of Alderman Sturzaker, hallkeeper and Thomas Rowe, town customer, for the last year's account	£50	14s	5d
Richard Rogerson, subcustomer	11	13	2
License and composition money	5	19	0
Presentments of juries	8	1	4
Freemen	73	13	4

Rent of stalls	19	6	6
Schoolmaster's money	5	13	3
Town's rents	10	4	8
On a ley	19	13	8
Overplus of subsidies		14	5
Of executors of Robert Sutton due on bond	60	0	0
Of Mr Kitchin & William Garner which was to balance the account at audit	41	0	0
Captain Edward Tarleton for fine of Margaret Loye's house	1	0	0
Of Richard Linaker, use of his bond		6	0
Of Mr Samuel Fazakerley for place as town clerk, for half year ending October last	2	10	0
Of Mr Edward Alcock part of his bill of £20	15	0	0
The whole receipt	£325	19	9
The whole disbursements	229	18	5½
Remaining to balance account now paid to the use of the bailiffs Thomas Birch, James Holt	96	1	3½

Debts in the former bailiffs' hands, and at this audit to the now bailiffs:
Edward Formbie's bond of £20
Mr Gilbert and Edward Formbie for restor. and rent of ferry boat £100
Richard Linaker's bond £10
Robert Sutton's two bonds, one payment of £6 10s, the other of £6 16s, £13 6s
Mr Chandler & Mr Blackmore note £2 12s 6d
Remainder of Mr Alcock's note £2
Richard Blevin's note £2

Auditors: John Sturzaker, mayor, Thomas Andoe, Henry Corles, John Chandler, Peter Lurting, aldermen, Samuel Fazakerley, town clerk.

p. 800
9 JUNE 1665
    An Assembly in the town hall before the mayor, aldermen and common council. On reading of Mr William Norman, the High Constable's precept, reciting a letter from the chancellor of his majesty's exchequer for raising money for his majesty's supply, it is ordered that Mr Mayor shall propose (at the next meeting of the

commissioners) such persons as he thinks fit for the paying in of nine months assessment, according to his majesty's proposal, and that such persons shall be indemnified and saved harmless. And further it is ordered that Mr Mayor, being one of his majesty's commissioners for the royal aid, may inform himself of what other course he finds meet at the next meeting of the commissioners in answer to the lord treasurer's letter, and what he shall then do is ratified. And it is also unanimously ordered that the same nine months assessment shall be collected with speed from all the inhabitants of the town according to the last assessment, that is to say, for every 12d in the last assessment, this time 3 shillings, which said nine months makes up the whole year ending at Christmas next. Signed: John Sturzaker, mayor, Tho. Andoe, Henry Corles, Robart Moore, Peter Lurting, T the mark of Thomas Birch, Ja. Hoult, Jo. Sandiford, John Blundell, John Lorting, Will. Gardner, William Eccleston, + the mark of Bayliff Owen, Tho. Johnson, Thomas Alcock, Tho. Preson, Tho. Bridge, Rob. Lyon, Raph Hall, Will. Fleetwood, Henry Riding, Richard Jones, William Accars, Sam. Fazakerley, William Mulliney, Thomas Roe.

MICHAEL TARLETON, GENTLEMAN, MAYOR [1665–66]

p. 801
LIVERPOOL. ELECTION COURT FOR TOWN AND BOROUGH OF LIVERPOOL IN COUNTY OF LANCASTER, WEDNESDAY 18 OCTOBER 1665, 17 CHARLES II, the feast day of St Luke the Evangelist, before John Sturzaker, gent., mayor, Thomas Birch and James Holt, bailiffs, according to custom in the common hall.

Michael Tarleton, gentleman, elected mayor by the votes of the freemen, sworn
Thomas Preeston is chosen by the said Mr Mayor chief bailiff, sworn
George Bennett is elected by the freemen the other bailiff, sworn.

John Entwisle, esq., recorder
Samuel Fazakerley, town clerk
William Mulliney, serjeant at mace
Thomas Roe, water bailiff, sworn town customer

   Officers chosen by the common council, Friday 20 October 1665:
John Leigh, minister
George Glover, schoolmaster
Mr John Sturzaker, hallkeeper, sworn
Thomas Rowe, town customer, sworn
Subcustomer respited
Thomas Holland, James Scairsbricke, stewards of the hall and ley gatherers

p. 802
Mr Thomas Johnson, Mr James Holt, Thomas Bridge, William Fleetwood, merchant appraisers, sworn

William Ackers, Ralph Johnson, registers of leather, sworn
Peter Allen, John Storie, aletasters, sworn
William Tyrer, Anthony Johnson, John Erlinn, James Fletcher, barleymen, sworn
John Mulliney, tailor, John Litherland, carpenter, overseers of the highways
Edward Barton, murenger
William Eccoes, Richard Tubman, Thomas Finloe, George King, scavengers, sworn
John Sanderson, Peter Walker, John Poole, Roger Bushell, William Symson, porters
Richard Rogerson, Thomas Banckes, leavelookers
William Chorley, John Higginson, boardsetters
Thomas Banckes, Thomas Wittar, boothsetters
Thomas Wittar, beadle and bellman.

p. 803
PORTMOOT COURT OR SESSIONS OF THE PEACE FOR TOWN AND BOROUGH OF LIVERPOOL IN COUNTY OF LANCASTER, 23 OCTOBER 17 CHARLES II, before the mayor and bailiffs.[108]

Inquisition of the jurors for the the lord king, Thomas Birch, William Rimer, James Smoult, Thomas Galloway, Brian Mercer, Robert Simpson, William Ackers, Robert Eccoes, William Leech, Robert Fleetwood, William Baylie, James Travers, William Crompton, John Johnson, Edward Buckley, Anthony Banister, Peter Allen, John Roson, William Dwarrihouse, Thomas Gildoes, Ralph Johnson, Roger Bushell, Richard Parr who say in English words.[109]

We present:
Jane Eccleston for selling ale by an unlawful quart, 6d; Edward Sutton, Henry Ryding, James Hey for the like, 12d apiece
Henry Crane for keeping 1 swine unrung, 12d; Jane Gerard, alias Haskeine, 1; Margery Formebie, 1; Richard Crompton, 6; Mr Gilbert Formebie, 1; John Lunt, 1; Anne Andoe, 2; William Garner, 3; Dorothy Johnson, 2; William Ackers,2; Mr John Sandiford, 3; Anne Moore, 1; Thomas Holland, 3; Mr Strangewaies, 1; Thomas Roe, 3; William Robinson, 2; John Williamson, 4; 12d a piece for every swine
Isabel Sutton and Widow Boane for letting their fence lie down between Mrs Bixsteth and the said Isabel
Mr Oliver Lyme for not making his street clean before the Tower, 6d
William Halsall, William Nicholls, Robert Kenion, Gregory Formbie for setting barrels in the street by their doors and not cleansing the street, 6d apiece
Mr Thomas Alcocke for not cleansing the street before his shop, 6d

108   Latin.
109   Latin.

Widow Heyes, Mr Laurence Breers, John Higginson, William Chorley, Richard Jones, John Lunt for the like, 6d apiece

Mrs Bicksteth for laying muck in Tithebarn Street, 6d

Mr John Lurting for not scouring his gutter at the end of his house in Dale Street which hinders the passage of the watercourse, 12d

Mr Samuel Fazakerley for not producing the record of several of the officers last year to this jury

John Tarleton, tanner, for selling leather unsealed, 3s 4d

Thomas Lurting for working unlawful leather

p. 804

Mr Samuel Fazakerley for a tussle on bailiff Alcock, 3s 4d

Mr Thomas Alcock for a tussle on him

Robert Ireland, Henry Webster, Edward Lea, Edmund Parr, Thomas Taylor, Edmund Lyon, John Tenant, and John Hodgson for not appearing to do their suit at this sessions, 3s 4d apiece

All other freemen who did not appear

Widow Birch in Dale Street for entertaining a woman and three children and not giving security to the town according to order, 20s

Alice Chamber for entertaining a man and his wife and child without security, 20s

We order:

That every freeman who employs any of the porters, if they cannot serve at a convenient time, they may employ any freeman they please and the porters shall have no allowance from that work

The porters shall give security for their trust in the work they undertake

There shall be erected two posts and a rail by the steps against the Tower at the waterside and the battlements by the steps shall be repaired before 12 November

All the quarry holes by the waterside near the highway to be filled by 25 November, on penalty on those who made them, 6s 8d

Any carter who refuses to help a freeman when his cart is empty shall forfeit to the town, 3s 4d

No carter shall go over a cable with his cart laden if there is another way, 3s 4d.

12 NOVEMBER 1665

Mr John Arrowsmith admitted and sworn a free burgess by the free consent of the mayor and aldermen, gratis, as a former benefactor of the town.

p. 805

THURSDAY 2 NOVEMBER 1665

At an Assembly in the common hall before the mayor, aldermen, bailiffs and the major part of the common council:

Because of the spreading contagion of the plague in divers neighbouring towns in Cheshire and other parts and of the great concourse of people from those parts at the time of the fairs kept in the town, it is ordered that the keeping of the fair here on St Martin's Day eve, and other usual days after shall on this present danger be absolutely forbidden by open publication in the open market on next market day.

Ordered that the swine of this town shall be kept on back sides or styes according to several former orders, and not allowed to go in the streets or on other men's ground or gardens on pain of 12d for every swine, to be paid by distress and sale, giving the overplus to the owners, one half of the fine for the poor of this town, and the other half for him employed by Mr Mayor to find out defaulters, and shall by his warrant distrain the goods of the offenders.

It is also ordered that the former orders that the mayor, aldermen, bailiffs, bailiffs peers, town clerk and serjeant at mace shall have gowns in the ancient manner, shall be put into execution, and that each shall provide themselves with fit gowns before 2 February, on pain of £5.

p. 806
THURSDAY — NOVEMBER

Richard Wainwright and Ralph, the one apprentice to Richard Lievesley and the other to his wife, formerly to Richard Leivesley, proved by indentures shown by Mr Evan Marsh to have duly served seven years, are admitted freemen, at the fine of 6s 8d apiece.

p. 807
PORTMOOT COURT OR SESSIONS OF THE PEACE, 22 JANUARY 17 CHARLES II, before mayor and bailiffs according to custom.[110]

Inquisition of the jurors of our lord king, Thomas Johnson, Thomas Alcocke, John Walles, William Tyrer, Thomas Scarisbricke, Thomas Simson, Richard Tubman, John Storie, John Kellie, William Eccles, Robert Hall, Thomas Tatlock, John Moniley, tailor, Ralph Johnson, Robert Fleetwood, who say in English words.[111]

We present:

Henry Crane, John Fairhurst, William Leech, James Middleton, fighting on the watch, 3s 4d apiece

John Roson for breaking the town's pound, 6s 8d

Roger Bushell for digging, cutting and encroaching on the highway on the east side of the castle, four yards in breadth, 6s 8d

Said Roger Bushell for making a ditch on the town's waste on the south side of the castle, 3s 4d

Robert Robinson for using the faculty of a freeman not being free, 3s 4d; Richard Strang of Bootle, William Kellie of this town, Robert Ballard of Derby, for the like, 3s 4d apiece

---

110 Latin.
111 Latin.

William Bushell for keeping 6 swine unrung, 3s; William Garner, 3, 1s 6d; Roger James, 3, 1s 6d; William Eccleston, 1, 6d; Mrs Dorothy Johnson, 2, 1s; William Milles, 2, 1s; James Apleton, 1, 6d; Anne Moore, 1, 6d; Mr John Sandiford, 2, 1s; Robert Bicksteth for the like.

James Heyes for selling ale by a quart under the assize, 1s

Thomas Fazakerley, shoemaker, for working unlawful leather, 2s 6d; James Stringfellow for the like, 2s 6d

Mr John Chandler for not cleansing the street before his house, 6d; Mrs Bicksteth for the like before her barn, 6d; Thomas Patrick for the like, 6d

p. 808

Those that keep streets foul continually: Richard Windle, William Ackers, Mrs Dorothy Johnson, Anthony Meyris, William Brise, 6d apiece

Thomas Bankes for not cleansing his part of the street, 6d

Thomas Aspe, skinner, for buying skins before the market time, 2s 6d; James Moorecroft, Thomas Norland, Humphrey Copple, for the like, 2s 6d apiece

Robert Hey of Ormskirk for bringing muttons and veals to market without their skins, 1s apiece

We order:

All the inhabitants of this town to mend as much of the street before their houses or barns to the gutter as is broken up, before 1 May, according to former order, in forfeit of 10s apiece to offenders; to be presented at next portmoot[112]

Roger Bushell to throw down the new ditch he made on south side of castle before 10 February, on pain of 20s, amerced 5s; and the same to throw down the coppe[113] he made on the highway on the east side of the castle into the castle trench, and throw up that part of the highway he threw down into the trench, before 15 February, on pain of 20s, amerced 5s

Headbolts and fences to be made up, ditches scoured, before 1 March, 3s 4d apiece

All who have entertained any inmates in their houses and not given security to the mayor according to former order, shall give security to the mayor before 2 February, in forfeit of 20s apiece; to be enquired by the bailiffs from house to house[114]

— Simpson to make up the shooting butts on the heath before 25 March

We agree to all ancient orders and laudable customs.

p. 809

AUDIT TAKEN TUESDAY 24 JANUARY 17 CHARLES II, 1665 OF MR JOHN STURZAKER, MAYOR, Thomas Birch, bailiff for himself, and James Holt, bailiff, deceased, in the common hall before the mayor, aldermen then present and auditors.

---

112 Note about presentment at next portmoot is added in margin.
113 Probably a hole made in the ground: OED.
114 Note about bailiffs' enquiry is added in margin.

	£	s	d
Recd. from Mr Sturzaker and Thomas Rowe for town's custom hallage, license and composition	£101	13s	0d
Of Richard Rogerson	11	6	10
From former bailiffs, Thomas Johnson & Mr Alcock	96	1	3
From Isabel Sutton on two bonds	13	6	0
From Mrs Jane Alcock on a note	2	0	0
For schoolmaster	5	13	3
The town's rent	9	19	6
Interest on Linaker's bond		6	0
Of Alderman Lurting's fine for town common	1	0	0
Of Mr Formebie for a piece of timber		17	0
For stalls	18	6	6
For freemen	81	6	8
For fines	7	7	6
From Mr Fazakerley	5	0	0
From Mrs Sturzaker for a bullock seized from Mr Weyborne for custom	1	10	0
The whole receipts	355	13	6
The whole disbursements as appear by particular accounts given by the bailiffs	206	15	9½
Remains to balance the account	148	17	8½

Paid to the now bailiffs, Mr Thomas Preeston and George Bennett in cash, £127 17s 8½d

Delivered to balance the rest of the account on bond from Robert Lyon of £5, and another bond from Thomas Row for £16 debt, £21.

Debts formerly delivered into the old bailiffs hands, and now delivered to the new bailiffs:

Edward Formbie's bond £20

Mr Gilbert and Edward Formbie's bond, £100

Richard Linaker's bond of £10

Mr Chandler and Mr Blackmore's bill, £2 12s 6d

Richard Blevin's bill, £4

The aforementioned accounts are allowed: Michael Tarleton, mayor, Henry Corles, Peter Lurting, John Sturzaker, Samuel Fazakerley, town clerk.[115]

115 Signatures.

p. 810
8 NOVEMBER 1665
Richard Wright, apprentice to Widow Leivesley, and after to Evan Marsh, was admitted a free burgess.

p. 811
PORTMOOT COURT OR SESSIONS OF THE PEACE, 26 MARCH 18 CHARLES II, before mayor, greater part of freemen, and bailiffs according to custom.[116]

Inquisition of jurors for our lord king, Thomas Johnson, Thomas Birch, John Lurting, Richard Jones, Thomas Bicksteth, Anthony Walles, Thomas Norbury, Richard Windle, Anthony Banister, William Dwarihouse, Peter Allen, John Erlum, George King, John Burton, Robert Davie, who say in English words.[117]

We present:
Roger Bushell for selling stinking herring in market, 12d; John Kenion for the like, 12d
Mr Thomas Christian, merchant, for not paying the town's duty of 6s 8d for hides sold to a foreign tanner, 10s
Thomas Birchall for selling shoes made of unlawful leather, 2s 6d
John Richardson for using the faculty of a freeman, 3s 4d;
Robert Robinson, Richard Strange, John Harrison of Formby, Mr Robinson, strongwaterman, remitted;[118] Robert Ballard, Jeffrey Clerkson, William Kelley of this town, all for the like, 3s 4d apiece
Roger Bushell for not obeying two former orders for the throwing down of the coppes at the east and south of the castle, 5s
Nathan Gleave for 2 swine unrung, 12d; John Sandiford, 2, 12d; Anne Andoe, widow, 12d
Thomas Bancks for not cleansing the street in the market, 6d; Mr Laurence Bryers, John Higginson, Thomas Patricke, William Chorley, Thomas Witter, all for the like, 6d apiece
Mr Oliver Lyme for not clearing wood from the street
Mr Done for not making up the headbolt between him and Edward Bancks, 12d
The barleymen for neglect of their office, John Earlom, William Tyrer, Anthony Johnson, James Fleetwood, 12d apiece

p. 812
Robert Woodside for selling ale unlicensed, 3s 4d; Robert Mercer, John Bleasdell,[119] David Cooke, John Poultney, for the like, 3s 4d apiece

116 Latin.
117 Latin.
118 Note about remitted is added in margin.
119 John Bleasdell is crossed out.

We order:

The bailiffs to take an account through the town of such as have entertained inmates without security; may give security by 16 April on forfeiture of 20s apiece, and 20s for the bailiffs if they neglect to take an account

Thomas Bridge to move his muck from John Kelly's wall by 14 April and lay no more there, 3s 4d

John Mulleney, sailor and John Litherland, carpenter, overseers of the highway, to give notice to the inhabitants to mend the highway where wanting before their houses and barns by 20 May, and to see that the town highways be put in good repair, on forfeiture of 10s

No person to tether horse or beast in the townfield at night, 3s 4d for each default

The water bailiff to see that John Walles and Richard Windle set up a sufficient pole at the quay end at their own cost by 1 May, 10s, amerced 3s 4d apiece

We agree to all ancient orders and laudable customs.

p. 813
28 FEBRUARY 1666

At an Assembly of the mayor, aldermen and major part of the common council assembled in the common hall, it was unanimously agreed that whereas the freemen of the city of Carlisle and town of Lancaster claim freedom from paying any tolls or town customs within this borough and have had former suits with the officers of this town, and still threaten to prosecute the said suits, from henceforth all officers employed by the mayor of this town to take tolls or town customs from any citizens of London, Carlisle or Lancaster shall be indemnified at the common charge of this borough, and all their costs shall be paid from the public stock of the town.

p. 814

p. 815

p. 816
TOWN RENTS
Edward Hobson, gent.
William Poultneye's and Boate's house
Mr Edward Tarleton for Margaret Loy's house
Edward More, esq. for town common, 3s 4d, and the little lane, 8d
Mr Edward Tarleton for Church Steele house
Mr Edward Tarleton for —
William Eccleston for Burscoe's
Mr William Strangwaies for Seacome's
Mr Cornell's child for Browne's croft
John Vose of Garston for Mr Norres
Kenion's house[120]

120 Kenion's house is added in margin.

Mr Gilbert Aspinwall for an enclosure
— for house in Castle Street; Richard Rose[121]
Widow Lurting, her house
Mr Henry Corley for Sickman's Lane and town common
Mr Peter Lurting for the town common in lease
Elen Blevin for the Mill dale
Widow Harrison for the corner shop
William Strangwaies for a cottage, 2s a year for 5 years; and Mr Winstanley[122]
Cooke's house and lands leased to Robert Suttons's children.

p. 817
TOWN'S CUSTOMS
   Whereas the owners and masters of ships belonging to the port and borough of Liverpool, being all or most free burgesses, have by their oaths at enfranchisement engaged to increase the liberties and customs of the town, and to aid the mayor and his officers to maintain the customs, nevertheless the same owners and masters have not only omitted to make their invoice of goods imported but also have been remiss (if not wilfully refusing), in assisting the officers in the collection of the duty of town's custom on cattle and other goods by them imported from Ireland. It is therefore, at a general meeting of the mayor, aldermen and major part of the common council of this borough, 18 May 1666, ordered that the respective owners and masters and pursers of vessels belonging to the port, being freemen of the borough, shall at their landing of any cattle brought from Ireland within the limits of this port, pay for such cattle, be the same on the Cheshire or the Lancashire side, on pain of 6s 8d for every default, and, if any question arise, any officer employed for collecting the same, or levying the penalty, shall be defended and saved harmless at the charge of the town.
   Ordered at the same time that Mr Mayor shall take such of the aldermen as he shall think meet to view a place of wasteground on the castle hill where Peter Allen desires to build a smithy.

p. 818

p. 819
PORTMOOT COURT AT LIVERPOOL IN COUNTY OF LANCASTER, 2 JULY 18 CHARLES II, before the mayor, burgesses and bailiffs according to custom.[123]

   Inquisition of the jury of our lord king: John Blundell, John Buckley, Timothy Tarleton, Francis Ryding, Thomas Coppull, John Williamson, William Travers, John Storie, John Litherland, Anthony Johnson, Anthony Banister, Robert Fleetwood, Thomas Finloe, Edward Buckley, Evan Gerard, who say in English words.[124]

---

121 Richard Rose is added in margin.
122 Mr Winstanley is added in margin.
123 Latin.
124 Latin.

We present:

John Rose of Prescot Lane in West Derby for a tussle on Thomas Rose of Low Hill in West Derby, 3s 4d

Thomas Rose for the like tussle on John Rose, 3s 4d

William Bushell, slater, for using the faculty of a freeman, not being free; Robert Bushell, James Hesketh, Mr Richard Robinson, free,[125] William Kelly, Margaret Granger, 6s 8d each; William Worrall, 3s 4d; Thomas Stockley, 3s 4d; Jeffrey Clerkson, 6s 8d, Robert Robinson, made free; John Harrison of Formby, 6s 8d; Jane Martin, 3s 4d; Mr Arthur Hutton, 6s 8d; Mr John Tempest, 6s 8d; Mr Anthony Nixon, 6s 8d; Mr William Strangwayes, 3s 4d; Mr Henry Jones, 6s 8d; all for the like.

Richard Crompton for keeping and selling by unlawful quarts, 12d; William Gardner, James Fletcher, Thomas Dicconson, for the like, 12d apiece

John Owen for neglect of sending his cart to the highway, 5s; John Lunt, William Middleton, John Roson, John Holland, Edward Banckes, William Mosse, Thomas Birch, John Kellie, for the like, 5s apiece

Mrs Tarleton for keeping her swine unrung, 6s; Peter Baite, 1, 6d; Thomas Wolfall, 2, 12d; Richard Morecroft, 1, 6d; Mrs Robinson, 3, 18d; John Potter, 4, 2s; John Harries, 1, 6d; William Gardner, 4, 2s; William Bushell, 2, 12d; William Ackers, 1, 6d; Margaret Granger, 1, 6d; Edward Jones, 1, 6d

Richard Widdowes for getting turves on this side of the common contrary to mayor's order

William Ackers and Ralph Johnson for neglect of their offices, 2s 6d apiece

Alehousekeepers unlicensed, Robert Johnson, Roger James, William Brewerton, William Mosse, 3s 4d apiece

p. 820

All landlords who have not given security to the mayor for their tenants, inmates, strangers not free, according to former orders, hereafter named:
In Chapel Street:

Thomas Lancelot for entertaining Thomas Robinson and 1 child, 6s 8d

Widow Dawson, for James Perry and 2 children

Mrs Bicksteth for John Bicksteth, discharged

Mr Thomas Sandiford for Thomas Smalshaw, Henry Chernock, 6s 8d

Mrs Asbrooke and executors of Thomas Asbrooke for James Apleton, 6s 8d

Mr William Bushell for Broockbanck for Robert Edwards and Robert Fell

Dorothy Bicksteth for John Prescott and Richard Kenion,[126] 6s 8d

Edmund Whalley, Thomas Holland departed from thence

Elen Blevin for T. Hurdis, William Mercer and William Richardson, 10s

John Litherland for Philip Harrison and 2 children, 6s 8d

William Halsall for Cuthbert Cuthbert[127] Kulcheth, his wife and children, and for Margaret Lansdale and Jeremy Finloe

125 Note about free is added in margin.
126 Richard Kenion is crossed out.
127 Cuthbert is repeated.

Thomas Patrick, Thomas Johnson, wife and 4 children, 10s

Richard Browne for Henry Huetson and Margaret Yongwoman and William Evans, 6s 8d

Edgar Sutton, Mr Preswick and wife

John Harries, George Place and wife and widow Higginson

Richard Wright for Thomas Taffee, 6s 8d

John Williamson for Richard Mallett, wife and 1 child, 6s 8d

Widow Harrison, George Wright and wife, Robert Robinson and John Hill, Tybergh, 10s

Mr William Strangwaies for Richard Tarleton, free.

p. 821

We present:

Samuel Postlethwaite, free burgess, for suing the mayor in the court of common pleas at Lancaster where the said mayor would hold pleas

Margaret Hunter, widow, for a bloodwipe on Ellen Lunt, 6s 8d

Thomas Roe, waterbailiff, for neglect of his office in suffering ballast to be cast on the wharf and if he find them out then we present the offenders, 6s 8d

All those who do not appear to their recognisance in this court

Roger Bushell for not obeying two former orders about his ditch on the town's waste, 6s 8d

We order:

That all those who take any apprentices cause them to be enrolled in the town's book according to former order within 12 months of the commencement of their terms, on pain of 5s

Thomas Darwin and all others that keep any mastiff dogs that they either keep them up, or muzzle them, 13s 4d

Henry Crane and Richard Williamson, churchwardens last year, that they execute the office of overseers of the poor, and that they go about the town once every month and give notice to Mr Mayor what poor have come into the town, and so the churchwardens after their office of churchwardenship is up shall be determined as overseers of the poor the year then after next, on pain of £5

Thomas, son of John Erlum, on 16 August 1666 was bound apprentice to Captain Edward Tarleton, to serve him for seven years.

p. 822

FREEMEN ADMITTED AND SWORN

28 February 1665:

John Arrowsmith, gentleman, free

Joseph Richardson, shoemaker, £7

William Carie, £2 10s

Thomas Tyrer, of Huyton, blacksmith, £4

9 October 1666:

Brian Fleetwood, butcher, £3

28 February 1665:
Henry Rycroft, apprentice of John Fey, 6s 8d
Huon Gerard, elected heyward, elected free
Henry Higginson, £3
   15 March 1665:
Thomas Drins of Colchester, free
John Sayre of Bolers hall, free
Ferdinand Stanley, free
   15 May 1666:
Robert Houll, 40s
Richard Robinson, £5
Ralph Anton, as apprentice, 6s 8d
Richard Wright, as apprentice, 6s 8d
   23 July 1666:
James Jones, butcher, £4
John Souper, mariner, £2 10s
Thomas Parrie, £3
   13 September 1666:
Thomas Marsh, 3s 4d
Ralph Eccleston, 3s 4d
Richard Tarleton, 3s 4d
James Brindle, as apprentice, 6s 8d
   14 September 1666:
Henry Hey, £10
Thomas Wright, gentleman, £6
John Tempest, £5
Robert Robinson, £6, the mayor remitting on a plea
   17 September 1666:
James Sanderson, apprentice of James Blevin, 6s 8d
   9 October 1666:
Charles Christian, £7
Thomas Glover, £3
Jeffrey Clerkson, £3
Peter Atherton, as apprentice, 6s 8d
   12 October 1666:
John Jones, free
William Preeston, 3s 4d.[128]

p. 823
TUESDAY 9 JULY 1666
   An Assembly before the mayor, the aldermen and bailiffs and the rest of the common council in the common hall. Whereas a suit is threatened by Lord

128 Latin.

Molyneux for the seigniory of this town of Liverpool in reference to the common or waste if the same be not yielded to him, on a proposal by Mr Mayor it is unanimously agreed and ordered that the ancient claim and title of seigniory of the commons of this town in the mayor, bailiffs and burgesses be maintained and defended at the charge of the town against Lord Molyneux or any other that shall endeavour to invade the same, and that all and every member of this borough concerned in the same suit on behalf of the town shall be indemnified and saved harmless. Michael Tarleton, mayor, Tho, Andoe, alderman, Henry Corles, John Chandler, Peter Lurting, John Sturzaker, Tho. Preeston, bailiff, Sam. Fazakerley, William Rimer, John Blundell, John Lorting, Robt. Lyon, John Owen, Tho. Johnson, Thomas Allcock, John Walls, William Eccleston, William A Harre, Willm. Fleetwood, Richard Jones, Thomas Bridge, Ralph Hall, Thomas Roe, William Mulliney, Thomas B Birch.[129]

Mr Robert Moore consented to the above but declined to subscribe his name.

p. 824

23 JULY 1666

An assembly of the mayor and common councilmen in the common hall:

It is ordered that Peter Allen, for 2s 6d a year, may build a smithy on a spot of ground on the Castle Hill, of 6 yards breadth to the front in such place as shall be set out by the bailiffs, and for that rent shall have a lease made to him by the mayor, bailiffs and burgesses for three lives, and the mayor, bailiffs and burgesses shall be indemnified by this town if any question or suit shall be, and that James Scarisbrick shall remove his timber there forthwith.

It is ordered that Mr Nicholls be admitted tenant for 3 lives of a spot of waste ground between the church wall and stairs, on such rent and fine as Mr Mayor and such as he shall take to view the same shall think meet.

It is ordered, according to former order, that no goods seized by Mr Sturzaker or any officer of this town for town's custom from Mr John Greenwood or any of the inhabitants of Lancaster, shall be redelivered, and if any suit arise Mr Sturzaker and every officer shall be indemnified by the town. The like order made in the suit between Carlisle and Mr Sturzaker and Thomas Rowe.

24 SEPTEMBER 1666

An Assembly of the mayor and common council in the common hall:

It is ordered that such as Mr Mayor shall appoint shall view and set out as much ground as convenient without damage to the street for John Mulliney to build a house near the church stile in Chapel Street with a small garden.

It is also ordered that Mr William Bushell be admitted tenant of 16 foot square of waste ground on the heath or common near the Stoops at the warping place to

129 Signatures.

build a house on, and shall have a lease from the mayor, bailiffs and burgesses at a reasonable rent.

George Seddon, his mark; John Prescott[130]

p. 825

p. 826

[CHARLES, EARL OF DERBY, MAYOR, 1666–67][131]

p. 827
ELECTION COURT FOR TOWN AND BOROUGH OF LIVERPOOL IN COUNTY OF LANCASTER IN THE COMMON HALL, THURSDAY 18 OCTOBER 1666, the feast of St Luke the Evangelist, before Michael Tarleton, mayor, Thomas Preeston and George Bennett, bailiffs, according to custom.

Charles, Earl of Derby[132] is elected mayor (no-one contradicting) by unanimous vote of the freemen
Thomas Bicksteth is nominated by the right honourable the mayor to be chief bailiff and sworn
John Bulckeley is elected by the freemen to be the other bailiff, sworn.

John Entwisle, esq., recorder
Samuel Fazakerley, town clerk
William Mulliney, serjeant at mace
Thomas Roe, water bailiff

Officers elected by the common council Friday 20 October 1666:
Minister, Mr John Leigh
Schoolmaster, Mr George Glover
Hallkeeper, Mr John Sturzaker, sworn
Town customer, Mr Thomas Rowe, to have £4 augmented to his former wages, sworn
Subcustomer, Richard Rogerson
Stewards of the hall and ley gatherers, William Crompton, Anthony Banister, sworn
Church clerk, William Poultney
Heyward, Evan Gerard

130 This entry added at foot of page, distinct from other entries.
131 There is no heading to this mayoral year.
132 This is written in large, bold letters.

Officers elected Monday 22 October 1666 at a portmoot court or quarter sessions in common hall:

Mr Thomas Birch, sworn, George Bennett, sworn, Mr William Rimer, refused 25 October,[133] John Walles, sworn, merchant appraisers

Joseph Richardson, sworn, Robert Holt, sworn, Edward Eccles, William Done, sworn, barleymen

William Price, William Tyrer, aletasters, sworn

Edward Jones, James Toppinge, surveyors of the highway

James Fletcher, William Robinson, registers of leather, sworn

Joseph Peacocke, Ralph Anton, Hugh Diggles, William Carr, scavengers

p. 828

p. 829

LIVERPOOL. PORTMOOT COURT OR QUARTER SESSIONS FOR BOROUGH OF LIVERPOOL IN COUNTY OF LANCASTER, IN THE COMMON HALL, MONDAY 22 OCTOBER 1666, before the Earl of Derby, mayor, Thomas Bicksteth and John Bulkeley, bailiffs, according to custom.

Inquisition of the jurors: Thomas Preeston, Thomas Birch, John Johnson, William Fleetwood, William Ackers, Robert Fleetwood, Robert Leadbeter, William Prise, John Storie, William Dwarrihouse, James Boates, Robert Burt, Thomas Holland, Robert Hall, Richard Robinson, Peter Allen, William Tyrer, John Moniley, William Eccoes, Edward Banckes, Jonathan Gleave, John Souper, James Fletcher, Evan Gerard.

We present:

James Fletcher for not buying, and working leather unsealed, 2s 6d

Thomas Ireland, tanner, for selling unlawful leather, 2s 6d

Edmund Laurenson for the like, 3s 4d

Mr John Sandiford for keeping his swine unrung, 1, 6d; Richard Browne, 1, 6d; William Ackers, 1, 6d; Elizabeth Sanderson, 1, 6d; William Granger, 10, 5s; Robert Kenion, 1, 6d; Katherine Rainford, 2, 1s; Timothy Holt, 2, 1s; Mrs Tarleton, 1, 6d; Henry Chernock, 1, 6d; John Roson, 1, 6d

Robert Lyon for breaking the common pound, 5s

Ellen Holland and Elizabeth Mosse for forestalling the market, 12d apiece

— Hey, widow, for buying in the market and selling the same day, 6d

Richard Diggles for using the faculty of a freeman not free, 12d; John Richardson, Randle Williamson, for the like, 3s 4d apiece; Jeremy Tomlison, 5s; Robert Prenton, 3s 4d

John Whitfield of Low Hill for cutting gorse and taking it off the town common, 3s 4d

133 Rimer's refusal is added in the margin.

William Mosse for setting his cart in the street, 6d; John Roson for the like
All freemen who have not made appearance at this court

p. 830
Mrs Alcock to pull down her lime kiln on the town waste within 10 days, penalty 30s

We order:
No lime kiln be erected between Chapel Street and the Pool, £5
No lime stones or other rubbish be heaved out of any ship or boat between the post or mark set up, £5
The water bailiff to take care that no lime stones or other rubbish be heaved out of any boat between the places aforesaid, 13s 4d, unless licensed by mayor
All persons who keep swine shall keep them up on market and sabbath days, 12d apiece
John Johnson of Everton to scour his ditch and cut his wood that it be no annoyance to Alderman Lurting, by candlemas, 13s 4d
Alderman Peter Lurting cause a fair cart way to be left at the head of his lands for John Johnson and others to pass to his field, 13s 4d
All freemen who take apprentices to cause them to be enrolled in the town book within 12 months, paying 6d for the enrolment, £5
Mr Moore of Bank Hall to cause a wall to be made about the well in Moore Street, 20s
Thomas Darwin to keep his dog muzzled, 6s 8d
All that have mastiff dogs to keep them muzzled, 6s 8d
The overseers of the poor to go once a month through the town to enquire of inmates lately come, and such as have not given security to the town, and make presentment to the mayor, 10s
The curfew to be rung as formerly
We agree to all ancient orders.

p. 831
PORTMOOT COURT OR SESSIONS OF THE PEACE AT LIVERPOOL IN COUNTY OF LANCASTER, 18 FEBRUARY 18 CHARLES II, in the presence of the mayor and bailiffs according to custom.[134]

Inquisition of the jury: John Owen, Thomas Birch, William Done, Anthony Walles, William Ackers, Robert Hoult, William Robinson, Hugo Diggles, James Krindle, Ralph Arton, John Burton, James Toppinge, James Scarisbricke, William Tyrer, Evan Gerard, who say in English words.[135]

134 Latin.
135 Latin.

We present:

    James Fletcher for a tussle on William Lurting, 3s 4d

    William Lurting for a tussle on James Fletcher, 3s 4d

    Humphrey Coppull for a tussle on William Lurting, 3s 4d

    James Jones, butcher, for blowing his meat and making it not fit to be sold, 3s 4d

    William Litherland for entertaining inmates, 1s

    James Glover for the like, 3s 4d

    Elizabeth Harrison for the like, 3s 4d

    John Johnson of Everton for not cleansing his ditch between Alderman Lurting and him, 6s 8d

    Thomas Rowe for not removing lime stones , 2s 6d

    John Richardson for using the faculty of a freeman, Randle Williamson, Gilbert Nayler, Richard Diggles, Thomas Cheshire, William Coppull, Ralph Tutchett, for the same, 3s 4d each; William Newport for the same, 1s

    Robert Bushell for encroaching on the highway beside the castle, 3s 4d

    William Nicholls for a tussle on Henry Fazakerley, 3s 4d

    Henry Fazakerley for a tussle on William Nicholls, 3s 4d

    Richard Rogerson for a tussle on Thomas Birch, 3s 4d

    Thomas Birch for a tussle on Richard Rogerson, 3s 4d

    Edward Scarisbrick for using the faculty of a freeman not being free, 1s

    Margery Hardman for one swine not rung, 6d

    William Tyler, gauger, and for all that have occasion for him, to allow him 2d the barrel by the town standard

We order:

    Three gates to be made before 10 March for the town field at the town's cost

    The quay to be made up with stones as formerly before 10 March for the town field

    Every man to make up his fences against the Moorecroft before 10 March

    All men who take apprentices to enrol them according to former order

    The town clerk to give notice to every freeman of every borough to enrol their apprentices

    Every freeman to make up sufficient headbolts against their own ground on the sea brow

    Headbolts to be made up before 5 March

    Shooting butts to be made up by 25 March as formerly by Robert Simson

    The overseers of the poor to go round once a month to look for inmates

    Mr Moore to make up a gate into the town field beside the Old Hall, according to ancient custom

    We agree to all ancient orders and laudable customs.

p. 832

APPRENTICES

    William Prescott, son of Mary Prescott of Halsall, on 5 April 1667 has put himself apprentice to Mr Thomas Andoe, alderman, for seven years from the feast of St Michael the Archangel past, in the science of a mariner. Mr Andoe is to find his apprentice meat drink and lodging and 20 shillings a year wages, at the Annunciation of the Virgin Mary and St Michael the Archangel by equal portions, and the apprentice shall have at every voyage one barrel portage free, provided it be his own goods. And in case Mr Andoe depart this life before the end of the term the apprentice shall not be assigned to any master or mistress other than Mrs Ann Andoe, his now mistress if she be then living.

Henry Cocke, son of Philip Cocke of this town, on 23 May 1667 has put himself apprentice to John Williamson of this town, mariner, from 1 May last for seven years, and the same John Williamson is to teach his apprentice in the science of a mariner in the best way he can, and to find meat, drink, lodging, washing and apparel during the term. And in regard the apprentice is still under fourteen years, and so not able to manage a seaman's duty at present, the said Henry Cocke is to serve his master for one year after the end of the seven years as his journeyman, and have for that year £3, with meat, drink and lodging. And the said master is to allow his apprentice one barrel portage with every voyage, provided it be his owne goods. Henry Cocke, John Williamson.[136] The aforesaid apprentice, being a poor orphan and left in the charge of the town bound himself apprentice as abovesaid with the consent of the mayor and commonalty of this borough, and he is to have a pair of cloth breeches and jumper of the same and 2 red waistcoats and 1 pair of red drawers and one pair of linen drawers with two shirts and one pair of shoes and stockings.

p. 833
AUDIT 13 MAY 1667 OF MICHAEL TARLETON, GENTLEMAN, LATE MAYOR, DECEASED, Thomas Preeston and George Bennett, bailiffs, from 18 October 1665 to 18 October 1666, taken before Thomas Andoe, deputy mayor to the right honourable Charles Earl of Derby, Henry Corleyes, John Chandler, Peter Lurtinge and John Sturzaker, aldermen, according to custom on 15 May 1667.

Recd. Mr Sturzaker, hallkeeper, ingates and outgates	£29	2s	10d
Thomas Rowe, town customer, ingates and outgates	42	1	10
Richard Rogerson, subcustomer for tolls	9	9	2
For freemen	69	13	4
Town rents	10	3	4
For stalls	18	15	0
For schoolmaster	5	13	3
Interest on Linaker's bond		6	0
Cash received	148	17	8½
Blevin's bond	2	0	0

136 Signatures.

Fines	8	4	10
Remaining of leys in bailiffs hands		11	1
The clerk's £5	5	0	0
Whole receipt	349	18	4½

The bailiffs' disbursements, as by their accounts, £210 17s 0½, £60 of which was paid to Thomas Bicksteth and John Bulkeley, the present bailiffs before this audit, and by us allowed, and to be accounted for as cash received by the bailiffs at the next audit:

	210	17	0½
Cash now paid to the new bailiffs	107	4	6
More paid to the new bailiffs	6	3	7

The aforesaid cash paid to the new bailiffs before and at this audit amounting to £173 8s 1d they are to account for at next audit

The whole disbursement	324	5	1

There is £12 remaining on Thomas Roe's bond of £16, now returned to the new bailiffs, £5 from Richard Robinson which is remitted, being part of the above account, £8 13s 3d in accounts allowed to Samuel Fazakerley, which said sums amount to £25 13s 3d and make up the balance of the abovesaid account

	349	18	4½

Edward Formbie's bond of £20
Mr Gilbert and Edward Formbie's bond £100
Richard Linaker's bond £10
Mr Chandler and Mr Blackmore's bill £2 12s 6d

The aforesaid accounts are allowed and the old bailiffs discharged at this audit. Thomas Andoe; Henry Corles, Peter Lurting, John Chandler, John Sturzaker, Sam. Fazakerley, town clerk.[137]

p. 834
FREEMEN
   19 November 1666:
Robert Roper, gent., admitted free
Paul Thunell

137 Signatures; The name of Thomas Andoe is clearly inserted with a specially made stamp.

Richard Wood
James Nowell
Peter Cropper
John Ormishaw
    20 June 1667:
Randle Williamson, joiner, £2 10s, sworn
Ellis Lyon, apprentice, 6s 8d, sworn
William Hunt, maltmaker, £2 10s, sworn
Gilbert Sutton, apprentice, 6s 8d, sworn
Thomas Jumper, apprentice, 6s 8d, sworn
John Heyes, £2, sworn
William Galley, saddlery maker, £3, sworn
Thomas Durninge, £2 10s, sworn
George Aspinwall, porter, £2 10s, sworn
Samuel Raban, apprentice, 6s 8d, sworn
Jeremy Hindley, apprentice, 6s 8d, sworn
    25 September 1667:
William Hardman, apprentice to William Poultney, carpenter, sworn and made free
before Thomas Andoe, deputy mayor, 6s 8d
    17 July 1667:
Robert Lord Cholmondley, free
Sir Philip Egerton, knt. free
Major Thomas Ashton, free
Edward Mainwaringe, free
Francis Adshead, free
Charles Jones, free
John Parr, free
Thomas Parr, free
Edward Formbie, free
Thomas Greenhalgh, esq. free
    8 October 1667:
Henry Mercer, tanner, son of Laurence Mercer a freeman, 3s 4d
Richard Mercer, another son of Laurence, 3s 4d
Henry Jobson, £2 10
John Richards, £2 10s
Robert Edwards, 6s 8d
    11 October 1667:
Thomas Stockley, £3
Thomas Hurdis, £1
Thomas Lyon, £2
    12 October 1667:
Richard Diggles, £8 10s
Thomas Linaker, £1
Nicholas Carreine, as apprentice, 6s 8d
William Rycroft, son of freeman, 3s 4d.

p. 835
PORTMOOT COURT OR SESSIONS OF THE PEACE, 12 AUGUST 29
CHARLES II, in presence of mayor and bailiffs according to custom.[138]

Inquisition of jurors: Thomas Sandiford, Thomas Johnson, William Williamson, William Crompton, Henry Higginson, William Price, Edward Carre, Gregory Formbie, Richard Bushell, Anthony Banister, Thomas Tatlocke, Robert Simpson, William Travers, Hugh Diggles, Edward Eccles, who say in English words.[139]

We present:
Randle Williamson for a tussle on George Greene, 3s 4d
John Lurtinge, bailiff, for tussle on John Roson, 3s 4d
John Roson for a tussle on John Lurting, 3s 4d
Mr Henry Johnes for using the faculty of a freeman, not free, 13s 4d; Arthur Hutton for the like, 13s 4d
William Yonger, carpenter, Anthony Nixon, servant to Mr Orson, Ralph Langshawe, Richard Diggles, glasier, for the like, 3s 4d each
Edward Moore, esq. for laying dung in the street, 12d; William Done, Ellen Blevin, widow, Robert Davies, John Roson, Henry Rydinge, 12d, Ralph Eccleston, John Heyes, William Mosse, William Nicholls, Widow Witter, all for the like, 12d each
Edward Moore, esq., for refusing to pay his ley for repair of the chapel, £1 3s 4d; Robert Barker, 3s 4d; Edmund Lievesey, 3s 4d; Richard Moorecroft, 1s; Widow Harrison, 6d; Edward Marsh, 8d; John Williamson, master of the *Supply*, 5s; James Toppinge, 6d; John Roson, 2s; Richard Crompton, 5s; John Tompson senior, 2s; Thomas Birche, esq., 3s 4d; Robert Edwards, 6d; Evan Swift, 1s; Henry Jones, 4s; William Bushell, 13s 4d; William Strangwaies, 3s 4d; all for the like
George Kinge for keeping one swine unrung, 6d; John Lunt, 1, 6d; Alice Chambers, 2, 1s; William Bushell, 8, 4s; Thomas Birch, 3, 1s 6d; Thomas Patericke, 5, 2s 6d; James Joanes, butcher, 1, 6d; Gilbert Formebie, 3, 1s 6d; Mr Blackemore, 2, 1s; Richard Bullocke, 1, 6d; Margaret Granger, 5, 2s 6d; Jane Haskeyne, 2, 1s; Alderman Sturzaker, 2, 1s; Richard Mercer, seaman, 1, 6d; William Younger, 1, 6d; Margaret Eccleston, 1, 6d; William Ackers, 4, 2s; Mr Thomas Williamson, 1, 6d, all for the like
Robert Leatherbarrowe of Wigan for forestalling the market, viz. buying goods on shipboard, 3s 4d
Isabel Sutton for not making the fence between her and Mrs Bicksteth, 1s
Elizabeth Mosse for forestalling the market, 1s
John Roson for keeping a scabbed horse on the common, 3s 4d
John Hill for getting turves on the common and selling them to those not free, 1s
Richard Moorecroft for bringing unlawful meat into the market, 3s 4d, and for giving to Mr Deputy Mayor abusive language, 20s

138 Latin.
139 Latin.

Thomas Aspe for buying skins in the market before market time, contrary to ancient orders, 2s 6d; George Woods, Thomas Ellison, Robert Fleetwood of Fazakerley, 2s 6d each for the like

Henry Denny for giving abusive language on 8 July against the mayor and government of the corporation, saying there was neither law nor justice in the town, and that the mayor acted neither lawfully nor justly, £5

p. 836
We order:

All beer brewers who sell wholesale to fill their barrels with 36 gallons of the king's standard gallon, and those that sell ale make their barrels 32 gallons according to statute

Within 14 days a gauger to be appointed and authorised by the mayor and common council to receive and gauge all beer and ale caskets put to sale, and no person to sell beer or ale in lesser caskets than by law provided on pain of 5s every offence

We present:

Mr Robert Seacome for setting his house to one who is not free, and has not given security to the corporation, 6s 8d

Thomas Alcocke and John Burton, overseers to Mr Alcocke's children, for the like, 6s 8d; Ellen Bleven, William Olliffe, Nicholas Banckes, Richard Williamson, chirurgeon, Thomas Pattricke, Mrs Elizabeth Tarleton, John Sandiford, 6s 8d, Richard Rimer, Anne Gallamore, John Bulkeley, William Poltney for Maudling Johnson, Thomas Blackemore, Timothy Holte, Widow Higginson, Widow Harrison, William Johnson, Widow Ball, Hanna Houlte, William Bushell, 6s 8d each for the like[140]

Samuel Postlethwaite for giving very abusive language to the last jurors, viz. saying the stocks were more fit for them than the court, £5

APPRENTICE
Memo. 12 August 1667 Richard Percivall of Liverpool, merchant, produced in the common hall before Mr Thomas Andoe, deputy mayor, and the bailiffs, certain indentures of apprenticeship, dated 1 May 1662, between Richard Percivall, his son, and Richard the father, and desired that his son be enrolled as an apprentice, which is granted; Witnessed, Ralph Massam, Edward Williamson, John Winstanley.

The same day the said Mr Percivall produced a like indenture, dated last of June 1665 between himself and Henry, son of John Cowpe of Bury, and desired the said apprentice be enrolled, which was granted. Witnessed, Edward Williamson, John Winstanley, George Bennett.

---

140   Crosses appear in the margin beside the names William Olliffe, Richard Rimer, John Bulkeley and Thomas Blackemore.

p. 837
THURSDAY 20 JUNE 1667
An Assembly of Thomas Andoe, gentleman, deputy mayor, the aldermen, bailiffs and major part of the common council in the common hall:

It is ordered that if it please God to grant peace and settlement in this kingdom, that, in return of the gracious offers of favour to the town by the right honourable the Earl of Derby, application be made to his lordship by the aldermen to acquaint his honour of the freedom of this assembly to have their charter renewed in his lordship's mayoralty, and such of this borough as his lordship shall direct may make application to council thereunto if it to his lordship may seem meet.

It is also ordered that this town shall be divided into five divisions: the first Chapel Street with Old Hall Street with those houses in the church yard; the second Jugler's Street with Tithebarn Street; the third Dale Street, Henry Fazakerley's house on the heath, William Garner's house and Tithebarn Lane; the fourth Castle Street, Castle Hill, Moore Street, Pool houses and Duke Street; the fifth Water Street, Pheonix Street with the other lands adjoining. And that for the residue of this year until next election day Mr Thomas Andoe, alderman, will take care of the first ward, Mr Henry Corleys, alderman, of the second ward, Mr Peter Lurting, alderman, of the third ward, Mr John Chandler, alderman, of the fourth ward, Mr John Sturzaker, alderman, of the fifth ward, and that each of the said aldermen shall every month survey their division and return the names of every landlord that receives inmates and the names of such inmates shall be received.

It is ordered that Mr Mayor or his deputy may call in all such tenants as pay rent to this town for house, housing, shop, lands or whatever they hold, to bring in their leases to show how they hold and for what term.

It is also ordered that William Nicholls and Samuel Fazakerley shall be admitted tenants to this town of all that piece of waste ground or rock between the corner of the churchyard wall, and the stairs from the sea to the church way at the town side, to build on, and for other conveniences there, and shall each have a lease for three lives that they nominate to pass under the common seal of this borough under the hands of the mayor and bailiffs, yielding each 6s 8d at the feasts of Our Lady and St Michael the Archangel by equal portions, with a covenant in the lease that in case any of the three lives in either lease expire then a new lease shall be made to both or either, for one new life to the respective lives then living, and if all the lives be dead in either lease then for one new life only, and with further covenant to have 4 or 5 yards on either side of the stairs towards the Tower for their convenience, not moving or altering the stairs, and to have two years to build in, the lease to be speedily sealed and executed.

It is ordered that order be made in the name of the mayor, bailiffs and commonalty of this borough for indemnifying Nicholas Valentyne, administrator of Philip Cockes, as by council shall be thought meet.

p. 838
In pursuance of an order made at an assembly on 9 November 1663 in the mayoralty of Peter Lurting, it is now ordered that a new survey be made of such as

hold stalls and they be warned to come before Mr Mayor to compound, and that a perfect inventory be made, but that no alteration be made of any stall already leased, the rent days for them be be at Christmas and Midsummer, and that now a whole year's rent will be due at Midsummer next.

It is ordered that till further order provision be made for the younger child of Thomas Litherland, deceased, and that application be made to the justices at the next quarter sessions of this county for relief of the same orphan and the older child out of a tenement which their grandmother holds.

Whereas Philip Cockes, late of Liverpool mariner, lately died in Liverpool intestate and left two small orphans and a small estate and too small to maintain them without the charity of his neighbours or relief from this town where they were born and had legal settlement, and whereas towards preserving of that small personal estate, immediately after his death, Mr Henry Corles, then mayor, with the advice of the aldermen and others, procured Nicholas Valentyne to take legal administration of the said Cockes' goods for the use of the children, with the promise of Mr Corles and the aldermen that the said Valentyne be saved harmless and indemnified for so doing, and for that the said Nicholas has already on behalf of the children sued for the administration of Cockes' goods and given security in the consistory court at Chester for due administration according to law, and has been exposed to several suits as administrator, viz. one against Thomas Christian, and another by Christian against him, and is still threatened with more suits, it is now ordered by the deputy mayor, Mr Thomas Andoe, the aldermen and common council that Nicholas Valentyne, his sureties and assigns, shall for ever be indemnified and saved harmless at the common charge of the town for all manner of costs, suits, troubles and damages which may happen to them.

Memo. that on 19 August 1667, Mr Thomas Andoe, deputy mayor, with the consent of Mr Henry Corleys, Peter Lurting and John Sturzaker, alderman, did put – daughter of Philip Cockes late of Liverpool deceased, apprentice to Elizabeth Parkinson of Liverpool for two years and has agreed for and towards the maintenance of the said infant with meat and clothes, to pay the said Elizabeth 20 shillings for the two years on the last day of September yearly, and the said Elizabeth for the said sum of 40 shillings has agreed to discharge this corporation for ever from the said child and every charge touching the same.

p. 839

30 SEPTEMBER 1667

Memo. Mr Thomas Andoe, deputy mayor, by the consent of the aldermen, Mr Henry Corleyes, Mr Chandler, Mr Lurting, Mr Sturzaker, delivered to Thomas Norbury, now churchwarden of the church or chapel of Liverpool, one great gilded bowl with a cover, one lesser gilded bowl, unserviceable, to be made into two convenient silver bowls for church use, and one little private mace for the town's use, the same being in weight 2lbs 10oz 2½drams, neither with any inscription showing them to be the gift of any particular person.

ACKNOWLEDGEMENT OF THOMAS DUKE

Know all men, that I Thomas Duke of Liverpool, carpenter, acknowledge that about eleven years ago John Sturzaker of Liverpool, gentleman, for 26 shillings or thereabouts, granted his interest made to him by the mayor and bailiffs of Liverpool of one acre of heath lately enclosed by direction of the mayor from the commons or waste of Liverpool, to me, Thomas Duke, yielding to the mayor and bailiffs of Liverpool 12d per acre at the usual rent days; and that Alice Lyon granted to me about the same time one cottage or cabin and one acre of heath ground late parcel of the said common and her life interest therein, at the like rent of 12d per acre to the mayor and bailiffs, and that I have no other estate or claim to any lands adjoining and lately enclosed but what I hold at will under the said mayor and bailiffs. In witness hereof I have hereto set my hand and seal, 17 October 19 Charles II, 1667. The mark of Thomas Duke. Sealed and delivered with the words and their successors interleaved in the presence of Edmund Whitehead, Thomas Carter, Samuel Fazakerly, Christopher Marsden.

Memo. The original of this is in the iron chest.

Memo. the same day Thomas Duke paid to Mr Andoe, deputy mayor, 2 shillings, which he and the aldermen present accepted in satisfaction of his arrears of the said rents of two shillings per annum until Michaelmas last. Witness, J. Fazakerley.

MEMO

That on 1 January 1667 the right honourable Charles, Earl of Derby, our noble lord and late mayor, presented to this town a most noble gift, viz. a great large mace of silver most richly gilt and engraved with his majesty's arms and the arms of the town, viz. the Leaver, with his own name inscribed thereon in two places specifying it to be his free gift.

p. 840

THURSDAY 10 OCTOBER 1667

An Assembly of Mr Thomas Andoe, deputy mayor, the aldermen and the rest of the common council in the common hall, both bailiffs also present:

Whereas several orders have been made by the late jurors at our late quarter sessions that all landlords should give security to the mayor or deputy for such foreigners as they have admitted on certain penalty imposed on defaulters, which orders have not been pursued, or the penalties collected, it is ordered that from henceforth any landlord who takes into any house or cottage in the town any foreigner not a freeman and does not within six days give good security to the present mayor or his deputy, shall be fined for each default, £5, which fine shall by warrant of the mayor or his deputy be directed to the bailiffs of the town, and collected by the bailiffs, and levied by distress and sale of goods or otherwise.

At the same assembly, on consideration of the gracious late favours and encouragement of the right honourable the Earl of Derby to us, we are unanimously resolved that all suitable preparation be forthwith made to renew our charter, the same to be done in his mayoralty, as the short time permits, and that his lordship shall be recorded in our great book of record as the principal promoter.

It is also ordered that if Mr Robert Seacome shall freely pay 12d per annum rent in the future all arrears shall be remitted him, viz. for his cottage on the heath, and that the said Mr Robert Seacome pay the ancient rent for Browne's Croft and all arrears be also remitted, the distress thereof, if any shall need, to be in the croft on back of Heyes' workhouse.

It is also ordered, in pursuance of a former order, that William Bushell shall have 16 foot square for a house on the heath near the warping place and shall have a lease thereof for three lives, paying 12d per annum rent at usual days.

It is also ordered that in case Thomas Duke shall submit himself to Mr Andoe and the alderman at their sending for him, and pay the arrears of his rent of 12d, the said rent and arrears be accepted if the aldermen find it meet.

THOMAS VISCOUNT COLCHESTER, MAYOR [1667–68]

p. 841
LIVERPOOL. ELECTION COURT FOR THE TOWN AND BOROUGH OF LIVERPOOL IN COUNTY OF LANCASTER, FRIDAY 18 OCTOBER 1667, feast day of St Luke the Evangelist, before the right honourable Charles, Earl of Derby, mayor, Thomas Bicksteth and John Bulkeley, gentlemen, bailiffs, according to their charters and ancient customs.

Thomas Lord Viscount Colchester is nominated and elected mayor and sworn and subscribed according to the late act of regulation
Timothy Tarleton is nominated and elected by the right honourable the mayor to be chief bailiff and sworn and subscribed
William Fleetwood is nominated and elected to be the town's bailiff, sworn and subscribed.

John Entwisle, esq., recorder
Samuel Fazakerley, town clerk
William Molliney, serjeant
Thomas Rowe, water bailiff

Officers nominated and elected by the Common Council, Friday 25 October 1667:
Mr John Leigh, minister
Mr George Glover, schoolmaster
Mr John Sturzaker, hallkeeper, sworn
Thomas Rowe, town customer, sworn
Richard Rogerson, subcustomer, sworn
James Travers, Peter Atherton, stewards of the hall & ley gatherers, sworn
William Poltney, church clerk
Evan Gerard, heyward

Officers chosen by the jury at quarter sessions, Monday 28 October 1667:
Thomas Preeston, John Bulkeley, William Ackers, Richard Jones, merchant appraisers, sworn
John Erlum, Joseph Peacock, alefounders, sworn
Joseph Richardson, Edward Buckley, registers of leather, sworn
William Hunt, Thomas Durninge, Thomas Lyon, John Banckes, barleymen, sworn
Ellis Lyon, Randle Williamson, overseers of the highways
Thomas Jumper, John Richards, Richard Diggles, John Heyes, scavengers, sworn
Robert Simpson, murenger
John Sanderson, Peter Walker, William Simpson, John Poole, porters
Thomas Banckes, Widow Wittar, boothsetters
William Chorley, John Higginson, boardsetters
Richard Rogerson, Thomas Banckes, leavelookers, sworn
Richard Widdowes, beadle and bellman.

p. 842

p. 843

p. 844

8 OCTOBER 1667. GOODS OF WILLIAM NEWPORT APPRAISED

	s	d
Nine pieces of pewter	6s	0½d
One looking glass at 2s, one handkerchief 6d	2	6
One piece Irish frieze at 2s, two cans,		
one greater, one brass	2	4
One bushel	1	4
One cupboard	10	0
One table cloth	1	0
One wheel	1	0
One chase bed	1	6
One white caddow[141]	5	0
One chest	2	6
One box		6
One old bed, two old chase pillows, one old		
white blanket	1	0
Three joined stools	4	6
One small table	1	0
Three chairs and two stools	3	0
Nine spades	6	0
Two truckle beds	5	0
One brass pan	2	0
One frying pan	1	0

141 A rough woollen cover: OED.

Old iron, 20 pound at 1d per pound	1	8
Old trumpery	2	6
Total £3	1s	4½d

p. 845

PLATE RECEIVED BY MR STURZAKER, DEPUTY MAYOR, 25 OCTOBER 1667
The bottom of one great salt double gilt
One great gilded cup with harts and cover
One wine bowl gilded
One bowl given by Mr Edwards
One can given by Mr Ralph Seacome
Twelve silver spoons, usually called Postle spoons
Two silver beakers
One handle cup with a cover
Two silver wine cups
The town's great seal
The mayor's seal
The greater part of the statute seal

Books delivered at same time:
Pulton's Statutes at Large
2 new books of statutes at large from Pulton to 1664
One new book in folio of Statutes from Pulton to 1667
The Country Justice
The Complete Justice
Third part of Lord Cooke's Institutes
Irwell & Harding in folio bought in Mr Corley's mayoralty
Two paper books now in the town clerk's hands, one for entering leases and contracts in the town, the other for bonds of inmates

All the abovesaid plate and books delivered by Mr Thomas Bicksteth, late mayor, to Mr Thomas Johnson, mayor, 21 October 1670. The books delivered to Mr Brownle, mayor 18 October 1671; since to Mr Richmond; since to Mr Jerrom; since 14 December to Mr Chandler, deputy mayor. Brass weights avoirdupois, delivered to Mr Bicksteth, mayor.

25 NOVEMBER 1667
Delivered to the hands of Mr James Jerrome, a little charter of King John, another of Henry III, another of Henry IV, and our last charter, dated 4 July 2 Charles I.

p. 846
William Litherland, apprentice of Edward Williamson, gentleman, admitted, 6s 8d

p. 847

p. 848
10 OCTOBER 67
William Worrall admitted a freeman and sworn, fine £4
Thomas Nicholson admitted free, as apprentice, 6s 8d

COPY OF THE ORDER FOR THE SETTLING OF THE PORT
After hearty commendations, having by a former letter taken notice of the differences between some officers and other interested persons in the port of West Chester and town of Liverpool concerning the bounds and limits of each port's place, and having declared our opinion and knowledge that Liverpool (however it may be accounted a member of West Chester) yet in the execution of all customs affairs has ever been distinct and absolute of itself, and that the whole River Mersey and the shores on both sides were and ought to be under the care, privilege and inspection of the officers of his majesty's customs at Liverpool, but finding our letter either misunderstood or not regarded and the same disputes and worse troubles fomented as well against the merchandise as officers there, with a very great prejudice to his majesty's service, we again positively order and desire that what ships, goods or merchandise soever shall be exported or imported from or into the river Mersey on either side the shore beginning on Wirral side at a place called the Redstones and not further southwards, be entered and accounted for at the custom house at Liverpool and to the officers there without any let or hindrance. And hereunto we expect your ready compliance, the quiet and welfare of his majesty's service being very much contained therein, and we rest, your very loving friends, Nicholas Crisp, John Shaw, Job Harris, John Wolstenholme, John Jacob. Custom House, London 12 December 1660. To the customs collectors and other of his majesty's officers in the port of West Chester.

p. 849
WEDNESDAY 6 NOVEMBER 1667
A meeting of Mr John Sturzaker, deputy mayor, the aldermen, bailiffs and the rest of the common council in the common hall:
It is ordered that Sir Gilbert Ireland, one of the burgesses in parliament for this town, and John Entwisle, esq., recorder of the same, be with speed consulted in order to renew our charter, and to advise us in the method and preparation thereunto.
It is also ordered that Mr James Jerrom shall be entrusted as principal agent to undertake the renewing of our charter with convenient expedition, and from time to time to receive our advice and direction, and what he shall spend therein to be paid out of the treasury of this town.
It is also ordered that Mr Sturzaker, deputy mayor, with assistance of such of the aldermen as he shall take to his assistance may put apprentice or provide for Robert Seale, a poor orphan in this borough, as to them shall seem meet, and the town shall be bound by their act.

p. 850

p. 851

p .852

p. 853

PORTMOOT COURT OR SESSIONS OF THE PEACE, 28 OCTOBER 19 CHARLES II 1667, before Thomas Viscount Colchester, mayor, Timothy Tarleton and William Fleetwood, bailiffs, according to custom.[142]

Inquisition of the jurors: Thomas Bicksteth, Thomas Birch, John Blundell, Anthony Carr, Edward Carr, Robert Fleetwood, Thomas Lurting, William Travers, William Done, William Dwarihouse, Richard Diggles, Joseph Richardson, Thomas Scarisbrick, Ralph Williamson, Edward Buckley, Robert Burt, Thomas Holland, John Mulliney, John Johnson, William Price, Edward Jones, Ralph Auton, William Robinson, Evan Gerard, who present on their oath in these English words:

We present:
Margery Loy, widow, for having unlawful quarts; Thomas Glover for the like, 12d; Peter Walker for the like, 12d

Richard Crompton for his fence lying down between him and Richard Rogerson, 2s 6d
William Yonge for having one swine unrung, 12d
John Tarleton of Halewood for bringing unlawful leather to the market, 2s 6d
Thomas Nicholson for using the faculty of freeman, not being free, amerced and admitted free; Robert Ballard for the same, Thomas Cheshire, Ralph Tutchett, William Coppull, Henry Fazakerley, all for the like, 3s 4d each
Captain William Fazakerley for suing Thomas Norbury out of this court contrary to his oath, both being freemen, 20s
Edmund Laurenson of Male for buying hides before the market time, 2s 6d; John Barker of Halewood, William Chadwick of Melling for the like, 2s 6d
Richard Aspinwall of Skelmersdale for buying skins before the market time and market time, 2s 6d; Henry Goore of Male, Robert Fleetwood of Fazakerley, P. Smith of Derby, John Deane of Melling, Humphrey Coppul of Holmerghe, John Tarleton of Halewood, Thomas Aspe of Kirkby, George Woods of Darby, Robert Worrall of Derby, 2s 6d apiece
Edward Worthington of Ormskirk for bringing carcases of meat to the market without the skins, 3s 4d
Mrs Tarleton, widow, for abuse to Mr John Bulkley, bailiff, when he was distraining for a fine; she pulled off his coat, locked him up, 40s
Mr Edmund Levesey for his wife abusing Mr John Bulkley, bailiff in execution of his office by locking him up and imprisoning him in her house, 40s
Widow Harrison, glasier, for abusive words to Mr Thomas Bicksteth and Mr John Buckley, late bailiffs, calling them rogues, thieves and rascals, 40s

142 Latin.

Henry Bolton of Darby for using the faculty of freeman, not being free, 3s 4d; Anthony Hartlett, Edmund Bispham, Arthur Hutton, William Hartlett, Major Henry Jones, all for the like, 3s 4d

p. 854
John Hoole, milner, who on 16 October 1667 imprisoned both the late bailiffs in Mr Moore's mill in Liverpool when they were making a distress there, 40s

Mr Thomas Andoe and Mr William Bushell for leaving their winglass in the open street, 6d apiece

John Blundell for muck lying in the street; John Banckes 6d; Alice Boare 6d for the like; Margaret Haire, nil

For entertaining those not free without giving security to the mayor according to former order: Widow Downes, William Poltney, William Ackers, Anne Holt, Mr Thomas Bicksteth, Ellen Blevin, Widow Higginson, Ralph Eccleston, Mr Richard Williamson, chirurgeon, Mrs Elizabeth Tarleton, widow, 6s 8d apiece

Mr John Owen for causing 5 cattle and 2 horses to be put in the town field before the corn was out, 6s 8d

Richard Rogerson, John Holland, John Kelley, John Roson, William Middleton, 6s 8d apiece for the like offence

John Williamson in Dale Street for abusive words to Mr Thomas Andoe, deputy mayor, £5

Mr William Prose for offering to lend money to one to beat his man after he was bound to peace, £5

We order:
All landlords to give in security for any new tenants they take into any dwelling according to former order, £5

If the porters refuse to serve a freeman on notice he may employ any other and the porters shall have no benefit of wages

Henry Crane and Bailiff Owen to cut their gutter a foot and a half deep, that the water out of Robert Johnson's ditch may have passage before 25 December, 10s

Robert Johnson of Everton to cut his wood and scour his ditch which annoys Henry Crane's ground, before 25 March, 20s

Mrs Sandiford to remove her muck, and cause some course to be taken to prevent water passage on Mr Corleye's barn before 2 February, 10s

James Heyes to remove his muck from the back side which annoys Widow Formeby, and to cause sufficient payment to prevent the water from annoying her, before 2 February, 10s

A gate and steel to be made and set up by Edward More esq. at the end of the town common as formerly, before 2 February, 10s

All those who have or shall put for the half pences in this town shall give in sufficient bond to the mayor or his deputy at any time for silver, before 14 November, £5

The curfew to be rung, and we agree to all ancient orders and laudable customs.

p. 855

p. 856

p. 857
20 NOVEMBER 1667
Memo. Robert Seale, son of Thomas Seale, bound himself apprentice to Henry Jobson, for seven years to the trade of ropemaker, and this was at the town's for that they paid to Henry Jobson £3, besides apparel for the boy.

p. 858
FREEMEN
William Worrall admitted, fine £4
William Litherland admitted as apprentice, 6s 8d
Sir John Arderne, knt., admitted gratis
Robert Heywood, esq., gratis
Laurence Rostherne, esq., gratis
    29 January 1667:
William Davenport of Hardin, esq., gratis
John Gardner of Manchester, barber, gratis
Byram Banister of Knowsley, gent., gratis
William Eccles of Bromhall, gratis
William Norres, clerk, gratis
William Pennington of Birch, gratis
George Hull of Bankhall, gratis
John Jones of Ormskirk, gratis
Robert Bellin, fine £5
    27 February 67:
Ralph Tutchett, house carpenter, £2
    6 July 1668:
George Lambert of Dundalk, merchant, sworn, £6
    9 May 1668:
Joseph Graves, sworn, £4
Henry Withington, sworn, £5
John Hartley, sworn, £6
William Bushell, slater, sworn, £2
James Pares, mercer, sworn, £6 13s 4d
Thomas Shawe, grocer, sworn, 3s 4d
Mr John Nott

p. 859
AUDIT OF RIGHT HONOURABLE CHARLES EARL OF DERBY, LATE MAYOR, TAKEN FRIDAY 14 FEBRUARY 20 CHARLES II, 1667, Thomas Bicksteth and John Bulkley, bailiffs, taken in the common hall before John Sturzaker, gent., deputy mayor, Thomas Andoe, Henry Corleyes, Peter Lurting and John Chandler, aldermen, according to custom.

	£	s	d
Recd. from Mr Sturzaker, hallkeeper, ingates & outgates	£23	9s	4d
From Thomas Rowe, town customer, ingates & outgates	31	17	5
Richard Rogerson, subcustomer, tolls	8	19	2
Freemen	43	13	4
Town rents	10	4	4
Stalls	19	11	8
School master	5	13	3
Interest on Linaker's bond		6	0
Cash at last audit	173	8	1
Fines	9	16	4
Remainder of leys	12	15	8
Thomas Rowe's bond, in part	4	0	0
William Poltneye's servant		6	8
The clerk's £5			
Total	349	1	3
The bailiffs' disbursements by their accounts	214	14	1
Remains to balance accounts	134	7	2
Which said sum of £134 7s 2d is at this audit paid over to the new bailiffs Timothy Tarleton and William Fleetwood, so total	349	1	3
Memo. Also paid to the new bailiffs in the hands of Samuel Fazakerley	3	8	8
So the total now charged on the new bailiffs	137	15	10

Bonds delivered to the new bailiffs:
Edward Formebie's bond, £20
Mr Gilbert and Edward Formebie's bond, £100
Richard Linaker's bond £10
Mr Chandler's and Mr Blackmore's bill, £2 12s 6d
Thomas Rees bond £16

The aforesaid accounts are allowed at this audit, and the old bailiffs discharged. Signed: John Sturzaker, deputy mayor, Thomas Andoe,[143] Henry Corles, Peter Lurting, Sam. Fazakerley, town clerk.

143 Thomas Andoe's stamp.

p. 860
30 APRIL 1668

William Poultney is admitted tenant of the house he now lives in, for 3 lives for the yearly rent of 20 shillings, with a covenant to build a bay and what more he thinks meet.

James Boates is also admitted to the house he lives in, in the churchyard, for three lives for 6s 8d yearly rent, with a covenant to build.

FREEMEN
   7 May 1668:
Joseph Graves admitted a freeman, paying £4, sworn
John Wheatley, £3, sworn
Henry Withington, £6, sworn
John Hartley, £6, sworn
William Bushell, £2, sworn
   2 June 1668:
James Pares, £6 13s 4d, sworn
   21 September 68:
John Nott, gratis
Thomas Shaw, admitted as apprentice, 3s 4d
   15 October 68:
Henry Pemberton, £4
Francis Meadowcroft, apprentice of Richard Percivall, 6s 8d
Thomas Topping, apprentice of Thomas Williamson, 6s 8d
Edward Rokon, apprentice of Thomas Christian, 6s 8d
Thomas Bolton, apprentice of John Royle, 6s 8d
William Valentyne, £3
William Lyon, £2
Roger Gorsuch, apprentice, 6s 8d
Robert Williamson, 3s 4d
Thomas Winstanley of Billing, whitesmith, £4
Henry Colberne, £10
Robert Turner, £2
Edward Simson, £2
Thomas Plombe, £2 10s
Thomas Ashton, £2
Thomas Nicholson, 6s 8d
Evan Herefort, 6s 8d

p. 861
THURSDAY 30 APRIL 1668
At a meeting of Mr John Sturzaker, alderman deputy mayor, Mr Thomas Andoe, Mr Henry Corleyes, Mr Peter Lurting, aldermen, and the major part of the common council in the common hall:

The said Mr Deputy Mayor, with the free consent of the aldermen and council, elects and nominates Mr Laurence Brownlow to succeed as bailiff in the room of Mr Timothy Tarleton, late deceased, for the remainder of the year.

John Lunt is the same day admitted tenant at will, from year to year only, to the lime kiln on Castle Hill, paying 2s 6d per annum during pleasure of this town, viz. he is admitted tenant to the large lime kiln, putting the lesser into repair which is to remain to the use of the town.

On consideration of several former orders of this assembly and of the great cost and charge William Nicholls and Samuel Fazakerley have been and are like to be at in building on the rock between the church wall and stairs from the sea to the church way, it is ordered that they shall have a lease for three lives, duly executed by the mayor, bailiffs and burgesses under the common seal, of one moiety of the rock or waste ground between the said churchyard and stairs, with such addition of four or five yards on this side of the stairs, and with such like covenant of addition of life or lives as is in the last order concerning the premises, for the yearly rent of 6s 8d apiece, as in the former order is also specified. And it is hereby ordered that the same moieties shall be warranted to them and their assigns during their respective terms against all persons. John Sturzaker, deputy mayor, Tho. Andoe, Henry Corles, Peter Lurting, Willm. Fleetwood, William Rimar, John Blundell, John Lorting, Tho. Johnson, the mark of John Owen, George Bennett, Tho. Bickesteth, Robert Lyon, John Walles, Raph Hall, Thomas Bridg, Richard Rimer, Sam. Fazakerley, Richard Jones, Thomas Roe, the mark of Thomas B Bierch, William Mulliney.[144]

p. 862

p. 863
PORTMOOT COURT OR SESSIONS OF THE PEACE, 13 JANUARY 19 CHARLES II 1667, before Thomas Viscount Colchester, mayor, Timothy Tarleton and William Fleetwood, bailiffs, according to custom.[145]

Inquisition of the jurors, John Bulkeley, John Owen, Thomas Johnson, Richard Windle, William Eccles, Thomas Tatlocke, John Walker, Thomas Bridge, John Erlum, John Richards, William Hunt, Randal Williamson, John Mulliney, Huon Gerard, who presented on their oath in the following English words:

We present:
    Richard Morris for a bloodwipe on Richard Abraham, 6s 8d
    Richard Abraham for a tussle on Richard Morris, 3s 4d
    James Rowe for a bloodwipe on Thomas Rainford, 6s 8d
    William Angsdale for five bloodwipes on two strangers at two times on the last fair day, 13s 4d

144 Signatures.
145 Latin.

Thomas Knowles for over-violent abusing and beating John Whitfield a servant boy to John Tempest, 3s 4d

John Tempest for a bloodwipe on Thomas Knowles, 6s 8d

Thomas Knowles for a tussle on John Tempest, 3s 4d

Richard Abraham for driving his cart on Thomas Rainford's mare's heels, being forewarned before he did it

James Swift, carter, for walking John Kellie's cart as it stood in the street, and drawing his horses when they were down with his own loaded cart, 6s 8d

John Harries of owning Mr Lang's goods for his own both outward and inward to wrong the town's carters of their due

Mr Thomas Clayton for forcibly hindering two horse loads of goods from paying town toll

Evan Gerard for cutting other men's grass in the town field

John Roson for setting his cart in the street at night to the prejudice of his neighbours

Edward Banester for selling shoes before market, 1s

Mr Gilbert Formeby for 1 swine unrung, 6d; James Fletcher, 3, 1s 6d; Thomas Roe, 1, 6d; William Watmough, 1, 6d; Mr William Fazakerley, Elizabeth Mercer, Thomas Galloway, Richard Bushell, each for 1, 6d

William Hunt, Thomas Durninge, Thomas Lyon, John Bancks, barleymen, for neglect of their office, 2s apiece, 8s

Mr Robert Ticknor for using the faculty of a freeman, 3s 4d; Mr Henry Jones, £1 6s 8d; Mr Arthur Hutton, £1 6s 8d; Mr William Strangewaies, 6s 8d; William Woodes, 3s 4d; John Whittle 0, all for the like offence

Elinor Loye for cursing her son, 5s

Anne Moore for entertaining inmates in her house, not giving security according to former order; Elinor Loye, William Poltney, Ralph Eccleston, William Bushell, bailiff, Ginnett Whitehead, each 3s 4d for the like offence

Mr Thomas Clayton for not cleansing streets, 6d; John Bancks, William Robinson, Margaret Farrer, William Hunt, 6d each for the like

John Lurting for not wearing a gown according to former order, 6s 8d; Thomas Birch, John Blundell, Thomas Bicksteth, each 6s 8d; present bailiffs, Mr Timothy Tarleton and William Fleetwood, for the like

John Lurtinge for not appearing at hall on his summons this day, 0

p. 864

Mr Thomas Blackemore and Isabel Sutton for letting their fence lie down to Mrs Bicksteth's croft, 12d apiece, 2s

John Mercer for letting his fence lie down in Tithebarn Street to Henry Jobson's house and back side, 1s

Thomas Jumper, John Richards, Richard Diggles, John Heyes, scavengers, for neglect of their office, 12d apiece, 4s

We order:

Mr Timothy Tarleton, Mr William Fleetwood, present bailiffs, Mr John Lurtinge, John Blundell, Thomas Birch, Thomas Bicksteth, bailiffs' peers, that they provide themselves gowns by 14 March on penalty of 50s apiece for every default

Esquire Moore to make up his fence gate and steel at the end of Mr Corleyes' common by 10 March, 6s 8d

Mr Blackmore and Isabel Sutton to make up their fence by Mrs Bicksteth's croft in Tithebarn Street by 20th of this month, 10s apiece

John Mercer to make up his wall against Henry Jobson's house by 26th of this month, 5s

All headbolts on the sea brow to be made up by every freeman and others against their own ground before 10 March, 3s 4d apiece

All other fences and headbolts to be made up before 1 March

The shooting butts to be made up at the town's cost by 10 March by Robert Simpson

2 long hooks and 12 new leather buckets to be provided at the town's cost as they formerly have been by 1 May

We agree to all other former orders and ancient customs.

p. 865
PORTMOOT COURT OR SESSIONS OF THE PEACE, 6 JULY 20 CHARLES II, 1668, before Thomas Viscount Colchester, mayor, Laurence Browneloe and William Fleetwood, bailiffs, according to custom.[146]

Inquisition of the jurors, William Gardner, Thomas Johnson, Richard Rimer, William Leech, William Hunt, Joseph Peacocke, Robert Holt, Hugo Diggles, John Heyes, Thomas Jumper, Robert Simpson, James Jones, Joseph Richardson, Thomas Lyon, Huon Gerard, who present on their oath in the following English words:[147]

We present:
Robert Briers for hindering the town of toll and dues of five cartloads, 6s 8d

The said Robert Briers for bringing several parcels of leather to town when as the registers required him to seal them he denied them, 6s 8d

John Moorecroft for using the faculty of a freeman, not free, 3s 4d; Henry Fazakerley, John March, Robert Ballard, Thomas Plumbe, Richard Strange, Edward Scarisbricke, Thomas Stainton, Thomas Storrey, James Cheshire, each 3s 4d; William Woods, John Whitley, cymbal man, Robert Ticknor, 6s 8d each; Mr Henry Jones, Arthur Hutton, £2 13s 4d each, all for the like

Henry Mason and his wife especially for entertaining lewd persons at unseasonable times in the night, amerced

Robert Mason, son of Henry Mason, Alice Singleton for their uncivil carriage at unseasonable times in the night in the abovesaid house, 6s 8d

John Calley, seaman, for the same, 6s 8d

146 Latin.
147 Latin.

Thomas Fazakerley for bringing unlawful shoes to the market, 2s

Thomas Rose of Kirkdale for the same, 2s

John Tarleton of Halewood for bringing unlawful leather to sell at the market, 2s; Henry Tatlocke, John Barker, for the like, 2s

William Fleetwood, butcher, for selling flesh meat on the week day, not being free

William Hunt, Thomas Durninge, Thomas Lyon, John Bankes, barleymen, for neglect of office, 2s 6d apiece

John Harries for entertaining William Lyon in his house and not giving security to Mr Mayor according to former order that he shall not be chargeable to the town

Richard Williamson, chirurgeon, for entertaining Elizabeth Erbie, widow, and one child, and Elizabeth Rimer, wife of James Rimer and one child

Ellen Blevin, widow, for entertaining George Penkeman and wife and child, and William Mercer, his wife and child

Mrs Greene for keeping and selling by unlawful quarts, 12d; Richard Rimer, Castle Street, Widow Scarisbricke, New Street, Jonathan Gleave, all for the like, 12d each

Ellis Lyon and Randle Williamson, overseers of the highway, for not appearing at this court

William Bushell for letting his druge[148] cart stand in the street to the prejudice of his neighbours, 12d; John Roson, William Mosse, 12d each, for the like

p. 866

Thomas Durninge for Derbie Street, John Bankes, Thomas Holland, barber, Edward Moore esq., for the like, 6d each

John Blundell for laying a midden in the street, 6d

Thomas Pattricke for setting a great piece of wood in the street to the prejudice of his neighbours, 6d

William Worrell for a bowsprit lying in the street, 6d, and formerly for letting several pieces of wood lie in the street, 6d

Thomas Bankes and Widow Witter for setting stalls and boards to William Price's wall to his prejudice, when formerly warned, 6d apiece

John Lurtinge, bailiff's peer, and all other freemen for not appearing in the town hall according to their oath and ancient custom; Thomas Preeston for the like

John Lurting, bailiff's peer, Mr Laurence Browneloe, bailiff, for not providing and wearing a gown according to order, 10s apiece; Thomas Birch, John Blundell, Thomas Bicksteth, each 10s for the like

William Chorley and John Higginson for setting stalls before Thomas Knowles' shop and to the prejudice of William Acker's house door, 6d apiece

Katherine Rainford, widow, for selling ale unlicensed, contrary to custom of the town and laws of the realm, 3s 4d; John Moorecroft, 3s 4d,[149] Richard Mercer,

---

148 Probably as in 'drug', a low truck for heavy goods: OED.
149 John Moorcroft is crossed through.

paid, William Carie, paid 1s; William Milles, 3s 4d; Robert Kenion, 3s 4d; Thomas Wainewright, 3s 4d; Thomas Parrey, 3s 4d; Widow Andoe, 3s 4d; Alice Deyntie, widow, 3s 4d, Widow Lurting, William Halsall, Widow Rainford, Robert Davies, all for the like.

We order:

Mr Lawrence Browneloe, bailiff, to provide himself a gown and wear it before 20 July, on forfeit of 50s for neglect; John Blundell, bailiff's peer, Thomas Birch, John Lurtinge, Thomas Bicksteth, the same, 50s for default, according to former orders made

Thomas Bankes and Widow Wittar not to set any more stalls or boards to William Price's wall, 3s 4d for every default without his leave

William Chorley and John Higginson not to set any stalls or boards to shop of Thomas Knowles or prejudice the door of William Ackers on forfeit of 3s 4d, without their leave

Observing that the butchers' stalls and stocks stand in the week days to the prejudice of the inhabitants and strangers every butcher, both freeman and foreigner, who has any stalls or stocks, to provide for them in their inn or elsewhere, that the streets or market place may be freed from them, before 20th instant July, 10s for neglect

Mr Lawrence Brownloe, Mr William Fleetwood, bailiffs, to give notice on Saturday 11 July to every butcher with a stall in the market to remove it according to this order, and to see it put into execution, 20s for neglect

John Roson, William Mosse to move their carts from the street forthwith and find convenient place to set them elsewhere, night and day, 10s for default

The order concerning mug carts, formerly neglected, to be executed and that full due be taken of every load that comes into town by Richard Rogerson

p. 867

Every carter not free, taking any load of wool, yarn, skins, hides, tallow, wine, vinegar, herring or other, out of the town, for every such cart load to pay to the town 2d, whether freemen's or foreigners' goods, towards the maintenance of the streets, over and above 4d a load bought and sold payable to the town. Richard Rogerson to see this order executed

Two long fire hooks, 12 new leather buckets to be provided at the town's cost, as formerly, before 29 September

Henry Crane forthwith to cause the stalls and boards to be laid up near his house that they do not lie on the town's ground, and that John Heyes, Thomas Jumper, scavengers, give notice to Henry Crane, and if the said Henry Crane lay the stalls or boards on the town's ground he shall pay 3s 4d

We choose Robert Hoult porter, and order that he or any other porter who works shall for every loading or load lightening receive wages according to their work, and the said persons may not make agreement one with another, but he that works let him have wages, and he that works not have nothing

We agree to all ancient orders and laudable customs.

p. 868

COPY OF A LETTER FROM THE LORDS OF HIS MAJESTY'S PRIVY COUNCIL

After hearty commendations his majesty, having received frequent information from several parts of the kingdom that divers persons, formerly displaced by the commissioners authorised for regulating corporations in pursuance of an act of parliament, and others, without taking the oath and declaration appointed by the statute of 13 Charles, endeavour to be elected to the several officer of mayor, bailiff, sheriff, alderman, town clerk and others in the respective cities and boroughs of this kingdom with design, as may be instantly apprehended, to disturb the peace and happiness of his majesty's government, his majesty thereupon has commanded us to require you to signify his pleasure to the mayor, bailiff, aldermen and other officers of every city and town corporate in the county palatine of Lancaster, that they do not henceforth admit any person into office but according to the rules prescribed by the act. And so, not doubting of your care herein, we bid you heartily farewell from the court of Whitehall, 22 September 1668, your ever loving friends, Gilbert Cant. Craven, Lauderdaill, Midleton, Arlington, T. Clifford, Jo. Berkelley, Will. Morrice, H. Coventry, W. Duncombe, Ormond, Bathe, Humph. London. Ex. W. Walker.

p. 869

FRIDAY 9 OCTOBER 1668

A meeting of Mr John Sturzaker, deputy mayor, the aldermen and common council in the town hall:

It is ordered that John Bamber, ropemaker, be admitted tenant of a spinning place on Old Hall Lane, leading to the townfield, at the yearly rent of 6d per annum at the will of the mayor and burgesses of the town, he not being an annoyance to those who shall pass with cart or carriage in or out of this town through the same lane.

It is also ordered that every carter not free, bringing in or taking out of this town any load of goods shall pay 2d for every load towards repair of the streets, and that the officers employed for collecting the same shall be saved harmless at the charge of the town.

It is ordered also that Thomas Birch, esq. be admitted tenant of the fish yards by Duke's House at 4d per annum for 99 years, he defending the town's title to the same fish yards against any who may claim it against the town, though it cost him one hundred pounds, which he now consents to.

It is ordered, on reading Thomas Duke's petition, that he shall not be admitted tenant of the last enclosed piece of waste, nor admitted to marl it, but it be reserved to further consideration of the next meeting, and that speedy order be taken for pulling down the said enclosure and laying the same waste, as also the corner of the barn there adjoining. The said enclosure and part of the barn was accordingly pulled down by order, 3 March 1668.[150]

---

150   Note about pulling down of barn is added in margin.

p. 870

p. 871
COPY OF THE RENTAL OF BOROUGH RENTS OF LIVERPOOL TO THE KING'S MAJESTY FOR ONE HALF YEAR
James Earl of Derby for Edward Chambers
John Woods Beck's cellar 6d. appraised[151]
John Moore, esq. for parcels of land and Town's End Mill and Horse Mill; more lands purchased from Turkey for pool house
Richard Crosse, esq. for his land
More for the house late Brooke's
The heirs of Mr Thomas Lee, late Mr Warren's, £1 4s. appraised[152]
The lands of Mr John Boores paid by John Higginson , Mr Eccleston and James Burton. appraised

Water Street appraised:
William Singleton, for Bird's house, 6s 4d
For the house where John Barton dwells, 1s
Mr Mossock for Thomas Brookbank for Mossock's Roe
Mr Robert Moore for the house where Mrs Dobson lives, 1s
Mr Walker for his two houses, 2s
Mr Chandler for Richard Lord Viscount Molyneux, 2s 4d
Roger Rose for where John Bird dwells, 1s
Margery Barker, 1s
The house where the barber dwells by Mr William Ireland. 1s 6d
John Crane's house, Mr Sorrocoles land, 5s 6d; more a mosse room
Mrs Dobson for the house where Richard Tarleton lives
Mr James Williamson for two houses, 2s
Mr Johnson for William Lurting, 9s
The same William Lurting for a house in Jugler Street, 6d
Mr James Southerne for Mr Fazakerley 1s

Castle Street appraised:
Mrs Eccleston for the house where Henry Rollin lives, 2s
For the house she lives in, 1s 8d
Ellin Rose and sister, 1s 6d
Wife of Morris
Wife of Moore, 1s
Mr Washington, 1s
Mr Strangewayes or the heir of Ralph Seacome for the house in Dale Street and Castle Street, 4s 6d

---

151 Appraised appears in margin.
152 Appraised appears in margin.

Ralph Mercer for Mrs Tarleton, 12s 4d
John Johnson, 7s 4d
Richard Kenion the house at Pool for Mr Blundell of Crosbie, 1s
Wife of Worrall, 2s

Dale Street appraised:
Mr William Moore for Thomas Asbrooke, 13s
Mr Blundell of Ince for John Higginson, 1s
Mr Mercer for Margaret Higginson, 1s
Susan Eccleston, 1s
Mr Thomas Blackmore for Mr Blundell of Crosby, 1s
Nicholas Lurting, 1s
Roger Lurting for Mr Garrett of Aughton, 1s
Edward Williamson for Hoberstalle's houses, 1s
Mr Sorocold for George Prescott
The next house for Thomas Garner
Mr William Fazakerley for Richard Rose, 4s
The heirs of Thomas Potter, 2s
Wife of Mercer for Mr Garrett of Aughton, 1s
Wife of Barker, 6d
Mr Carsles for a croft, 6d
Wife of Nicholson for Brown's croft where William Monely lived, 1s
Mr Lathom of Earlom for Richard Norres, 1s
Wife of Widdowes for Mr Hocknall, 6d
Mr Dobson for Henry Cook's house where John Corker dwelt being part of land of Mr Mollyneux of the Wood, 1s
Thomas Tarlton for the house where John Tarlton dwells, 1s
Thomas Brookbank for the house where John Williamson dwells, 1s

Juggler and Tithebarn Streets appraised:
Wife of Tarton, 1s
Mr Mossock for James Southerne, 3s
Dorothy Bickesteth for the house where Cutler dwells, 6d
Mr Sharples for Needomes Hall and her houses, 1s 8d
Edward Alcock for house and shop, 10d
Mr Norres for Richard Blevine, 6d
The house late Robert Melling for Thomas Rose, 1s
Mr Williamson for the house Robert Eccowes dwells in; more for land in the field, 8s; more, his own house
Mosse house
Mr Bickesteth for a barn, 6d
Mrs Sandiford for lands purchased from Roger Rose in Tithebarn Street, 1s 6d; more lands in Mill Street
Henry Anderton for Richard Anderton, 1s
Mr Sorocold for Robert Eccowes for the house where Thomas Bridge is, 1s

Wife of Cooke, 2s
Richard Lunt, 6d
John Higginson for Mr Blundell of Ince for a house and barn and yard, 1s
Tyrer of Counscough for Thomas Coppoll for a house and burgess
at Srueshill, 4s 6d

Chapel and Hall Street appraised:
John Lurting, 3s
The heirs of Thomas Pickavance, 1s
Thomas Tarlton for the house where Mrs Blanckard lived, 1s 2d
Alice Williamson, 1s
John Higginson for Care's house, 1s
Wife of Balshawe, her house for Mr Tarlton, 1s; more for the barn bought of
Mr Sorocold, 2s
The butcher's shop for 2 years
Mrs Dobson for the corner shop, 12s
Edmund Raphson for the little shop, 6s
Richard Rose or Rodger for great shop, 12s; more the little shop, 6s
Robert Marten, 6s
John Higginson, 12s
Mr Williamson for John Sturzaker, 6s; more the Eastham Mill for Mr Fazakerley of
the Spellow House; more the ferry boats.

p. 872

p. 873

p. 874

WILLIAM STANLEY LORD STRANGE, MAYOR [1668–69]

p. 875
LIVERPOOL. ELECTION HELD ON THE DAY OF ST LUKE, 18 OCTOBER
1668, before the Right Honourable William Lord Strange, mayor, Thomas Atherton
and Richard Bushell, gent., bailiffs, according to custom.

William Lord Strange elected mayor and sworn
Thomas Atherton, gent., mayor's bailiff, sworn
Richard Bushell, town's bailiff, sworn

John Entwisle, esq., recorder, confirmed
Samuel Fazakerley, town clerk, confirmed
William Mulliney, serjeant at mace, confirmed
Thomas Rowe, water bailiff, confirmed.

Officers chosen by the common council, Friday after the election according to custom:
John Leigh is continued minister
George Glover, schoolmaster
John Sturzaker, hallkeeper
Thomas Rowe, town customer, sworn
Richard Rogerson, subcustomer
William Poultney, church clerk and sexton
William Shaw, William Price, stewards of the hall
Evan Gerard, heyward.

p. 876
FREEMEN
   7 November 1668:
Giles Reece of Chester, combmaker, admitted freeman and sworn, £4
   30 November 1668:
William Woods of Liverpool, mariner, £2, sworn
   12 December 1668:
Richard Erby, apprentice to Bryan Mercer, 6s 8d
   23 March 1668:
Daniel Swift, apprentice 6 years, £1
Peter Scarisbrick, apprentice, 6s 8d
Edward Winstanley, son of a freeman and apprentice, 3s 4d
Robert Bushell, a slater £3
   29 March 1669:
William Yonger, sworn, 20s, marrying a freeman's daughter and freeman's widow,
therefore other 20s was remitted by consent of council
   10 May 1669:
Thomas Norland, sworn, £4
John Jackson, £5
Henry Stevenson, £2
   11 October 1669:
William Mercer, sworn, £2
John Peeres, sworn, £1 10s
Richard Thrilwynd, sworn, £3
William Heath, sworn, £3
Thomas Mathewes, sworn, £3
Edward Bowker, sworn, £6 13s 4d
Ralph Henchaw, sworn, £3
Henry Hardman, sworn, free
John Mollineux, sworn, £4
Evan Stock, sworn, £4
James Whitfield, sworn, 2
Christopher Marshden, sworn, £5
Thomas Williamson, sworn, 3s 4d
James Storie, sworn, 3s 4d.

p. 877

p. 878
27 OCTOBER 1668
Memo. That John Gamond, apprentice to Joseph Peacock of Liverpool, mariner deceased, now of Anne, the widow and relict of Joseph, is this day by the assent of his nearest relations to serve the said widow and work as a cooper for two years from the nativity of our saviour Jesus Christ next, and at the end of the term the said widow is to be at the charge of making the said John Gamond a freeman.

p. 879
PORTMOOT COURT OR SESSIONS OF THE PEACE HELD AT LIVERPOOL IN COUNTY OF LANCASTER, 26 OCTOBER 1668, before William Stanley, Lord Strange, mayor, Thomas Atherton and Richard Bushell, gentleman, bailiffs, according to custom.[153]

Inquisition taken on the oath of Laurence Brownloe, John Lurting, William Gardner, Thomas Preeston, Robert Leadbeter, John Molliney, Richard Crompton, John Johnson, Thomas Galloway, William Dwarrihouse, William Crompton, John South, John Bancks, Thomas Durninge, Edward Bulkley, Randle Williamson, Richard Diggles, George Prenton, William Parker, John Litherland, William Mills, Robert Burt, John Burton, Evan Gerard, who say on oath in the following English words:[154]

We present:
John Tarleton of Halewood for bringing unlawful leather to the market, 2s
Henry Cowper for bringing unlawful work to the town, 2s
Richard Parr, locksmith, for bloodwipe on William Mosse, 6s 8d
John Moorecroft, butcher, for using faculty of freeman, not being free, 0s 0d; Roger Tyrer, 0s 0d; John Phillipps; Mr Arthur Hutton, £2 13s 4d; Henry Fazakerley on the heath, 3s 4d; Thomas Martindale, currier, 0s 0d; Thomas Feantone, 0s 0d; Mr Henry Jones, £2 13s 4d; Mr Tickner, 0s 0d; Henry Stevenson, seaman, 0s 0d; all for the like
For swine unrung: Mrs Greene, 1, 12d; Mrs Tarleton, 3, 3s; Richard Crompton, 1, 12d; Captain Fazakerley, 1, 12d; Margaret Granger, 1, 12d; Robert Bicksteth, 1, 12d; Mr Ticknor, 1, 12d; Edward Holrobin, 1, 12d; Mr William Bushell, 8, 8s; Mr John Tempest, 1, 12d; William Ackers, 3, 3s; Margery Horrockes, 4, 4s; John Williamson, 1, 12d; Richard Bullocke, 1, 12d; Thomas Patricke, 2, 2s; Gregory Formeby, 1, 12d
Ellen Nicholson for entertaining Mr Jackson and his wife, not free, amerced, 0
William Poultney, landlord, for letting Madline Garrens with a child of her daughter, bring strangers to live in his house, without security given to the town, 0

153 Latin.
154 Latin.

Adam Smith, journeyman, to Richard Lurtinge, the like, 0

Edward Carr for entertaining one John Pilkington and his wife and child, concealing them nearly three months in his house though there was enquiry made for them, 13s 4d

John Holland for heaving out a load of hides after they were laden, and left them on the sands, 6s 8d

For not cleaning the streets according to order: Mr Thomas Johnson, 6d; Isabel Sutton for not cleansing her sink, 6d; William Mosse for having a midden in his street, 6d; William Ackers for the like, 6d; Alderman Andoe for a piece of timber lying in Chapel Street, 6d; John Roson for his cart standing in the street, 12d; Mr William Bushell for the like, 6d; Mr Edward Moore for not causing the street to be cleansed before his croft in Dale Street, 6d

p. 880

Mr Edward Moore for encroaching on the town's land by a building in Pool Lane, 0s 0d

Thomas Duke for an enclosure on the common, 6s 8d

Thomas Roe, water bailiff, for suffering limestones and ballast to be heaved overboard in places not convenient and contrary to former orders.

We order:

So much of the new building as appears to be on the town's waste in Pool Lane to be pulled down before the last of this month

The new enclosure on the town common by Thomas Duke with the new barn erected to be both pulled down before 20 November

Owner John Moneley and Richard Diggles, to fill up the sluice in the highway going towards the water side from the castle hill through the field, and to take away the rubbish from there before the 10th of next month, on penalty of 3s 8d

Anne Moore to remove the rubbish between her and Mr Corleyes within ten days, 6s 8d

The curfew to be rung as formerly

We agree to all ancient orders and laudable customs of this borough.

OFFICERS CHOSEN BY THE JURY, 26 OCTOBER 1668
Mr Thomas Bicksteth, Mr William Fleetwood, Mr John Lurtinge, Richard Rimer, merchant appraisers
Edward Holrobin, Thomas Nicholson, registers of leather
Roger Gorsuch, Robert Bellin, alefounders
Hugh Diggles, Richard Jackson, overseers of the highway
John Holland, John Kellie, William Carie, William Kellie, barleymen
William Simson, murenger

p. 881
Gilbert Sutton, Edward Simson, Thomas Glover, John Whittle scavengers
John Sanderson, Peter Walker, John Poole, William Simson, Robert Hoult, porters

Thomas Bankes, Widow Witter, boothsetters
William Chorley, John Higginson, boardsetters
Richard Widdowes, beadle and bellman.

p. 882
MEMO.
On 20 January 1668 James Cooper bound himself apprentice to James Scarisbrick for seven years.

MEMO.
That on 3 March 1668 William Halsall, James Whitfield, John Tompson, and John Hodgson of Truwell in the field of this county broke down an enclosure lately made by Thomas Duke and also part of a barn erected on the waste of this town, and this was done by special order of the mayor, aldermen, bailiffs and burgesses of this town, in preservation of their claim and right to the said commons according to ancient custom used against all encroachers. John Hodgson,[155] William Halsall his mark, James Whitefield his mark.

p. 883
PORTMOOT COURT OR SESSIONS OF THE PEACE HELD AT LIVERPOOL IN COUNTY OF LANCASTER, 8 MARCH 21 CHARLES II 1668, before William Stanley Lord Strange, mayor, Thomas Atherton and Richard Bushell, gentlemen, bailiffs, according to custom.[156]

Inquisition of jurors, William Fleetwood, Thomas Birch, Richard Windle, Thomas Bridge, Peter Atherton, Thomas Shawe, Roger Gorsuch, Hugo Diggles, Thomas Holland, Peter Allen, Gilbert Sutton, William Carie, Thomas Nicholson, Edward Banckes, Evan Gerard, who present on oath in the following English words:[157]

We present:
    Christopher Orme for a bloodwipe on John Glover, 6s 8d
    John Heyes for a bloodwipe on Thomas Handcocke, 6s 8d
    Thomas Handcocke for a bloodwipe on John Heyes, 6s 8d
    Richard Williamson, chirurgeon, for a tussle and abusive language against Mr John Chandler, an alderman, by calling him a turd of an alderman and peers are turds of aldermen, £25
    Mr John Chandler for a bloodwipe on Richard Williamson, chirurgeon, 6s 8d
    Richard Mercer, millner for a tussle on Thomas Everard, 3s 4d
    Thomas Everard, millner for tussle on Richard Mercer, 3s 4d

155 Signature.
156 Latin.
157 Latin.

Mr Chorley, distiller, for usurping the privilege of a freeman, not being free, 0s 0d; Mr Robert Ticknor for the like, 3s 4d; Thomas Fenton for the like, 3s 4d; Mr Henry Jones for the like, £5 6s 8d; Edward Ratchdale or Mr John Winstanley for entertaining him, for the like, £5; Daniel Curtis, 3s 4d; Mr Abraham Alred, 3s 4d; Thomas Whitehead, shoemaker, 3s 4d; Mr Arthur Hutton, £5 6s 8d; John Tue, 3s 4d

John Meadow, butcher, for keeping false weights, 3s 4d

William Scarisbricke, butcher, for bringing meat to the town, not marketable, 1s

Edward Worthington for bringing meat without skins, 2s 6d; Philip Heyes for the like, 2s 6d

The setters of the stalls for not cleansing the market place in due time; also Mr Lawrence Breeres, 0d; John Moorecroft, 6d; Esther Hardman, 6d; Thomas Durninge, 6d; Isabel Sutton, 6d; Widow Chambers 0d; Widow Hunt, 6d, all for the like

Mr Deputy Mayor for having his swine unrung, 4s; also Mr Atherton, 2, 4s; Margaret Granger, 1, 2s; Mr Richard Crompton, 5, 10s; John Litherland, 3, 6s; Widow Chambers, 3, 0s; Widow Potter, 1, 2s; William Middleton, 1, 2s; Widow Greaton, 3, 6s; Mr Thomas Galloway, 2, 4s; Captain William Fazakerley, 2, 4s; Edward Clarkson, 1, 2s; Ellen Williamson, 1, 2s; Henry Jobson, 2, 4s; George King, 2, 4s; John Mercer, 1, 2s; Mr John Tempest, 3, 6s; William Ackers, 3, 6s; Mr Thomas Blackmore, 2, 4s; John Moorecroft, 1, 2s; Peter Walker, 1, 2s; Mr William Bushell, 10, £1; Mr John Owen, 1, 2s; Widow Formeby, 1, 2s; Mr Robert Ticknor, 2, 4s; Widow Blevin or Mr Alred, 2, 4s; John Harries, 2, 4s; Mr Thomas Bixteth, 1, 2s; Mr William Garner, 1, 2s; Mrs Elizabeth Tarleton, 5, 10s; Widow Andoe, 1, 2s; William Halsall, 1, 2s; Edward Bulkeley, 1, 2s, all for the like

p. 884

Mr Thomas Atherton for small quarts, 3s 4d

Peter Winstanley, Mr John Harris, Thomas Kirby, Mr Prigion alias Tomson, all concerned in the breaking of fish stones, 20s apiece

Mr Thomas Johnson, Mr George Bennett, Mr John Pemberton, Mr Richard Crumpton, Mr William Bushell, Mr Edward Williamson, Peter Atherton, all for putting forth half pennies without the town's license, 40s apiece

All sellers of beer unlicensed in the town, 3s 4d

The present bailiffs for not having gowns in readiness, £5

We order:

The stalls standing before Peter Atherton's house side to be speedily removed, being both an annoyance to him and an inconvenience to the town

The present bailiffs to provide gowns according to custom by Easter day next, 11 April, on penalty £5 apiece

Everyone within the liberties of the borough to make up their headbolts and fences by 20 March, 6s 8d

The stalls to be speedily removed from Mr Shaw's shop side

No more stone to be taken from the foot of the Town's End mill being an annoyance to all travellers, and those who have taken already to repair and speedily fill up the breech

Thomas Stockley to be confirmed porter for the town

The field gate stoops be set up where wanting

Every person in the town with dogs which can devour children or disturb others shall muzzle or tie them, many having complained of such a crime

All householders with swine to keep them off the streets especially on Saturdays and Sabbath days, otherwise to take the damage done to them in their own hands

Richard Browne to scour his rubbish from the house side of Richard Jackson

The shooting butts be made up by 20th instant

We agree to all ancient orders and laudable customs of the town.

p. 885

p. 886

p. 887

TUESDAY 23 MARCH 1668

An assembly of Mr John Sturzaker, alderman, deputy mayor, the aldermen and the rest of the common council in common hall:

Whereas information is given to this assembly that Lord Molyneux intends to erect a new bridge over part of the pool on the waste or common of Liverpool without the licence of the mayor and burgesses of the town, they having time out of mind been reputed to have the rightful seigniory of the same common under his majesty, and since the making of a bridge without license of or composition with the mayor seems to invade the ancient privileges of the town, it is unanimously ordered that if any attempt be made to lay any foundation or build any part of the bridge the same will be obtructed and pulled down by such as the mayor shall appoint for that purpose, and if any suit shall arise by Lord Molyneux against the mayor or his deputy they shall be defended and indemnified at the charge of the town. John Sturzaker, deputy mayor, Tho. Andoe, Henry Corles, John Chandler, Peter Lurting, Robert Moore, John Blundell, Richard Bushell, Sam. Fazakerley, William Rimar, John Lorting, Thomas Christian, Edw. Tarleton, Tho. Johnson, Thomas Birch, Tho. Preeston, George Bennett, Tho. Bickesteth, Law. Brownlowes, Willm. Fleetwood, Tho. Bridge, John Walls, John Owen, Will. Gardner, Robert Lyon, William Ackeres, Tho. Roe, Ralph Hall, William Mulliney, Richard Jones.[158]

It is ordered the same day that John Chorley, the distiller, shall remove out of this town and be admitted to sell strongwaters or spirits.

p. 888

MONDAY 5 APRIL 1669

An assembly of Mr John Sturzaker, alderman, deputy mayor, the aldermen and common council in the town hall. It is ordered that whereas Mr John Tatlock, one

158 Signatures; four councillors made a mark: Thomas Birch, Thomas Preeston, Thomas Bridge and Robert Lyon.

of Lord Molyneux's commissioners has on behalf of his lordship moved Mr John
Sturzaker, deputy mayor, for a treaty between the town and his lordship, on
Tuesday in Easter week, concerning the building of a bridge which his lordship
would build on the heath or waste of Liverpool, Mr Alderman Sturzaker shall, with
the aldermen and such of the charterers of this town as he shall think meet, treat
with Lord Molyneux in the town hall or other convenient place.

p. 889

p. 890

p. 891
AUDIT OF THOMAS LORD VISCOUNT COLCHESTER, LATE MAYOR,
10 JULY 1669, before John Sturzaker, alderman, deputy to Lord Strange, mayor, Henry
Corles, John Chandler and Peter Lurting, aldermen, auditors according to custom.

Thomas Roe, ingates and outgates	£36	15s	3½d
Hallidge, ingates and outgates	32	14	8½
Subcustomer for tolls	7	14	9
Same for carts	1	9	4
Rents received	9	17	2
Freemen	80	3	4
Stalls	20	16	4
Surplusage of leys	1	0	0
Fines	12	16	6
Schoolmaster	5	13	3
Clerk	5	0	0
Linaker's bond received	5	6	0
Paid in by former bailiffs	137	15	10
Total	357	2	6
Disbursed by the bailiffs	317	0	6
Remains to the bailiffs	40	2	0

Memo. The above £40 2s balance is at this audit secured to the new bailiffs and
£113 0s 8d in cash is now paid by the old bailiffs into their hands so that the new
bailiffs now stand chargeable with £153 2s 8d. And so the old bailiffs are
discharged. John Sturzaker deputy mayor, Henry Corles, John Chandler, Peter
Lurting, aldermen, Samuel Fazakerley, town clerk.

Bonds delivered to the new bailiffs:
Bond from Edward Formeby £100

Thomas Roe's bond £32
Edward Formbie's bond £20
Mr John Chandler £2 10s

p. 892

p. 893
11 OCTOBER 1669
An Assembly before John Sturzaker, alderman, deputy mayor, Henry Corles, Peter Lurting, aldermen, the bailiffs and the rest of the common council:
It is unanimously ordered that whereas Mr Thomas Bicksteth has lately paid to the right honourable the Earl of Derby £3 5s for five acres of copyhold land in West Derby, lately the inheritance of Mr John Williamson, alderman, and stands charged with a yearly rent of £4 to the present minister of the church or chapel of Liverpool, which is near to the yearly value of the said land, the present bailiffs shall repay Thomas Bicksteth the sum of £3 5s out of the stock of the town.
It is also ordered that it shall be in the power of the mayor of the town or his deputy to treat and make composition with masons, stone getters and brickmakers who get stone or break ground on the waste or common at such rates as the mayor or deputy, with such others as he shall take to his assistance, shall charge.
It is also unanimously ordered that a ley of £50 shall be forthwith assessed by the common assessors or ley layers of the town on all freemen living out of the precincts of the town as well as those within, for the necessary repair of the chapel of Liverpool, called Our Lady and St Nicholas, and for other necessities of this corporation, and if any of the said freemen shall obstinately refuse to pay, contrary to their oaths at enfranchisement, they shall be disenfranchised and made incapable of any benefit of their freedom for ever, their former admittance notwithstanding.
It is ordered that Richard Lurting shall have 13 yards to the front on Castle Hill, on the east side of Peter Allen's smithy, if so much can be spared without prejudice to the highway.
It is ordered that John Kellie have 15 yards to the front, 4 yards west from Peter Allen's, if so much may be spared on survey made by Mr Mayor or his deputy's order, on Castle Hill.
It is also ordered that Ralph Johnson shall have 12 yards to the front, there to build westwards from John Kellie, at 6d per yard per annum rent, in like manner as Peter Allen holds the same.

p. 894

p. 895
15 OCTOBER 1669
A meeting before John Sturzaker, deputy mayor, the aldermen, bailiffs and common council:
It is ordered, whereas lately James Whitfield and Edward Marsh have been arrested by warrant of quominus from his majesty's court of Exchequer at

Westminster at the suit of Mr John Tatlock, and Mr John Sturzaker, together with Edward Moore esq., has given bond for the appearance of James Whitfield and Edward Marsh, that Mr John Sturzaker his executors and administrators shall be hereafter saved harmless and indemnified from any cost or trouble which may happen to him by reason of the bond, and that the said suit shall be defended at the charge of this borough. Henry Corles, John Chandler, Peter Lurting, Robert Moore, Richard Bushell, John Blundell, John Lorting, Thomas Christian, Will. Gardner, Tho. Johnson, Thomas Preeson, Thomas Berch, Tho. Bickesteth, Edw. Tarleton, Law. Brownlowe, George Bennett, Willm. Fleetwood, Sam. Fazakerley, Robt. Lyon, Willm. Ackers, Tho. Roe, Ralph Hall, William Mulliney.[159]

It is ordered the same day that Mr Laurence Browneloe and William Fleetwood, late bailiffs of this borough, shall be reimbursed for costs expended or to be incurred concerning the escape of Richard Blundell by any suit commenced against them by Mr Thomas Patten, and that they shall order their attorney to take out non pres. against Mr Patten where he has filed and not proceeded.

It is ordered the same day that Mr Robert Williamson or his tenant may enlarge the steps to his cellar in Chapel Street, one step more towards the street, and so far as may not be a nuisance to the passage or neighbourhood.

It is ordered the same day that Mr Arthur Hatton shall be admitted to proceed as factor or agent as formerly he has done, so that he does not retail, paying yearly to the bailiffs £3 besides the usual town duty, during pleasure of this town, providing Mr Entwisle, our recorder, shall not advise this order to be prejudicial and if the said Mr Recorder judges it meet he may be admitted a freeman on taking the oath, paying such fine as may be imposed.

p. 896[160]

[THOMAS BICKSTETH, MAYOR, 1669–70][161]

p. 899
ELECTION COURT ON DAY OF ST LUKE, 18 OCTOBER 1669, 21 CHARLES II, before the worshipful Thomas Bicksteth, esq., mayor, Richard Windle and Robert Fleetwood, bailiffs, according to custom.

Thomas Bicksteth, mayor, sworn
Richard Windle, bailiff of the mayor, sworn
Robert Fleetwood, bailiff of the freemen, sworn

John Entwisle, recorder, confirmed

159 Signatures.
160 Pages 897 and 898 do not appear.
161 No heading is provided for Thomas Bicksteth's year of office.

Samuel Fazakerley, town clerk, continued and sworn
William Molliney, serjeant at mace, confirmed, sworn
Thomas Rowe, water bailiff, confirmed, sworn.[162]

Officers chosen by the common council, on Friday after the said election according to custom:
John Leigh, minister, continued
George Glover, schoolmaster, continued
John Sturzaker, hallkeeper, continued, sworn
Thomas Roe, town customer, continued, sworn
Richard Rogerson, subcustomer, continued, provisionally[163] sworn
William Poltney, church clerk and sexton, continued
Richard Lurting, Ellis Lyon, stewards of the hall, continued
Evan Gerard, heyward, continued

p. 900
Officers chosen by the grand jury, 25 October 1669:
Mr Lawrence Brownlowe, Mr Richard Bushell, Edward Tarleton, Thomas Bridge, merchant appraisers, sworn
William Ackers, Henry Hardman, registers of leather, sworn
Thomas Tyrer, Henry Jobson, alefounders, sworn
Edward Bowker, Thomas Hurdis, overseers of the highways, sworn
Robert Simson, William Bushell, slater, Thomas Ashton, Ralph Henshawe, barleymen, sworn
Thomas Gildoes, William Heath, Thomas Mathewes, George Hull, scavengers, sworn
William Simson, murenger, sworn
John Sanderson, Peter Walker, William Simson, Robert Hoult, George Aspinwall, John Carter, Thomas Stockley, porters, sworn
Richard Rogerson, Thomas Bankes, leavelookers, sworn
Thomas Bankes, Widow Witter, boothsetters, sworn
William Chorley, John Higginson, boardsetters, sworn
Richard Widdowes, beadle and bellman, sworn.

p. 901
PORTMOOT COURT OR SESSIONS OF THE PEACE HELD AT LIVERPOOL IN COUNTY OF LANCASTER, 25 OCTOBER 21 CHARLES II, 1669, before the worshipful Thomas Bicksteth, mayor, Richard Windle and Robert Fleetwood, gentlemen bailiffs, according to custom.[164]

Jurors of the the lord king who present on oath in these English words: Mr John Blundell, Mr John Lurtinge, Thomas Birch, Mathew Gleave, Roger Gorsuch,

162 Latin.
163 Latin.
164 Latin.

Richard Jackson, William Simson, John Kellie, Gilbert Sutton, James Storie, John Johnson, Edward Flitcroft, Edward Buckley, Edward Litherland, Edward Carr, John Jackson, Robert Burt, Edward Winstanley, Robert Houghton, William Worrall, Thomas Hurdis, Thomas Norbury, Edward Simson, Evan Gerard

We present:

Gilbert Sutton for a tussle on George Mort, millner, 3s 4d

Mr Robert Breeres for tussle on John Carter, 3s 4d

John Carter for the like on Mr Robert Breeres, 3s 4d

Mr James Jerrom for stones lying within the floodmark to the danger of shipping, because stones were removed on notice, nil

John Widowson for laying clay and rubbish at Chapel Street end to the disturbance of the highway, 2s

Richard Everard for the like, 2s

John Gamond, cooper, for using the faculty of freeman, not being free, 2s; Joseph Pryor, 2s; Evan Swift, 2s; Robert Brownbill, 2s; Henry Fazakerley, 2s; Robert Worrall, 2s; Robert Prenton, 2s; John Marsh, 2s, all for the like

John Barton of Ormskirk, for buying skins before market time, 2s; Robert Worrall, 2s; Robert Fleetwood of Fazakerley, 2s; George Woods, 2s; all for the like

James Hey of Ormskirk for bringing meat to the market without the skins, 1s

Thomas Fazakerley for working unlawful leather, 1s; Henry Cooper, 1s; Henry Pemberton, 1s; Thomas Lurtinge, 1s; all for the like

p. 902

Joseph Richardson for his swine being unrung, 8d; William Bradocke, 2; Richard Wright, 3; Richard Moorecroft, 1; Robert Leadbeater, 2; Katherin Rainford, 1; William Ackers, 1; John Tempest, 1; Mr William Bushell, 1; John Harries, 1; Robert Ticknor, 1; Ellen Nicholson, 1; Mrs Bicksteth, 4; Margaret Goore, 1; William Garner, 3; William Baily, 2; Widow Andoe, 1; Thomas Galloway, 1; Jame Gerard, 1; Margery Formeby, 3; James Fletcher, 2; Anthony Walles, 2; Mr Gilbert Formeby, 1; Mr John Sturzaker, 1; Mr Thomas Atherton, 1; Richard Crumpton, 2; Jane Hunt, 3; Thomas Gregson, 1; Thomas Bridge, 1; Henry Jobson, 1; Thomas Roe, 1; John Goore, 1; George Kinge, 1; Widow Jumpe, 1; Ralph Eccleston, 2; all for the like, amerced at 4d a piece for every swine

Thomas Tarleton for carrying stones of the hills out of the liberties of this corporation, 2s; Ellis Brookes for the like, 2s

George Penkiman for getting turves on the waste and selling them out of the liberties, 6d

The said George Penkiman for loitering on the sabbath day, on coursing in reference to Mr Mayor what to return of this, 3s 4d

Edward Whalley of Wavertree Lane for carrying turves off the waste, 6d

William Mercer of Lowe for taking Thomas Birche's turves out of Mr Crosse's room and carrying them out of the liberties, 6d

Mr Edward Moore of Bank Hall for muck lying against his croft in Dale Street, 6d; William Chorley, John Higginson, Richard Formeby, William Forber, Richard

Mercer, James Winsfield, Mr Thomas Bickesteth, mayor, William Price, Richard Widdowes, all 6d for the like

Richard Jackson and Hugh Diggles for neglect of their office as overseers of the highways, nil

William Bushell, slater, for neglect of the town's work, nil

All freemen who have not made their appearance this day.

p. 903
We order:

The quay to be repaired by 1 February

All carters who trespass on ships' cables by carting over them shall forfeit 3s 4d per time, unless the carter calls to the vessel and gets a bar to save the cables

Mr Robert Williamson to have liberty to make one more step to his cellar door in Chapel Street according to former order

Mr John Lurting to make a gutter to carry his easing dropping off Mr Robert Williamson's house by 1 March

Curfew to be rung as formerly

We agree to all ancient orders and laudable customs of this borough.

p. 904
7 NOVEMBER

At an Assembly before the mayor, aldermen, bailiffs and common council it is ordered that the rubbish lately cast up out of the Castle ditch be cast in again to the trench and those who cast the same in there by order of Mr Mayor shall be indemnified. Thomas Bickesteth, Henry Corles, John Chandler, Peter Lurting, John Sturzaker, Robart Moore, Rich. Windall, Robt. Fleetwood, William Rimar, Thomas Christian, John Blundell, John Lorting, Tho. Johnson, Tho. Preeson, George Bennett, Willm. Fleetwood, Richard Borshett, Ralph Hall, Thomas Bridge, Tho. Burch, Robert Lyon, Tho. Roe, Willm. Ackers, Richard Jones, William Mulliney, Sam. Fazakerley, Edward Tarleton.[165]

p. 905
MONDAY 15 NOVEMBER 1669, 21 CHARLES II

An Assembly in the town hall before the worshipful Thomas Bickesteth, mayor, John Entwisle, esq., recorder, Henry Corleyes, John Chandler, Peter Lurting and John Sturzaker, aldermen, Richard Windall and Robert Fleetwood, bailiffs, and the rest of the common council. Whereas a servant of the right honourable the Earl of Derby came to Mr Bicksteth, mayor of this borough, on 9 November with a paper in these words, viz. I have sent to Liverpool to let them know I would not take advantage where either myself or my heir is in possession of the staff of Liverpool now in possession of the town, I have ordered you to demand of them, which in justice they cannot deny, to cause quiet possession to be delivered to you upon my

---

165 Signatures.

behalf of those houses lately erected between my house called the Tower and the sea, and to this I cannot but expect a ready compliance from them, Lathom 9 November 69, E. Derby, and demanded an answer of the possession of the houses abovementioned, it is ordered that Mr Bailiff Windall and Mr Samuel Fazakerley or other appointed by Mr Mayor shall attend his honour with a paper in these words following: that the ground whereupon the several houses are built is the right of the corporation and that they are seized thereof in fee, and that they cannot deliver the possession without betraying the right of the corporation. This afterwards put off and only verbal answer sent to Mr Jones.[166] Thomas Bickesteth, Henry Corles, John Chandler, Peter Lurting, John Sturzaker, Robart Moore, Rich. Windall, Robt. Fleetwood, William Rimar, Thomas Christian, John Blundell, John Lorting, Tho. Johnson, Tho. Preeson, George Bennett, Willm. Fleetwood, Richard Bushell, Ralph Hall, Thomas Bridge, Thomas Burch, Robert Lyon, Tho. Roe, Willi. Ackers, Richard Jones, Sam. Fazakerley, Edward Tarleton, William Mulliney.[167]

p. 906

p. 907
30 NOVEMBER 1669
An Assembly of the mayor, aldermen and common council. Whereas we have received letters from one burgess and Colonel John Birch, a member of parliament, of complaints against us to his majesty's privy council concerning our late election of Mr Thomas Bickesteth our mayor, and whereas the said Mr Mayor was lately by process in the consistory court of Chester summoned to appear, and likewise Mr John Leigh, our minister, and accordingly articles exhibited against the said Mr Leigh, but not proved against Mr Mayor, yet in regard the same articles seem to relate to our said election and to the title and electing a minister of our chapel of Liverpool granted to us by her late majesty of glorious memory, Queen Elizabeth, it is hereby ordered that it shall be lawful for the said Mr Bicksteth, mayor, at all times hereafter during the time of his mayoralty, for quieting of the said complaint against the mayor or Mr Leigh or any other of this town in reference to the election or any other concern of this town, to employ a solicitor or solicitors as he sees meet in defence of the said matters, and all charges expended by order of Mr Mayor shall be paid out of the town's treasury. And whereas letters are frequent to Mr Mayor from our burgesses and Mr Birch and others in reference to the town's concern, we further order that Mr Mayor may answer the same as he shall think meet, taking to his assistance some of the council as he thinks meet, four at the least, without calling a full assembly, and we hereby ratify what they do in reference thereunto. Thomas Bickesteth, Henry Corles, John Chandler, Peter Lurting, John Sturzaker, Tho. Atherton, Robart

166 Note about verbal answer is added in margin.
167 Signatures.

Moore, Rich. Windall, William Rimar, Sam. Fazakerley, John Blundell, John Lorting, John Owen, Tho. Preeston, Tho. Johnson, Tho. Birch, Law. Brownelowe, George Bennett, Robert Lyon, Richard Jones, Ralph Hall, Thomas Bridge,[168] Tho. Rooe, William Mulliney.[169]

30 November '69. Mr Lawrence Brownlowe and William Fleetwood, late bailiffs, to be saved harmless by this town in case any suit arise between Mr Henry Jones and them in reference to some late fines against Mr Jones.[170]

p. 908

TUESDAY 21 DECEMBER 1669

An Assembly in the town hall before Mr Thomas Bixteth, mayor, the aldermen, bailiffs and burgesses. Upon consideration of the former order of 30 November which we ratify and for that Mr Marsden, the vicar of Walton, has lately made claim to the right of appointing a minister in our chapel, and has peremptorily demanded the keys thereof as his own right contrary to our ancient grant in the 7th year of Queen Elizabeth and our constant usage ever since, we hereby with much and unanimous resolution declare that, in the appointing of minister and schoolmaster having been enjoyed for above a hundred years, it would not only be a loss but a great dishonour to this ancient corporation to be deprived thereof without a fair and legal trial, and we therefore order that if any suit arise concerning the same against Mr Mayor or other officer about the keys or possession of the said chapel at the suspension of Mr Leigh by Mr Marsden or rector of Walton or any other person, in due defence of our right Mr Mayor and all other freemen of the town sued in any of his majesty's courts temporal or spiritual shall be indemnified and defended at the charge of the town, to be paid out of the common treasury of the town. Thomas Bickesteth, Henry Corles, John Chandler, Peter Lurting, John Sturzaker, Robart Moore, Rich. Windall, Rob. Flitwood, William Rimar, John Blundell, Tho. Christian, John Lorting, John Owen, Tho. Johnson, Tho. Preeson, Tho. Berch, George Bennett, Willm. Fleetwood, Robert Lyon, Tho. Bridge, Ralph Hall, William Ackers, Richard Jones, Tho. Roe, William Mulliney.[171]

p. 909

TUESDAY 18 JANUARY 1669

An Assembly. It is ordered that Mr Arthur Borren and Samuel Fazakerley, our town clerk, shall be employed as solicitors to the town in the suits between Mr John Tatlock, on behalf of Lord Molyneux, against James Whitfield and Edward Marsh or any other of this town that may be impleaded on Lord Molyneux's account, and what they shall disburse with their reasonable fees shall

168 Thomas Bridge's mark.
169 Signatures.
170 Note about bailiffs is added in margin.
171 Signatures.

be repaid from the town's treasury; and we order that the grant of Queen Elizabeth for provision for the minister and schoolmaster of the town shall be sent by the town clerk to be showed to the bishop. Thomas Bickesteth, Henry Corles, Peter Lurting, John Sturzaker, Robart Moore, Rich. Windall, Robte. Fleetwood, Sam. Fazakerley, John Blundell, John Lorting, Thomas Christian, Tho. Johnson, Willm. Fleetwood, Thomas Burch, Thomas Preeson, Ralph Hall, Richard Rimer, William Ackers, Tho. Bridge, Richard Jones, Ri. Lyon, Tho. Roe, William Mulliney.[172]

p. 910
WEDNESDAY 9 FEBRUARY 1669
An Assembly. In pursuance of an order made in the mayoralty of William Lord Strange, 11 October 1669, for assessing of a ley of £50 on the free burgesses of Liverpool within and without the liberties, it is further ordered by Mr Thomas Bicksteth, mayor, the aldermen and bailiffs and major part of the council that the said ley be forthwith assessed by the ley layers and such others as Mr Mayor thinks fit, and collected by such persons as Mr Mayor appoints. Thomas Bickesteth, Henry Corles, Peter Lurting, John Sturzaker, Robt. Fleetwood, William Rimar, John Blundell, John Lorting, Tho. Johnson, Tho. Birch, Tho. Preeson, George Bennett, Willm. Fleetwood, Richard Jones, Robert Lyon, Tho. Bridge, Ralph Hall, William Ackers, James Travers, Tho. Roe, William Mulliney.[173]

3 MARCH 1669
An Assembly. In pursuance of an order of this assembly, 9 February 1669, for the assessing of a ley of £50 on the burgesses, it is ordered that the sum be forthwith taxed on the freemen inhabiting within the town by the usual ley layers and others Mr Mayor shall appoint to assist, and that it be immediately collected by the bailiffs and stewards of the hall or ley gatherers, and that all other freemen who live out of the town be assessed and taxed for £20 by such as Mr Mayor and the major part of the common council appoint. Thomas Bickesteth, mayor, Henry Corles, John Chandler, Peter Lurting, John Sturzaker, Tho. Atherton, Robert Moore, Robt. Fleetwood, John Blundell, Tho. Johnson, John Lurtinge, Tho. Birch, Law. Brownlowe, Willm. Fleetwood, Richard Bushell, Tho. Preeson, Geo. Bennett, Richard Jones, Richd. Rimar, Robt. Lyon, Tho. Bridge, Sam. Fazakerley, William Mulliney, Tho. Roe.[174]

p. 911
FRIDAY 26 MAY 1671
An Assembly. It is ordered by the worshipful Mr Thomas Johnson, mayor, the aldermen, bailiffs and the rest of the common council that, whereas there is a suit now commenced by Lord Caryll Molyneux against the mayor, aldermen and

172 Signatures.
173 Signatures.
174 Signatures.

bailiffs on behalf of the corporation, that the charges expended in defence of the said suit shall be paid by the said corporation, and likewise, if Lord Mollineux offer to take any tolls of the corporation or any employed by him, they shall be resisted by the said mayor or his order and be indemnified. Thomas Johnson, mayor, Tho. Andoe, Henry Corles, Peter Lurting, John Sturzaker, Thomas Bickesteth, Robert Williamson, Tho. Atherton, Robart Moore, Law. Brownlowe, Thomas Christian, Thomas Prison, Tho. Bridge, William Ackers, Robt. Lyon, Willm. Fleetwood, John Blundell, John Lourtinge, Robert Fleetwood, Ralph Hall, Richard Jones, William Mulliney, Tho. Roe.[175]

p. 912

p. 913
PORTMOOT COURT OR SESSIONS OF THE PEACE AT LIVERPOOL IN COUNTY OF LANCASTER, 11 APRIL 22 CHARLES II, 1670 before Thomas Bicksteth, mayor, Richard Windle and Robert Fleetwood, gentlemen, bailiffs, according to custom.[176]

Jurors of the lord king who present on their oath in the following English words:[177] Mr Thomas Johnson, Mr Thomas Preeston, Mr Edward Tarleton, Thomas Marsh, Roger Gorsuch, Henry Hardman, Henry Jobson, Edward Bowker, William Heath, Hugh Diggles, John Story, Richard Jackson, Peter Atherton, Ralph Henshawe, Evan Gerard.

We present:
   Henry Bannester for striking Richard Rogerson and calling him coward, 3s 4d
   William Brewerton for a bloodwipe on Edward Bowker, 6s 8d
   Edward Bowker for a bloodwipe on William Brewerton, 6s 8d
   Alderman Thomas Andoe for not keeping his street clean against White Cross, 6d; Ralph Henshawe, Thomas Durninge, Jonathan Gleave, William Eccles, Thomas Birch, Ellis Lyon, John Kellie, Peter Walker, 6d each, all for the like
   William Bushell for letting his cart stand in the street to the annoyance of people passing, several times forewarned, 1s
   William Bradocke for laying rubbish in Pool Lane to the prejudice of the highway, 1s; Robert Kenion for the like, 1s
   John Wainewright of Edge lane for laying rubbish in Pool Lane, 6d
   John Gamond, cooper, for using the faculty of a freeman, not being free, 0; Robert Berry of Ratcliffe, Samuel Lightbourne of Manchester, Thomas Clough of Leeds in Yorkshire, William Keakwicke of Everton, Edward Ogden, tailor, Evan Swift, Robert Brownbill, William Holland, John Phillips, Abraham Alred, 3s 4d each for the like

175 Signatures. This entry is out of sequence.
176 Latin.
177 Latin.

p. 914

Edward Stringfellow for working unlawful leather, 2s; Thomas Rose, 2s; William Seddon, 2s, for the like

Richard Clough of Winstanley for shipping goods privately, not paying the town's duty, 0

Jane Haskeine, widow, for letting her swine out on market day contrary to order, her swine pulling sacks in pieces, 2s; Thomas Gregson for the like, 2s

Mr Thomas Atherton for selling ale and beer by quarts under the assize, 1s; Edward Simpson, William Nicholls, John Jackson, Abraham Alred, Thomas Stockley, Widow Scarisbrick, 1s each, for the like

Widow Holrobin for keeping one swine unrung, 6d; Thomas Patricke, 1, 6d; Robert Bickesteth, 1, 6d; Edward Litherland, 2, 1s; Mrs Elizabeth Tarleton, 2, 1s; Widow Anne Jumper, 1, 6d, all for the like

John Litherland for selling ale, not licensed, contrary to statute, 2s; Thomas Lyon, Ralph Eccleston, Robert Mercer, Gilbert Sutton, Robert Bushell, Widow Fairhurst, Widow Andoe, John Phillipps, William Worrall, James Brindle, Robert Kenion, John Bankes, William Brewerton, 2s each for the like

Jane Hunt, widow, for keeping an unsealed measure and offering to buy and sell by it, 3s 4d

The scavengers for neglect of their office, nil

The barleymen for neglect of their office, nil

Nicholas Valentyne for employing a foreigner to glaze his house, neither being free, nil

We order:

James Boates to build his intended house two foot six inches further into the churchyard than the groundwork of the old house was, measuring from the outside of the old groundwork to the outside of the new groundwork and from thence backwards following the line of the old groundwork, 21 foot

How much further James Boates goes with his gable end till the square of Captain Tarleton's house shall be built at his own proper cost, and when Captain Tarleton has occasion to lay into the said gable end he is to pay one half of the charges that Boates has been at and no more, that is Captain Tarleton is to pay one half of the charges that he takes of Boates' gable end, and further that Captain Tarleton is to lay any goods or coals to the said Boates' gable end that he has occasion to lay, and that the said Boates shall make good Captain Tarleton's wall, all that he pulls down

p. 915

Widow Scarisbricke to remove her dung from Mr John Pemberton's garden wall before 20 April, 3s 4d

Mr John Lurtinge, draper, to remove his dung from Mr John Sandiford's barn now erected by Mr Jerrom before 16 April, 3s 4d

Robert Johnson to scour his ditch at the further end of the townfield, and that those lands between Alderman Lurting and Robert Johnson's ditch to be guttered that Alderman Lurting come to no damage from the water, by last of April, 6s 8d

Those who have any lands lying to the sea bank to make a lawful fence by 1 May, 3s 4d apiece

The worshipful Mr Mayor and the present bailiffs to provide themselves with gowns before 24 June, £3 for each default, and the bailiff's peers the like

All the inhabitants who keep swine shall not let them out on Saturday or Sabbath day, but keep them up on their back sides or some convenient place, and if any be found in the streets then any one who takes them to the common pound or the darkhouse shall receive for each 2s 6d from the owner, the owner paying for poundage of such swine over and above

We have chosen William Carter a porter

We agree to all ancient laws and laudable customs.

p. 916

p. 917
AUDIT OF RIGHT HONOURABLE WILLIAM STANLEY, LORD STRANGE, MAYOR, 1 JUNE 1670, Thomas Atherton and Richard Bushell, gentlemen, bailiffs, in the common hall, before Thomas Bixteth, gentleman, mayor, Thomas Andoe, Henry Corleyes, Peter Lurting and John Sturzaker, aldermen.

	£	s	d
Ingates and outgates Mr Sturzaker and Thomas Roe	£65	11s	5d
Richard Rogerson	12	0	2
Stalls	21	4	0
Freemen	73	6	8
Overplus of leys		9	1
Town's rents	10	3	8
Fines	6	11	0
Schoolmaster's money	5	13	3
At last audit paid to new bailiffs, cash	153	2	8
Total	348	1	11
Disbursed by the old bailiffs	232	1	6
Paid by them to the new bailiffs in cash	110	7	2
Paid more by town clerk, schoolmaster's money	5	13	3
Which balances the account to	348	1	11
Cash paid to the new bailiffs which they are to account for at the next audit	186	0	5
More paid to them in cash at this audit	2	0	0
	188	0	5

Bonds received:
Edward Formbie's bond £20
Mr Gilbert and Edward Formbie's £100
Mr Chandler's bill, £2 12 6
Thomas Roe's bond, £16; £8 only due[178]

The aforesaid accounts allowed and the old bailiffs discharged. Thomas Bickesteth, mayor, Tho. Andoe, Henry Corles, Peter Lurting, John Sturzaker, Sam Fazakerley, town clerk.[179]

p. 918

p. 919
MONDAY 11 JULY 1670
Assembly of common council in portmoot hall:
   In pursuance of our ancient right of nomination, election and appointing of a fit person to minister in the borough with the advice and assent of the bishop of Chester, we whose names are undersubscribed, being the mayor and council of the said borough, do unanimously nominate and elect Mr Robert Hunter, late of Macclesfield, clerk, to be our minister, and accordingly we humbly present the said Mr Robert Hunter to the Right Reverend Father in God, John, Lord Bishop of Chester, and desire his lordship's assent.
   Ordered the same day that all butchers and others who have stalls or standings shall carry the same to their lodgings or other convenient places out of the streets at the end of market days so that they shall not be an annoyance to any on week days, 12d on defaulters.
   Thomas Bickesteth, Thomas Andoe, Henry Corles, Peter Lurting, John Sturzaker, Robert Moore, Richard Windall, Robert Fleetwood, Samuel Fazakerley, James Jerrom, Laurence Brownlowe, Thomas Christian, Thomas Preeston, George Bennet, William Rimer, Thomas Birch, Thomas Bridge, Ralph Hall, William Ackers, John Lurting, John Blundell, Richard Lyon, William Fleetwood, Richard Jones, Thomas Roe, William Molliney.

p. 920
JULY 1670
   An Assembly in the common hall before the mayor, aldermen, bailiffs and major part of the common council. It is ordered that the present bailiffs shall be defended and saved harmless against any person whatsoever who may sue them by reason of an escape of Mathew Storie, and Samuel Whitfield, late prisoners for debt in the prison at Liverpool, and likewise all other officers of this borough, at the town's charge. Thomas Bickesteth, mayor, Tho. Andoe, Henry Corles, Peter Lurting, John

178   £8 due is added in margin.
179   Signatures.

Sturzaker, Robart Moore, Rich. Windall, Robt. Fleetwood, Sam. Fazakerley, William Rimar, John Blundell, Tho. Johnson, Law. Brownlowe, Thomas Christian, Tho. Preeston, George Bennett, Willm. Fleetwood, Tho. Birch, William Accars, Ri. Rimar, William Mulliney, Tho. Roe; only John Lurting dissenting.[180]

p. 921

p. 922
FREEMEN ADMITTED AND SWORN
John Williamson, 3s 4d
Joseph Pryor, £7
George Naylor, £3
Henry Fazakerley, 10s
Hugh Richardson, £3
William Carter, £2 10s
Robert Lunt, £4
Thomas Edwardson, £4
Thomas Nowell, £2 10s
Richard Boulton, £3
Thomas Hollis, £4
Matthew Mainwaring, 3s 4d
David Hall, £2
George Wright, £2
Henry Orme, £5
William Finloe, £5
Jonathan Wainwright, £3
William Lupton, £15
William Christian, 6s 8d
John Henshaw, £2
Abraham Alred, £4
Edward Halsall, £3
Robert Halsall, £8
John Tue, £1 16 8
John Travis, 6s 8d
Richard Ryding, £2
Richard Ryding his son, 3s 4d
John Walls, 3s 4d
John Ward, £10
Thomas Walles, 6s 8d
George Brethwaite, 6s 8d
Henry Cragg, 6s 8d
Henry Christian, 6s 8d

180 Signatures.

Christopher Barrow, 6s 8d
Bryan Berwick, 6s 8d
John Philipps, £1 16 8
Anthony Wood, £20
William Formeby, 3s 4d
Richard Percivall, 3s 4d
Thomas Percivall, 3s 4d
Mr Nathaniel Jenson, £15
Joseph Litler, £3
John Ashworth, £8
John Whitfield, £3
Robert Carter, £3
Robert Brownbill, £2
Nicholas Mercer, £2
Nicholas Banckes, £2
Henry Potter, £2
Thomas Cowper, £1
Thomas Back, 3s 4d
Mr William Patten, £11
Garnett, £3
William Answorth, £4

Edward Herle, esq., gratis
Henry Gerard, his servant, gratis
John Hesketh, gent., gratis
John Crosse, esq., gratis
John Astley, his servant, gratis
Mr George Buck, gratis
John Jeoffreys, esq., gratis
Edward Jeoffreyes, gent., gratis
George Jeoffreyes, gent., gratis
Mr Gilbert Aspinwall, gratis
Mr Thomas Cooke, gratis
Mr Robert Crossman, gratis

[THOMAS JOHNSON, MAYOR, 1670–71][181]

p. 923
LIVERPOOL. ELECTION COURT ON DAY OF ST LUKE, 18 OCTOBER 22
CHARLES II, before the worshipful Thomas Johnson, mayor, Robert Williamson
and Thomas Norbury, bailiffs, according to custom.

---

181   No heading is provided for Thomas Johnson's year of office.

Thomas Johnson, elected mayor and sworn
Robert Williamson elected mayor's bailiff and sworn
Thomas Norbury elected freemen's bailiff and sworn

John Entwisle recorder, continued
Samuel Fazakerley, town clerk, continued
William Molliney, serjeant at mace, continued
Thomas Roe, water bailiff, continued

    Officers chosen by the common council, Friday after the said election:
Robert Hunter, clerk, minister of the chapel of Liverpool, continued
George Glover, schoolmaster
John Sturzaker, hallkeeper, continued
Thomas Roe, town customer, continued
Richard Rogerson, subcustomer, continued, provisionally[182]
William Poltney, church clerk, continued, and sexton also

    Officers chosen by the common council, Friday after the said election:[183]
Joseph Pryor, Samuel Rathbone, stewards of the hall
Mr Robert Seacome, chosen one of the council, sworn

p. 924

p. 925
29 FEBRUARY 1670
    This day Magdalen, wife of Thomas Duke, on behalf of her husband, came to the mayor, Thomas Johnson, and petitoned that her husband be allowed to dig for marl on Liverpool heath for improving part of the enclosure which he holds by a former lease from the mayor of this town, witnessed by the hand of Magdalen 29 February 1670. And the said Magdalen for her husband agrees to pay for the marl what the council shall think meet. The mark of Magdalen Duke.

29 APRIL 1671
    Thomas Ashcroft of Bootle came to petition me, Thomas Johnson, this 29th April 1671, and desired leave from John Fazakerley, stonegetter on Liverpool heath, by contract with the mayor that the said Thomas Ashcroft might buy four or five loads of stones from the said John at his desire if the said mayor granted him leave.

22 SEPTEMBER 1671
    John Kelly this 22nd September 1671 to Thomas Johnson, mayor, prayed leave to have five loads of stones of the quarry on the town waste to be carried into Lord

182 Latin.
183 Heading is repeated.

Molyneux Street, and has agreed to give 12d per load, and has paid the same to the bailiffs.

p. 926
MONDAY 14 NOVEMBER 1670
An Assembly of the mayor and common council. It is unanimously ordered that where orders for enrolling apprentices with the town clerk have several times been made, and that no apprentice should be admitted as a freeman notwithstanding they have served seven years unless enrolled in the book provided and in the said clerk's custody for that purpose, the aforesaid orders shall be now revived and strictly put into execution, and no apprentice shall hereafter be enfranchised unless he has first repaired to the town clerk and procured himself enrolled as aforesaid, and paid to the clerk 12d fee for such enrolment, and the said clerk is ordered to keep a book for that purpose and to cause this order to be set up in the public places of this town. Tho. Johnson, mayor, Tho. Andoe, Henry Corles, John Sturzaker, Thomas Bickesteth, Robt.Seacome, Robert Williamson, Thomas Norbury, Law.Brownlowe, John Blundell, Willm. Fleetwood, Robt.Lyon, Tho.Bridge, Robert Moore, Sil.Richmond, Edw. Tarleton, John Lurting, Tho.Preeston, Tho.Birch, Geo.Bennett, Richard Rimer, Ri.Jones, Wm.Ackers, Tho.Roe, Wm.Molliney.[184]

p. 927
12 APRIL
An Assembly of the common council before Thomas Johnson, mayor and the rest of the common council. Whereas at the last assizes Lord Molyneux by Mr John Tatlock, his trustee, had a trial against Edward Marsh and James Whitfield on behalf of the corporation, which after full evidence was non suited, and whereas Mr Mayor was advised by counsel to pull down the bridge made on the waste of Liverpool by order of Lord Molyneux and to claim the stones and bricks dug up on the same waste without leave of the mayor, it is hereby ordered that the said act of the mayor to pull down the bridge and claim the stone and bricks shall be adjudged an act done for the good of the corporation. And we do further order that what further act or acts Mr Mayor, with the assistance of the aldermen, shall do in reference to the premises shall be allowed by this assembly, and every person who shall act in the premises by order of the mayor shall be indemnified and saved harmless at the charge of the corporation. Tho. Johnson, mayor, Thomas Andoe, Henry Corles, Peter Lurting, John Sturzaker, Thomas Bickesteth, Robart Moore, Robert Williamson, Thomas Shaw, Wm.Blundell, Sam.Fazakerley, John Lorting, John Blundell, William Rimar, Thomas Preeston, George Bennett, Willm. Fleetwood, Rich.Windall, Robt.Fleetwood, Thomas Bridge, Richard Rymer, William Ackers, Ralph Hall, Richard Jones, Thomas Roe, James Tra, lliam M.[185]

---

184 Signatures.
185 Signatures; the incomplete signatures are probably those of James Travers and William Mulliney.

p. 928

p. 929
3 DECEMBER 1670
Writ of election came to this town between 5 and 6 o'clock for the election of a burgess of parliament in the room of Mr William Stanley.

A copy of the warrant for election:

Lancaster. Henry Slater, knt., sheriff of the county, to the mayor and bailiffs of Liverpool, greeting. Since William Stanley esq., lately elected a burgess for the town of Liverpool for the present parliament held at Westminster on 8 May 17 Charles II, prorogued to 10 October 21 Charles, and continued from 19 October to 14 February last, has died, one of the burgess places is empty. Therefore by virtue of this writ I order you to elect another burgess in William Stanley's place according to the statutes laid down. And the name of the burgess is to be set down in an indenture between me and the electors so that he shall have full power to act on behalf of the borough. And you are to send me, sealed with your seals and the seals of those who make the election, one part of the indenture with this writ. Given under the seal of the sheriff's office, 3 December 22 Charles II.[186]

p. 930
James Plover of this town, 3 August 1671 to get stone in the quarry near Fall Well for 12d till St Luke's day next, the said James having paid 12d the same day to the bailiffs.

p. 931
MONDAY 16 JANUARY
An Assembly, Thomas Johnson, gentleman, mayor, the aldermen and rest of the common council. It is ordered that whereas there are now several suits between Lord Molyneux and the corporation both in law and equity, and also a contest before the lord commissioners for sale of some of his majesty's fee farm rents, all or some of which are expected to be made this Hilary term, Thomas Carter, late servant to the town clerk, Mr Fazakerley, who has last term been employed in London in the concerns of the town, especially concerning the preemption of the burgage and chantry rents, shall with all expedition be sent to London to attend Sir William Bucknell, our burgess in parliament, and other our friends, and on his advice to solicit and act in our concerns, and to take the assistance of such attorneys as may be meet in that behalf, and that the costs and charges thereof shall be paid out of the treasury of this town. And it is also ordered that Mr Mayor with privity of the aldermen and four of the common council shall be empowered to answer letters and direct and advise in any thing relating to the said matters. And all freemen hereafter admitted to this corporation shall first make their address by petition to the mayor of the

186 Latin.

corporation, or not be admitted, except freemen's sons and apprentices. Tho.Johnson, mayor, Tho.Andoe, Hen.Corleyes, Peter Lurting, John Sturzaker, Tho.Bickesteth, Robart Moore, Robert Williamson, Thomas Norbury, Sam.Fazakerley, town clerk, Tho.Christian, Law.Brownlowe, John Blundell, Edw.Tarleton, Willm.Fleetwood, Rich.Windall, Robt.Fleetwood, Richard Rimer, William Mulliney, William Ackers, John Lorting, Tho.Preeston, Geo.Bennett, Tho.Bridge, Ralph Hall, Richard Jones, Thomas Roe.[187]

p. 932

p. 933
20 FEBRUARY 1670
   An Assembly. It is ordered that a ley of £60 shall be forthwith assessed on the inhabitants of this town towards repair of our church called Our Lady and St Nicholas, repair of the streets, relief of the poor and other necessary uses, and that the usual assessors, Mr George Bennett, Mr William Fleetwood and Mr Richard Windall shall assess the inhabitants, and in case any shall refuse such freemen shall ipso facto be disenfranchised and made incapable of any benefit of their freedom. It is further ordered that William Watnough and William Dwarihouse, churchwardens, shall assist in taxing and assessing. Mr George Bennett, Watergate; Mr William Fleetwood, Castle; Mr Richard Windall, Dale Street. Tho.Johnson, mayor, Tho.Andoe, Henry Corles, Peter Lurting, John Sturzaker, Thomas Bickesteth, Robert Williamson, Thomas Norbury, Sam. Fazakerley, Silvester Richmond, Willm.Fleetwood, Ralph Hall, William Rimar, John Blundell, John Lorting, Tho.Preeston, Robt. Lyon, Willm.Mulliney, Mr Robt.Moore, Richard Bushell, Richd.Rimar, Rich.Windall, George Bennett, Thomas Shaw, Tho.Roe, Tho.Bridge, Wm. Accars, Richard Jones.[188]

p. 934
   MEMO. That 28 March 1671 Thomas Edward of Tandergee in Ireland on behalf of William Martyn of the same paid £5 4s 4½d to Mr Peter Atherton of Liverpool by a bill of 25 March 1670, and the said William Martyn is discharged therefore of the bill. Witness, Sam. Fazakerley, town clerk.

28 MARCH 1671
   At an Assembly of the mayor, aldermen and common council in common hall it is ordered that Richard Rogerson, formerly one of the leavelookers and subcustomer, being now unable to execute his offices and desirous of being discharged, is from henceforth discharged from his offices, and William Galley is elected to execute the offices until next election day.

187 Signatures.
188 Signatures.

p. 935
TUESDAY EIGH — [189] MARCH 1671
Liverpool. An Assembly in common hall before Thomas Johnson, mayor, the aldermen, bailiffs — of the common council. Whereas several suits have been moved between John Tatlock against James Marsh and Edward Whitfield on behalf of Lord Molyneux, and also by Henry Parr, as lessee of John Tatlocke, against Samuel Fazakerley, all of which concern the interest and title of the corporation of Liverpool as to their claim in the waste grounds of Liverpool, and also other suits are threatened against the mayor for withholding tolls and other duties and customs of this town by the Lord Molyneux or some on his behalf, and whereas it is agreed that in case a verdict should pass against the said defendants or any of them at the next assizes that a writ or writs of error shall be sued and recognisances given for prosecuting thereof according to the statute, it is now ordered that the said mayor and Samuel Fazakerley be indemnified at the charge of this corporation from any charges they shall be exposed to by reason of the said suits, and from any recognisance or bond they shall enter into for prosecuting the said writ of error, and further that the said mayor and every other person employed by him in or about the premises shall be indemnified. And that in case of any overture of peace or final agreement in the said suits at the next assizes it shall be in the power of the mayor, on behalf of the corporation to elect and name one or more arbitrators to agree if it seems to him convenient, and the corporation shall be bound by the order or umpirage, and whatever costs shall be expended by the said mayor or by his order about the premises shall be paid by the corporation, and the said mayor may take to his assistance at the next assizes such of the aldermen or other of the town as he shall think meet. Tho. Johnson, mayor, Tho. Andoe, Peter Lurting, John Sturzaker, Thomas Bickesteth, Robart Moore, Robert Williamson, Edw. Tarleton, John Blundell, John Lurtinge, Thomas Shaw, Thomas Bridge, Richard Jones, Tho. Preeston, George Bennett, Willm. Fleetwood, Rich. Windall, Sil. Richmond, Willi. Ackers, Ralph Hall, Tho. Roe, William Mulliney.[190]

p. 936
14 APRIL 1671
Let the quarry, 14 April 1671, to John Fazakerley and William Kenyon, both of Walton, masons, where they have got and now get stones for the rent of 18d to the 18 October next, being a half year, to be paid to the mayor of Liverpool or the bailiffs at St James tide next, the said John Fazakerley and William Kenyon not selling any stone to foreigners without the consent of the mayor, nor any load of stone into the Lord Molyneux Street except they obtain leave of the mayor, witness our hands, the mark of William Kenyon, the mark of John Fazakerley.

189 Damp has eroded the pages of the town book from this point and some text is lost. Such loss is indicated by a dash.
190 Signatures.

The abovesaid John Fazakerley and William Kenion, 3 May 1671, are admitted to carry from the Quarry hill three cart loads of stones already dressed into the Lord Molyneux Street, and agreed to pay three shillings before 13th instant. Received 15 May 1671.

1 MAY 1671

It is ordered at this Assembly that it be referred to Mr Mayor and the aldermen to contract with Mr Herles or other to build a house on the waste ground or rock at the schoolhouse side on the north side, and to set out and allow so much ground for the same towards the church stile as to the mayor and aldermen seems meet, on such terms as they shall conclude.

It is ordered the same day that the mayor and Mr Corleyes may treat on behalf of the corporation with Mr Nicholas Fazakerley and Mr John Tatlock on behalf of Lord Molyneux to compose or end the suits between this corporation and Lord Molyneux or on his behalf, and what the mayor and Mr Corleyes shall agree to shall be binding as if by the consent of this whole assembly, the aforesaid treaty to be in this town tomorrow at the house of Mrs Margery Formeby.

It is ordered the same day that the mayor, by the consent of this assembly, shall give warrants for the distress of the goods of any freeman inhabiting this town who has not paid sums taxed at the last ley for the repair of the church and other necessary uses. And it is also ordered that the town clerk shall be sent up to London (if occasion be) to solicit the business of this town, either this week or beginning of the next.

p. 937

INDENTURE 12 AUGUST, 3 ELIZABETH

Between Ralph Sekerston, mayor, and his brethren and commonalty on the one part, and — Seacome on the other part. Witness that William Moore, esq., mayor of Liverpool in times past, and his brethren and commonalty, being of one whole mind, granted to Hugh Davidson, late of Liverpool, baker deceased, and his heirs and assigns in fee farm for ever all those lands lying at the east end of the Gallow Field eastward to a close called Gorstie Hey and in breadth from the land of Richard Starke, esq., to the heath and long ditch called Common Ditch on the south part of Gallowfield and so extending eastwards to the south corner of Gorstie Hey, which lands by good conveyance descended to Gilbert Hughson, one of the legitimate sons of Hugh Davidson, which Gilbert for a certain sum of money bargained and sold the lands to the said Thomas, his heirs and assigns, in corroboration whereof Ralf Sekerston, his brethren and commonalty have confirmed, and by their deed give to Thomas Secome the same lands to have with all appurtenances to him and his heirs and assigns in fee farm for ever, yielding yearly to Ralph Sekerston, mayor, his brethen and commonalty and their successors 6s 8d at the feast of St Michael the Archangel and the Annunciation of the Blessed Virgin by even portions, which rent, with the annual rents of the town is to be employed for the use and preservation of the bayeghs in the port of Liverpool, defence of the walls on the western side, for the repair of the pavements without and within the streets of the town and other repairs to the common hall. And for want of rent and no sufficient distress being found on the lands, within twelve days after the said feast days the mayor, brethren and commonalty can repossess the said lands. And furthermore, Ralph Sekerston, mayor, his brethren and commonalty have put their faith full in Christ, Richard Samuelson and John Heygh, lawful attorneys, to enter in the said lands in their name and to deliver them to Thomas Secom or his attorney according to this deed and both sides are bound to the other by this deed in £50. In witness whereof Ralph Sekerston, his brethren and commonalty have affixed and put — of the same borough and port town of Liverpool on the above date. Possession was taken and delivered by the attorneys in the presence of Robert Corbett, Ralph Jameson, Ralph Egekers, Thomas Englefield, and others.[191] Copy of the original, 24 April 1671, by us, Thomas Johnson, mayor, Thomas Carter.

p. 938
26 APRIL 1671
An Assembly. Whereas there have been suits and controversies, some yet pending, between the corporation of Liverpool and Lord Molyneux, and it has recently been signified to Mr Thomas Johnson, mayor, by some from Lord Molyneux that he is willing to have a treaty to accommodate the differences, it is decided that the mayor take to his assistance Mr Percivall, Mr Richmond the town clerk and one of the bailiffs to treat with Lord Molyneux to proceed in the conclusion of the differences, and whatsoever the said mayor shall do shall be valid and binding as if done with the consent of this assembly. Tho. Johnson, mayor, Tho. Andoe, Henry Corles, Peter Lurting, John Sturzaker, Thomas Bickesteth, Robart Moore, Robert Williamson, Thomas Shaw, Sam. Fazakerley, William Rimar, John Blundell, John Lurtinge, Tho. Preeston, Willm. Fleetwood, Rich. Windall, Robt. Fleetwood, Ralph Hall, Tho. Roe, S. Richmond, Rob. Seacom, Tho. Bridge, James Travers, William Mulliney.[192]

p. 939
A CATALOGUE OF THE FREE BURGESSES OF LIVERPOOL IN THE —
Mr Thomas Johnson, mayor, Charles Earl of Derby, alderman, Thomas Lord Colchester, alderman, William Stanley, Lord Strange, alderman, John Entwisle, esq., recorder, Sir Gilbert Ireland, burgess in parliament; Thomas Andoe, Henry Corbyes, Peter Lurting, John Sturzaker, Thomas Bixteth, John Chandler, aldermen; Robert Hunter, minister; Robert Williamson, Thomas Norbury, bailiffs; Samuel Fazakerley, town clerk, George Glover, schoolmaster, William Molleny, Thomas Roe, town customer, Mr Thomas Blackmore, Mr Thomas Williamson, Mr Ralph Massam, Mr Gilbert Formby, Mr Richard Percivall, Mr Richard Williamson, Evan Marsh, William Rymer, John Blundell, William Bushell, John Lurting, Mr Thomas

191 Note about possession is added in margin.
192 Signatures.

Sandiford, Edmund Lievesley, William Gardner, John Pemberton, Thomas Birch, Thomas Preston, George Bennet, Laurence Brownloe, Mr Thomas Atherton, Richard Bushell, William Fleetwood, Richard Windle, Robert Fleetwood, Mr John Winstanley, Mr Robert Moore, John Bradill, William Brookes, esq., Bartholomew Hesketh, Jeffery Halcroft, Sir John Booth, Thomas Birch senior, Sir Peter Brooke, Henry Ogle, John Lord Murrey, earl of Atholl, John Murry, esq., John Greenalgh, clerk, Ferdinand Colcatt, William Bell, Henry Bolton, Thomas Cleyton, Richard Burkenfield, Thomas Warburton, Richard Fleetwood, Thomas Blakburne, John Brookes, Richard Hockenhall, George Hally, Elline Walley, Edward Moore, esq., William Rigby, esq., Thomas Massock, gent., Edward Dickonson, gent., William West, esq., Richard Stankey, John Sharples, Henry Hulcroft, Hugh Cooper, Nicholas, Sherburne, John Bexwicke, Robert Clerke, captain, John —, John Birch, Henry Stanley, Roger Wingreene, William Lea, Andrew Ashton, Jeffrey Birchall, John Eaton, John Newton, John Daniell, Edward Ogle, Richard Ratcliffe, William Massey, William Fife, Alexander Bonner, Robert Gardner, Gregory Holcroft, John Ashurst, mayor, James Johnson, Richard Washington, Thomas Higginson, Henry Rollin, Thomas Coppull, Henry Johnson, Alice Nicholson, Thomas Chapman, John Barrow, Humphrey Webster, Edward Ogden, Joseph Wade, esq., Richard Holland, Bryan Mercer, Robert Johnson, Henry Webster, John Henshaw, Robert Bixsteth, Henry Birchall, Robert Fleetwood,

p. 940

George Prescott, Robert Seacome, Robert Eccles, Thomas Duke, Robert Taylor, Robert Fidler, Richard Brown, Henry Ratcliffe, Thomas Taylor, Thomas Carr, John Lurt, John Bankes, Edward Lyon, maltster, William Widnesse, Peter Rowe, Henry Fernhead, Thomas Gardner, Michael Barker, Richard Fazakerley, Richard Moorcroft, John Bate, Edward Taylor, Henry Ambrose, Richard Fairer, Henry Cooper, Thomas Cheaney, Thomas Rainford, John Johnson of Everton, Thomas Lurting, Peter Bolton, Robert Lyon, William Chorly, John Cann, Richard Widdow, John Rice, Abel Lyon, Henry Wilcock, William Jumper, John Cooke, Thomas Morecroft, Henry Kilshaw, sadler, James Ainsdale, Henry Crane, Thomas Cropper, John Halle, John Burgesse, William Mosse, Edward Tyrer, John Heskines, Darby Caton, Thomas Lancelott, Thomas Darbishire, Richard Farrer, Edward Tarleton, Thomas Galloway, Gilbert Tarleton, John Bitchfield, William Marshall, Richard Tyrer, Robert Washington, Richard Compton, William Sadder, Anthony Carr, John Lyon, tanner, Christopher Bennet, Thomas Learer, Robert Hall, Cuthbert Holland, William Riding, cooper, Thomas Roe, Gregory Formby, John Smith, shoemaker, Gilbert Coote, John Tenant, tailor, Edward Lea, George Tarleton, Jeremy Berston, William Oliffe, Richard Rymer, Henry Oyle, Robert Barrow, John Sutton, Edward Sutton, John Eccles, Richard Galloway, Thomas Chapman, junior, James Hey, Percival Crosse, Richard Symkin, Robert Kenion, Thomas Percivall, Robert Swift, William Whalley, John Sanderson, Peter Walker, Enoch Bolton, John Kenion, William Moore, William Ackers, Richard Atherton, James Blevine, Walter Mathews, John Melling, Richard Scarsbacke, John Heyes, mort, William Faith, clerk, Robert Kenion, cooper, John Holland, Robert Sympson, Edward Bankes, Andrew Over, Ralph Be —

p. 941
Hugh Reynold, John Crane, Jonathan Gleave, Thomas Johnson, George Smith, Lawrence Jumper, Richard Browne, John Cary, Thomas Andoe, Ralph Halle, William Parker, Thomas Mossed, Edward Rideing, John Goultney, Thomas Farr, Robert Eaton, clerk, Henry Gregson, Thomas Bridge, Richard Gooer, eston, James Litherland, Richard Rogerson, John Griffith, Edward Car, Philip Peircy, Samuel Sandiford, William Poultney, William Lewis, Thomas Crompton, clerk, John Williamson, George Thorpe, Jonathan Greene, John Rymer, Roger James, Thomas Blackmore, lyme, Henry Nield, Thomas Coventry, John Walker, Thomas Stedman, William Nichols, Thomas Tatlocke, William Fazakerley, shoemaker, Thomas Litherland, Thomas Dobb, John Moniley, mariner, Robert Haughton, Robert Leadbeter, Thomas Dickonson, joiner, Richard Jones, painter, Thomas Wilson, mariner, William Marsh, William Mills, mariner, John Williamson, mariner, Edward Clerkson, Joseph Ambrose, clerk, John Waring, gent., John Stirrup, Steven Platt, Thomas W, John Coote, tailor, William Williamson, mariner, Thomas Sharp, John Rymer, sailor, John Starky, gent., Richard Williamson, chirurgeon, Laurence Williamson, mariner, William Welsh, mariner, Edward Flitcroft, skinner, James Scarisbrirch, blockmaker, John Rymer, ropemaker, Sir James Graham, knight, Thomas Bromhall, doctor in physic, Mathew Dodsworte, Henry Bryan, William Watmough, A G, Mr Sam Birch, William Baylie, William Travis, William Simpson, James Collier, gent., Thomas Hought, gent., Henry Ambrose, John Melling, William Price, cutler, John Francy, Thomas Lathom, Robert Secome, gent., James Lydiat, James Jerrome, Anthony Drubabin, Michell Hinkison, William Leech, H C, Joseph Wilson, Laurence Brownloe, Robert Murrey, John Mercer, Richard Foxe, Thomas Worthington, Josias Fogg, Edward Litherland, John Litherland, William Shoomaker, Walter Mothy, Simon Arrowsmith, John Heywood, clerk, Richard Whitfield, Edward Prenton, Isaac — ld, Hugh — yson

p. 942
W.A., Robert and John Mercer, sons of Ralph, William Blundell, mariner, Robert Lurting, John Higginson, William Dwarrihouse, John Crane, John Haking, George Smith, Richard Dobb, Thomas Wolfall, William Bruerton, Francis Hunter, Richard Formby, John Erby, Richard Mercer, Robert Woodside, William Plumb, bodymaker, John Kelly, carter, John Bamber, ropemaker, Richard Walles, Anthony Johnson, Richard Parr, Patrick Reynolds, W.S. 4 November 14 Charles I, now, Sir Roger Bradshaigh, Hugh Dickonson, Henry Blundell esq., James Anderton of Birchall, Thomas Leigh of Lyme, knt., Roger Molyneux of Wood, knt., Nicholas Fazakerley of Spella, knt., William Woolfall of Wolfall, knt., William Gerard of Brymeard, H. Norries of West Derby, John Townly of Townly, Charles Townly of Townly, William Fazakerley of Spella, Richard Norres of West Derby, Thomas Cawarden of Croxteth, Henry Parr of same, William Curghew of same, Thomas Turner of Preston, George Colcheth of Townly, Thomas Butler, — ke of Walton g —, — hom servant to Esquire Gerard, — Marshall of Prescot, — footly of Heatly, — Kirkby, — Smith of Swepg —, Henry Blundell of West Derby, John Hodgson,

William Bridges, James Parr, Mr Stanley's servant, John Fairhurst, John Leigh, clerk, Edward Wally, Edward Eccles, Thomas Patricke, Thomas Holland, Ralph Johnson, Thomas Gildoes, John Sandiford, Peter Allen, Edward Buckly, James Travis, Oliver Lyme, Henry Knowles, William Lord Brabaso, George Collinwood, Henry Hocknell, James Smoot, John Story, Anthony Banister, Gilbert Blundell, James Boates, Robert Burt, William Forber, Matthew Gleave, Thomas Lurting, William Spenser, esq., William Parker of Bradkeh, Clodius Dennis, James Ball, Thomas Finloe, John Moniley, Richard Marsh, William Williamson, Thomas Wainwright, James Topping, Thomas Darwin, Edward Stockly, Thomas Gregson, George King, William Eccles, William Done, James Fletcher, Jane Smith, Nicholas Stone, David Cooke, Thomas Norbury, Robert Breers, William Tyrer, John Widowson, Edward Archer, William Birchall, William Sturtall, esq., William Bankes, esq., Peeres Leigh, esq., William Kirkby, esq., Thomas Lyon senior, Sir William Stanley, John Molyneux, Thomas Lyon junior, Peter Jones, Hugh Diggles, Silvester Richmond, William Crompton, Edward Jones, John Arrowsmith, John Richa —, William Cary, Thomas Tyrer

p. 943

Bryan Fleetwood, Henry Ricroft, feltmaker, Owen Gerard, Henry Higginson, John Sayre, esq., Ferdinand Stanley, esq., Richard Robinson, Ralph Anton, Richard Wright, James Jones, John South, Thomas Parry, Thomas Marsh, Richard Eccleson, Richard Tarleton, James Brindle, Thomas Wright, John Tempest, Charles Christian, Thomas Glover, Jeffrey Clerkson, John James, gentleman, William Preeston, Peter Allerton, Edward Derby, Robert Roper, Paul Chuvall, Richard Wood, James Nowell, Peter Cropper, John Ormishaw, Randle Williamson, Ellis Lyon, Gilbert Sutton, Thomas Jumper, John Heyes, William Galley, Thomas Durninge, George Aspinalle, Samuel Robem, Jeremy Findly, William Hardman, Robert Lord Cholmely, Sir Philip Egerton, Mayor Thomas Ashton, Edward Mayneringe, Francis Ashed, Charles Jones, John Parr, Edward Formby, Henry Mercer, Richard Mercer, Henry Jobson, John Richards, Robert Edwards, Richard Bullocke, Thomas Stockly, Thomas Hurdis, Thomas Lyon, Richard Diggles, Thomas Linaker, Nicolas Currein, William Ricroft, William Worrall, William Litherland, Sir John Ardern, Robert Heywood, esq., William Davenport of Ardin, John Gardner of Manchester, Brian Banister of Knowsley, William Eccles of Bromhall, William Norres, clerk, William Bennington of Birch, George Hull, John Jones of Ormskirk, Robert Bellin, Ralph Tutchell, George Lambert, Henry Wilington, John Hartly, William Bushell, slater, James Pares, mercer, Thomas Shaw, grocer, John Nott, Henry Pemberton, Francis Medower, Thomas Topping, Edward Racon, Thomas Bolton, William Valentine, William Lyon, Roger Gorsuch, Robert Williamson, Thomas Winstanley, locksmith, Henry Colborne, Roger Turner, Edward Simpson, Thomas Plombe, Thomas Ashur, Thomas Nicholson, Edward Herrison, Giles Reece, combmaker, William Woods, Richard Erby, Daniel Swift, Peter Scarisbrick, Edward Winstanly, Roger Bushell, William Yonger, Thomas Norland, John Jackson, Henry Stevenson, William Mercer, John Peeres.

p. 944
— MAY 1671

Thomas Carter, late servant to the town clerk, was admitted and sworn an attorney of the court of record at Liverpool before the mayor, aldermen and bailiffs.

William Nicolas came before me Thomas Johnson, mayor, this 27 May 1671 and desired that Thomas Lidiatt of Lidiate might buy from William Turner three loads of stones for window stuff. The said William, paying a rent for his quarry to the mayor, was allowed to carry three loads of the quarry to Lydiate.[193]

TUESDAY 8 AUGUST 1671
An Assembly:

It is ordered that a ley or tax of £60 be forthwith assessed on the inhabitants of the town by the usual assessors for repair of bridges about the town, the town hall, defending the rights of the corporation and other necessary uses in and about this town, and that the same shall be collected and paid to the bailiffs. Tho. Johnson, mayor, Tho. Andoe, Henry Corles, Peter Lurting, John Sturzaker, Thomas Bickesteth, Robart Moore, Robert Williamson, Thomas Shaw, Law. Brownlowe, Robt. Seacome, Sam. Fazakerley, Will. Gardner, George Bennett, Willm. Fleetwood, Thomas Bridge, William Ackers, Robert Lyon, William Mulliney, Tho. Roe, James Travers, Richard J — .[194]

Also ordered that the mayor and aldermen shall view the — at the sea side where Richard Lurting has built a smithy, and contract with him for a lease of so much as is on the town waste on such terms as they think meet.

That Ralph Johnson shall have a lease of his house on Castle Hill according to his contract.

That William Bushell shall have a lease according to his contract.

That William Ainsdale shall have a place on the Castle Hill to build a house on, against Mr Alcocke's house, 15 yards to the front, — bd 4 yards, for three lives, building the house of stone, slate and oak.

p. 945
12 AUGUST 1671

Memo. That John Wilson of Chester came before the worshipful Thomas Johnson, mayor, and submitted himself to Mr Mayor — trespass in getting sods on the waste of Liverpool near Lord Molyneux — licence, and paid fine 6s 8d.

THE BOUNDARIES OF LIVERPOOL

The perambulation is from Water Street end to Beeton gutter on the N — of Liverpool, thence to the Grove and the mere stone in Mr Moore's mead —, thence

193 Note about William carrying stones from the quarry to Lidiate is in a different hand.
194 Signatures.

to Kirkdale Lane to the mere stone there against the beacon, th — to a mere stone in Syre's ditch adjoining the Beck, thence through — thence through several closes to a mere stone up Everton causey, thence through several fields to Liverpool Common, and so after the common side to the merestone at Johnson's field end on the east side of the town, and so up the gutter to the Mosslake to a place called Hollin Hedge, and thence straight to the Park wall, and all along the Park wall and through two crofts to Booth's Mill, and so to the sea side, and all along the sea side over the pool and thence along the sea side to Water Street end. Our liberty at sea to arrest within the flood mark is on both sides of the river Mersey as far upwards as the same flows with custom or toll on either side of the river with other usual privileges of the river.

p. 946

p. 947

PORTMOOT COURT OR QUARTER SESSIONS HELD AT LIVERPOOL IN COUNTY OF LANCASTER IN THE COMMON HALL, 24 OCTOBER 1670, before Thomas Johnson, — Williamson and Thomas Norbury, gentlemen, bailiffs, according to —

Inquisition of the jurors, Mr Richard Windle, Mr Jo —, Thomas Birch, Mr John Lurting, Thomas Brige, William Ackers, Ellis —, Henry Jobson, Thomas Hurdis, Ralph Henshaw, William Healy, George —, William Simpson, Thomas Stockly, Hugh Diggles, Huon Gerrard, James —, Simon Arrowsmith, Robert Woodside, Peter Atherton, Thomas Nor — , Anthony Car, William Valentine.

We present:
Richard Boulton for keeping an unlawful quart, 6d
Thomas Stockley for muck lying in the street, 4d; Margaret Boulton, Ellis Lyon, Thomas Patrick, Thomas Birch, Thomas Holland, James Hall, Richard Windle, John Richards, James Fletcher, Robert Bickesteth, Ellen Nicholson, all 4d, for the like offence
Mr John Winstanley for his swine unrung, 1, 4d; Thomas Patrick, 1, 4d; John Tempest, 1, 4d; Thomas Gregson, 4, 1s 4d; Richard Rimer, 3, 1s; Widow Jumper, 1, 4d; Widow Barton, 1, 4d; Widow Brookes, 1, 4d; Mr Thomas Atherton, 1, 4d; Mr John Sturzaker, 1, 4d; Widow Hoult, 1, 4d; Widow Jarret, 1, 4d; o —lland, 6, 2s; Richard Crompton, 1, 4d; Anthony Walles, 1, 4d; Widow Tarlton, 1, 4d; Evan Marsh, 1, 4d; Thomas Roe, 1, 4d; Richard Rimer, 1, 4d; Richard Crompton, 12, 4s; Mrs Bickesteth, 3, 1s; Thomasin Hoult, 1, 4d; John Morecroft, 2, 8d; Mr Thomas Bickesteth, 2, 8d; Margaret Eccleston, 2, 8d; Edward Buckley, 1, 4d; John Morecroft, 1, 4d; Widow Bullock, 1, 4d; Peter Walker, 1, 4d; Thomas Stockly, 5, 1s 8d; Edward Litherland, 2, —, Margaret Granger, 2, —, Jane Walles, 1, —, Mr John Sturzaker, 6, 2s; — s Andoe, 1, — , Thomas Hollis, 5, 1s — , Abigail Martin, 1, —, all for the like.
Edward Bowker for neglect of office of overseer of —

The scavengers for neglect of their office, viz. Thomas Gilds, Thomas Mathews, George Hull, William Heath

Henry Jobson and Thomas Tyrer for neglect of their office

John Hatton, hatter, for using the faculty of a freeman, not—John Spencer, Robert Righly, Mrs Blackborne, John Woods, for the like

William Kelly and John Everid for lading a pit on the town's — mayor's licence

Edward Moore, esq., for not paying his ley assessed on him for the repair of the chapel and the privileges — corporation; Captain William Fazakerley, Henry Mercer, Widow Postlethwait, Thomas Sandiford for the Angel, — Ward, — wick, administrator, — of Everton, Robert Fleetwood, Doctor Heywood, Robert Eccles, adm. exec., Widow Hardning, — Harrison, — mpson, — Wmson, — Kelly

p. 948

Jane Haskeine, John Bankes, John Higginson, Widow Dwarrihouse, exec., Brian Fleetwood, Thomas Parry, Thomas Lancelott, John Williamson junior, William Jumper, William Mercer, William Ryding, Robert Jellison, Thomas Rowell, Samuel Birch, collector, Mr Thomas Latham, John Starkie, Thomas Finloe, all for the like offence

John Banckes for entertaining inmates; Mrs Bicksteth, Anthony Banister, Widow Ellen Litherland, John Goore, Elinor Garrett, Ann Gallomore, Isabel Sutton, Thomas Lancelott, Mr John Tempest, Robert Swayne, William Eccleston, William Carie, Richard Browne, Alice Johnson, John Hall, Ann Brookes, Bryan Mercer, Thomas Hurdis, Evan Swift or Richard Crompton, all for the like

All the freemen of this corporation not appearing this 24 October 1670: Henry Webster, John Holland, George Thorp, Edward Prenton, Edward Lea of Holland, Ralph Bellin, John Stirrupp, William Bridge

Robert Fleetwood, John Blundell, Thomas Christian, Mr Robert Secome, merchant appraisers[195]

High Diggles, Ralph Johnson, registers of leather

Richard Anton, Henry Knowles, alefounders

Thomas Norland, Richard Diggles, overseers of the highway

Robert Brownbill, Richard Bolton, Evan Stock, Edward Archer, scavengers

Thomas Hollis, John Wanewright, Nicholas Banckes, Peter Scarisbrick, barleymen

William Simson, murenger

John Sanderson, Peter Walker, Thomas Stockley, William Simson,— A —

— Ricroft, — Holland, porters

p. 949

Richard Rogerson, Edward Halsall, leavelookers

Richard Widdowes, beadle and bellman

---

195 These are elections made by the portmoot court, but are usually included immediately after the election court at the beginning of the mayoral year.

William Kelly, Franc — Wittar, boothsetters
William Chorley, John Higginson, boardsetters

We order:
Elizabeth Bridge to make a wall fence between Richard Finloe and her before 25 March
Edward Moore esq. to make clear the water course between Robert Bellin and Robert B — March next
The carters not to go over ship cables on pain of —, according to former order
Swine to be kept up on Saturdays and sabbath days
Simon Arrowsmith to have a free easing drop — Harrison to lay no rubbish or muck to stop the gutter
Mr Ralph Massam to move his well pins to make a way to the right hand of an old well, and down to John Williamson — 2 February
The curfew to be rung through the whole year, at 4 and 8 o'clock as formerly

We present Thomas Ackers for breaking the door of the common —, and making his escape on Saturday 22 October 1670

We agree to all ancient orders and laudable customs.

p. 950
AUDIT OF THOMAS BICKESTETH, ESQ., MAYOR, 11 JANUARY 1670, Richard Windfall and Robert Fleetwood, bailiffs, taken in the common hall before Thomas Johnson, gentleman, mayor, Robert Williamson, Thomas Norbury, bailiffs, Thomas Andoe, Henry Corles, Peter Lurting, John Sturzaker, aldermen, according to custom.

Ingates and outgates, Mr Sturzaker and Thomas Roe	£65	5s	8d
Richard Rogerson, subcustomer,	11	0	7
Stalls	20	4	10
Freemen	181	6	8
Town rents	9	19	4
Fines	6	3	2
Mr Hutton's 2 year's rents	6	0	0
Received of the town clerk	2	4	0
Paid to the late bailiffs	188	0	5
Received by late bailiffs of a town ley	41	13	9
Total	531	18	5
The whole disbursements of the late bailiffs	427	17	11
Rest to balance	104	0	6

The balance of this account paid by the said late bailiffs to the aforesaid new bailiffs and the late bailiffs are discharged

104 0 6 — by the late bailiffs to the — bailiffs:

Edward Formbye's bond, £20
Mr Formbye's bond, ferry boat, £100
Mr Chandler's bond, £2 12s 6d
Thomas Roe's bond, £16 8s, part paid, £16

The abovesaid account is allowed by us the auditors underwritten, and the late bailiffs are discharged: Thomas Johnson, mayor, Thomas Andoe, Henry Corles, Peter Lurting, John Sturzaker, Thomas Bickesteth.[196]

p. 951
ENTRY OF FREEMEN
  In Mr Brownloe's time, entered in the new book:
Joshua Tunstall, £7
Edward Browne
Joseph Moxon, £15
Gilbert Lowe, £10, dead[197]
John Mollyneux, hatter
Thomas Hancock, dead[198]
David Poole
John Hackner
John Orme
John Dichfield
Nathaniel Palmer
Robert Prenton
Thomas Clerk
Peter Leyland
John Reynolds
John Tarleton
Edward Tarleton
Gilbert Tarleton
Hugh Langford
John Wakefield
Robert Waad

  Freemen, gratis:
Sir William Osbaldaston

196 Signatures; Thomas Andoe is recorded with his stamp.
197 Note of death is written in margin.
198 Note of death is written in margin.

Edward Osbaldaston esq.
Ralph Astley, cap.
Edward Ogden
Nicholas Willington
Richard Hodkinson
Thomas Hodgkinson
Arthur Burron
Samuel Andrews
Edward Lord Herbert
John Rede
Edward Price
Richard Jones
Thomas Pawlett, rector

Freemen, Mr Johnson's time:
Henry Houghton, £2
Richard Gill, £3
Edward Owen, 6s 8d
George Browne, £5
Abraham Brodley, 6s 8d
John Davies, 6s 8d
John Fisher, 6s 8d
Robert Ticknor, £2
Henry Cope, £3
Henry Tompson, £3
Edward Heyes, £4
Edward Rycroft, 3s 4d
Thomas Ditchfield, 6s 8d
William Christian, £5
Christopher Jans, £5
Griffith Ubbebin, £5
Thomas Brookbank, 3s 4d
John Higginson, 3s 4d
Thomas Robinson, 3s 4d
John Jones, £5
Richard Higginson, £5
William Stevenson, 6s —
Edmund Travers, £10
John Glover, £4
Thomas Tottie, £14
Thomas Hasloe, £5
Richard Marsh, 6s 8d
William Trueman, £3
William Houghton, £5
John Gamond, 6 —

Edward Ogden, £4
Peter Dawson, £2
Richard Windle, cooper, £5
Nicholas Withington —
Charles Green —
Ralph Astly —
Ralph Sheperd —
Thomas Sutton —
Stephen Shawcroft, £3
William Southerd, 6 —
James Maddock, £4
Henry Hilton, 6s 8d
Nicholas Needham, £5
John Battersby, £4

    Freemen gratis:
Thomas Ashurst esq.
Thomas Witherden, London grocer
Sir William Buckp —
John Breden, alderman —
John Bowck, clerk
Thomas Corbett of London
Samuel Newton
Mr George Birch
John Kellett undersheriff
Randle L — ter
Henry S — esq.
Sir Roger —
—
—

p. 952

p. 953
2 AUGUST 1671
Assembly:
    It is ordered that 10 shillings be paid by the bailiffs to Peter — for charges he has had in being kept out of the town smithy on Castle Hill.
    It is also ordered that William Price shall not proceed with jettying over on the town's new building.

PORTMOOT COURT OR QUARTER SESSIONS FOR THE BOROUGH OF LIVERPOOL IN COUNTY OF LANCASTER, IN THE COMMON HALL, MONDAY 14 AUGUST 1671, before Thomas Johnson, mayor, Robert Williamson, Thomas Shaw, gentlemen — , according to custom.

Inquisition of the jurors, Mr Bailiff Gardner, Mr Bailiff Bennett, Mr F — , Thomas Brige, Mr Henry Higginson, Richard Jones, Roger Gorsuch, James — , Thomas Norland, Anthony Banister, Ralph Auton, Thomas Hurdis, — Hollis, Mr Samuel Ralphborne, Hugh Diggles.

We present:
Richard Crompton for laying his limestone on the south side of the pool at the water side contrary to former order; John Lunt, Richard Diggles, Thomas Hurdis, Michael Jenkinson, William Bushell, 3s 4d each for the like offence
Robert Denton for using the faculty of a freeman, not being free; William Hurdis, Thomas Lyon for the like offence
Gerrard Ford for opening and selling his goods at the fairs contrary to laudable customs of this town; John Weakefeild of Wigan for the like
Gilbert Lowe for using the faculty of a freeman and is none
Robert Ticknor for keeping unlawful gaming at unreasonable times; John Morecroft for the same offence, 6s 8d
Mr John Ward for retaining goods and borrowing money of James Greene, servant to Mr Thomas Johnson
Jacob Middleton for aiding James Greene — to Mr Thomas Johnson illegally
James Whitfeild, watchmaker, after warning — Storie's servant
Henry Bootle for being a confederate with Jam —
Widow Earlome for harbouring and receiving goods of — from his servant James Greene illegally and at unlawful times
John Hill for delivering and carrying away clods of the Co—— thout licence from the mayor
Edward Buckly for a bloodwipe in Mr Ticknor's house against John Buson of West Derby
Edward Halsall for neglect of his office in seeing bad meat in the market and not disposing of it according to the statute in that case
Thomas Tyrer for making bread short of statute weight; James Jones, Edward Simpson, Richard Boulton, Esther Hardman, each 3s 4d for the like
William Nicholls for keeping 3 quarts that are not measured according to the statute; Thomas Christian, 1 quart, John Jackson the same, John Litherland 1 quart, Anne Midleton 1 quart, Robert Burt 1 quart, Jane Haskeine for 1 quart, each 3s 4d for the like offence
William Ackers for keeping and selling bad ale; Robert for the like offence
William Trimew for keeping one swine unrung; Richard Crompton for 2, 12d; — ton for 3 swine

p. 954
Jane Heskeine for having three swine in the market contrary to order of former jury, 2s; Thomas Roe, 1 swine, James Fletcher, 1, John Goore, 1, Thomas Gregson, 1, 1s each for the like offence
Anthony Walles for his 10 swine trespassing on John Williamson's corn, 5s; Mr William Gardner for 5 swine trespassing on ditto, 2s 6d; John Jumper for 6 swine trespassing on ditto, 3s

Alice Parry for getting paze on the sabbath, 6d; Elizabeth Robbinson, Margaret Holland 6d each for the like

Robert Litherbarrow for bringing leather not well tanned according to statute, 3s 4d

John Rowell for working unlawful leather, 3s 4d

These persons following for keeping inmates: — Hunt, — therland, — urting, — Carter, — Litherland, Anthony Johnson, John Astley, John G — re executors of Edward Alcock, at 6s 8d apiece, Widow Norbury, Thomas Lancelott, Thomas Jumper, Elizabeth Alco — , — , — , William Polney, Mrs Elizabeth Tarlton, Henry Harrison, Mr Ambrose, James Jones, Michael Rumby, Roger Gorsuch, Widow Gallomore, Elizabeth Clarke, Thomas Hurdis, Edward Scarisbrick, Isabel Sutton, Mrs Bickesteth, all 6s 8d for the like offence

— all and every person who are in order as —

p. 955
19 SEPTEMBER 1671
An Assembly:

It is ordered that a lease be made to Thomas Norland of Lurtings — in Dale Street with the lands and appurtenances belonging, for the lives of John Norland, Ann Norland, his son and daughter, to the use of his said children.

It is also ordered that Peter Ardem[199] shall have a lease of the smithy on — to be put in possession thereof.

It is also ordered that Mr Thomas Johnson, now mayor, shall have that ground for three lives and 21 years at 12d per yard, building there — oak timber, which was set out for John Kellie.

It is also ordered that if the present mayor, bailiffs or any member of the — shall be at any time fined or impleaded for any matter — by him or them on behalf of the corporation he or they shall be indemnified at the charge of the corporation.

It is also ordered that Richard Lurting shall have at the sea side — upon 5 yards on the waste from Tarleton's field in length, and 8 yards towards the sea, and when has occasion to build a wall 7 yards more — the end of his smithy, 23 yards in length, paying 5s per annum — lease for 3 lives and 21 years, to begin at Michaelmas next, vizt. 23 — per annum after.

It is also ordered that Thomas Duke shall have a lease for his life of — hereto adjoining and appertaining, containing about 3 acres at 3s per annum.

It is also ordered that the mayor and aldermen shall take a view of convenient places for making lime kilns on the waste, and hereof as they see meet, and also to appoint places to lay their limestones near to the limekilns.

Memo. That Mr Thomas Bicksteth, alderman, dissented to the 21 years after 3 lives.

Tho. Jon —, Tho. Andoe, Henry Corles, Peter Lurtin —, John Sturz —, Thomas Bickestet — , Robart Moore, Sil. Richmond, Robert Williams —, Thomas Sha —, Sam, Fazakerley, Wil —, Fleetwoo —, John Blundell, Law. Brownlowe, Will.

199 Peter Ardem is written over.

Gardner, Richard Rimer, Thomas Preeston, George Bennett, Robart Lyon, Rob. Seacome, Richard Jones, Thomas Bridge, James Travers, Willi. —, R —[200]

p. 956
We order:
That Robert Carter cleanse his ditch sufficiently lying from Sickman's Lane — about his field adjoining to the town field and also shall make sufficient plat — the water out of his ditch before Michaelmas Day next, or in not so doing — 30s

Jonathan Gleave to ditch his ditch from the watering pool in Tithebarn Lane as far as his ground lies towards Richard Moorecroft's house, sufficiently to carry water along before Michaelmas, 20s

Richard Moorecroft to take away the rubbish lying in the lane at his house and barn side and make a sufficient ditch to carry the water out of the High Lane so far as his ground lies before M —, 20s

Bailiff Robert Fleetwood to make a sufficient ditch or gutter to carry the water so that it be not noisome to the highway in Tithe — Street as far as he is possessed of before Michaelmas Day, or forfeit —

Thomas Durning to carry his dung out of the highway over against the barn in Tithebarn Lane and that he lays no more dung to annoy the highway before 25 September next, 10s

Robert Burt to forthwith open the watercourse lying at the side of Richard Wright adjoining to the said Burt's yard according to usual former custom and watercourse before 20 of instant August, 40s

James Fletcher to take his dung lying under Mr Thomas — window, and clear the water course before — August, 10s

That if any person after 30 August shall carry any gravel, earth or rubbish to the waterside without the licence of the mayor, he shall forfeit 12d every load

All millers within the corporation shall bring their toll dishes — to be cut and sealed according to the statute in the town hall before 20 August next, 20s

The smithy against the town hall being found noisome to all and several shops and other tradesmen, and the market side, that the owner of the smithy shall not after 25 December next let it to any smith to work but shall convert the same to some other use, £5 for every six months

William Bushell to forthwith take and carry away the gorse and in the future not to lay any more gorse near his oven back, it being conceived to be dangerous to his neighbours, 20s

Henry Harrison to make his gable end adjoining to Simon — straight and upright so that the said Simon shall — before 20 March next, —

p. 957
Simon Arrowsmith shall make — side adjoining to Henry Harrison's gable end straight by 25 March next, 40s

200 Signatures.

The lime kilns on Castle Hill shall be — down and not to burn any more limestone, from 29 September next, 20s

Whereas there have been several complaints by town carter and carriers on the state and negligence of — to the great damage of the said carters or carriers, that after 25th instant August such complaints made to the present magistrate of such porters causing the carters to stay above — one hour, shall for every such offence forfeit 5s

If any freeman or foreigner after the 2 — of this instant August carry or lay any dung that may be — to the highway or stop any water course, on complaint made of such person to the present magistrate, shall forfeit 10s

Whereas there was this day a complaint made — and John Prestley that Mr Robert Seacome delivered a — as his own land, lying at the bottom of a yard of a house where William Kelly now lives, it does — by four evidences of Mr William Strangwayes, John —, Elinor Winstanley, widow, that such a parcel, from the elder tree straight on, is Mr Crosse's land, declared on oath to the jury, and accordingly we conceive the same to be Mr Crosse's

We agree to all ancient and laudable laws.

p. 958
7 SEPTEMBER
— ordered that Mr Mayor shall take to his assistance Alderman Thomas —, to treat with Mr Nicholas Fazakerley and one such other as he shall bring to treat in reference to an accommodation of the differences between this corporation and the Lord Molyneux, and whatsoever the said Mr Mayor and Mr Bicksteth shall order therein on behalf of the corporation shall be binding, with the consent of this whole assembly.

It is ordered that Alderman Andoe, Alderman Bickesteth and Mr Thomas Preston shall view the ground and set out where William Ainsdale shall build so that he leave a convenient space for the street or highway there.

That the rent for Browne's croft be deferred till Mr Thomas Williamson be further consulted.

19 SEPTEMBER 1692
Then showed at the execution of a commission at Liverpool issued out of the Exchequer in a cause between the attorney general at the relation of the borough of Liverpool and John Hodgson, comp. and the borough of Lancaster, Augustine Greenwood, John Bryer, defendants, and deposed unto by Joshua Mand and Thomas Sherwin. Before us: Wm. Preston, John Roberts, John Knowles, John Kirkham.[201]

— ril 1696 then showed at the execution of a commission at Liverpool — of the Exchequer at Westminster, between Nathaniel Stanes, — omas Plasts and the mayor, bailiffs and burgesses of Liverpool, deposed by Mr William Heyes. Edward H —, James Croxton, David Parry, Frs. Winckley.[202]

201 Signatures.
202 Signatures.

INDEX

264, juror, 184, 191, 212, 230, 236, register of leather, 172, 209; John, 204, bailiff, 196, 197, 201, 208, 212, 214, juror, 191, 217, merchant appraiser, 209; Joseph, 178; Mary, 138; Richard, 62, 68, 88
Bucknell (Buckp —), William, Sir, 249, 263
Building, 217, 228, 233, 267; pulling down, 228
Buird, John, 66
Bull, James, 164
Bullock (Bullocke), John, 5, 77, 80, 88, 123; Richard, 203, 227, 256; widow, 258
Bullock, seized, 188
Bulshawe, Edward, 127
Bultney, William, 142
Burgage rents, 97–8, 110, 138, 140, 249; dispute, 142, receipts, 42, 60; rentals, 138, 139
Burges (Burgess), John, 35, 53, 62, 254; Ralph, 41, 51, 79; Thomas, 4
Burgesses (*see* Freemen), selling not free, 117
Burial dues, 58
Burkenfield, Richard, 254
Burninge, Thomas, barleyman, 220
Burran (Burron), Arthur, 3, 52, 262
Burscoe (Burscow, Burscowe, Burscough), Henry, 11, 22; Mr, 97; Thomas, 77, 100
Burscough's house, 16
Burt (Burte), Robert, 150, 163, 227, 256, 264, 266, juror, 197, 212, 236
Burton, James, 3, 8, 19, 21, 37, 48, 49, 53, 62, 76, 79, 80, 145, 223; Jane, widow, 88, 90; John, 48, 66, 89, 136, 140, 145, 157, 174, 227, juror, 168, 198, overseer, 204; Margery, 79, 102; Robert, 54, 140; Thomas, 4, 5, 6, 8, 19, 30, 34, 37, 42, 53, 98, churchwarden, 29, register of leather, 1, 34, 41, shoemaker, 57; widow, 175; — , 48
Bury, 204
Bushell (Bushel, Bushall), Elizabeth, 113; Henry, 149; Mr, 120; Richard, 130, 132, 218, 231, 238, 240, 250, 254, bailiff, 225, 227, 229, 243, juror, 203, merchant appraiser, 235; Robert, 192, 199, 242, slater, 226; Roger, 174, 179, 186, 187, 189, 193, 256, juror, 184, porter, 184; William, 4, 10, 21, 36, 77, 83, 89, 90, 100, 101, 102, 103, 104, 105, 113, 123, 132, 133, 136, 152, 155, 159, 168, 175, 180, 187, 192, 195, 203, 204, 208, 213, 216, 220, 227, 228, 230, 236, 241, 253, 257, 264, 266, bailiff, 91, 99, 218, barleyman, 235, juror, 124, 130, 145, 165, mariner, 87, merchant appraiser, 99, 144, scavenger, 1, 19, slater, 192, 214, 235, 256
Buson, John, of West Derby, 264
Busyhell, Richard, 234
Butchers, 64, 100; mean, 90; shop, 33, 225; stalls, 221, 244
Butler, Thomas, 255, servant, 148
Butlerage, 11, 44, 59, 70, 82, 83, 86, 93, 94, 95,

107, 108, 109, 118, 133; and prisage, 110; license and compositions receipts, 78; purchase, 18, 41, 106–7, 109
Butter, 10
Butterworth, Edward, esq, 2, 51
Byrom, Henry, 129

Cables, 137, 185
Calcott (Colcatt), Fardinando, 128, 254
Calley, John, 219
Cancett, John, 141
Candlemas, 198
Candowe, John,
Cann, John, 254
Cannage, George, capt, 3
Car (Care, Carie, Carr, Carre), Anthony, 4, 37, 53, 76, 88, 178, 254, juror, 137, 145, 212, 258; Edmund, 173; Edward, 54, 89, 100, 228, 255, juror, 137, 145, 203, 212, 236; John, 4, 53, 56, 72, beadle & bellman, 75, 61, leavelooker, 47, 61, 75; Ralph, 53, shoemaker, 72; Thomas, 4, 6, 7, 48, 50, 53, 67, 80, 88, 98, 101, 254, barleyman, 1, juror, 20, 34; William, 193, 221, 259, barleyman, 228, juror, 229, scavenger, 197
Care's house, 225
Carlisle, 170, 190, 195
Carpets and cushions, 96
Carreine, Nicholas, apprentice, 202
Carrington, William, 52, lt col, 3
Carrion, burial, 81, 113, 124
Carsles, Mr, 224
Carter, James, 179; Joan, widow, 141; John, 236, porter, 235; Robert, 246, 266; Thomas, 98, 207, 253, servant, 249, 257; William, 245, 243; — , 265
Carters, 137, 218, 237, 260; complaints, 267; duties, 185, toll on non free, 221–2
Carts, 160, 165, 168, 173, 185, 192; country, 139; dangerous driving, 218; levy, 153; mugs levy, 181; receipts, 232
Cartway, 123, 198; diversion, 7; maintaining, 90, 102; widening, 76
Cary, John, 54, 77, 255, victualler, late servant to Mr. Windas, 84; William, 256
Case, John, captain, 166, gent, 128, Mr, 133, 152
Castle, *see* Liverpool castle; Castle Street, *see* Liverpool streets
Cater, Tracie, 4; William, 9
Caton, Darbie (Darby), 4, 8, 19, 34, 38, 50, 53, 63, 131, 254
Cattle, 116, 213; burial, 77, 102; in town field, 5; leasowing, 80; on Cheshire side, 174; on Wirral, 166
Causeway, constructing, 90
Cawarden, Thomas, of Croxteth, 255
Cawdey, John, 62

208, 211, 225, 234, 237, 253, Mr, 234,
  recorder, 247
Erbie (Erby), Elizabeth, widow, 220; John, 255,
  apprentice, 146; Richard, 256, apprentice, 226
Erlam (Earlom), 98, 224
Erlin (Erlinn), John, 176, 178, barleyman, 184
Erlum (Erlun), John, 173, 193, alefounder, 209,
  juror, 217; Peter, juror, 189
Escape, 234
Ettles, Robert, 158
Evans, John, 23, shoemaker, 73; William, 193
Everard (Evererd), John, 4, 53, 62, 136, 179;
  Richard, 175, 236; Thomas, 229
Everett, John, 35, 51, 91
Everid, John, 259
Everton, 48, 50, 68, 76, 78, 88, 90, 112, 122, 145,
  151, 154, 165, 168, 198–9, 213, 241, 254, 259;
  causey, 258
Evesdropping, 68, 141
Exchequer, 182, 233, 267

Factor, 234
Fagg, John, 7
Fairclough (Farclough), Gilbert, 3; Thomas, 179
Fairehurst (Fairhurst, Fayrehurst, Farehust), John,
  152, 157, 186, 256; Oliver, 4, 7, 21, 36, 40, 50,
  53, 79, juror, 30; Robert, 4, 35, 53, 62, 100;
  Richard, 254; widow, 242
Fairish, Charles, 160, 162
Fairs, St Martin's day, 186; selling contrary to
  custom, 264
Faith, William, clerk, 254
Fall Well, 69, 90, 249; cleaning, 69
Farer (Farrer), James, of Alker, 168; Margaret,
  40, 218; Peter, 4, 8, 40, 49, 53, 102; Richard, 3,
  53, 68, 76, 254, boothsetter, 47, 61, 75,
  leavelooker, 47, 61, 75; Thomas, 255, of
  Ormskirk, woollen draper, 84
Farren, Thomas, 3
Farrington, Robert, 3, 19, 35, 53
Fazakerley, 26, 171, 204, 212, 236
Fazakerley (Fazakerly), capt, 227; Edward, 8, 20;
  Henry, 140, 199, 205, 212, 219, 227, 236, 245,
  Capt, 212; J, 207; John, 251–2, stonegetter,
  247; Margaret, 62, 68; Mr, 50, 97, 188, 223,
  225; Nicholas, 142, 156, 252, 267, of Spella,
  knt, 255, of Spellowhouse, esq, 148; Richard,
  3, 53, 62, 254, of Fazakerley, 26; Roger, mayor,
  39; Samuel (Sam), 159, 183, 285, 195, 201,
  205, 207, 215, 217, 231, 234, 237–40, 244–5,
  248, 250–1, 253, 257, 265, auditor, 182, bailiff,
  210, of Allerton, 152, town clerk, 162, 164,
  167, 170–1, 183, 188, 196, 208, 215, 225, 232,
  235, 239, 247, 249–50, 253; Thomas, 4–5, 7–9,
  19, 21, 30, 76, 136, 220, 236, barleyman, 17,
  30, miller, 19, shoemaker, 150, 159, 187,

supervisor, 29; William, 19, 26, 30, 48, 98, 108,
  131, 218, 224, capt, 230, 259, gentleman, 100,
  of Kirkby, 39, of Spellowhouse, gent, 148, of
  Spella, 255, shoemaker, 255
Feantone, Thomas, 227
Fearnehead (Fearnhead, Fernhead), Henry, 3, 53,
  62, 254
Fell (Felle), Robert, 192; Thomas, 50, esq, 2, 51
Fells, Isabel, 48, 50, 63
Fences, 31, 40, 73, 168; down, 20, 31, 49, 62,
  66–8, 79–80, 127, 179–80, 180, 184, 212;
  making, 137, 242; repair, 7, 22, 35, 37, 50, 64,
  66, 76, 78, 90, 101–2, 113, 115, 132, 138, 142,
  151, 175, 187, 199, 203, 219, 230; sea bank,
  20, 22, 36–7, 41, 48, 242
Fenton, Thomas, 230
Ferry boats, 70, 225, 261; cattle, 141; farming,
  81; lease, 55; purchase, 59; receipts, 28, 42, 60,
  79; rents, 110, 182; toll, 141
Fey, John, 194
Fidler, Robert, 3, 53, 254
Field (Town field, *see* Liverpool lands), 160; gate
  stoops, 231
Fife (Fyfe), William, 254, physician, 3, 52
Finch (Fynch), Mr. 107; William, 53, clerk, vicar
  of Walton, 72
Findley (Findly, Finley), Archibald, 5, 8, 19;
  Jeremy, 256
Fines, buying goods, 11; buying pink, 43; on
  tallow, 15; on Wirral goods, 15; receipts, 60,
  79, 182, 188, 201, 215, 232, 243, 260;
  suspended, 26
Finloe (Finlow), Jeremy, 192; Richard, 260;
  Thomas, 168, 256, 259, scavenger, 184, juror,
  191; William, 245
Finlon, Thomas, 164
Finney, Edward, 3
Fire, buckets and hooks, 9, 64, 96, 137, 219, 221;
  ladders, 64
Fish stones, 230; yards, 222
Fisher, Edward, 3; John, 262; Richard, 43
Flag stones, 62
Flax, 180
Fleetcrofe, Peter, 3
Fleetwood (Fleetewood, Fletwoode), Brian
  (Bryan), 115, 256, 259, butcher, 193; James,
  barleyman, 189; Lord Deputy, 85; Richard, 2,
  52, 254; Robert, 3, 40, 48, 52, 62, 81, 88, 100,
  123–4, 131, 168, 237–8, 240–1, 244–5, 248,
  250, 253–4, 259, bailiff, 234–5, 237, 241, 260,
  266, juror, 34, 140, 145, 159, 184, 186, 191,
  197, 212, merchant appraiser, 259, of
  Fazakerley, 204, 212, 236, overseer of
  highways, 111, scavenger, 88, skinner, 108,
  steward of hall, 1, 122; William, 4, 53, 62,
  79–80, 101, 114, 143, 147, 153–4, 164, 170,

Griffith, David, mayor of Liverpool, 38–9; John, 54, 89, 91, 114, 137–8, 255, alefounder, 129, 137, barleyman, 87, 100, carpenter, 85, juror, 131, sailor, 7, junior, 34
Ground, use of, 113
Grove, the, 257
Gurling, Mr, 15, 43; certificate, 15
Gutters and walls, 8, 50–1, 67, 77, 81, 90–1, 131–2, 142, 151, 160, 185, 213, 237, 242

H — , Edward, Mr, 267
Hackin (Hacking), Ellen, 90, 113, 138, widow, 112; John, 173, 157, 255, apprentice, 146; widow, 63
Hackner, John, 261
Haddock, widow, 165
Haghton, Evan, mayor, 39
Haigh, 148
Haire, Margaret, 213
Haldifield, 39
Halewood, 212, 220, 227
Half pennies, 213, without license, 230
Hall field, 102
Hall and hallkeeper, *see* Liverpool corporation
Hall (Halle, Halles), David, 49, 245, foreigner, 136; Davie, 66; Geoffrey, 9; James, 258, bailiff, 180; John, 4, 53, 254, 259; Margaram, 9; Peter, 8, 19–21, 30, 40, 48–51, 63; Ralph, 54, 76, 143, 153–4, 164, 255, 170, 178, 183, 195, 217, 231, 234, 237–41, 244, 248, 250–1, 253, bailiff, 147, merchant appraiser, 158, waiter in port, 84; Robert, 4, 6, 8, 18, 21, 37, 53, 63, 67, 88, 100, 102, 115, 127, 130, 254, barleyman, 61, juror, 30, 123, 186, 197, locksmith, 9, overseer of highways, 75 scavenger, 1, 19, steward of the hall, 99, supervisor of highways, 17, 21; Samuel, 3, 52
Halley (Hally), George, 3, 52, 62, 254; Mr, 16
Halliwell, Richard, 54, 131, of Manchester, innkeeper, 84
Halloway, Alice, 5
Halls hey, 41, 80
Halsall, Edward, 6, 245, 264, leavelooker, 259; Henry, 126; William, 136, 150, 180, 184, 192, 221, 229–30, esq, recorder, 33, 47, 51, 61, 75, 86, esq, of Harleton, 24; Mr, 24
Hambleton, Mr, 166
Hamlett, Deane, 19: Edward, 176; John, base son of Edward, 176
Hancock (Handcocke), Alexander, 114; Thomas, 4, 18, 23, 35, 53, 102, 117, juror, 30, 34, 112, 229
Hanett, Mr, 16
Harbouring goods, 264
Hardin (Harding), —, 214, 96, 210
Hardman, Esther, 80, 88–9, 91, 100–2, 112, 115, 130, 132, 138, 230, 264, widow, 114, 136, 140,

149; Francis, 175; Henry, 132, 179, 226, juror, 241, register of leather, 235; Margery, 199; widow, 259; William, 256, apprentice, 202
Harebron (Harebrowne), James, mayor, 38–9; William, 39
Harkine, Ellen, widow, 88
Harracks, Alexander, 79
Harre (Harrs), John, 150; William A., 195
Harrington, Cuthbert, 8; John, esq, 148
Harris (Harries), Job, 211; John, 192–3, 218, 220, 230, 236
Harrison (Hareson, Harrinson, Herrison), Edward, 138, 256; Elizabeth, 40, 180, 199; George, 49; Henry, 265–6; Humfrey, 49; John, 3, 54, 133, 149, 168, 179, of Formby, 192, 189; Lucas, 4; Luke, 20; Michael, 49; Philip, 23, 72, 180, 192; Robert, 49; Roger, 3, 11, 32, 40, 44, 48, 50, 53, 67, 79, 86, 89, 101, 106–7, 117, 164, 181, merchant appraiser, 87; Thomas, 35, 168; widow, 191, 193, 203–4, glasier, 212; William, 115, 119, 124, 127, 130, 132–3, 136, 138, 140, 159, glasier, 114, 149; — , 259–60
Harrox, Alexander, 79
Harrwood, Thomas, 83, 92
Hartlett, Anthony, 213; William, 213
Hartley, John, 214, 216, 256; Mr, 55
Harvey (Harvie), Arthur, 83; Mr, 116; Robert, 40, 53, 62, 67, 80, 89, 91, 115, 117, 126, grocer, 44, juror, 130–1, 136, sidesman, 61, steward of hall, 47
Harware, Mr, customs officer, 118
Haskaine (Haskeine, Haskeyne, Haskine, Haskins), Jane, 7–8, 19, 33, 37, 49, 63, 68, 90, 106, 159, 203, 259, 264, widow, 5, 159, 242; John, 4, 35, 62, 254; Katherin, 159; Thomas, 3, 35, 53; widow, 32
Haslam, Thomas, 162
Hasledeine, Thomas, 179
Hasloe, Thomas, 262
Hatton, Arthur, 140, 234; John, hatter, 259
Haughton, Robert, 63, 255, juror, 172
Hawarden, Thomas, 156, of Croxteth, gent, 148; Mr, 142
Hawett, Nicholas, 13
Hawkshead, William, 3, 35
Hawney, John, 139, ironmonger, 140
Hay, cartload, 131
Headbolts, 35; repair, 7, 37, 101, 115, 125, 132, 138, 166, 175, 187, 199, 219, 230
Healey, 149
Healy, William, juror, 258
Heapey (Heapie, Heapy), Elizabeth, 67, 80, 90, widow, 7–8, 19; Thomas, 175; Mrs, 40, 66, 102, 113–14
Heath, William, 226, juror, 241, scavenger, 235, 259

192, juror, 30, 34, overseer of highways, 75, 122; widow, 127; — , 98
Mossed, Thomas, 255
Mossey, William, 52
Mosslake, 258
Mossley, Nicholas, commissioner, 147
Mossock, Mr, 24, 98, 223; Thomas, 35, 52, chirurgeon, 3
Mossock's Roe, 223
Mothy, Walter, 255
Motley, Walter, of Dublin, merchant, 143
Moxon, Joseph, 261
Moyer (Moyers), Anthony, 53, 62, joiner, 57, 77
Moyries, Anthony, 138
Muck, 80, 88, 90, 166, 168, 180, 190, 213, 236–6
Mugs, 153, 181; carts, 221
Murrey (Murry), James, Lord, earl of Athol, 128; John, esq, 128, 254, earl of Athol, 254; Robert, 143, 255
Muttons and veals, 187

Na. Berkley, 174
Nagbor, George, 112
Nantwich, 144
Naris, Richard, 98
Nayler (Naylor), Gilbert, 199; Henry, 2, minister, 52; George, 115, 245
Needham (Needomes) Hall, 98, 224
Needham, Nicholas, 263
Neile, George, 146
Nelson, Roger, 39
Netherfield Steele, 76, 160
Newcomen, lieut, 85
Newis (Neweis, Newys), Nicholas, 11; William, 4, 7, 10, 20, 22, 40, 53, alefounder, 34, juror, 34, supervisor of highways, 17, 21
Newport, William, 124, 165, 179, 180, 199, 209; wife of, 165
Newton, John, 3, 52, 254; Mr, 93–4; Samuel, 263
Nicholas (Nicolas), 254; Sir, priest, 39; William, 257
Nicholason, Thomas, 114
Nicholls (Nichols), Mr, 195; William, 114, 150, 160, 180, 184, 199, 203, 205, 217, 242, 255, 264, alefounder, 145, scavenger, 111, steward of hall, 158, wine cooper, 108
Nicholson (Nicholsonn), Alice, 254; Ellen, 127, 227, 236, 258; land of, 7; Nicholas, 7, 54; Thomas, 4–5, 7–8, 14, 18–19, 21–2, 30, 37, 48, 50, 53, 62, 68, 76, 88–90, 98, 100, 108, 117, 123, 126, 130, 136, 212, 216, 256, alderman, 48, apprentice, 211, juror, 30, 123, 131, 136, 165, 172, 229, register of leather, 1, 29, 47, 87, 111, 129, 158, 228, shoemaker, 18, 26; wife of, 224; William, juror, 159

Nickson (Nixon), 168, Anthony, 192, servant, 203; capt, 179
Nield (Neild), Henry, 255; apprentice, 108
Nine Lands, 64
Nor — , Thomas, juror, 258
Norbury (Norbery, Norburie), Thomas, 136, 140, 149, 178, 212, 248, 250, 256, bailiff, 246–7, 253, 260, churchwarden, 206, gent bailiff, 258, juror, 189, 236; widow, 265
Norland, Ann, 265; John, 265; Thomas, 123, 136, 140, 187, 226, 256, 264, of Lurtings, 265, overseer of highways, 259
Norlum, Thomas, 173
Norman, William, 182
Norres (Norries, Norris, Noris), Edward, mayor, 39; Henry (H), of West Derby, gent, 148, 255; Mr, 190, 224, of Derby, 98; Richard, 10, 43, 72, 92, 224, of Formby, 23, of West Derby, 148, 255; Thomas, 147–8, 156, commissioner, 147, esq, 143; William, 19, clerk, 214, 256
Nott, John, 214, 216, 256
Nowell, James, 202, 256; Thomas, 245
Nutter, Thomas, boothsetter, 99
Occupations (of individuals): administrator, 153, 205; alehousekeeper, 8, 180, 192; apothecary, 84; attorney, 34, 49, 253; baker, 252; barber, 220; beerbrewer, 72; blockmaker, 84, 128, 255; boatman, 159; bodice maker, 146, 255; butcher, 3, 5, 8, 20, 22, 30, 33, 37, 40, 52, 57, 64, 108, 149–50, 194, 199, 203, 227, 230, 220; captain, 3–4, 6, 24, 52, 69, 71–2, 79, 85, 93, 95, 103, 106–7, 116, 121, 124, 126, 134, 136, 139, 166–8, 179, 180, 182, 193, 212, 224, 230, 254, 259; carpenter, 85, 133, 184, 190, 202–3, house, 214; carter, 80, 89, 100, 218, 255; chapman, 154; chirugeon, 3, 67, 128, 143, 159, 204, 213, 220, 229, 255; clothier, 9, 41; cobbler, 74; collarmaker, 120; combmaker, 226, 256; cooper, 4, 9, 21, 30, 36, 53, 57, 65–7, 72, 75, 102, 108, 114, 127, 160, 241, 254, 263; cumbal man, 219; currier, 57, 227; customs officer, 118; cutler, 3, 6, 8, 14, 21, 52, 90, 133, 255; doctor, 259; draper, 52, 61, 67, 80, 102, 112, 115, 124, 127, 136, 242; feltmaker, 9, 57, 72, 256; ferryman, 19, 141; gauger, 199; glasier, 31, 114, 145, 149, 203, 241; grocer, 84, 256, 263; gunsmith, 21, 57, 133; hatter, 8, 259; hosier, 91; husbandman, 3, 6, 27, 44, 84–5, 123, 127, 146; innkeeper, 84, 99; ironmonger, 140; joiner, 57, 77, 120, 202, 255; locksmith, 9, 227, 256; maltster, 4, 35, 53, 202, 254; mariner, 1, 3–5, 8, 18, 20, 26–7, 41, 52, 57, 65, 84, 87, 89, 108, 111, 115, 117, 120, 128, 136, 143–4, 146, 158–9, 167, 194, 199–200, 226–7, 255; mason, 4, 251; mercer, 214, 220; merchant, 3–4, 10, 26–8, 38, 44, 58,

25, 52, younger, 50, attorney, 34; Robert, 254; widow, 90; — , junior, 5

Watch, 177, 181, 186

Water bailiffs, *see* Liverpool corporation

Water course/channel, 7–8, 64, 77, 115–16, 123–4, 132, 138, 141–2, 266; cleaning, 6, 41, 50, 68–9, 77–8, 102, 113–15, 125, 127, 131, 141, 260

Water Street, *see* Liverpool streets

Water gate, 250; pump, 138; side, 81, 124, 185, 228; sough, 124

Waterhouse, John, 24; Mr, 23

Watering pool, 90, 101, 115, 266

Watmough (Watmowe, Watnough), Thomas, 48; William, 129, 218, 255, alefounder, 135, blacksmith, 159, churchwarden, 250, juror, 131, 140, 172, scavenger, 129

Watson, James, 3; Philip, 3

Wavertree Lane, 236

Way, Mr, 12

Ways, repair, 80, 151

Weaver, Thomas, alderman, 147

Weaver, river, 166

Webster, Brian, 141; Henry, 3, 19, 52, 100, 131, 185, 254, 259, juror, 112, of Knowsley, yeoman, 161; Humphrey, 3, 52, 131, 254; John, 20, 30, 36–7; William, 3, 53

Weights (*see* Measures), 104, 179, 209, 230

Wells, 90, 162, 198, 260

Wells, Mr, 14, 15

Welsh, William, 123, 124, mariner, 128, 255

West, Abraham, 4, feltmaker, apprentice, 9, scavenger, 29; William, 3, esq, 52, 254

West Chester, 211

West Derby, 65, 109, 148–9, 160, 173, 192, 233, 255, 264

Westminister, 134, 161, 234, 249, 267

Weston, Mr, 12

Wetherby, Lawrence, 102

Wexford, 103

Weyborne, Mr, 188

Whalley, 61, 158

Whalley, Edmund, 21, 100, 158, 162–3, 192, boothsetter, 158, leavelooker, 158; Edward, 62, of Wavertree Lane, 236; Randle, 51, 62; William, 32, 53, 63, 254, town customer, 33, 61

Wharf (*see* Jetty, Quay), 193

Wheatley, John, 216

Whiston, 32, 44

White Cross, 55, 112, 241

Whitefield, James, 229

Whitehall, court of, 222

Whitehead (Whytehead), Edmund, 207; Ginnett (Jeanette), 40, 218; Richard, 73, 88; Robert, 88; Thomas, shoemaker, 230; John, cumbal man, 219

Whitestone (Whytestone), John, 22, 162

Whitfield, Edward, 251; James, 226, 229, 233–4, 239, 248, watchmaker, 264; John, 246, of Low Hill, 197, servant, 218; Richard, 143, 255; Samuel, 244; Thomas, 19, 30

Whittakers, the, 54

Whittle, John, 218, scavenger, 228

Whitworth, captain, 24, 72

Whyte, Mrs, 10

Wicklow, 71

Widdow, Richard, 254, juror, 30

Widdowes (Widowes, Widoes), John, 131; Richard, 4, 5–6, 17, 21, 48, 53, 63, 66, 68, 76, 91, 100, 112–13, 192, 237, beadle & bellman, 145, 158, 209, 229, 235, 259, board/boothsetter, 2, 30, 47, 61; Thomas, 64; widow, 98; — , 100, wife of, 224

Widnes (Widnesse), William, 3, 53, 100, 254

Widowson (Widdowson), John, 90, 173, 178, 236, 256, butcher, 64

Wigan, 31, 149, 170, 203

Wilcock, Henry, 4, 6, 53, 254; Mr, of Dublin, 23

Williams, Richard, 4, 8, 37, 53, 66, 69; Robert, 265; widow, 127

Williamson (Wiliamson, Willinson, Wmson), alderman, 31; Alice, 225; Edward, 2, 11, 13, 18–19, 23, 44, 107, 27, 32–4, 45, 60, 83, 98, 105–7, 146, 172, 204, 224, 230, alderman, 63, 69, 74, 81, 105, 107, 109, 138, bailiff, 106, 126, 142, gent, 210, gent mayor, 47, 54–6, 60, 74, mayor, 47, 51; Ellen, 230; James, 2, 7–8, 48, 55, 70, 79, 82, 85, 118, 223, alderman, 51, 69, 81, 97, 100, 118, gent mayor, 16, 21, 29, mayor, 18, 26, 83; Jane, 63, 66, 77; John, 2, 18, 37, 41, 54, 56, 65, 70–1, 94, 98, 100, 112, 115, 127–8, 130, 132, 139, 155, 172, 180, 184, 193, 200, 213, 224, 227, 245, 255, 260, 264, alderman, 54, 233, gent, 155, hall keeper, 1, 17, 28, 33, 45, junior, 19, 80, 124, 145, 149, 191, 259, mariner, 115, 120, 255, master, 203, scavenger, 122, 130, seaman, 114, senior, 77, steward of hall, 99, younger, 112; Laurence, 124, 127, 130, juror, 149, mariner, 128, 255; Margaret, Mrs, 113–14, 127, 132, 137, 151, widow, 66, 136; Margery, 8; Marie, 78; Matthew, 118; Mr, 83, 98, 224–5; Mrs, 113–14; Ralph, juror, 212; Randle, 197, 199, 203, 227, joiner, 202, juror, 217, overseer of highways, 209, 220; Richard, 2, 7, 13, 15, 18, 23–4, 30, 36, 50, 52–3, 69, 78, 86, 91, 100, 105, 116, 120, 126, 143, 159, 253, chirurgeon, 128, 159, 204, 213, 220, 229, 255, churchwarden, 193, junior, steward of hall, 144, juror, 30, 145, 168, mason, 4; Robert, 71, 100, 65, 69, 216, 234, 237, 241, 248, 250–1, 253, 256–7, bailiff, 246–7, 253, 260, gent, 263, mariner, 65, the